CURRENTS OF ENCOUNTER

Studies on the Contact between Christianity and Other Religions, Beliefs, and Cultures

VOLUME 8

CURRENTS OF ENCOUNTER

VOLUMES PUBLISHED OR AT PRESS

1 J.D. Gort, *et al.*, eds. — *Dialogue and Syncretism: An Interdisciplinary Approach* (copublished with Eerdmans)
2 Hendrik M. Vroom — *Religions and the Truth: Philosophical Reflections and Perspectives* (with Eerdmans)
3 Sutarman S. Partonadi — *Sadrach's Community and its Contextual Roots: A Nineteenth-Century Javanese Expression of Christianity*
4 J.D. Gort, *et al.*, eds. — *On Sharing Religious Experience: Possibilities of Interfaith Mutuality* (with Eerdmans)
5 S. Wesley Ariarajah — *Hindus and Christians: A Century of Protestant Ecumenical Thought* (with Eerdmans)
6 Makoto Ozaki — *Introduction to the Philosophy of Tanabe, according to the English Translation of the Seventh Chapter of the* Demonstratio *of Christianity*
7 Karel Steenbrink — *Dutch Colonialism and Indonesian Islam: Contacts and Conflicts, 1596-1950*
8 A.A. An-Na'im *et al.*, eds. — *Human Rights and Religious Values: An Uneasy Relationship?*
9 Rein Fernhout — *Canonical Texts: Bearers of Absolute Authority (Bible, Koran, Veda, Tipiṭaka). A Phenomenological Study*

Volumes in this series unavailable from Eerdmans can be obtained from Editions Rodopi, Keizersgracht 302-304, 1016 EX Amsterdam, the Netherlands, or 233 Peachtree Street, N.E., Suite 404, Atlanta, GA 30303-1504

Human Rights and Religious Values

An Uneasy Relationship?

edited by

Abdullahi A. An-Na'im, Jerald D. Gort,
Henry Jansen, Hendrik M. Vroom

EDITIONS RODOPI, AMSTERDAM

WILLIAM B. EERDMANS PUBLISHING COMPANY
GRAND RAPIDS, MICHIGAN

[redacted]

255 Jefferson Ave. S.E., Grand Rapids, Michigan 49503

Published 1995 jointly by
Wm. B. Eerdmans Publishing Co.
and Editions Rodopi
Keizersgracht 302-304, 1016 EX Amsterdam, the Netherlands
or 233 Peachtree Street, N.E., Suite 404, Atlanta, GA 30303-1504

Printed in the United States of America

00 99 98 97 96 95 7 6 5 4 3 2 1

Library of Congress Cataloging-in-Publication Data

Human rights and religious values: an uneasy relationship? /
edited by Abdullahi A. An-Na'im . . . [et al.].
p. cm. — (Currents of encounter; vol. 8)
Essays presented at a workshop held at the Free University, Amsterdam,
Apr. 21-23, 1993.
Includes bibliographical references and index.
ISBN 0-8028-0506-X (paper)
1. Human rights — Religious aspects — Congresses. 2. Religious ethics —
Congresses. 3. Religions — Congresses.
I. Na'im, 'Abd All#h A?mad, 1946– . II. Series.
BL65.H78H86 1994
291.1'77 — dc20 94-21228
CIP

Editions Rodopi ISBN 90-5183-777-1

Contents

Preface

The theme of this symposium, *Human Rights and Religious Values* does not require an extensive introduction to establish its relevance and urgency. Developments throughout the world indicate the existence of a number of real problems, which, while perhaps quite predictable, have become clearly manifest today. Religious adherents claim universal validity for their beliefs and view their ethical codes as universally valid. In situations in which the latter do not correspond fully with Human Rights, which are also considered to be universally valid and applicable, both religious ethical codes and human rights claim the highest authority over human life. This cannot but give rise to conflict, though frequently this tension is camouflaged by the general agreement that all human beings should be kind and congenial, should not steal and ought not to be egocentric. Though such sentiments are in themselves very sound and praiseworthy cannot hide the fact that religious ideals of human life differ very deeply. A realistic and honest approach demands that these deep differences should be faced squarely.

For the furtherance of peace in this world and the reception of human rights into all cultures, these difficult questions should be discussed in a dialogical way, that is, openly, with mutual understanding, reciprocal witnessing and critical questioning. In such a dialogue Western individualism will be subject to correction, and hierarchical social-religious philosophies will be questioned on the matter of the rights of individuals, especially the place held by the poor in society. Religious traditions are hermeneutical processes: they do develop, change and - sometimes - improve in response to circumstances and in dialogue with their context. Critical dialogue does not mean a flight from fixed, unchanging positions but rather a mutual search for a better understanding of human life, a just and merciful society, nature, and ultimate reality. In this volume the authors have not been content to write in an uncritical manner regarding the degree of support religious traditions give to the idea and realization of Human Rights. It is our hope that these papers serve to further such an open, congenial and critical dialogue.

In this preface we include, first, the position paper, co-written by Hendrik M. Vroom and Johannes S. Reinders, which was sent beforehand to the other authors of this collection, with a view to clarifying some of the salient issues involved in the ambiguous relationship between human rights and religious ideas of life. The central question of the paper is: *can human rights be interpreted and justified from within religious traditions, such that they are supported, rather than undermined, as the 'common core' of a universal morality among these traditions?* Second, we will offer a brief synopsis of each of the various contributions to the symposium.

POSITION PAPER

Moral Codes and Religious Traditions

One of the characteristics of religious traditions is that they determine, at least in part, the moral norms and values to which their followers adhere. In a society where communities from different traditions coexist, the question arises as to how their moral norms and values are related. Do they overlap or do they conflict? Is there a common core of moral truth accepted by all, or are differences so substantial that one can only speak of a fundamental gap between them? If the latter, how ought this religious diversity in morals to be assessed?

In order to address these questions one can turn to the ideal of human existence and fulfilment that religious traditions provide. This ideal of what we call the good life is embedded in a religious understanding of various dimensions of human existence, like the yearning for truth, happiness and salvation, but also the experience of finitude and fallibility. The understanding of these issues in various religious traditions provides a powerful framework for analyzing the relations between their respective ideals of the good life and the norms and values in support of this ideal.

Besides starting from the interpretation of human existence, however, another approach is also required. The fact is that not only do traditions probe morality, but in a pluralist society the reverse is also the case: the traditions themselves are criticized by what appear to be general moral standards. This sort of criticism is neccesary. Some people do, after all, hold beliefs entailing significant moral consequences, both for themselves and for others. Therefore, religious traditions have to be judged by standards of what is morally acceptable in a pluralist society. Given the fact of pluralism and the necessity of coexistence, traditions will have to pass the test of some sort of universal moral code.

The problem with this two-way perspective on religious morality is, of course, how to identify a moral standard that is sufficiently independent from any particular tradition. The need for such a standard in interreligious dialogue is obvious. For without it, the approbation of religious morality can only mean that one tradition judges, by its own standards, the moral code of another. In this way any tradition can acquire a *de facto* normative superiority over another, but why accept this as a *de jure* superiority if not on the basis of an independent standard?

The very notion of a tradition-independent moral standard, however, has recently come under attack as ultimately incoherent. What counts as morally acceptable in any given society is largely determined by dominant cultural ideas, both religious and secular, including ideals of the good life. Consequently it is quite difficult, if not impossible, to defend any moral standard as independent from any particular view on these matters.

Human Rights between Universality and Tradition

One of the obvious candidates to qualify as a universal moral code is provided by the 1948 Universal Declaration of Human Rights. The norms and values expressed by this Declaration are claimed as valid for all human beings. Such was, and still is, the main contention. But the fact cannot be overlooked that the doctrine of human rights is the product of a particular period in the history of Western culture and philosophy. Eighteenth-century Enlightenment philosophy searched for a foundation of moral and religious truth in human nature, aspiring to establish a 'natural' religion and morality. But the ensuing conception of human nature, with its strong appeal to free and independent reason, turned out to be very much embedded in the cultural tradition from which it emerged. Given these cultural antecedents, questions arise as to the universal validity of a rights doctrine that is based on Enlightenment anthropology. Two examples will serve to illustrate the point.

Article 1 of the Universal Declaration states that all human beings are born free and equal in dignity and rights. If one interprets this claim in light of the notion of *karma* in Hinduism, which implies that the birth of the individual is determined by the *karma* that has been developed in previous lives, then the phrase 'born free and equal' requires significant qualification. This does not mean that for Hindus the Declaration cannot be valid on the point of freedom and equality. But it does mean that in order to determine its validity and its practical consequences, Hindus can only interpret its claims within their own religious framework. They cannot do otherwise, without giving up an important element of their religious tradition. The Universal Declaration of Human Rights has to be interpreted from all possible points of view and integrated into all possible traditional frameworks, in order to acquire universal validity. If not, it remains the product of an alien culture, valid only for those who adhere to the views inherent to that particular culture.

The second example comes from Article 18 of the Declaration, which states that all human beings have the freedom of thought, conscience and religion. This implies the freedom to express one's religion or belief, either individually or collectively, either in public or in private, in education, practice and in worship. Freedom of religion is thus a human right. In many Western societies this right is interpreted in the wider context of individual freedom and equality, implying - among other things - an equal status of men and women within the religious community. If we take into account the fact that some religious communities do not acknowledge equal status for women (as is the case with many orthodox religious communities - Islamic, Protestant, Jewish or Roman

Catholic), it appears that the right of these communities to religious freedom would be infringed, if the state would decide to enforce equality for women. Consequently, some hermeneutical space must be granted these orthodox communities in order to discern what individual freedom and equality means to them. If not, the right to express their religion must remain alien to them in the sense that they cannot recognize its relevance for their own religious practices: it would merely be a freedom to express their religion on other people's terms. To make good its claim to universal validity, the doctrine of human rights must allow for contextual interpretations. If not, this implies that the interpretation of one particular tradition gains universal dominance, but from the point of view of all the others the doctrine must remain a *corpus alienum*, so to speak, something belonging to another tradition.

In any event, however, it is difficult to conceive of the Universal Declaration of Human Rights as the source from which a 'common core' can be derived. Even if one can argue that, in a legal sense, the doctrine of universal human rights is clearly established in international law, this does not mean that the same can be said of it in terms of a universal moral standard. To summarize our point: human rights are contextually interpreted and it is from that context that they acquire their practical meaning and content. This necessarily presupposes a hermeneutical space, without which they could never be part of the positive morality of particular traditions. At the same time, however, contextual interpretations cannot but jeopardize the universality of the doctrine, at least in some respects. Positive morality in any case is always tradition-dependent, and thus particular rather than universal.

Social Morality and Ideals of Human Existence

The problem outlined in the previous section can be further explored in terms of a distinction that is well-known in philosophical ethics: the distinction between a 'narrow' and a 'broad' conception of morality. Morality in a narrow sense addresses questions regarding the principles and rules by which people ought to live in order to render social intercourse as peaceful and beneficial as possible. It guides moral judgment on institutions, practices and actions, and finds its characteristic expression in duties, obligations and rights as central moral categories. It seeks to base its claims on points of view shared by all members of society, regardless of their identity as members of particular communities and traditions.

In contrast, the broad conception of morality addresses questions that one can answer only by referring explicitly to one's particular identity. Whereas narrow morality asks what one ought or ought not to do as a member of society, broad morality asks what sort of person one should be. Its main concern is the good life as a means to attain human perfection and fulfilment. Unlike narrow morality, which is primarily a morality of constraint, broad morality is a morality of direction. Virtue and character, rather than principles and rules, are its central categories.

The assumptions on which this distinction is based are pertinent to the liberal tradition with its strong sensitivity to moral and religious pluralism. Within this tradition social morality is often understood in terms of a pacification model: individuals with conflicting interests and differing ideals of the good life must cooperate, while there is no generally accepted system of beliefs to guide them. Consequently, the ideal of the good life is taken to be a matter of individual choice, for which only private - as opposed to public - reasons can be given. Hence, within liberal society only matters that are of concern to all members of society alike are capable of public justification. Whereas in a religious moral community a broad conception may be capable of guiding social life, liberals take this to be impossible in modern society where unifying perspectives on human existence are no longer universally accepted.

Though the distinction between narrow and broad morality stems from the liberal tradition, this does not mean that it can only be relevant to understand the problems of religious pluralism in Western liberal society. The reason is that religious pluralism is as much a characteristic of non-Western societies as it is of liberal society. But apart from this, it can very well serve as an analytical tool to explore the problem outlined in the previous section. Like the doctrine of human rights, the distinction between 'narrow' and 'broad' also is based upon a supposedly tradition-independent conception of human nature. Without such a conception, the idea of a narrow morality as a pacification model could not make sense. Likewise, the doctrine of human rights seems only possible as a 'common core' between the moral codes of particular traditions, when it succeeds in terms of a narrow morality.

In order to see whether or not it can succeed as such, several points can be made. The first point is that morality in a narrow sense seems to lack the force of inspiring people to devote their lives to any ideal of the good life. Since religious moralities are always moralities in the broad sense, they are clearly superior in this respect. At the same time, however, these traditions suffer a loss of function when they are removed from the domain of public life, as is clearly the case in liberal society. So the question arises as to how the doctrine of human rights can inspire people to embrace it as the core of social morality, if therefore in public life they have to set aside their religious ideals of the good life. In particular it becomes unclear how the doctrine can inspire people to embrace public life as part of their religious ideals.

The second point is closely related to the first. Morality in the narrow sense is not by itself able to motivate people sufficiently to be good people. This is due to its predominantly legalistic character. Like legal institutions constraining action to remain within the boundaries of the law, morality in the narrow sense constrains action to its own system of duties, obligation and rights. When seen from the broad perspective of religious traditions, however, narrow morality is incapable of guiding people in a positive direction. For this requires education and training to become good people, which is something quite different from obeying moral rules and principles. By dismissing ideals of the good life from its agenda, narrow morality creates for itself a problem which it cannot by itself resolve.

The third point is that any conception of narrow morality characteristically requires moral judgment to be universal and impartial. When considering one's moral duty in a given context the question to ask is not 'what is required of me?' but 'what ought anyone to do in cases that are in relevant respects the same as this one?'. Only on the basis of what anyone ought to do can I infer what I ought to do. The problem is that this universality and impartiality robs people of their particular identity. To be a moral person one must detach oneself from one's particular set of values and ideals that determine who one actually is as a moral person. The first question, therefore, is whether or not the notion of a moral person can be explained meaningfully at all, without referring to concrete circumstances and contexts. The second question is whether or not the impersonal moral life which narrow morality seems to require can in any way uphold people's particular identity. Again, tradition and community seem to be a much more fruitful ground both for explaining and developing people's identity as moral persons.

The fourth and last point is again closely connected with the foregoing. The problematic aspect of impersonal moral identity affects claims as to the universality and impartiality of narrow morality. Moral convictions that are said to meet these requirements often turn out to be the convictions of cultural, academic or political elites. Given this fact, the very notion of a universal and impartial moral code can be used to dominate the people who do not belong to any such elite. Once the moral rationality of 'what anyone should do' turns out to be the rationality of a particular elite, even the doctrine of human rights - as a 'narrow' morality - could prove to be less universal and partial than the elite would have it. Inasmuch as it would alienate people from their cultural and religious roots, it could become an instrument of oppression. The question is whether or not it can be used otherwise.

The Problem of a Religious Dialogue on Human Rights

When seen from broader traditional perspectives, then, narrow morality lacks motivational force. It is less capable of directing people to the good life, alienates them from their own roots and, consequently, it may be turned into an instrument of domination.

All these points do not suffice, however, to deny the fact that none of the traditional broader perspectives is universally accepted. In almost any part of our world, East and West, North and South, societies lack a unifying moral perspective that contains a defined ideal of the good life as well as rules and principles for communal life. We are consequently confronted with fierce struggles between adherents to different traditions with grave consequences for all. This fact stresses the necessity of exploring the conditions for peaceful coexistence which, it will be recalled, is precisely what narrow morality seeks to establish, despite all its difficulties.

From this analysis it follows that, on the one hand, narrow and broad morality are in need of support from one another, while on the other hand, they tend to undermine one another. The same holds *mutatis mutandis* for the relation between the doctrine of human rights and the moral norms and values of traditional religious moral codes. The question resulting from this analysis can therefore be stated as follows: *Can human rights be interpreted and justified from within religious traditions, such that they are supported, rather than undermined, as the 'common core' of a universal morality among these traditions?*

One way to contribute to answering this question is to look for aspects which religious traditions have in common, in particular with regard to ideals of human existence and fulfilment or 'true humanity'. All religions speak of salvation, the good life, and living well. Inquiry into correlations, analogies, differences and agreements with regard to these issues is an urgent task, given the fact of pluralism. Since scientists of religous studies have confined themselves to the task of describing and explaining aspects of religious life, while excluding normative questions from their research and since theologians have mostly worked exclusively from within the normative framework of their own tradition, much work is still to be done in this field. Interdisciplinary cooperation is a precondition for any progress in this connection, requiring the contribution of anthropology, theology, moral philosophy and the philosophy of religion. Moreover, given the problematic relation between particularity and universality as outlined above, interreligious dialogue appears to be the most promising approach to conduct this type of research. No self-evident points of view from which to proceed are available for this dialogue, except for the evidence that all religious traditions share this problem at least: how to establish the conditions of a peaceful coexistence with one another.

Diversity in Religious Anthropologies

The precondition of a real dialogical study of religious diversity is the full appreciation of the divergencies among traditions. Interreligious dialogue on morality should not begin with simple statements about supposedly common notions and thus avoid awkward issues. In dialogue on morality up to the present these questions have not been dealt with very extensively. The problem is whether the diverse religious anthropologies give way to a common core of 'universal' rights and stimulate adherents to acknowledge them in their cultural context, or prevent adherents from doing so. Therefore, this symposium will focus on the implications of religious anthropologies for the possibibility to acknowledge human rights. We will now give some examples of belief about humankind which may be inconsistent with the claims of universal validity of human rights.

We will concentrate on the religious traditions of Hinduism, Buddhism, Judaism, Christianity, and Islam.

SYNOPSIS OF THE ESSAYS

The first two essays deal with the general themes of ethical universality, pluralism and relativism: *Ethical and Philosophical Perspectives.*

Johannes S. Reinders outlines some examples of different views of morality and then evaluates one author who tries to establish the presence of a common deep structure to the ethics found in the various religious traditions. Because that claim is not substantiated by an analysis of the various ethical systems, Reinders supports a dialogue on religious ideas and ideals of morality.

Hendrik M. Vroom shows that religious ideas of humanity are more than philosophical; they incorporate the practical wisdom of their traditions as how to become truly human. Religious traditions may support human rights, but will reinterpret them, select their own priorities, and possibly reject some.

Part II of this volume discusses the *Juridical and Cultural Perspectives* of religious pluralism.

Paul de Waart is a professor of international law and as such is concerned with the clarity of human rights formulations in court. In two appendices he provides checklists of points which help in the practical application of human rights. These practical points are a good and perhaps the only starting point for interreligious dialogue on human rights. Human rights have their ground in certain basic needs related to human well-being. While the variety of cultures should be acknowledged, the formulations of human rights should be interpreted and supported by all cultures.

Bas de Gaay Fortman, professor of political economy and former member of Parliament in the Netherlands, takes up the question of the practical reception of human rights in all countries. He argues that, while the formulations of human are not sacrosanct, the underlying principles are. He describes the institutional requirements that are needed if people are to make effective claims for their rights. Human rights must meet with support in the hearts of human beings and here religious traditions play a major role.

The cultural anthropologist **André Droogers** argues against the relativist claim that makes all critique obsolete. Ethnic minorities are present in each culture and, therefore, intercultural and interreligious encounter is a fact, and the questions of good and evil in relation to people of other faiths cannot be avoided. Cultural anthropology has learned how to understand and how to share.

Part III is concerned with specific religious traditions in their critical, ambiguous or supportive attitude toward human rights. This section thus deals with *Case Studies from Religious Traditions*.

The Indologist **Victor van Bijlert** writes on the Hindu renewal movement of Raja Rammohun Roy in India. Social injustice has been criticized within Hindu culture for a long time. Roy criticized traditional society and especially the traditional practice of burning widows. He supported the British colonial Governor's decision to outlaw this practice. In this renewal movement the widow's right to live was been recognized on the basis of the Hindu traditions themselves and the contextual influence of Western colonial culture.

Corstiaan van der Burg asks what possibilities are offered by Hinduism for a religious underpinning of human rights. Examining two recent cases, the reaction to the Mandal Commission report and the Ayodhya question, he concludes that fundamentalist Hinduism is hostile to the implementation of human rights. There are interpretations of Hindu texts, however, which are supportive for human rights.

On the basis of his broad knowledge of the use of Holy Scriptures in religious traditions **Rein Fernhout** discusses one very special case. The *Bhagavadgita* (along with the Sermon on the Mount) was the source of Gandhi's inspiration for *ahimsa*, even during the revolution, but also provided Scriptural support for his murderer. Both readings of the *Bhagavadgita* are to be criticized from the point of view of traditional exegesis for different reasons, but who would not support Gandhi's innovative reading?

From the perspective of Theravada Buddhism **Padmasiri de Silva** agrees with the basic core values expressed in human rights. Because Buddhism is not as anthropocentric as Western society, he pleads for a wider perspective than the merely human one and for environmental ethics. Although the ethics of care and compassion is more important than accentuating one's rights, in his view Buddhism can integrate many human rights.

As a Zen philosopher, **Masao Abe** recognizes that the first commandment in Buddhism is not to destroy *any* life. Thus environmental issues are as important as human rights. Claiming one's rights is always in danger of becoming individualistic. Abe shows how the cultivation of wisdom is valued more highly than the struggle for justice in Buddhism. The latter inevitably leads to dichotonomous thinking.

Jacques Kamstra deals with the concept of Japan as the Divine Country (*shinkoku*) in some Japanese Buddhist traditions, especially that of Nichiren Buddhism. He describes the roots of these ideas in some Buddhist doctrines and their contextual reception in Japan. All ideas of a holy land or country constitute a possible threat to the rights of other peoples, other countries and nature.

Reender Kranenborg is a specialist on oriental religious movements in the West. He describes the attempts in Europe to limit the freedom of sects to exercise influence over their members. The right of freedom of religion makes such measures unacceptable. Legislation that is already in existence is sufficient for making legal decisions regarding any unacceptable policies of religious movements.

Arnulf Camps states that efforts to further the reception of human rights in Asia should take into account the three realities of Asia: the poverty of the masses, the deep religiosity of the people, and the character of Asian cultures. Full humanity is conceived in terms of one's relation with the whole community and not in individualistic isolation. The notions of collective rights and solidarity with the poor as well as the *dalit* should be integrated into new formulations of human rights.

In a survey of Calvinist ideas **Aad van Egmond** shows how the worth of the human person in Calvinist Christian theology is grounded in the idea that every human being is created in the image of God. Although Abraham Kuyper was not opposed to the idea of human rights as such, he was opposed to their modernist formulation. The doctrine of common grace, by which God sustains creation and human beings everywhere in the world, leads to the acknowledgement and accentuation of the ethical responsibility of all human beings. Reformed theology thus has little difficulty in accepting and supporting human rights.

Jerald Gort describes the history of the reception of human rights within the Protestant ecumenical movement. Initially, there was an almost exclusive emphasis on religious liberty and, somewhat later, on individual rights. Since the late 1960's ecumenical understanding of the *content* of human rights has broadened dramatically to include socio-economic, political, environmental, and future-generation rights. Recent thinking regarding the *relationship between* human rights is that they are indivisible; this also holds for human rights infractions. The ecumenical view of the proper *methodological approach* to the implementation of human rights has also undergone a great deal of change throughout the years. Finally, the *root causes* of human rights infringements are seen to be unjust national and global structures; this has led to the establishment of 'preferential solidarity with the poor' as strategic priority in human rights efforts.

Because human rights require support by and integration into various cultures and religious traditions, **Abdullahi An-Na'im** stresses the possibilities of underscoring them from different perspectives. He denies that it is possible or even valuable to have a (supposedly) neutral formulation. Rights need the support of value systems. An-Na'im proposes a hermeneutical method that would allow human rights to be reconciled with Islam and, by extension, other religious communities as well. The movement to further the acceptance of human rights is a truly global and mutual venture and not a struggle to promote one of the cultural or religious interpretations of these rights.

Anton Wessels describes the work and thought of another Islamic reformer, 'Ali Shari'ati and his struggle against the three major powers of oppression, wealth and hypocrisy. Shari'ti reinterpreted the Qu'ranic expression 'God of *al-nas*' (God of humankind) as '*God of the masses*'. In contrast to the Western individualistic interpretation, he thus interpreted the struggle for rights from an Islamic Third World perspective. One should not simply accept traditional religious understanding as it is, for it is often in need of critique.

Part IV offers some *Concluding Observations: Strategy for the Future.*

In his closing essay, **John Clayton** takes up the issue of the tension between the local and the universal in human rights discussions. This issue, in his view, arises from the preceding essays, leaving us with the question of what the strategy for the future ought to be. After offering some suggestions, he further explores the issue of the universality of human rights in terms of its Enlightenment roots and the question of relativism.

The essays in this volume were presented to and discussed at an international workshop held at the Free University, Amsterdam from April 21 - 23, 1993. The workshop and this publication were made possible by the deeply appreciated support of the Abraham Kuyper Foundation and the Executive Board of the Free University. One of our editors, Henry Jansen, had the additional task of correcting the manuscripts of non-English speakers and preparing the camera-ready text of this volume for publication. In this he had the assistance of his wife, Lucy, to whom the editors express their deepfelt appreciation.

The editors

Abdullahi A. An-Na'im
Jerald D. Gort
Henry Jansen
Hendrik M. Vroom

Part 1

Ethical and Philosophical Perspectives

CHAPTER I

Human Rights from the Perspective Of a Narrow Conception of Religious Morality

Johannes S. Reinders

INTRODUCTION

The doctrine of human rights appears to be grounded in the belief that different cultural and religious traditions share a common morality. This much at least seems to follow from the fact that in 1948 the United Nations did not adopt a declaration on universal human rights but a *Universal Declaration*, apparently expressing thereby a set of moral convictions which they held in common. Although the original declaration was rather limited in the sense that it was only supported by a limited number of nations, in the past forty years the doctrine of human rights has become acknowledged virtually all over the world. An international consensus gradually emerged in which no single government could afford to dismiss accusations of violating human rights simply by saying that the people it represented did not share the moral convictions underlying this doctrine. Only very recently, however, as occurred at the United Nations Conference on Human Rights in Vienna in June 1993, several countries have been claiming precisely this defence, thus threatening this consensus. These countries argue that every nation is entitled to its own convictions and beliefs, and that, consequently, human rights cannot mean the same thing in different contexts. These countries - foremost among them China and Indonesia - thus seem to be challenging the assumption that the doctrine of human rights is an expression of common moral convictions.[1]

---

[1] This is not to say that we should understand their claim as one concerned with moral truth, because it is nothing of the sort. Their main purpose is to undermine the results of the Human Rights Conference of Teheran (1968) that led to the extensive monitoring of the implementation of human rights all over the world. Countries like China and Indonesia do not opt out of a universal consensus because of their different values but because they consider criticism of their human rights record as intervention in internal affairs. Their position betrays a conception of national sovereignty that is inconsistent with *any* commitment to universal human rights, whatever one's moral convictions.

There are other political phenomena that help to undermine the credibility of this assumption further. One need mention only the considerable political strife between people of different religious traditions in today's world: Hindus and Muslims in India, Muslims and Jews in the Middle East, Christians and Muslims in former Yugoslavia, etc. In addition, there are the rapidly spreading 'nationalist' conflicts in various parts of Eastern Europe that give little support to an international consensus on human rights based on common moral convictions. How can one then justify this assumption?

Apart from political developments, there is a philosophical reason for raising this issue. If one investigates the literature on the doctrine of human rights, one typically finds essays asking how this doctrine is received in this or that tradition. The conclusions of these essays, however, give the impression that there is anything but an expression of common moral convictions. Instead they indicate a wide range of moral diversity. One way of explaining such diversity is to argue that it exists only on the surface; underneath, however, there are universal moral beliefs founded upon the canons of moral reason. In this article I wish to examine this explanation, i.e., the view that underlying various interpretations of human rights there are common principles of moral reasoning by means of which one can assess their differences.

My examination of this argument will proceed along the following lines. I will first describe three particular interpretations of the doctrine of human rights from, respectively, oriental, Islamic and Christian perspectives. These examples are arbitrarily chosen and could be replaced by many others. Next, I will describe a theory that has been proposed recently to account for observations of the kind made in this introduction. This theory purports to show that, notwithstanding apparent diversity in cultural and religious traditions, there is a 'deep structure' of moral reasoning that underscores any of these traditions. In the third part I will discuss this theory in some detail in order to evaluate its claims. Finally, I will draw some conclusions on the rationality of interreligious moral dialogue on human rights.

Before I start, let me make one remark on terminology. In speaking of 'the doctrine of human rights' I do not refer to the enumerations of rights in documents such as the *Universal Declaration* and subsequent documents from the United Nations or other organizations.[2] As I use it, the term refers to a wider framework of ethical thought that includes answers to questions as to why people have human rights, what rights they have, and how important these are in

[2] There have been several declarations by religious organizations, of which the most famous is the *Universal Islamic Declaration of Human Rights* (London: Islamic Foundation, 1980). Also, several Christian organizations, such as the World Council of Churches have issued their own 'catalogue' of human rights. Cf. *Human Rights and Christian Responsibility* (Geneva: WCC Publications, 1974).

relation to other moral values. Thus, the question to be discussed is: which elements of this framework, if any, are shared by the various religious and cultural traditions.

CONTEXTUAL INTERPRETATIONS OF HUMAN RIGHTS

There is an initial assumption which provides our inquiry with a useful point of departure. This assumption is that it would be difficult to understand how the language of human rights could become part and parcel of otherwise different traditions unless there is some degree of commensurability between them. Building on this, Ryosuke Inagaki, a philosopher of law at Tokyo University, explains what he understands to be the ethical background of human rights in Japanese thought (Inagaki, 179-92). Human rights were introduced into Japanese legal thought in the early nineteenth century and Inagaki asks how this could have occurred if any notion of the equality between human beings, or of the fundamental rights of human beings, had been completely alien to pre-modern thought in Japan. The question is not easy to answer, since pre-modern Japanese philosophy was largely given to the ideology of feudalism, which was associated with hierarchical societal structures rather than social and political equality.

Human Rights and Japanese Thought

A positive exception to feudalist thought was Shoeki Ando (b. 1701), a 'rural philosopher', who spent most of his life in the agricultural north of the country. Shoeki's religious-ethical philosophy evolved from the concept of nature which he understood as the essential harmony and oneness of all being. Humans are capable of participating in this harmony when they follow the 'way of nature'. To understand this way of nature they must acquire the knowledge and skills of agricultural life, which teaches humans to develop appropriate moral feelings and attitudes that create harmony and peace among people (e.g. the natural affections of parents to children and husband to wife). In Shoeki's thought, the agricultural family provides the basic ethical model for human existence.

With this 'romantic' view of rural life, Shoeki intended to oppose what he called the 'law', as taught by Confucian and Buddhist sages. Although this law was also said to be based on nature, it interpreted the order of nature in terms of social hierarchy, which, in Shoeki's view, was clearly false. Nature itself does not display hierarchical structures but relativity and reciprocity. Based on its misconception of nature, the 'law' of Confucianism and Buddhism set out to justify the institutions that lay at the root of social and political evil. Due to this distinction between the 'reign of nature' and the 'reign of law', Inagaki reads Shoeki as an oriental Jean Jacques Rousseau, who also appealed to the 'original' social forms of agricultural life as the true source of human freedom.

On account of his egalitarianism, Shoeki Ando appears as a pre-modern proponent of the doctrine of human rights. He opposed the domination of humans by other humans and rejected the feudal system erected upon this foundation. He criticized any form of political domination and acknowledged the right to revolt - not only against tyrants but against any ruler. Shoeki would have said that the land belongs to those who cultivate and work it, and not to the feudal lords who, in his view, were mere usurpers. Given his attachment to the agricultural family, Shoeki could only conceive of legitimate authority in terms of the *pater familias*. Apart from his glaring difference in this respect from Rousseau - who was after all a republican - Shoeki appears to have understood the establishment of political authority as an intrusion upon the 'natural' authority of the head of the family. When asked how the nation should be ruled, Shoeki simply answered, "Do not rule the nation at all" (Inagaki, 189).

Despite his alleged quarrels with both Confucianism and Buddhism, Shoeki's philosophy shows a remarkable correspondence with early Chinese political thought, which also views government as something alien to the moral life of the community. When the community lives in accord with the agricultural way of life, it has little to gain from political power - as an early popular Chinese lyric states:

> working as the day breaks, retire as the evening comes.
> We dig wells in order to drink; we cultivate the land to eat.
> What can the emperor do to us?
>
> (Woo, 114)

Political rulers are required, therefore, to make themselves agreeable to the people. Thus the ethical model of the legitimate ruler in Chinese political philosophy is that of the virtuous prince, a compassionate and benevolent ruler who, like a good *pater familias*, knows how to govern without force so that his rule contributes to peace and harmony.

An important implication of this view, which seems to be characteristic for oriental thought as such, has been that the concept of righteousness was never defined in terms of justice, but always in terms of appropriateness. This general inclination toward a philosophy of harmony meant that philosophers who advanced the idea of just human relations never gained any real influence in Chinese thought (Woo, 116-17; Rosemont, 167-82). Buddhism seems to have confirmed this tradition in later periods (Gerlitz, 320-28). This does not necessarily imply that the notion of rights was entirely alien to Chinese thought but it does imply that it

> was always regarded merely as a stage of awareness in moving toward the higher concept of 'propriety'. The latter is stressed much more, since it would lead to harmony, whereas 'righteousness' is a concept that usually implies an enforced legal activity. To strive for righteousness for oneself or for others is directly opposed to what is a natural and moral attitude of life, because this activity destroys the presumption of the natural harmony. (Woo, 120)

The same holds true for the reception of human rights in modern Japanese thought. Inagaki says that the notion of an individual self, distinct from other selves and possessing inalienable rights, is much less prominent in Japanese thought than the notion of one's moral duty to contribute to social harmony. Before the middle of the nineteenth century, therefore, the Japanese language lacked an equivalent for 'right', while there were many for 'duty' and 'obligation'. These observations lead Inagaki to conclude that

> The absence of the term [right (JSR)] seems to be due to the fact that to claim and defend one's rights openly and publicly was not considered virtuous, or even decent. The root of the problem lies in the fact that traditional Japanese moral, political and social ideas were developed in the context of the 'family-society'. It is characteristic of the 'family-society' that the idea of 'other' in the strict sense is absent; that is, there is no clear distinction between what belongs to me and to others (....) Where all social relations have been conceived after the pattern of a family, as has been the case in Japan, the development of a well-defined idea of justice and right has had little chance. (Inagaki, 191)

With this conclusion Inagaki confirms the distinctive meaning of rights as it is understood by Western social philosophers, such as, for example, Joel Feinberg. According to Feinberg, a society where rights are unknown is a society where the practice of claiming one's due is absent (Feinberg, 243-57). Japanese society appears to be very much this type of society. As Inagaki puts it, rather than claiming what is rightfully theirs, people in Japanese society are expected to sacrifice these claims readily in the spirit of communal virtue and self-denial (Inagaki, 192). This conclusion is supported by the fact that the enactment of human rights in the Japanese constitution after World War II was clearly and exclusively the result of foreign occupation (Inagaki, 183; Van Wolferen, ch. 8). Inagaki's initial assumption that the Japanese people must have had some "disposition or aptitude" for accepting the doctrine, therefore, seems unwarranted. One cannot avoid the impression that human rights are a *corpus alienum* in traditional Japanese thought.

An Islamic Interpretation of Human Freedom

A quick look at the body of literature on the subject of Islam and human rights is sufficient to warrant the view that there is no such thing as *the* Islamic view on this subject. The interpretation that will be described here seems to be a more 'conservative' one. Its author is the originally Iranian scholar, Seyyed Hossein Nasr, who attacks what he sees as the Western interpretation of the doctrine (1980, 95-101). Insofar as his criticisms also extend to some of the liberal authors within the Islamic world, they provide a good example of the wide diversity of interpretations that exist even among Islamic authors.

Nasr rightly perceives the doctrine as it is understood in the West to be dependent on a notion of human freedom as self-government. It presupposes a conception of humans as beings that create their own future, which Nasr terms the conception of "promethean man" (1981, 160-88). To understand freedom solely in terms of action, however, Nasr argues, is reductionist. He explains this by distinguishing between "the freedom to act" and "the freedom to be", which is characterized by the experience of "pure existence itself". We are thus dealing with a mystic (Nasr appeals in particular to the tradition of Sufi mysticism) whose main concern is personal and not political freedom:

> Personal freedom lies, in fact, in surrendering to the Divine Will and in purifying oneself to an ever greater degree inwardly so as to become liberated from all external conditions, including those of the carnal soul (*nafs*), which press upon and limit one's freedom. (Nasr, 1980, 96)

Personal freedom, which Nasr also defines as "absolute or infinite freedom", can only be found in spiritual life. At a "lower" level of existence, the freedom to act exists within the limits imposed upon human beings by external reality. Absolute or infinite freedom is of a different nature, but this should not be taken to mean that this mystical conception of freedom has no social and political relevance. According to Nasr, it is at the heart of all Islamic jurisprudence, which is based on human freedom, viewed not as an innate personal right but as the wish to surrender to the will of God.

Nasr's conception of human freedom obviously has far-reaching implications for his account of human rights in Islamic law. Contrary to, for example, the Western tradition of natural law, human rights can never be the basis for social obligations. The reverse, rather, obtains:

> Human rights are, according to the Shariah, a *consequence* of human obligations and not their antecedent. We possess certain obligations toward God, nature, and other humans, all of which are delineated by the Shariah. As *a result of fulfilling these obligations*, we gain certain rights and freedoms that are again outlined by the Divine law. Those who do not fulfill these obligations have no legitimate rights (....) in the same way that those persons who refuse to recognize their theomorphic nature and act accordingly are only 'accidentally' human. (Nasr, 1980, 97, italics added)

Nasr is not at all impressed by the widespread criticism of the lack of individual freedom in Islamic society nor is he inclined to support legal reform in Islam. In his view, the crucial test for Islam is whether it will be able to keep alive the way of attaining absolute inner freedom. In this respect he considers Islamic society to be eminently successful: it has been able to preserve its spiritual ways of attaining this freedom "despite all the obstacles that the gradual darkening of man's outward nature has placed before authentic spiritual paths" (Nasr, 1980, 101).

This way of phrasing his appreciation for the Islamic tradition betrays his attachment to a particular conception of history - 'the *gradual darkening* of man's outward nature" - which is partly the reason for presenting his views here. This conception is that of history as the ongoing attempt to revive the 'Golden Age' of Islam. In Nasr's philosophy, the normative model for Islamic society lies in the past, providing this society with a retrospective rather than a prospective ideal. In the Age of the Prophet that lasted till the end of the reign of the four righteous caliphs, Islamic justice obtained its purest form. In the subsequent ruling dynasties only the deterioration of justice as it existed in this 'Golden Age' occurred.

In discussing this issue, Fouad Zakaria, professor of philosophy at Kuwait University, argues that it is particularly this retrospective conception of history that accounts for the conservative interpretations of human rights in Islam (Zakaria, 227-41). In his view, the idea of a 'Golden Age' is detrimental to any viable understanding of history, because it rules out any positive historical development: history, on this view, is a history of decline. As a result, the understanding of human rights in Islamic conservatism is essentially "static" in that they are derived from the "ancient" and "sacred origin" of the classical sources of Islamic law. There is no room for adaptation to changing circumstances and appreciation of the evolution of rights in society:

> ... man's acquisition of his rights is complete at the outset; any adjustment thereafter is only a gradual diminution of them. Subsequent historical development gives us witness to retreats from and misinterpretations in the practice of them, with the result that history has not been able to exercise its function of giving firm ground to the right and making it articulate; it has only made it more shaky and obscure. (Zakaria, 237)

This peculiar feature of Nasr's conservatism - the embodiment of right in 'original' divine law - reveals a deep conflict with modern democratic thinking in the Western tradition. If human rights are conditional upon obedience to the Divine Will, as Nasr maintains, than it is difficult to see how the rights of *human beings qua human beings* can ever be the source of political legitimacy as they are in the West. This conclusion arises not only because it is the fulfilment of religious duty that is regarded as the proper source of rights, but also because it is only the human being *who lives by the Shari'a* who can claim these rights. It is not only that one needs to earn one's rights as a citizen, but Islamic law also determines what rights citizens can have. It is only with difficulty that one can conceive of the doctrine of human rights forming the 'legitimizing' framework of constitutional law, as it has been in most Western democracies. Conversely, the legitimacy of human rights is explained by Islamic law.

Besides the conservative Nasr, other Islamic voices are being raised, particularly those who have been calling for legislative reform (An-Na'im, 1990).[3] And in this connection the position of both women and religious minorities in Islam are two notorious issues (Hassan, 51-66; Keddie, 76-93). But my intention has not been to suggest that the interpretation described here is in any way authoritative or representative for the Islamic world. It has only been to show how particular theological and philosophical frameworks determine particular interpretations of human rights.

Human Rights from an Eschatological Point of View

My third example is in sharp contrast with Nasr's view - not so much because it stems from a different religious tradition but because it is guided by a radically different conception of human history. It is inferred from documents issued by the World Alliance of Reformed Churches, based mainly on materials prepared by the German theologian Jürgen Moltmann. This theological interpretation of human rights is grounded in what is called "das Recht Gottes auf den Menschen" (Moltmann, 1976a, 44-60). While this indicates a religious foundation not unlike Nasr's, it is completely different in that it operates with a conception of history that is radically anticipatory.

To establish his theological view, Moltmann draws on the notions of creation and redemption as understood in biblical theology. The former implies that human beings are destined to be free from all kinds of bondage, while the latter implies that, because of human sinfulness, no human project is capable of realizing this freedom completely. The human destiny to be free remains an eschatological prospective and history is thus the story of divine liberation from human bondage, mirrored in the ongoing struggle for human rights.

Given this ongoing struggle, there is no room in Moltmann's conception for a definite set of human rights, such as were enumerated in the *Universal Declaration* of 1948. The doctrine remains open to constant reinterpretation, so that currently, for example, great emphasis needs to be placed upon what might be called "ecological rights". In Moltmann's own explanation, he attempts to establish the universality of human rights in such a way that it is not tainted by the contingencies of any historical interpretation (Moltmann, 1976b, 280-82). In his view, it is necessarily true that any attempt to ground a universal doctrine of human rights on particular historical experiences must fail because of the limited nature of these experiences. A truly universal perspective on human freedom, therefore, can only be one that encompasses history itself. The eschatological model for such a perspective is provided by the Christian narrative of liberation from sin and death (Moltmann, 1977, 495-96; Tödt, 266-69).

---

[3] Cf. also A.A. An-Na'im's essay in this volume, pp. 229-42.

Having established this model, Moltmann is in a position to explain the practical relevance of his interpretation. Writing at the time of the Helsinki Conference on human rights (1975), he refers to the conflict between liberal and Marxist interpretations of human rights, which dominated the international debate at that time. To these two perspectives he adds a 'Third World' perspective and then claims that each of these perspectives are to be supplemented by the others. Accordingly, Western democracies are criticized for their limited efforts to secure social and economic rights (the right to employment, for example). Socialist countries are criticized for their lack of respect for civil liberties. Third World countries demand other priorities, such as the position of minorities. Different priorities in different circumstances are derived from the same universal perspective of liberation by means of this "dialectical openness":

> Wo individuelle Rechte auf Kosten der sozialen Menschenrechte realisiert wurden, sind diese geltend zu machen. Wo individuelle Menschenrechte zugunsten der sozialen außer Kraft gesetzt wurden, sind sie einzufordern. Wo Menschen die ökonomischen Grundrechte auf Leben, Nahrung auf Arbeit vermissen, haben diese Priorität. (Moltmann, 1976b, 281)

Christian interpretations of human rights cannot as a matter of principle assign priority to any particular right but will seek in any given situation to combat the actual injustices of social and political systems and regimes. Accordingly, Christian churches are not to identify with any of these particular historical perspectives. Instead, they should ask in each situation which people, individuals and groups, have their human rights most severely violated or endangered. The characteristically eschatological view implies - in line with the *perichoresis* of the Divine Trinity - "the mutual permeance of complementary rights" (Lochman, 1979, 17-25).

THE 'DEEP STRUCTURE' OF RELIGIOUS MORAL REASON

Given the various differences between the interpretations described above, the question is: how is the practice of intercultural and interreligious dialogue on human rights to be understood? What kind of rationality, if any, would effect such dialogue? In this section we will examine the answer developed by Ronald M. Green in his book *Religion and Moral Reason* (1988), which he presented as a "new method of comparative study of religion".

Green argues that religious traditions differ considerably in what he calls their "surface teachings", but this does not rule out that underlying them is a "deep structure" of religious moral reason. Notwithstanding the diversity of expression, the basic processes of both religious and moral reasoning are the same everywhere:

> This process of religious reasoning has its beginning in a method of moral judgment that, because it reflects the rational constraints on conduct in any communal situation, is common to all human beings and human cultures. Specific moral norms are the complex *outcome* of this process after it has been applied to different circumstances in different contexts, and for this reason specific norms can differ. But the underlying method of decision and judgment is the same everywhere. (Green, xii)

In my examination of Green's theory I will confine myself to an analysis of this "deep structure", which enables any religious tradition to deal effectively with the perennial problems of communal life. These problems concern three particular phenomena: the pursuit of self-interest, the willingness to sacrifice and the experience of moral failure. Together, these problems and the way in which religious moral reason seeks to overcome them constitute the latter's deep structure. In what follows I will turn to each of them as characterized in Green's analysis. I will then take up the question of how this analysis applies to the diverse interpretations of human rights outlined above.

The Moral Point of View

The function of morality, both in social and personal life, is primarily to restrain the pursuit of self-interest. In our personal lives, we must learn to control our tendencies to satisfy wants and desires immediately, in order to obtain happiness and self-fulfillment.[4] In social life, we must practice self-restraint with regard to our fellow human beings in order to maintain social order and stability. Both forms of restraint require that our reasoning as to how we should act proceeds from a particular perspective - what Western philosophers have recently termed "the moral point of view" (Baier, 1958).

Green explains this requirement by reference to the fundamental principle of Kantian ethics, which states that the appropriate guide for any action is whether it can be justified from a universal point of view. Contrary to what many of Kant's critics have argued, Green insists that the Kantian requirement should not be taken to say merely that similar cases are to be treated similarly. The categorical imperative is not merely the requirement of logical consistency, for we should not only assess our conduct

> from the egocentric perspective of our own situation but also from the standpoint of others we might affect. In Kantian terms, what one wills must be capable of becoming 'universal law' not only because it must apply to all other

[4] Green's pervasive use of first-person plural pronouns - 'we', 'us' and 'our' - obviously presupposes that his own convictions and beliefs on the matter are recognized by anybody else as true, regardless of any cultural or religious differences.

> persons, but also because it is something they might 'vote for' or accept - a law *for, of,* and *by* everyone. (Green, 6)

In view of widespread moral diversity, however, many people seem to lean toward ethical relativism, rather than accepting this method of universal moral reasoning. This is a mistake, according to Green, because the diversity of morals does not represent "fundamentally different ways" of moral reasoning. To establish this claim, Green refers to well-known examples from the ethical literature such as, for example, the fact that all traditions prohibit wanton killing. Due to different circumstances, they have to develop different rules with regard to what counts as 'wanton'. While the practical content of these rules may differ, this does not show that the logic by which they operate cannot be the same. This logic requires that one transcends one's own immediate desires to make "impartial" choices from a social or communal point of view.

The Reason to be Moral

It is necessary to make our choices from this particular perspective if we are to be prepared to consider ways of conduct that go against our own interests. In Green's view, our willingness to sacrifice is essential to morality. The resultant problem is that moral action can be irrational from the point of view of our self-interest. So the question arises: Why be moral in the first place? Green claims that the problem of moral motivation, as it is called, cannot be answered satisfactorily from a philosophical point of view. Neither prudence nor moral reason can supply an argument for being moral. While the latter cannot supply such an argument without being caught in circularity, the appeal to the former is self-defeating. To sacrifice one's own interests for the interests of others is in many cases not prudent at all. So, in asking where the answer to the question of moral motivation is to be found, Green points to religion:

> Religious belief enters at precisely this point. We can think of religion as the effort by a rational being to act in a fully rational manner. (....) It is human reason's effort to resolve its own internal dispute and to make possible coherent rational choice. (....) Although the individual may appear to run terrible risks in choosing to be moral, these risks are not the last word on the matter. Beyond sacrifice lie possibilities of fulfillment directly proportional to moral effort. Moral retribution is certain. The righteous are rewarded. Those who risk their lives shall gain them. (Green, 15)

Also, with regard to this doctrine of moral retribution, different ideas and metaphors are present in various religious traditions, but Green again insists that these differences cannot make us overlook that the underlying logic, the 'deep structure', is essentially the same: the religious belief in moral retribution is necessary to bridge the gap between rationality and morality.

The Awareness of Failure

The belief in moral retribution implies the view that "the world is ruled by a moral geometry". But the experience of the suffering of the righteous tends to undermine this belief. Therefore an explanation is required in order to be able to uphold one's belief in this "moral geometry". In this connection, the awareness of failure weighs heavily on religious conscience. Our experience teaches us the "omnipresence and inescapability of sin", according to Green, which implies that even the righteous do not deserve their award as yet:

> In moments of honest moral insight, we know ourselves to be called to total moral commitment, but the awareness of our rational freedom to choose otherwise and the powerful attractions of self-interest work together to produce a sense that we may not be up to this demand. As a result, we can never confidently assert our own moral goodness. (Green, 19)

Green's claim here is that we all know, by experience, of our own weakness of will. Hence the "pervasive sense of moral inadequacy" that occupies the conscience of anyone who seriously contemplates his or her motives to be moral. In facing this inadequacy, the religious person clings to her belief in a divine mercy that will take her confession of sinfulness into account. This divine will is "beyond morality", not only in the sense that it is free not to judge us by our own standards but also in the sense that it provides the ultimate ground for obeying the moral law. The notion of forgiveness does not mean that obedience to this law does not finally count, but it does mean that our ability to obey this law depends on our being liberated from sin, which cannot be achieved within the domain of the moral itself.

LAYING FOUNDATIONS AND OFFERING REASONS

I have described Green's theory of the deep structure of religious moral reason in some detail in order to uncover in particular the presuppositions on which it is based. This I will do, again under three headings: the conception of morality, the Kantian account of moral reason, and the universality of basic moral rules. By applying this deep structure to the diverse interpetations of human rights portrayed in the previous section, I intend to show that Green fails to establish his thesis that there is a method of moral judgment common to all human beings and human cultures.

'Morality of Constraint' versus 'Morality of Direction'

Despite appearances, Green's conception of morality belongs to a tradition of moral philosophy that has its origins not so much in Kant but in the ethical naturalism of philosophers like Thomas Hobbes and David Hume. This tradition has been revived in recent times by such thinkers as Geoffrey Warnock (1971) and John Mackie (1977). Within this view, the purpose of morality is to constrain the acts of individuals in order to secure the conditions necessary for a stable society. The concept of morality emerging from this tradition has at least five distinguishing features each of which can be found in Green's text. First, morality consists of rules pertaining to acts. Secondly, these acts are identified by the fact that they affect other people. Thirdly, the purpose of these moral rules is to constrain self-interest. Fourthly, the reason for considering the well-being of others ('why be moral?') is believed to be 'external' to morality itself. Fifthly, moral actions beyond what is minimally required ('acts of supererogation') are of secondary importance only. When viewed together and in combination, these features amount to what Peter Strawson has called the "narrow conception of morality", which arose in Western liberal society since the seventeenth century together with religious pluralism and is characterized, therefore, by the fact that it expels religious ideals of the good life from social morality (Strawson, 1970, 98-119). With regard to the last feature Green, for example, argues that, although there are sharp differences between religious traditions about the saintly life, this does not imply differences on the basic moral norms. All traditions condemn wanton killing, cheating, or abuse of other persons, which establishes the compartmentalization of morality in what is socially necessary and what is the good life for human beings (Green, 10).

Returning to the interpretations of the doctrine of human rights in the second paragraph of this essay, it will be immediately clear that at least two of them presuppose quite different conceptions of morality. Seyyed Nasr, for example, explicitly criticizes Western liberal thought for interpreting freedom with regard to the question of what one may or may not justifiably do. In contrast, he argues for a conception of spiritual freedom, the "freedom to be" as the highest goal of morality. Human nature is essentially spiritual, which implies that it can attain fulfilment only by being liberated from what is only accidental to it, namely its limitations in the 'external' world. Accordingly, true freedom is attained not by struggling for social and political liberation but by seeking reconciliation with God.

At this point there is also a crucial difference with the oriental conception of morality as it appears in Inagaki's description. Morality here is also primarily a question of 'being' rather than 'acting'. By living in accord with nature as it is revealed in agricultural life, humans will attain fulfilment in unity and harmony with being itself. In pre-modern Japanese thought as described by Inagaki, the morality of the ruler is founded on virtue and good character rather than on constraint vis-à-vis the freedom of the citizen. Likewise, the oriental perspective on morality in general does not seem to be primarily occupied with constraining action with regard to the interests of others. Green's account of the Taoist view of 'the Way' as a cosmological order of which the order of nature is a reflection, therefore, raises the question of how this cosmology fits the narrow conception of morality supposedly operative in the deep structure of religious moral reason (Green, 70-71). Its main concern is not to ask what it is from which *other* people ought to remain free or against which they are to be protected, but how one achieves harmony and oneness with 'being' as the *telos* of human existence. From this broader perspective of morality as it is found both in Islamic and oriental views, Green's conception of morality cannot appear as anything but legalistic. It will be seen to be the concern of lawyers rather than 'moralists'.

Moreover, one should note that the Western ethical tradition itself has been deeply divided on this point. Pre-modern Western conceptions of morality were not so much concerned with constraining self-interested individuals as they were with attaining human fulfillment. In this respect, medieval ethical thought, of which Aquinas' moral theory is the most outstanding example, pursued the same course as that of the Greeks. With respect to the latter, the American philosopher William K. Frankena says that

> The Greeks were seeking the *rational* way to live, without making special mention of the *moral* way to live; their solutions do not center on our relations to other persons. However, the moderns conceive of a specifically *moral* way to live that is largely a matter of our relations to our fellow human beings. A prevailing egoism in Greek ethics runs counter to the altruism in modern ethics. (Frankena, 1980, 11)

Ignoring the self-congratulatory tone of this statement, Frankena's adherence to the narrow conception of morality tends to make him even deny the classical tradition a moral view at all. But this is clearly false. Within both the Aristotelian and Thomist framework there is no distinction between living a good life and acting morally, but this does not mean that the latter is without importance. In order to act morally one has to be virtuous, while the aim of being virtuous is to attain the good life, which - far from being merely egoistic - aims at human perfection. Throughout its history Christianity has espoused less a social ethics than an ethics of virtue (MacIntyre, 1981; 1988).

It is difficult to see, therefore, how the Kantian view on moral universality could be common to all human beings and human cultures *because* it reflects the rational constraints on conduct in any community. For this is true only if morality is universally understood to be concerned with constraining self-interested individuals in the pursuit of their private projects. This is clearly not the case. In his account of Confucius' teachings, for example, Green himself points out that the 'Golden Rule' in Confucian thought is an expression of "the moral point of view" as explained by Kantian ethics. But he also shows that both the *scope* and *range* of this rule are controlled by the 'virtue' and 'propriety' of the nobleman that he exhibits in following customs both as a political and religious leader (Green, 51-52; see also Ames, 199-216). Not all people have understood their practices of moral judgment, therefore, as the operation of "impartialist reason". Against this objection Green might answer that, while not all human beings in all cultures may have *understood* morality in terms of Kantian moral philosophy, this does not preclude the possibility that this philosophy *explains* the logical structure of their moral beliefs correctly. It is at this point that I have my second quarrel with Green's theory, with respect to his defense against the objection of the empty formalism of Kantian moral theory.

Foundationalist Ethics

As already indicated, the objection states that, as a strictly formal requirement of moral reason, the categorical imperative is inadequate for distinguishing between the moral and the immoral. For example, a white racist could hold that apartheid is not morally objectionable, because, if he were black, he would prefer to live under that system.[5] The point is that someone can consistently justify certain immoral acts by accepting their adverse consequences for himself in the case that he happens to be the recipient of these acts.

Green's response to this objection, as we saw, is that the categorical imperative does not only entail impartiality but also the more radical requirement of "omnipartiality". It compels us to consider our actions from the *actual point of view* of all those who will be affected by them. There is a serious defect in this defense, however, because respect for persons in Kant's view means respect for *reasonable* persons. This follows from the third formulation of the categorical imperative, the so-called principle of humanity, which reads: "Act so that you treat humanity, whether in your own person or in that of another, always as an end and never as a means only" (Kant, 1959, 47). Thus Kant did not mean to state that other persons enter into our moral reasoning as empirical egos: he explicitly stresses that the principle of humanity can only be objective insofar as it is based on what is an end in itself, i.e., "rational nature" (Kant, *ibid.*). Consequently, on this view "omnipartiality" can only mean that one ought to take into account the will of others insofar as it characterizes them as reasonable persons. In other words, what others actually want for themselves is morally considerable *if and only if* it is reasonable.

Green ignores this condition, however, by substituting the notion of "what the others *actually* will for themselves" for "the will of reasonable persons". While this substitution interprets the objectivity of morals in terms of intersubjectivity, it presupposes a completely different conception of moral reason. Kantian moral reason is essentially what Seyla Benhabib has called *monological reason*, which one cannot turn into *dialogical reason* without implicitly rejecting the Kantian account (Benhabib, 1-31). Nonetheless, this is what Green intends to do. In order to justify in moral terms a particular course of action and the rule it entails, one must not only ask whether it could be anybody's action, but whether it is acceptable to all persons affected by this action. Thus, the categorical imperative is changed from a logical into a social device for moral justification. In

[5] The adequacy of this counter-example depends, of course, on the presupposition that apartheid as a social and political system *is* morally objectionable.

other words, the objection to the empty formalism of the Kantian account of moral reason is met by explaining it in terms of a consensus theory of moral justification. But that is certainly not what Kant meant by his categorical imperative. Everybody's point of view is plainly not the same as anybody's point of view, which indicates the difference between dialogical and monological reasoning. To explain the latter in terms of the former is not a radical interpretation: it is to change it into something completely different.

Furthermore, Green's manoeuvre to save Kant from formalism is not without consequences for his own thesis regarding the deep structure of religious moral reason. The shift from monological to dialogical reason implies that we can only justify our moral beliefs vis-à-vis the beliefs that people from other cultural or religious traditions actually have. This conclusion has a very important consequence for our standards of moral justification, for it means that these standards are themselves subject to and cannot be exempt from moral dialogue. Consequently, the moral principle implied in the deep structure cannot be presented as only an *explanation* of the logical structure of traditional moral beliefs. In the dialogical process it is one account among others, open to discussion with respect to its validity. In other words, the Kantian account of moral reason is not the description of moral logic that underscores all possible moral positions but is itself expressive of one of these positions.

If this argument holds, it has one further implication for Green's account of the deep structure: this account does not merely *describe* the logic inherent in particular religious convictions, but also criticizes these convictions from a *normative* point of view. There are several examples to this effect in his work. In his chapter on Confucian thought, for example, he is forced to conclude that it "neglected" two elements of the deep structure of religious moral reason, among which is the notion of moral retribution in relation to sin and forgiveness (Green, 55, 61). Consider also his observation regarding the "failure" of Taoism as an indigenous religion: "Where indigenous cultured religion fails to meet the conceptual needs dictated by reason's deep structure, the void is typically filled by alternative movements and tendencies" (Green, 74).

A third example showing his account to be normative rather than descriptive concerns the Divine will as moral authority. Orthodox believers like the Muslim Seyyed Nasr might well contest the moral authority of the rational will of human beings and want to submit it to the authority of the will of God. Green comments that divine command as the source of moral authority is only acceptable if God is obeyed because He is righteous (Green, 80). It is the moral content of the divine will that obtains. While this is undoubtedly true from the point of view of universal moral reason, the orthodox believer may well have reasons to deny the possibility of an independent standard of righteousness. It is hard to see how Green could answer this objection without running into the same difficulties we encountered with regard to the monological nature of Kantian moral reason.

The last point in this connection regards the claim that the categorical imperative is not only a precondition of social life, but also "a firm and essential part of *our rational structure*" (Green, 15, italics added). This apparently means that his account of the moral law represents a fact about our reason that is not optional: it just happens to operate according to this law. This identification of what is seen as a metaphysical and a social fact strikes one as a clear example of what Richard Rorty has described as the typical manoeuvre of foundationalist epistemology: the attempt to show that our knowledge of the world is mirrored and therefore "grounded" in our reasoning processes (Rorty, 1979).

Contrary to what Green intends, however, his assertion ironically shows that the Kantian foundation of the moral law is indeed optional. If there are certain requirements that amount to a *necessary* condition of social life - such as the requirement to constrain individual self-interest for the sake of social order and stability - then one adds nothing by saying that these requirements are confirmed by the formal logic of moral reason. Nor are they necessarily explained in these terms, which is supported by the fact that we find the same requirements to be "grounded" in quite different moral theories as is shown, for example, by the ethical naturalism of Thomas Hobbes, who does not know anything of the formal logic of moral reason in the Kantian sense, but has much to say about the necessary constraints on the pursuit of individual self-interest.

Universal Rules

Finally, there is a point to be made about the universality of the basic moral rules. The logic of these rules, as Green explains, is simple. "Do not wantonly kill another human being" means that killing without moral justification is forbidden. This rule can be found in any culture - which is probably true - but cultures will differ in what they accept as moral justification. Since they have to adapt themselves to different circumstances, says Green, moral diversity with respect to the content of this rule should be expected (Green, 9; see also Milne, 1986; Reinders, 86-89). To illustrate the point he uses the famous example of the Eskimo community, in which the killing of the elderly is not only accepted, but considered a duty towards one's parents once they are no longer able to sustain themselves. Given the circumstances of this community, particularly its existence on the edge of survival and the necessity of all members to partake in securing food, the justification of killing the elderly is understandable and, according to Green, does not display anything like a "fundamentally different way of thinking about moral choice".

What is remarkable in connection with this example, however, is that Green confines his comments to ethical relativism and does not mention ethical pluralism. His justification for the Eskimo's acceptance of killing the elderly is clearly utilitarian: it is justified by the community's interest in survival. Even when this is accepted as a valid justification by all members of this community, this does not by any means rule out a "fundamentally different way" of thinking about the morality of killing when compared with other communities. Surely there are those that do not accept utilitarian reasons for killing other people as moral justification. As a matter of fact, Green himself seems to oppose utilitarian reasoning in cases like the one under consideration, when he says that at times it is reasonable to forego the interests of a majority. This is when we feel "that many basic human rights should not be subject to majority rule and why we believe - against the utilitarians - that certain principles of right and justice should be respected even if they do not always benefit the majority" (Green, 7).

The prohibition of wanton killing may be judged by different moral standards derived from distinct and incommensurable moral values (Nagel, 128-137). Contrary to what Green asserts, differences in moral beliefs cannot always be explained as differences in factual circumstances, but may be dependent on different values underlying different types of moral justification.

CONCLUDING REMARKS

I started this essay with the question of whether there are common moral convictions underlying the doctrine of human rights on which interreligious dialogue can draw, notwithstanding the considerable differences between various traditions. The foregoing analysis yields a clear answer to this question. Whether there are or are not such common convictions is a matter *to be discovered* in moral dialogue; probably it cannot be established by neutral philosophical analysis. The analysis presented by Green suggests that the moral views of particular traditions can be tested by a critical method, which in turn is established by independent philosophical reason. This suggestion turns out to be implausible, however. There is no such thing as 'the' method of moral reason used at all times and places, nor 'the' foundation of morality. Given different worldviews within which moral systems are developed, what can most likely be expected is a corresponding set of 'foundations'. No foundation of a moral system or code in fact *transcends* the particular convictions of the tradition within which it is developed. It only *reflects* these convictions on a more abstract level and reconstructs them in a more sophisticated way. In order to combat moral diversity, it may be more effective to practice dialogical reasoning than to continue digging for philosophical foundations. If the truth of moral convictions cannot be established by independent reason, then there is no truth to be found except through dialogue. As we have seen, to conceive of moral reasoning in dialogical terms changes the question of justification from a logical into a social and historical issue. In fact, that is how the universal doctrine of human rights has been developed in the last forty years.

A few concluding remarks may be added to this. The first is that the rejection of foundationalism in moral theory does not mean that one is imprisoned by one's own moral tradition. Even though the critical counterpart of my tradition is not a supreme principle founded in universal moral reason, it does not follow that there is no critical counterpart at all. Traditions are not necessarily given to idiosyncrasy but can be both critical and receptive towards one another. Recognition of particularity in one's own and in other traditions is a precondition rather than a limitation of mutual understanding. Closely related to this is a second remark. The shift from monological towards dialogical reason implies what might be called the *epistemic competence* of all participants in moral dialogue. If the subject matter of human rights is the universal quest for what it means to be a human being, then every human being must have a say in the answer to this question. Therefore interreligious dialogue cannot but oscillate between the universal and the particular. The fact that religious traditions hold their own view of human nature to be true for all human beings means that they all are driven towards universality. At the same time, however, they all are confronted by the otherness of convictions held by people from other traditions. Each tradition therefore has to account for the relation between the universal and the particular within its own framework. It is this problem at least which they all share. Furthermore, the acceptance of epistemic competence in interreligious dialogue rules out the possibility of playing down the differences between particular convictions as insignificant, because only through the recognition of otherness will it be possible to test moral truth. In my view, this is finally the answer to the question of whether the doctrine of human rights can be supported by religious traditions. Stated somewhat paradoxically: only through recognizing otherness does it become possible to aspire to moral universality.

The question that interreligious dialogue on human rights poses before us, then, is not only how we from within our own religious tradition interpret the doctrine. It is also how we think people from other traditions will interpret it, as well as what they may think about our own interpretations.

BIBLIOGRAPHY

Ames, R.T., "Rites as Rights: The Confucian Alternative." In: L.S. Rouner (ed.). *Human Rights and the World's Religions*. Notre Dame, IN: University of Notre Dame Press, 1988. Pp.199-216.

An-Na'im, A.A. *Toward an Islamic Reformation: Civil Liberties, Human Rights and International Law*. Syracuse, New Jersey: Syracuse University Press, 1990.

Baier, K. *The Moral Point of View*. London: Ithaca Press, 1958.

Benhabib, S. "In the Shadow of Aristotle and Hegel: Communicative Ethics and Current Controversies in Practical Philosophy." *The Philosophical Forum* 21 (1989): 1-31.

Feinberg, J. "The Nature and Value of Rights." *Journal of Value Inquiry* 4 (1970): 243-57.

Frankena, W.K. *Thinking about Morality*, Ann Arbor: University of Michigan Press, 1980.

Gerlitz, P. "Die Ethik des Buddha: Philosophische Grundlagen und sittliche Normen in frühen Buddhismus." In: C.H. Ratschow (ed.). *Ethik der Religionen*. Stuttgart/Berlin: Kohlhammer Verlag, 1980. Pp. 320-28.

Green, R.M. *Religion and Moral Reason: A New Method for Comparative Study*. New York/Oxford: Oxford University Press, 1988.

Hassan, R. "On Human Rights and the Qur'an Perspective." In: A. Swidler (ed.). *Human Rights in Religious Traditions*. New York: Pilgrim Press, 1982. Pp. 51-66.

Inagaki, R. "Some Aspects of Human Rights in Japan." In: P. Ricoeur (ed.). *Philo sophical Foundations of Human Rights*. Paris: UNESCO, 1986. Pp. 179-192.

Kant, I. *Foundations of the Metaphysics of Morals*. Tr. by Lewis White Beck. Indianopolis: Bobbs-Merrill Educational Publishing, 1959.

Keddie, N.R. "The Rights of Women in Contemporary Islam." In: L.S. Rouner (ed.). *Human Rights and the World's Religions*. Notre Dame, IN: University of Notre Dame Press, 1988. Pp. 76-93.

Lochman, J.M. "Ideology or Theology of Human Rights. Contemporary Problems of the Concept of Human Rights." *Concilium* 15 (1979): 17-25.

MacIntyre, A. *After Virtue: A Study in Moral Theory*. London: Duckworth Press, 1981.

——. *Whose Justice? Which Rationality?* Notre Dame, IN: University of Notre Dame Press, 1988.

Mackie, J.L. *Ethics: Inventing Right and Wrong*, Harmondsworth: Penguin Books, 1977.

Milne, A.J.M. *Human Rights and Human Diversity: An Essay in the Philosophy of Human Rights*. London: MacMillan, 1986.

Moltmann, J. "Theologische Erklärung zu den Menschenrechte." In: J.M. Lochman and J. Moltmann (eds.). *Gottes Recht und Menschenrechte, Studien und Empfehlungen des Reformierten Weltbundes*. Neukirchen/Vluyn: Kreuz Verlag, 1976. Pp. 44-60.

——. "Welches Recht hat das Ebenbild Gottes? Erklärungen des Reformierten Weltbundes zu den Menschenrechten." *Evangelische Kommentare* 9 (1976): 280-82.

——. "Streit um Menschenrechte." *Evangelische Kommentare* 10 (1977): 495-96.

Nagel, T. *Moral Questions* Cambridge: Cambridge University Press.

Nasr, S.H. "The Concept and Reality of Freedom in Islam and Islamic Civilization." In: A.S. Rosenbaum (ed.). *The Philosophy of Human Rights - International Perspectives*. Westport, Connecticut: Greenwood Press, 1980. Pp. 95-101.

——. *Knowledge and the Sacred.* The 1981 Gifford Lectures. Edinburgh: Edinburgh University Press, 1981.

Reinders, J.S. "Ethical Universalism and Human Rights." In: A. Musschenga *et al.* (eds.). *Morality, Worldview and Law*. Assen/Maastricht: Van Gorcum, 1992. Pp. 81-98.

Ricoeur, P. (ed.). *Philosophical Foundations of Human Rights*. Paris: UNESCO, 1986.

Rorty, R. *Philosophy and the Mirror of Nature*. Princeton: Princeton University Press, 1979.

Rosemont, H., Jr. "Why Take Rights seriously? A Confucian Critique." In: L.S. Rouner (ed.). *Human Rights and the World's Religions*. Notre Dame, IN: University of Notre Dame Press, 1988. Pp. 167-82.

Rosenbaum, A.S. (ed.). *The Philosophy of Human Rights - International Perspectives*. Westport, Connecticut: Greenwood Press, 1980.

Rouner, L.S. (ed.). *Human Rights and the World's Religions*. Notre Dame, IN: University of Notre Dame Press, 1988.

Strawson, P.F. "Social Morality and Individual Ideal." In: G. Wallace & A.D.M. Walker (eds.). *The Definition of Morality*. London, 1970. Pp. 98-119.

Swidler, A. (ed.). *Human Rights in Religious Traditions*. New York: Pilgrim Press, 1982.

Tödt, H.E. "Die Grundwerte im Menschenrecht: Zum Streit um juristische und theologische Auslegungen." *Evangelische Kommentare* 10 (1977): 266-69.

Warnock, G.J. *The Object of Morality*. London: Methuen, 1971.

Wolferen, K.G. van. *The Enigma of Japanese Power*. London: MacMillan, 1989.

Woo, P.K.Y. "A Metaphysical Approach To Human Rights from a Chinese Point of View." In: A.S. Rosenbaum (ed.). *The Philosophy of Human Rights - International Perspectives*. Westport, Connecticut: Greenwood Press, 1980. Pp. 113-124.

Zakaria, F. "Human Rights in the Arab World: The Islamic Context." In: P. Ricoeur (ed.). *Philosophical Foundations of Human Rights*. Paris: UNESCO, 1986. Pp. 227-41.

CHAPTER II

Religious Ways of Life and Human Rights

Hendrik M. Vroom

As outlined in the introduction to the theme of this workshop, a tension exists between the religious claim to truth and autonomy on the one hand and the use of human rights as a universal standard to determine what is acceptable behaviour on the other. In international affairs, this standard is non-negotiable. Human rights as such express minimal rights and thus give expression to a 'thin' morality that requires 'thickening' with respect to content in order to achieve more specificity and force. The question is whether religious traditions can provide this thickening and whether they mesh with the formulations of human rights that originated in Western culture.

This paper attempts to elucidate the nature and content of religious concepts of humanity from the viewpoint of the theory of religion, with the intention that the discussion of religious concepts of humanity more closely approximate experience and that the different perspectives of religious concepts of humanity and human rights can be made clear. We will see that religious concepts of humanity imply a view of 'the rights and responsibilities of people' which does not square automatically with the view of 'human rights'. By the expression 'human rights' we mean the rights of human beings as they have been established in the United Nations Charter of the Rights of Man. We are aware, moreover, that there have been various developments since 1948 with respect to reflection on these rights and to jurisprudence in international justice, in which 'human rights' have been interpreted and applied. This whole complex will be indicated by the term 'human rights' (even though the content of this term has not been finally fixed). In distinction from this we will indicate the rights (and responsibilities) of people within the religious traditions by the expression 'rights of humans'.

We will first describe the content and nature of religious concepts of humanity in greater detail. Secondly, we will discuss their claims to describe humanity as it is and their claims to universal validity and show how religious teaching on how to live places human existence within a larger framework. In the following section we will demonstrate by means of some (Christian) treatments the tension between the claims to universality in religious views of the rights of humans and such claims in 'human rights'. Finally, we will draw a number of conclusions about the relationship between religious concepts of humanity and human rights.

THE NATURE OF A RELIGIOUS CONCEPT OF HUMANITY

We will first describe, from the perspective of the theory of religion, the content of religious concepts of humanity, which display a number of fixed characteristics.

1. In a way similar to philosophical anthropologies, religious concepts of humanity express views of the composition of human beings, views which could be termed *religious anthropologies*. One often encounters the idea that human beings consist of two or more parts, of which only one, the physical, can be observed empirically. In addition to the mortal body, humans have one or more parts that are either immortal or less mortal. According to some religious traditions, humans have souls that are judged after death, enter into an intermediate state perhaps and finally - whether or not in possession of some sort of body - are able to live eternally. An important qualification of this is that within human spiritual existence further distinctions are introduced, e.g. within the spiritual aspect of humanity is a very fine substance which unites human beings with their transcendent origin. Other religious traditions, however, reject the soul-body distinction. The very idea itself that there is something immortal in humans is sometimes viewed as the root of egoism and suffering. A religious concept of humanity is determined to a large degree by its conception of the compositional elements of human beings.

2. Religious concepts of humanity describe the framework within which human existence must be seen. This can be called *religious metaphysics*. In some religious traditions reality is termed creation (as distinguished from God), in others as a manifestation of the divine, and in still others as a pure manifestation (*tathata*). They thus point to the ground of existence. In monotheistic traditions this placing of the human existence within a larger framework occurs through reference to the origin of existence, the creation, and its end - judgement or a hereafter. Reality is thus primarily seen in historical terms. In Hindu thought, this placing of the individual life within such a framework can occur in one or two ways: first, by belief in reincarnation - on the basis of which people orient themselves to a good subsequent life by living in conformity to the cosmic order; secondly, in a broader way, through the prospect of permanent bliss (*moksha*) which entails a liberation from the world and the cycle of reincarnation. Some important Buddhist traditions do not point to an external destiny for humans but to an alternative way of undergoing reality. The framework within which the different traditions portray existence decisively influences the view of the rights, duties and objectives of human beings.

3. The third element of religious concepts lies in the tradition as it is practised, i.e., the actual transmission of the tradition. This is in the foreground more than the other two elements, because the image of humanity is here concretized and connected to life as it is lived. This element - the most important - can be called the tradition's instruction about how to live. Here it concerns the practical wisdom, the insights, norms and values of a tradition as it is transmitted in daily life. One should not think here of the activity of spiritual leaders, but of the activity of all who adhere to a religious tradition or have been influenced by it. It involves the insights of a tradition-in-interpretation in the day-to-day life and context of the people themselves. These insights are associated with religious customs - sacrifice, prayers, meditation -and (other) rituals and ceremonies, through which attention is drawn to the dangers, mistakes and wrong assessments of priorities. The people help one another in making difficult decisions and in moments when the heart and the head do not agree. In this way the practical wisdom of the tradition is passed on. In living religions this instruction is interwoven with the content of belief. It is characteristic of philosophies of life that they distinguish between authentic and non-authentic ways of living and give instruction as to the proper way. They clarify what is wrong in the world and indicate the origin of the misery, which for the most part lies in wrong attitudes. One can find an example of such instruction on how to live properly in the 'eightfold path' of Buddhism: right view, right aim, right speech, right action, right living, right effort, right mindfulness and right concentration (*samadhi*). The Ten Commandments in Christianity constitute another example. In the Buddhist formulation one notices first that religion is to effect a disposition and, secondly, that much more elaboration is required to clarify what is meant by right speech, right action, etc., in different contexts. Religious traditions convey what is wrong with (outward) ordinary human existence and teach how one can be a better or even simply a good person. This instruction can take shape in different ways. It may consist of rules of conduct and prohibitions; in that case being a good person consists of following the moral code and the acquiring of a specific habit of mind (as in the surrender of faith and obedience in Islam). The way of life that is recommended can also refer to the rites that people must perform in order to internalise the insights of a religious tradition or, for example, to maintain the cosmic order. In the more mystical and pietistic movements of religious traditions there are more explicit instructions for the development of one's personality.

The texts in which mystics tell about their lives and experiences give insight into both the wrong way of life which they have left behind - mostly only through intense struggle- and the path they have followed in order to better their lives as the way of life that they have in mind. Instruction on how to live comprises a configuration of fundamental insights in life that are transmitted by the tradition. Examples of this are the Buddhist reference to attachment, or thirst, and ignorance as the root of suffering, the Jewish insight that each person is created in the image of God, the Christian insight that no proper life is possible without suffering, and the Moslem emphasis on the surrender of faith (*Islam*) as the condition for a righteous and merciful life. Religions teach people ways to deal with the important aspects of life. This applies primarily to the tensions in the discordant moments in human existence when emotions run high: the difference between justice and injustice, love and impartiality, the tension between sacrifice and claiming one's rights, between having and giving, being able and being unable, attachment and detachment. These moments also include not only human shortcomings, powerlessness, dependence, lostness, abandonment, loneliness, the uncertainty of existence, unhappiness, loss and death but the wonder at all that is good in life, gratitude, and the awareness of the meaning of one's existence as well. Religions communicate ways to deal with all these fundamental givens of life (Vroom, 1992a, 25-30).

Such traditions, of course, undergo historical development in which they are strongly influenced by circumstances and other ideological traditions with which they interact. Here lies the reason for the fact that religious traditions contain a large variety of views and interpretations. It continues to obtain that religious traditions transmit a way of life that is intended to help people through life. Meditation and rituals, in which religious writings are read or recited, play a primary role here. The exegesis of these writings (insofar as they do not prescribe rituals but contain a message) is contextual; the scriptures are applied, via a hermeneutic, to the changing contexts in which people live. The same applies to jurisprudence, for example, in the Halakah and the Shariah (An-Na'im, 59, 62 f.). In transmitting the right way to live, the different religious traditions make use of stories, in which difficult life-situations are portrayed through persons who have become entangled in them, have found solutions to them, or else have managed to bear up under the difficulties. The Jewish tradition has the Haggadah and the Hassidic narratives, while the Moslem tradition has the *hadith* and the Roman Catholic tradition the lives of the saints. Both the Buddhist and the Hindu traditions have an abundance of stories. These stories deal with the complexities of life, the (un)happy convergence of circumstances, human reflections, and the good and bad ideas of people. Thus religious traditions have at their disposal a varied and almost inexhaustible supply of stories that exist alongside the rules of conduct and the more dogmatic side of the tradition. The meaning of the general terms of the commandments are interpreted in jurisprudence and stories. The dogma of a tradition is 'translated' within the context of life and religious experience. There are some stories, doctrines and rules of conduct that are essential to a tradition. The seed of a religious concept of humanity does not primarily consist in general rules and doctrines but in the great paradigmatic stories, such as the stories about Krishna, the Buddha, Moses, Jesus and Mohammed. The doctrine is secondary (Vroom, 1989, CH. 10).

This discussion on the elements of a religious concept of humanity will suffice. Such a concept of humanity can be called a *normative concept* because it states how a person *should* live. In living traditions, such concepts of humanity are not transmitted as theory: they are implied in the primary religious texts, as we can see in the following quote from a sermon by Augustine on Psalm 42:

> Run to the fountain; long for the fountain; but do it not anyhow, be not satisfied with running like any ordinary animal; run thou "like the hart." What is meant by "like the hart"? Let there be no sloth in thy running; run with all thy might: long for the fountain with all thy might. For we find in "the hart" an emblem of swiftness. But perhaps Scripture meant us to consider in the stag not this point only, but another also. Hear what else there is in the hart. It destroys serpents, and after the killing of serpents, it is inflamed with thirst more violent; having destroyed serpents, it runs to the "water-brooks," with thirst more keen than before. The serpents are vices, destroy the serpents of iniquity; then wilt thou long yet more for "the Fountain of Truth" [...] Whilst, therefore, thou art yet indulgent to thy vices, thy covetousness or thy appetite, when am I to find in thee "a longing" such as this, that might make thee run to the water-brooks? [...] "My soul is athirst for the living God". What I am saying, that "as the hart panteth after the water-brooks, so longs my soul after Thee, O God," means this, "My soul is athirst for the living God".[1]

In the first lines the audience is exhorted to abandon the wrong way of life so that they can achieve humanity's goal through living properly. The deer (in the psalm an image of human longing for salvation) serves as an example: it is not slow. Thus the human, who is slow to follow the path to the spring, i.e, to true humanity, is here the object of exhortation. The thirst for true humanity must be cultivated and this cultivation is, for that matter, a task for religious customs, rites and meditations.

This sermon contains an implicit analysis of the wrong way of life. From the deer one can learn that it kills the serpents, by which, as Augustine explicitly says, he means the vices of injustice, greed and avarice. To these he adds malice, that which stands over against truth, improper desires and acquiescence in the life of this estranged world (living as if there was nothing else to desire beyond this world). Thus this text contains an analysis of the wrong way of life and instruction in a way of life that leads to the goal (salvation): victory over the vices and the cultivation of the desire for complete salvation. This text presupposes several other elements from the tradition, which clarify what improper desires are and how one can struggle against them. The text also stands within the framework of the doctrines of the tradition: an anthropology and a metaphysics

---

[1] This (abbreviated) English translation is from Augustine, *Expositions on the Book of Psalms*, Nicene and Post-Nicene Fathers, Vol. VIII, tr. A. Cleveland Coxe (Grand Rapids: Eerdmans, repr. 1983), 132 f. For the full Latin text see *Patrologia Latina* 36, ed. J.B. Migne (Paris: 1945), 464-76. See also G. Ruhbach and J. Subrack, *Christliche Mystik: Texte aus zwei Jahrtausende* (Munich: Beck, 1989), 76 f.

are in the background. God is the source of existence: both the origin and the destiny of human beings. Elsewhere in this sermon is the distinction between body and soul; the fact that the soul is the most important part of the human being underscores the importance of the struggle against the desires of the flesh.[2] The dogmatic-philosophical elaboration of this view of the body and soul is of secondary importance. At bottom lies the basic insight that people can be conscious of the desires of their body and should control them. Here the indicative is implied, and has, of course, been the object of discussion in many different ways, but the doctrinal insight, however, is not primary. Rather, at issue here are the practical (basic) insight into human existence and the path that is indicated in order to move from an undesirable situation to a better.

One can find similar instructions for the proper way of life everywhere in religious traditions. The concern here does not just involve morality but a fundamental religious attitude to life. These teachings can be found, for example, in many places in the Koran and in writings by religious people. I will quote a few lines from a Muslim sufi, Ibn 'Ata'illah (d. 1258):

> Far be it from our Lord
> to recompense with credit
> the servant who deals with Him in cash!
> When He gives, He shows you His kindness;
> when He deprives, He shows you His power;
> and in all that, He is making Himself known to you
> and coming to you with His gentleness.
> When He alienates you from His creatures,
> then know that He wants
> to open you the door of intimacy with Himself.
> When the forgetful man gets up in the morning,
> he reflects on what he is going to do,
> whereas the intelligent man *sees* what God is doing with him.
> (Ibn 'Ata'illah, nos. 89, 93, 101, 114)

Such a text does not in the first place offer dogma or moral theology but instruction on living: the effort of the believer is not immediately rewarded - God will reward him later. If one prospers ("When He gives"), then it is a gift from God (thus neither the result of one's own achievements nor a right that humans enjoy); if life is not prosperous, it is God who withholds the good. If one is alone - in a state of loneliness and abandonment - then it is God who is in the background with his salvific intention. The first thing the believer learns is to

---

[2] Cf. Augustine in Ruhbach and Subrack, 79: "Ich kehre in mich selber ein; und ich erforsche, wer ich selbst nun bin, der dies alles sucht. Ich entdecke, daß, ich Leib und Seele habe, daß die Seele wertvoller ist als der Leib; sie ist es doch, die solche Fragen stellt, die Seele und nicht der Leib."

trust God: the relation to God does not concern rights but a surrender of faith, as one can see if we paraphrase the last three lines in the following way:

> When the forgetful man gets up in the morning,
> he reflects on what are his rights,
> whereas the intelligent man *sees* what God will do with him that day.

In both Augustine and 'Ata'illah we can see how the reader or listener is called to re-orient his life away from an estranged life in which one's own I or group to which one belongs is central (inclusive of the rights one has) to God, the kingdom of God, the divine, or the true reality. All these cannot, for the most part, be *discovered* by people - and if people can discover them, they can do so only with difficulty. This is the case whether it involves the Bible, the Koran, the Bhagavadgita or the conversations with the Buddha. Within such religious concepts of humanity there can be no discussion of the rights of people apart from the framework of the religious instruction on how to live. Within this teaching the basic insights and the closely connected instruction for the proper attitude are more essential than the explicit concept of humanity that one can extract from it. This is why various controversies can arise in religious philosophies which do not immediately affect the practical religious life. Thus in Buddhist thought one can argue over how *karma* is transferred to a following life without *atman* and in christian theology whether and how body and soul are joined but yet distinguished. Such differences of opinion need not affect the practical side very much because the fundamental ideas themselves are not directly affected. *Karma* states that what one does has consequences that come back to the person who acted in the first place; the distinction between body and soul basically claims that one can know how to deal with the needs and desires of "the flesh" and, connected to the idea of judgement, that one is held responsible for one's way of life. These are examples of basic insights that are discernible under the centuries-long discussion on these ideas. They lie at the basis of such discussion and to a considerable degree are independent of the dogmatic-philosophical positions. To give an example, one can believe in the providence of God without knowing precisely how God in fact guides events. The fundamental idea here is that the course of events is not a matter of coincidence. Neither are basic moral insights immediately affected by shifts in dogmatics or religious philosophy. The code of the eightfold path or the Ten Commandments are largely autonomous with respect to explicit concepts of humanity and of God, while, on the other hand, they are very much bound up with the statements on human existence in the teaching in the different traditions on how to live. The relative weight of the different moral rules are determined by the views on humanity and the world. Therefore, on the whole concepts of humanity and morality form *normative concepts of humanity*. The expression 'a whole' must not be understood, as indicated above, as a scholastic dogmatic system but as a configuration of basic insights closely bound up with one another.

Thus we have seen that in religious concepts of humanity three elements can be distinguished: an anthropology, a metaphysics, and instruction on how to live. In all three religious and moral instruction is interwoven. Characteristic for such instruction is that it places human existence within a view of the whole of reality and indicates how one can change from a way of life labelled as wrong to a proper way. Such normative concepts of humanity involve truth claims; they state what the condition of humanity and the world is (in fundamental respects) and how people should live. This sometimes brings them into conflict with human rights. Here is it interesting to note that religious traditions often have high ideals (e.g., *ahimsa* and the Sermon on the Mount) which they either do not always consider to be obligatory for everyone or else they remove the sharp edge of the high ideals for ordinary people (keeping silent about the Sermon on the Mount, limiting *ahimsa* to ascetics). On the one hand, one can note here the wisdom of a tradition that does not demand too much of people. On the other hand, such compromise invites those who do not take their faith seriously. Popular religiosity and civil religion are ambiguous phenomena.

THE HUMAN PERSON WITHIN THE LARGER CONTEXT

A religious concept of humanity interprets existence. The individual person is allotted a place within a larger context, which, depending on the religion, can be the tribe, the Jewish people, the Kingdom of God, the oemma, dharma and *rita* or the chain of causality.[3] The concept of humanity in the world religions is related to a view of reality as it really is. Normative concepts of humanity claim to describe a) what reality is, b) the compositional elements of the human person, and c) what is wrong with the wrong way of life and how it can be made good (cf. Vroom, 1989, 226-28). Thus they include ontological and metaphysical statements, an anthropology and instruction on how to live. A religion's teaching on how to live is bound up with the claim that reality is as the tradition maintains it is (*ibid.*, 270 f.). It claims to know the compositional elements of human beings with respect to relevant points. A complete anthropology that covers all aspects of human existence is not necessary but only one that addresses relevant concerns. Insofar a concept of humanity is present, it is an anthropology that is universally valid, an anthropology that consequently, holds true for all people. Hindus who believe in reincarnation do not exclude Christians from it. Moslems

---

[3] For a short description of these contents of belief, cf. my ***Religions and the Truth***, the second paragraphs of CHS. 3-7. For a treatment of the earlier mentioned basic insights see CHS. 9-10 and for the idea of a "belief-system" as a configuration of basic insights and its implications for the relationship of religions cf. also CH. 12.

who believe in a final judgement expect that non-Moslems will also be judged after their death. Jews who observe the Halakah hold that non-Jews are also created in the image of God and must observe the Noahitic prohibitions (Fishbane, 25). Each ideological tradition makes universal claims about personal human existence, society and morality.

One of the tasks in the dialogue between adherents and students of religious traditions is to pursue the question of where the different concepts of humanity and views on virtues and moral rules overlap or contradict one another. In connection with human rights one of the central questions, of course, is the extent to which a basis for them can be found in the different traditions.

We will first elaborate further on the placing of human existence within the larger whole. The larger context in which humans live is decisive for the view on the rights and duties of individuals - in cases where, within specific traditions, people are viewed as individual persons. Also, the value that attaches itself to human individuality within religious traditions - which lies at the basis of the notion of human rights - depends at any rate on the view of reality as a whole. In connection with the question of the foundation of the individual rights of the human being, one must also consider completely different interpretations of human personality and individuality than in the Western culture. Within a tribal culture, the individual is not seen as an individual in the Western sense. The notions of individual autonomy and conscience is at odds with the traditional African ethos (Bujo, 12-21). While Zen Buddhism does not deny individuality, it understands it in a completely different way, as one can see in the following, often cited, story:

> Kyozan Ejaku asked Sansho Enen "What is your name?"
> Sansho said, "Ejaku!"
> "Ejaku!" replied Kyozan, "that is *my* name."
> "Well then," said Sansho, "my name is Enen."
> Kyozan roared with laughter.
> (Nishitani, 48).

Nishitani quotes this story in order to show how much the Western emphasis on individuality contrasts with the experience of the person within Zen Buddhism.

He gives some examples of this. If, in the tradition of Martin Buber, one describes the I in relation to the Thou, then the I and the Thou are regarded as absolute, precisely because they stand in relation to each other. In contemporary religious thought the I is related to God as the absolute Thou. Within this religious framework, individual subjectivity is seen to be absolute. The same absoluteness is ascribed to the individual in Kant, for whom morality is a characteristic of the autonomous person. Nishitani holds, however, that absoluteness is not to be ascribed to the human being. In Kant as well as in the relational view of persons individual subjectivity is regarded as absolute: "nothing else can take its place". Nevertheless, in these views and in belief in God, there is a universal quality (God, the moral law, or relationality *itself*) above or in the person that relativizes both the complete individuality as well as the (unique) relation between people (*ibid.*, 49). Nishitani argues from this that the actual freedom and autonomy of humans can not be understood as long as they are related to an absolute - God, the moral law or the encounter with the other. Therefore, the self must be understood in an entirely different way, as emptiness. This emptiness is not intended first of all as a dogmatic concept - it is primarily a practical and ethical concept (Waldenfels, 206). Lack of space prohibits us from elaborating further on Nishitani's views. We have only discussed him here to show that views on the value and nature of human individuality, autonomy and freedom are subject to criticism on the basis of religious traditions.

The idea of autonomy is also at odds with the idea of theonomy, in which the person lets himself be guided by the laws of God (because God knows what is best).[4] The idea of human individuality and (as a consequence) that of human autonomy are alien to Hindu thought, for which everything is based on the cosmic order. The individual, writes M. Biardeau, "is only a unit within his group, caste or lineage, which determines his place in the hierarchy" (Biardeau, 120). In contrast, the Jewish tradition holds to the value of the individual: every human is created in the image of God. The Mishna reads:

> The human is created as an individual, in order to teach you that everyone who destroys one soul proceeds as if he had destroyed the whole world. And that he who saves one soul is viewed as if he had saved the whole world. (Aschkenasy and Whitlau, 19)

It is the task of the Jewish people to show in their own lives how a righteous and merciful world can be achieved by means of the Torah. Only in the concreteness of a community, as Aschkenasy asserts, can it be shown what the completion of the creation signifies (*ibid.*, 21 f.). This is the task of the Jewish people - both the joy of the law as well as often a road of suffering.

Thus each religious tradition determines the values of the human person within the whole of a view of human beings and the world. It still makes a difference whether one holds that one lives only once, has a special place in the whole of creation and furthers the cause of righteousness in the world or whether one views humans from the perspective of their karmic connection to the

[4] The idea that one does good by doing the will of God is under discussion. Cf. Plato, "Euthyphro"; Kuitert, 1975; Bartley, 1971; Vroom, 1992a.

cosmic order, or from a humanistic understanding of human beings.[5] If the basic idea is that the task of the human is determined by the *rita*, than his own perspective and preference is secondary in comparison with the insight into *dharma* that is transmitted by the religious spokesmen.[6] Both individuality as well as anthropocentric thinking are interwoven with post-Enlightenment Western culture. The question is whether Christianity can subscribe to the Western individualistic view of individuality without undermining some essential elements of the content of Christian belief - which does not so much inspire the language of rights as that of gifts and responsibilities. Thus the religious concepts of humanity differ in their evaluation of human individuality. That is not to say that there are no common insights. None of the great religious traditions endorse an egocentric view. John Hick correctly states that religions attempt to effect a complete turn-about from "ego-centeredness" to "reality-centeredness" (Hick, 301). Religious traditions allow no place for those who claim their rights without recognizing their responsibility for their fellow human beings and nature. Thus there is still the possibility that religious traditions share a number of insights which can serve as a basis for a common ethos. Given the divergent views of human individuality this common ground will not be very broad and there will continue to be different evaluations of specific human rights and, when conflict arises, different priorities - as should be apparent from interreligious dialogue. One basic principle of dialogue is that the achievements of one tradition may not be used as criteria to judge other cultural and religious traditions. Each has a voice in that which is a common concern for all. Because the origin of human rights lies in a specific cultural tradition, that of the Western democracies (cf. Moltmann, 1990, 103; L. Swidler, 20-28), their formulation and the more detailed elaboration of their content is open to dispute, both in jurisprudence as well as in the conversation of people from different cultural and religious traditions.

CHRISTIAN FAITH AND A CRITICAL ACCEPTANCE OF HUMAN RIGHTS

A critique of the individualistic undertone of human rights is needed. After all, Western culture, in which the concept of human rights originated, suffers from

---

[5] Cf. J.P. van Praag, 1978. See also the obligations that are ascribed to humans in D. Bronder, 58 ff.: "What meaning is my existence to have? This: to become a person(ality) and to be a kind fellow-traveller with my fellow human beings ...." He speaks, moreover, of rights and duties (*ibid.*, 60).

[6] Cf. J.B. Carman, 113-28. It is quite improbable that the concept 'human' within a world and life view in which one can be reincarnated as a plant, animal, human or divinity has the same content as that in traditions which sharply distinguish humans from other beings.

serious ills. Economic life commands the most attention within Western society. In the economically affluent areas of the world, the economy continues to be dependent on growth and thus on increased production and trade, the consequence of which is an increased use of natural resources, greater mobility and further ecological damage. It is inconceivable that all of humankind can share in this Western form of 'prosperity' without destroying nature and humanity itself. The negative consequences of the Western way of life are clear and in obvious ways it is a wrong life-style. If that is so, how can one avoid the question of whether there is something wrong with the basis of Western culture, with individualism and thinking in terms of individual rights in particular? In the Christian tradition, the latter is a relatively recent development. One need not look far for the reservations Christian thinkers exercised with regard to human rights: for example, they spoke of 'human rights' instead of 'the human rights' or required them to be further specified. To demonstrate this I will go somewhat deeper into the foundation of human rights in Christian theology. We will first see how the recent encyclical *Centigesimus Annus* deals with the question of human rights, then how rights were seen in Neo-Calvinist theology and finally their treatment in Moltmann, who, on the one hand, accepts them but, on the other, considers them to be too limited.

In the encyclical *Centigesimus Annus* the idea of the human rights is accepted, but not without qualification. After having rejected freedom of conscience as a contagious error in the first half of the nineteenth century, the Catholic Church changed with the times by recognizing, in the encyclical *Rerum Novarum*, freedom of religion and association as well as the right to a just wage.[7] In the *Centigesimus Annus* (=*CA*) the pope warns against a view of human freedom "that removes it from obedience to the truth and thus also from the duty to respect the rights of others" (*CA*, 15). In that case freedom becomes a love of oneself, with the result that one despises God and one's neighbour, makes self-interest prior to all else and restricts duty to justice. At the same time, the state is to guard human rights. The encyclical itself indicates which are the principal rights: the right to life, the right to one's own parents, a favourable moral environment, the right to seek and to know the truth, the right to work with the opportunity to provide for oneself and one's own, and the right to raise a family. These privileges have their basis in the Christian faith: "The source and synthesis of these rights is in a certain sense the freedom of religion, understood as the right to live according to the truth of one's own faith and in correspondence with the transcendent worth of the individual person" (*CA*, 39). Thus a prioritizing and interpretation of human rights occurs here, through

---

[7] Cf. John Paul II, *Encycliek Centigesimus Annus* in *Kerkelijke Documentatie* 19 (1991): 18 f. Cf also L. Swidler, 26 ff. One should not, however, too quickly draw the conclusion that this entailed support for all human rights.

which they are brought more closely in line with the Catholic concept of humanity. Nowhere does the document say that the Church does not adopt all the human rights, as formulated in the United Nations Charter of the Rights of Man, but from the summary of the principal rights it appears to exercise restraint with respect to other rights. Thus the emphasis is on the unborn, young children, and the family as an institution, over against both a view of the rights of women that implies that they can terminate their pregnancies and the freedom of married couples to end their marriage (cf. Congregation of the Doctrine of the Faith, 36). Another caveat is that the encyclical recognizes the responsibility of the state to guard the exercise of human rights in the economic sector but at the same time limits this role - in line with the principle of subsidiarity[8] - through giving primary responsibility to individuals and different social groups rather than to the state (*CA*, 39). The encyclical lays a great deal of emphasis on the non-economic needs of the human heart, an area where the church has a special responsibility. The message of the church concerns the truth about the creation of the world, the redemption of humanity and the co-responsibility that includes all people (*CA*, 42). In this way the Encyclical approaches the question of human rights from the viewpoint of its own concept of humanity. The starting point is that the correct view of the individual and his unique value forms the weft and guiding principle of the encyclical because "the human being on earth is the only creature that is willed by God for his own sake."[9]

In the above position one can see the ambivalent attitude of the Catholic Church with respect to human rights insofar as they are formulated by other institutions and traditions. The Roman Catholic Church claims to know the truth concerning humans and the world, on the basis of which it constructs a hierarchy of human rights and a specific interpretation of them. Other interpretations of human rights are implicitly rejected. In addition to rights, it also formulates human responsibilities and obligations. The encyclical ignores the issue of discrimination against women. In the terminology of our previous sections, it provides a concept of humanity (the human being is the image of God, with gifts and shortcomings), places human existence within the larger system of the whole of reality - created by God - and advocates freedom via the principle of susidiarity so that it can transmit and develop its own teaching on how to live within the ecclesiastical community. The encyclical itself is a part of the living tradition through the fact that it articulates new emphases in the context of the modern world.

---

[8] The principle of subsidiarity states (*CA*, 40 (§ 48), that "a social context on a higher level ... [must] not intervene in a social context on a lower level and must not rob this of its authority."

[9] *CA*, 10, quoting the Pastoral Constitution on the Church in the world at this time from the Second Vatican Council, *Gaudium et spes*, p. 23.

With respect to the structure of the above approach, a corresponding position in the churches of the Reformation can be noted. The Neo-Calvinist Abraham Kuyper devoted a significant area in his theology to what he called common grace, that is, the idea that grace of God extends to all creatures, even though not in the same measure. Because of common grace, the continuing effects of sin are held in check, the human being is able to perform good acts relating to his citizenship "and he receives by divine providence those rights and freedoms which he requires for his civil existence" (Kuyper, III, 75; cf. Ridderbos, 110). On the basis of his appreciation of the pluriformity of culture (influenced by Romanticism) Kuyper rejected the (French) revolutionary ideals of equality and unity. If the distinction between cultures was not kept in mind, it was possible to overlook the fact that the rights and privileges of human beings could differ according to culture and historical period. Although this last statement could easily be misused in legitimizing the separate development of ethnic groups, it is important to note that Kuyper does not ground the rights of human beings in the autonomous person - who is primarily a sinner - but in God's providential grace. These rights and privileges belong to the people themselves and not to the government, which is to respect these rights and privileges (Kuyper, III, 77). In the context of the divine attributes, Kuyper's close associate Herman Bavinck speaks of rights that God gave, as it were, to his creatures. Here Bavinck intends more than simply human beings. For Bavinck as well, rights do not belong to autonomous human beings; to the contrary, God's grace is the source of all justice (Bavinck, 1967[5], II, 197). This justice consists in a just order that encompasses all creation: every creature has received its own nature. There are statutes, laws and ordinances in the world which God preserves. The justice that is expressed in this order is transparent enough - it is because of sin that people cannot see or do it.[10]

In Kuyper and Bavinck the discussion on the rights of human beings is linked to four important insights: 1) the recognition of sin; 2) the recognition of creaturely dependence on grace; 3) the association of the rights of human beings with the rights of all creatures or with the idea of a creational order; 4) the ascription of rights and privileges to people (and not to governments or groups) with the result that the state must respect these rights. Seen in this way, no one can claim rights or privileges at the expense of other people or creatures. The rights of humans are viewed from the perspective of the broad system that is characteristic of religious anthropology: because they are grounded in God's grace, there is an immediate connection with the non-human aspect of creation and every *interpretation* of rights and privileges is directly under suspicion of sinful self-interest. The advantage of such an approach springs to mind immedi-

[10] Bavinck also taught the doctrine of common grace. Cf. Bavinck, 1967[5], I, 272-94; II, 196; III, 198 f. Cf. as well Bavinck, 1921, 125.

ately if one compares it with that of J. Moltmann. Moltmann accepts human rights: because of the explosive world situation, peace and justice require that human rights be placed above all particular interests of peoples, groups, religions and cultures. He writes that the religious claims to particular absoluteness and the compassionless advance of particular political interests now threaten the very existence of humanity itself (1990, 103). In the history of freedom in Europe and North America, the emphasis was initially placed one-sidedly on the individual rights of persons, while neglecting the granting of equal rights socially. Because of ecological issues, an additional dimension has to be addressed today. Moltmann does not only discuss the exploitation of human workers but also that of natural resources (*ibid.*, 110). He coins the term "ecological justice" and speaks of the rights that belong to animals as living beings. He grounds this meticulousness in the involvement with nature, not in human discretion and in calculated self-interest but in nothing less than the *worth of creation*, which he indicates as the source of the natural rights of living beings other than humans and of the earth (*ibid.*, 110 f.). At this point, however, Moltmann abandons the general and neutral basis that he intended in speaking about human rights. The word "creation" after all arises within a specific historical-religious context that is shared by Jews, Christians, and Moslems but not by agnostics, Buddhists, and humanists. Thus Moltmann breaks through the anthropocentric formulation of human rights only by appealing to a religious tradition, through which the determination of human rights as a universal norm is threatened. One is therefore not surprised when he acknowledges that the further development of human rights and those of humankind is referred to the creative contribution of the different worldviews: from such contributions by other traditions he expects a correction of Western anthropocentrism (*ibid.*, 113). As far as I can see, this entails that the conception of human rights as a universal norm is open to discussion.[11]

In summary, there are three lines of approach to the question of human rights in the Christian tradition. (1) All people should be treated with respect and love. The basis for this lies in the belief that the human is created in the image of God. This belief provides a support for the ethic that the people must be treated as one would be treated oneself. (2) People are part of God's creation and must respect the order on which creation is based. (3) Human autonomy and individualism, greed, waste, and lack of solidarity, justice and mercy fall under the category of sin. On the basis of the Christian tradition one apparently arrives at a specific approach to human rights that at the same time implies a prioritizing and thus a distinctive approach in case of a conflict regarding specific rights (cf. Reinders, 199).

---

[11] Cf. also Moltmann, 1976, 44-60 and Reinders, 1989, 194-99.

CONCLUSION

A great number of human rights, as formulated in different declarations (cf. Lochman and Moltmann, 71-100), is for much of Western understanding non-negotiable and self-evident. Freedom from enslavement, freedom of religion, the condemnation of torture, discrimination and arbitrary prosecution by authorities, equal access to education according to ability and similar aspects are permanent fixtures of our thought as moral and legal principles of modern society. However, their foundation in various religious traditions is not as clear as many would like it to be; much careful work has to be done on that issue. In any event, some other formulations in the Charter of 1948 appear problematic. In article 1 the Charter states that all people are endowed with reason and conscience. But, one may ask, what is the foundation for this claim and what does one understand by it? In article 3 the right to life, liberty and personal security are established but not defined, while there is no mention of the conditions for the possibility of their realization. One could ask for some specification with respect to the right to the free development of personality (art. 22). The right to work and the free choice of employment (art. 23) are not introduced in connection with one's responsibility to contribute to society with his or her gifts but in connection with the individual (who must, nevertheless, at least choose work that lies within his own ability and is required by the society within which he lives). Only in article 29 is there mention of obligations: "Everyone has duties to the community in which alone the free and full development of his personality is possible." The content of these obligations, however, is not specified.

In comparison with the broad contexts in which religious concepts of humanity are situated and the wealth of life experience that is transmitted in the stories and examples of their doctrines of life, the formulation of human rights is bare and 'thin'. The danger of this formulation is that anthropocentrism and individualism are strengthened. In ordinary life people do not live primarily in terms of rights over against others and the community but in terms of mutual relationships. With their gifts, limitations and shortcomings they exist within these relationships right from the start, vulnerable and approachable. They live between self-sacrifice and self-preservation, between mercy and justice. They wish for themselves and their loved ones happiness and health, prosperity and peace. The great religious traditions teach people, with good reason, that such things are not a matter of course and, above all, are not a question of rights. Therefore, the discussion in terms of rights without mention of obligations, love and sacrifice always trails behind actual life.

In view of the inculturation of human rights and a less anthropocentric formulation of them it is necessary to study the concepts of humanity and the moral views of different religious traditions. Only in this way can one pursue the question of how far the different ideals of humanity overlap. The idea of the *humanum* as the common basis for an ethos borne by all the religions has already been discussed (Küng, 1989, 262; 1990, 101; Kuschel, 86 f.). The critical question is: How 'broad' is such a common concept of 'the *humanum*'? Each religious tradition has, as we saw, its 'own' idea of what it is to be a good human being (cf. Vroom, 1989, 278 f.). The question as to how much the concepts of humanity in the different religious traditions have in common must be taken up and this study must be supplemented with interreligious dialogue, in which others are approached with understanding while the hard questions are not avoided. Some of these question are clear from the preceding, but there are others. Is there a connection between *karma*, reincarnation and the acceptance of social inequality (cf. Biardeau, *passim*)? If, according to some Buddhist traditions, wisdom and *mahakaruna* (great compassion) become possible through the giving up of oneself, complete openness towards the other and complete detachment, how does *mahakaruna* relate to Christian agapè (which is neither egoistic nor detached) and justice in the sense of *sedaqah*?[12] Elaboration of this demands a great deal of study. A consequence of dialogue and of the confrontation between religious traditions in a pluralistic culture could be that they learn from one another's critique and take up valuable insights of others into their own tradition. The corollary of this is the danger that the multiplicity of world and life views makes all deeper questions obsolete.

The power of religious concepts of humanity lies in the fact that they describe wrong ways of living (against which the concept of human rights is intended to protect people) with thoroughness and informed by the experience of life. In contrast to the concept of human rights, they also recommend a way of living through which one can attempt to achieve a proper human existence; one cannot live by human rights alone. They arise from a tradition that underscores human autonomy and individualism. Individualism, however, appears to be an ambiguous phenomenon. While it is good to stand up for the worth of the individual person who has suffered at the hands of others, the individualistic Western culture has serious shortcomings with respect to both social and ecological questions. Therefore, as the basis of a common morality, human rights require 'thickening'. In a pluralistic, secularised culture one is referred to the wealth of wisdom, insight and emotiveness of the great traditions, which can help to overcome anthropocentrism and egoism. The morality that corresponds to human rights is too narrow a basis for this - without a religious framework it remains the minimum of humanity. One feels that the rule "Do not do to others as you would not have them do to you" is more general than its positive form "Do to others as you would have them do to you" (cf. Starkey).

---

[12] Cf. Laube's description (p. 13) of absolute emptiness as love in Hajima Tanabe; Kitaro Nishida, p. 135. See as well the essays by Christa Anbeek and Jan van Bragt in Anbeek *et al.*

BIBLIOGRAPHY

An-Na'im, A.A. "Koran, Sharia en mensenrechten: fundamenten, gebreken en perspectieven." *Concilium* 2 (1990): 58-64.

Anbeek, C. *et al. Voorbij goed en kwaad? Christendom en Boedhisme*. Kampen: Kok, 1991.

Aschkenasy, Y., and W.A.C. Whitlau. "'Geliefd is de mens.' Over een spreuk van Rab bi Akiba." In: Y. Aschkanesy *et al.* (eds.). *Geliefd is de mens. Artikelen rondom de Joodse traditie*. Hilversum: Folkertsma Stichting, 1983².

Augustine. *Expositions on the Book of Psalms*. Nicene and Post-Nicene Fathers, Vol. VIII. Tr. A. Cleveland Coxe. Grand Rapids: Eerdmans, repr. 1983.

Bartley, W.W. *Morality and Religion*. Basingstoke: 1971.

Bavinck, H. *Gereformeerde Dogmatiek*. Kampen: Kok, 1967⁵.

———. *Verzamelde opstellen*. Kampen: Kok, 1921.

Biardeau, M. *Hinduism: The Anthropology of a Civilisation* Tr. R. Nice. Delhi: Oxford University Press, 1992³.

Bronder, D. *Humanistische Antworten: Ein Leitfaden für den freireligiösen Jugendunterricht*. Hanover: Freireligiösen Landesgemeinschaft Niedersachsen, 1975.

Bujo, B. "The Understanding of Conscience in African Ethics." *Studies in Interreligious Dialogue* 2 (1992): 5-30.

Carman, J.B. "Duties and Rights in Hindu Society." In: L.S. Rouner (ed.). *Human Rights and the World's Religions*. Notre Dame, IN: University of Notre Dame Press, 1988. Pp. 113-28.

Congregation for the Doctrine of the Faith. *Instruction on Respect for Human Life in its Origin and on the Dignity of Procreation*. Vatican City: 1987.

Fishbane, M. "The Image of the Human and the Rights of the Individual in Jewish Tradition." In: L.S. Rouner (ed.). *Human Rights and the World's Religions*. Notre Dame, IN: University of Notre Dame Press, 1988. Pp. 17-32.

"Handvest van de rechten van de mens van de Verenigde Naties (1948)." *Concilium* 2 (1990): 14-19.

Hassan, R. "On Human Rights and the Qu'ranic Perspective." In: A. Swidler (ed.). *Hu man Rights in Religious Traditions*. Ed. A. Swidler. New York: Pilgrim Press, 1982. Pp. 51-65.

Hick, J. *An Interpretation of Religions*. Houndmills: Macmillan, 1989.

Ibn 'Ata'illah. *The Book of Wisdom*. Tr. V. Danner. London: SPCK, 1979.

John Paul II *Encycliek Centigesimus Annus*. In: *Kerkelijke Documentatie* 19 (1990).

Küng, H. *Kentering in de theologie*. Tr. from *Theologie im Aufbruch* (1987). Hilver sum: Gooi en Sticht, 1989.

———. "Op zoek naar een universeel basisethos van de wereldgodsdiensten." *Concilium* 2 (1990): 89-102.

———. *Projekt Weltethos*. Munich: Piper Verlag, 1990.

Kuitert, H.M. "Gods wil doen." In: *Ad Interim*. Festschrift R. Schippers. Kampen: Kok, 1975. Pp. 180-95.

Kuschel, K.-J. "Documentatie: Wereldgodsdiensten, mensenrechten en het humanum. Verslag van een symposium te Parijs." *Concilium* 2 (1990): 83-88.

Kuyper, A. *De gemeene gratie*, Vol. I-III. Amsterdam/Pretoria: Wormser, 1904.

Laube, J. "Hajima Tanabe's View of 'Radical Evil'." *Studies in Religious Dialogue* 1 (1991): 101-15.

J.M. Lochman and J. Moltmann (eds.). *Gottes Recht und Menschenrechte. Studien und Empfehlungen des reformierten Weltbundes*. Neukirchen: Neukirchener Verlag, 1976.

Moltmann, J. "Theologische Erklärung zu den Menschenrechten." In: J.M. Lochman and J. Moltmann (eds.). *Gottes Recht und Menschenrechte. Studien und Empfehlungen des reformierten Weltbundes*. Neukirchen: Neukirchener Verlag, 1976. Pp. 44-60.

——. "Mensenrechten, rechten van de mensheid en rechten van de natuur." *Concilium* 2 (1990): 103-14.

Nishida, Kitaro. *An Inquiry into the Good*. New Haven: Yale University Press, 1990.

Nishitani, Keiji. "The I-Thou Relation in Zen Buddhism." In: F. Frank (ed.). *The Buddha Eye: An Anthology of the Kyoto School*. New York: Crossroad, 1982. Pp. 47-60.

Plato "Euthypro." In: *Verzameld Werk* Vol. I. Haarlem: Tjeenk Willink, 1965. Pp. 293-316.

Reinders, J.S. "Theologie en mensenrechten." In: K.U. Gäbler *et al.* (ed.). *Geloof dat te denken geeft*. Festschrift H.M. Kuitert. Baarn: Ten Have, 1989. Pp. 192-210.

Ridderbos, S.J. *De theologische cultuurbeschouwing van Abraham Kuyper*. Kampen: Kok, 1947.

Ruhbach, G. and J. Sudbrack (eds.). *Christliche Mystik: Texte aus zwei Jahrtausende*. Munich: Beck, 1989.

Rouner, L.S. (ed.). *Human Rights and the World's Religions*. Notre Dame, IN: University of Notre Dame Press, 1988.

Starkey, P. "Agapè: A Christian Criterion for Truth in the other World Religions." *International Review of Mission* 74 (1985): 425-463.

Swidler, A. (ed.). *Human Rights in Religious Traditions*. New York: Pilgrim Press, 1982.

Swidler, L. "De mensenrechten: een historical schets." *Concilium* 2 (1990): 20-28.

Van Praag, J.P. *Grondslagen van humanisme*. Meppel: Boom, 1978.

Vroom, H.M. *Religions and the Truth*. Tr. J. Rebel. Grand Rapids/Amsterdam: Eerdmans/Rodopi, 1989.

——. "God and Goodness." In: G. van den Brink *et al.* (eds.). *Christian Faith and Philosophical Theology*. Festschrift V. Brümmer. Kampen: Kok, 1992. Pp. 240-57.

——. *Religie als duiding van de dood*. Amsterdam: VU Uitgeverij, 1992.

Waldenfels, H. "Can Religious Experience Be Shared?" In: J.D. Gort *et al.* (eds.). *On Sharing Religious Experience*. Grand Rapids/Amsterdam: Eerdmans/Rodopi, 1992. Pp. 203-14.

Part 2

Juridical and Cultural Perspectives

CHAPTER III

International Order and Human Rights

A Matter of Good Governance

P.J.I.M. de Waart

THE WILL OF THE PEOPLE

According to the 1948 Universal Declaration of Human Rights (UDHR) the will of the people is to be the basis of the authority of government and, correspondingly, of a social and international order in which the rights and freedoms set forth in this Declaration could be fully realized. The exercise of these rights and freedoms are subject only to

> such limitations as are determined by law solely for the purpose of securing due recognition and respect for the rights and freedoms of others and of meeting the just requirements of morality, public order and the general welfare in a *democratic society*. (italics added)

Each state would have the right to choose "its economic system as well as its political, social and cultural systems in accordance with the will of its people, without outside interference, coercion or threat in any form whatsoever" (1974 Charter of Economic Rights and Duties of States). The wills of different peoples has brought forth quite a variety of political systems, all claiming conformity to the UDHR as "a common understanding of the peoples of the world concerning the inalienable and inviolable rights of all members of the human family" (1968 Proclamation of Teheran).

The Parties to the 1966 International Covenants on Economic, Social and Cultural Rights (ICESCR) and Civil and Political Rights (ICCPR) respectively include command economies and free market economies, theocratic and secular systems as well as single-party and multi-party systems. These developments raise the question as to what extent the present international order actually underlies a common understanding of states as a basis for their implementation of the UDHR, ICESCR and ICCPR , which together constitute the International Bill of Human Rights.

The question has become all the more urgent since the (alleged) bankruptcy of communism. Western countries, in particular the United States, initially hailed the fall of communism as the beginning of a new international order based on *Western* achievements, i.e., democracy, a free market and human rights. Their euphoria seems to be fleeting. Other states and peoples have discovered, to their chagrin, that the collapse of the Soviet bloc has shifted the balance of power to the United States rather than the United Nations (UN). Thus it has, as of yet, far from increased the UN's influence on the international maintenance of peace and security.

Within the framework of development co-operation, the Council of the European Community (EC) launched the concept of good governance on 28 November 1991 (Bull. EC 11-1991). The Council considered general principles of good governance to be the following:

* Sensible economic and social policies
* democratic decision-making
* adequate governmental transparency
* financial accountability
* creation of a market-friendly environment for development
* measures to combat corruption
* respect for
    - the rule of law
    - human rights
    - freedom of the press and expression.

These principles led developing countries to fear that the chief result would be Western interference in their domestic affairs. The recent efforts of Western states to put a strong check on immigration, for instance, has mercilessly disclosed the limited value of the (free) market-friendly environment for development with respect to a truly social and international order in which universally recognized human rights, particularly the right to work, can be sufficiently implemented.

In the next section of this paper we will deal with the UN's position on democratization. We will subsequently raise the issue of the relationship between individuals and communities. Fourthly, we will define the concepts of minority and people in connection with the protection of human rights. In the final section we will discuss the principles of substitution and good governance as elements of a decent international order.

TIDAL WAVE OF DEMOCRATIZATION

A 'tidal wave of democratization' is now flooding across the former socialist countries and the UN:

> Thirst for democracy has been a major cause of change, and will continue to be a force for the construction of a better world. The United Nations must foster, through its peace-building measures, the process of democratization in situations characterized by long-standing conflicts, both within and among nations. (Boutros-Ghali, Report on the Work of the Organization, 1992b, 67)

New Era of Democracy, Peace and Unity

In its Charter of Paris for a New Europe[1] the Conference on Security and Co-operation in Europe (CSCE) launched ten principles intended to guide Europe to "a new era of democracy, peace and unity". The very first principle defines the relationship between human rights, democracy and the rule of law.

The Moscow Meeting on the Human Dimension of the CSCE emphasized that issues relating to human rights, fundamental freedoms, democracy and the rule of law were of international concern, "as respect for these rights and freedoms constitutes one of the foundations of the international order".[2] The CSCE Seminar of Experts on Democratic Institutions considered the development of a democratic culture a necessary element for the functioning of all democratic governments and noted the importance of the reciprocal relationship between international human rights norms and national practices in this regard (*ILM* 1992/2, 377; cf. also de Waart, 1992, 191-98.).

The 1991 Maastricht Summit of the European Community offered the Commonwealth of Independent States (CIS) a dialogue on mutual relationship whenever the CIS republics express democratically and peacefully their will to accede to full sovereignty. As general principles of Community Law the Maastricht Treaty on European Union enacted the fundamental human rights that had been guaranteed by the 1950 European Convention for the Protection of Human Rights and Fundamental Freedoms (ECHR) and are entailed in the constitutional traditions common to the member states. This enactment may be more than symbolic, due to the establishment of Citizenship in the Union for every person who bears the nationality of a member state (*ILM* 1992/2, 256, 258-60).

---

[1] The Charter for a New Europe was adopted in the context of the CSCE at Paris on 21 November 1990 (*International Legal materials* (*ILM*), 1991/1, 190-208).

[2] Document of the Moscow Meeting on the Human Dimension, Emphasizing Respect for Human Rights, Pluralistic Democracy, the Rule of Law, and Procedures for Fact-finding of 30 October 1991, *ILM* 1991/6, 1672 and 1683.

Referring to ICCPR, in its 1992 session the Commission on Human Rights appealed to all states to ensure respect and support for the rights of all persons "who exercise the right to freedom of opinion and expression and the rights to freedom of thought, conscience and religion, peaceful assembly and association, and the right to take part in the conduct of public affairs" (Res. 1992/22, paragraph 5). It also affirmed that full respect for the rights contained in the ICESCR is inextricably linked to the process of development,

> the realization of which is the realization of the potentialities of the human person in harmony with the effective participation of all members of society in relevant decision-making processes as agents and beneficiaries of development, as well as fair distribution of the benefits of development. (Res. 1992/10, para. 8)

The International Development Strategy for the Nineties shows the growing awareness of the UN General Assembly (UNGA) that democratic rights and freedoms are essential to effective approaches to economic and social development. The objectives of the 1993 Conference on Human Rights include examination of

> the relation between development and the enjoyment by everyone of economic, social and cultural rights as well as civil and political rights recognizing the importance of creating the conditions whereby everyone may enjoy these rights as set out in the International Covenants on Human Rights. (UNGA Res. 45/155 of 18 December 1990, para. 1(b))

UNGA is convinced that periodic and genuine elections are a necessary and indispensable element of sustained efforts to protect the rights and interests of the governed and that, as a matter of practical experience,

> the right of everyone to take part in the government of his or her country is a crucial factor in the effective enjoyment by all of a wide range of other human rights and fundamental freedoms, embracing political, economic, social and cultural rights. (UNGA Res. 46/137 of 17 December 1991)

In doing so, however, it affirmed that electoral verification by the UN should remain exceptional, undertaken primarily in situations with a clear international dimension. Moreover, electoral assistance should be provided only at the request of member states "in the context of full respect for their sovereignty".

Human Rights: Legitimate International Concern

The full realization of human rights has been recognized as a legitimate concern of the world community. The guidelines for such realization should be the principles of non-selectivity, impartiality and objectivity, and human rights "should not be used for political ends" (UNGA Res. 46/129 of 17 December 1991). In this context, the Commission on Human Rights underlined the continuing need for impartial and objective information on the political, economic and social situations and events in all countries (Res. 1992/92, paragraph 7).

In his Agenda for Peace the UN Secretary-General Boutros-Ghali rightly stated that respect for democratic principles at all levels of social existence is crucial "in communities, within States and within the community of States. Our constant duty should be to maintain the integrity of each while finding a balanced design for all" (Boutros-Ghali, 1992a, 10). This design should be dynamic, taking into account the ever-changing outcome of the interaction between globalism and nationalism. This very interaction is the pivot point of the UN Charter.

The implementation of the ICCPR and ICESCR depends entirely on democracy within nations and among nations. Therefore, democratic institutions are indispensable both at national and international levels. This is not all that is needed, however. For a democracy requires not only a democratic government or executive but also a democratic society. The expression 'in a democratic society' in international human rights documents restricts the application of limitation and derogation provisions, although only on the level of individual nations.

A society imposing limitations must demonstrate that the limitations do not impair its functioning as a democracy (Chowdhury, 1989, 14-15).[3] A democratic way of life cannot be confined to respect for political participation and freedom of speech, press, assembly and association. The realization of such rights largely depends on securing a majority. Tyranny of the majority does exist (Humphrey, 173). Majorities do not automatically have all the facts at their command in dealing with cultural traits which the members of groups in pluralist societies hold in common, such as language, religion, a common history, national symbols (Berting, 100-01).

Democracy within the family of nations means the application of its principles within the world organisation itself:

> This requires the fullest consultation, participation and engagement of all States, large and small, in the work of the Organization. All organs of the United Nations must be accorded, and play, their full and proper role so that the trust of all nations will be retained and deserved. The principles of the Charter must be applied consistently, not selectively, for if the perception should be of the latter, trust will wane and with it the moral authority which is of the greatest and most unique authority. Democracy at all levels is essen-

---

[3] "Siracusa Principles on the limitation and derogation provisions in ICCPR, Principles 19 and 20," *Human Rights Quarterly* (*HRQ*) 7 (1985): 5, 19; "Limburg Principles on the implementation of ICESCR, Principles 53 and 54," *HRQ* 9 (1987): 128, 143.

> tial to attain peace for a new era of prosperity and justice. (Boutros-Ghali, 1992a, 47)

Participation is indeed a condition for the exercise of human rights, at both the national and international levels. After all, the implementation of human rights requires legislative, policy, administrative and other measures within and among nations.

The UN and the specialized agencies are not parties to ICCPR and ICESCR. Despite the recognition of human rights as a legitimate international concern no UN organ can as yet make binding decisions in the field of human rights. The 1990 Global Consultation on the Realization of the Right to Development as a Human Right took a first step to overcome this shortcoming, recommending that UN bodies and agencies, including financial and trade institutions, should respect the International Covenants on Human Rights and other basic conventions in the field of human rights as if they themselves were parties (Doc. E/CN.4/1990/Rev.1, 50).

INDIVIDUAL *VS.* COMMUNITY

Human rights are defined as "those liberties, immunities and benefits which, by accepted contemporary values, all human beings should be able to claim 'as of right' of the society in which they live" (Henkin, 1985, 268). In the wake of the American and French revolutions, the Western doctrine of human rights has viewed civil and political rights as a shield protecting the liberty of the individual from his or her state (Vasak, 302). This may explain why little attention has been paid to human responsibilities. However, it is questionable whether states constitute the main threat to individuals. Other collectivities such as peoples, tribes, minorities, political parties, families, enterprises and settings such as neighbourhood and the (free) market may also be involved. *Cuius regio, eius religio* may be associated with the king (state) but the fact that *he who pays the piper calls the tune* indicates that the state does not constitute the only threat to freedom of expression.

Socialism (communism) rejected the western emphasis on individual liberty as well. Rights, duties and liberties were seen as means to establish relations between the state and the individual on the basis of mutual responsibility. This very responsibility underlies the idea of the collective human rights of peoples to development and to self-determination.

The 1990 Global Consultation left no margin for error in stating that all developing models were to conform to international human rights standards. In doing so, however, it rightly stressed that all cultures have a dignity and value of their own that must be respected. This implies that the UDHR is to be interpreted from the points of views of all cultures. These points of view still differ widely as to the relationship between the individual and the community.

Islam

In Islamic states the idea of the individuals' obligations to God and the state as God's obedient servant prevail over that of human rights: "Islamic states should allow their citizens to exercise freedom of opinion and expression in accordance with the teachings of Islam, since the exercise of these freedoms is a duty, and failure to exercise them is considered a sin."[4] The Islamic approach to human rights differs widely from the Western one, which is more secular (Arzt, 205-07). In principle it formulates, defines and protects human rights

> by inducing in the believers the disposition to obey the law of God, the Practice of his Last Prophet, and show obedience to those "constituted authorities" within the realm who themselves are bound to obey the law of God and the Practice of the Prophet and conduct man's affairs according to the Book of God and the Practice of the Prophet. (Brohi, 60)

Needless to say, this opinion concerns the relationship between the Islamic state and its Islamic nationals. In international relations between Islamic and other states twentieth-century Islam "has found itself completely reconciled to the Western secular system (...) These developments have committed Islam to the cause of peace and international security through adherence to treaties and the rule of law" (Khadduri, 232-33).

According to the 1980 Seminar on Human Rights in Islam, Islam considers itself as "man's only hope of salvation from social and economic exploitation" (Recommendation 1). This approach implies that civil and political rights are not viewed as an entirely separate category from economic, social and cultural rights. Every Islamic state is called upon to reform its economic system to achieve social justice and guarantee human dignity. With these ends in mind, the seminar recommended consideration of the following measures (Recommendation 6):

(1) Conservation and careful use of natural resources while taking account of the requirements of state security and the national economy;
(2) Redistribution of income and wealth on an equitable basis and in conformity with the principles of Islam;
(3) Revision of wages policies to meet the needs of the individual and guarantee him a decent life;
(4) A reappraisal of private ownership with a view to serving the interests of the community and guaranteeing proprietor's rights;
(5) Cooperation between private and public enterprise to promote economic development, increase production, raising living standards, and promote the well-being of all citizens;

[4] Recommendation 33 of the 1980 Seminar on Human Rights in Islam, International Commission of Jurists, 18.

(6) Combatting monopolies and imposing duties on capital, so as to promote state and public interests;
(7) Increase of governmental expenditure on public services, such as education and health, so that they are available to all;
(8) Enhancement of social security, and realisation of social and economic justice.

The right to development of peoples underlies a similar agenda as that of the Seminar on Human Rights in Islam. It recognizes the human person as the central subject of development but in the context of the community. According to that right states should formulate, adopt and implement policy, legislative and other measures at the national and international levels to create conditions for development as a

> comprehensive economic, social, cultural and political process, which aims at the constant improvement of the well-being of the entire population and of all individuals on the basis of their active, free and meaningful participation in development and in the fair distribution of benefits resulting therefrom. (UNDR-D, Articles 2 and 10)[5]

Because the term 'peoples' is left undefined, it is said that this capacity for development is very controversial. In my opinion, one should not attach undue weight to this argument, for international law and human rights law are not adversely affected by the absence of legal definitions of the main litigants, i.e. states, individuals, and collectivities of human beings, including peoples (de Waart, 1991, 472-73). After all, the existence of such collectivities is a question of fact and not of law (Thornberry, 165).

Persons before International Law

The present, horizontally-structured, international order implies that states should rigorously respect each other's sovereignty and territorial integrity. This explains why the concepts of sovereignty and territorial integrity determine the tenor of the UN Charter time and again: the effectiveness of international supervision on the implementation of human rights depends on the capacity of the bearers of these rights to bring international claims. In legal terms, the key questions are not so much whether and to what extent individuals and human collectivities other than states are capable of possessing international rights but whether they have the capacity to maintain these rights themselves by bringing international claims.

---

[5] See also the 1986 Declaration of the International Law Association (ILA), Seoul, 2-12, on the Progressive Development of Principles of International Law relating to a New International Economic Order, Principle 6: the right to development.

The latter have become burning questions since the 1648 *Peace of Westphalia* gave birth to the modern state by replacing "the idea of a hierarchical structure of Christian society under the Holy Roman Emperor" with the sovereign equality of states as the organizational basis of international society (cf. de Zayas). The Swiss jurist Emery de Vattel (1714-1767) was so influenced by the concept of the Westphalian international order of sovereign states that he removed, as it were, the human being from the ambit of Grotius' *De jure belli ac pacis* (Remec, 231-36). Vattel humanized states by 'nationalizing' human beings. International law thus became only a matter of law between states. This reversal of values has certainly left deep marks on modern international law. States appeal to it time and again as a means for arguing that their implementation of human rights is a matter lying essentially within their domestic jurisdiction.

The right to universal recognition as a person before the law apparently holds true only within national legal systems, unless a state has accepted treaty provisions on international supervision. Admittedly, states may not deny this right even in emergency situations (ICCPR, Article 4), but this prohibition does not as yet enable the UN to intervene effectively even when mass violations of human rights occur. Moreover, the ICESCR does not contain a provision regarding a government's proclamation of a state of public emergency. It confines itself to asserting that the state "may subject these rights only to such limitations as are determined by law only in so far as this may be compatible with the nature of these rights and solely for the purpose of promoting the general welfare in a democratic society" (Article 4). It is obvious that a society ceases to be democratic as soon as it refuses to recognize individuals as persons before the law. However it is still under discussion whether collectivities of human beings other than states, such as peoples, tribes and minorities are persons before international law and thus may bring international claims to implement collective human rights which are essential to good governance in a democratic society, such as the rights of peoples to development and to self-determination.

PROTECTION OF MINORITIES AND PEOPLES

The end of the Cold War paved the way for the UN to develop into an effective international body for the first time in its history. The specific concern now is to achieve a balance between the right to a people's self-determination and the prohibiting of arbitrary secession from states. Self-determination is an international legal right of peoples, while secession is only an *ultimum remedium* (Franck, 20).

The course of events in former Yugoslavia and the former Soviet Union illustrates the necessity of balancing the pros and cons of secession in a specific case. The tragedy of this situation lies in the fact that these very states had been proud to have solved the minorities problem through including them in decision-making once and for all. Be this as it may, the UN is now beginning to pay for the fact that its Charter has been tailored to states and not to peoples, let alone individuals. After all, this approach has kept the UN from taking timely, adequate, and effective action in order to cope with the dissolution of states as a result of peoples invoking their right to self-determination improperly or prematurely.

The recent events in the Middle East, Africa and Europe are illustrative. The end of the Cold War enabled the UN to take action against Iraqi aggression in Kuwait, but the UN is strongly influenced by the allied powers, in particular the United States. The last days of the Bush administration let that be known in no uncertain terms. This last-minute resolve stands out in sharp contrast with the continued irresolute stand towards Serbia and Israel. The allied powers thus prevented the UN from acting in accordance with the democratic principles of non-selectivity, impartiality and objectivity.

Minorities

The end of the European religious wars in 1648 gave shape to the protection of religious minorities in *bilateral* treaties. The end of World War I resulted in a radical reallocation of Central and Eastern Europe, including the Balkans. National minorities emerged within the new borders and their protection was vested in the League of Nations by virtue of *multilateral* treaties. The concept of national minorities appeared to be too open to serious abuse. Hitler seized on it eagerly in order to exert heavy pressure on neighbour states of the Third Reich and his policy finally led to the dramatic World War II. It was for that very reason that the 1942 *Declaration of the United Nations* shifted the emphasis from protection of minorities to that of individuals.

The expression minorities does not appear in the UN Charter (Wolfrum, 158). Already at its first session (February, 1947) the UN Commission on Human Rights established its Subcommittee on the Prevention of Discrimination and Protection of Minorities. Nevertheless, the UDHR only laid down the rights of individuals to protection by society and the state with the right of the family, as "the natural and fundamental group unit of society" (Article 16, paragraph 3), as the sole exception.

The ICCPR distinguishes between peoples and minorities: peoples have the right to self-determination and may, for their own ends, freely dispose of their natural wealth and resources (paragraph 2). Minorities do not possess this and have no right to protection except in terms of their individual members:

> In those States in which ethnic, religious or linguistic minorities exist, *persons belonging to such minorities* shall not be denied the right, in community with the other members of their group, to enjoy their own culture, to profess and practice their own religion, or to use their own language. (Article 27, italics added)

There is no question of an *actio popularis* (Klabbers/Lefeber, 70). This situation is likely to change, although the establishment of a sovereign and independent state by virtue of the right to self-determination will remain reserved for peoples only (De Zayas, 1993, 286-87). Unlike peoples, minorities do not have a territorial claim for establishing a state (De Waart, 1992, 7, 8; Higgins, 32-33; Hannum, 334-35).

The CSCE Meeting of Experts on National Minorities stated that issues concerning national minorities, as well as compliance with international obligations and commitments concerning the rights of persons belonging to them, are matters of legitimate international concern and consequently do not constitute exclusively an internal affair of the respective state (Report of the CSCE Meeting of Experts on National Minorities, 19 July 1991, *ILM* 1991/6, 1695-96).

The reluctance of states to assign group rights to minorities stems from their fear of separation movements. Immigration countries like the United States, Latin American states and EC members have preferred that members of minorities integrate into their society through a process of assimilation as soon as possible.

Peoples

Groups of human beings, like families, minorities, tribes and peoples may be bearers of collective human rights. However, their protection usually depends on the action of individuals. This holds true for religious societies as well. As legal persons, such societies may have rights. The European Commission on Human Rights holds that a church body is capable of possessing and exercising "in its own capacity as a representation of its ministers" the rights contained in Article 9 (1) of the 1950 ECHR, according to which everyone has the right to freedom of thought, conscience and religion. In doing so, the Commission moved from its earlier decision that a *legal person* does not possess such rights (Fawcett, 239).

Unlike peoples, human collectivities such as minorities and churches are not entitled to sovereignty. Sovereignty is reserved for peoples on the basis of their right to self-determination, which includes the free disposal of their natural wealth and resources. This free disposal results from the link between a people and a defined territory. Peoples thus have a special position among societies of man by virtue of their right to change, liquidate or create states. The heart of the right to self-determination of peoples is "freely to determine, without external interference, their political status and to pursue their economic, social and cultural development" (1970 Declaration on Principles of International Law concerning Friendly relations and Co-operation among States in accordance with the UN Charter). However, this right is not to be construed as

> authorizing or encouraging any action which would dismember or impair, totally or in part, the territorial integrity or political unity of sovereign and

> independent States conducting themselves in compliance with the right to self-determination of peoples (...) and *thus* possessed of a government representing the whole people belonging to the territory without distinction as to race, creed or colour. (italics added)

When this happens to be the case, the prohibition of secession freezes the establishment of a sovereign and independent state, the free association or integration with an independent state or the emergence into any other political status freely determined by a people as modes of implementing the right to self-determination. For the rest, the right to self-determination shares with individual human rights the condition that it shall not be exercised unrestrictedly, at least with respect to its impact on the composition of the society of states.

TOWARDS A DECENT INTERNATIONAL ORDER

International order and national orders are increasingly converging together. Local and national societies and communities should be able and willing to settle their own affairs, while the international order should be mainly concerned with the regulation of trans-boundary effects of local and national orders. The distinction between international and domestic affairs is losing value. Nevertheless, states cannot give up their sovereignty and for that reason the UN Charter deals with the maintenance of *international* peace and security. When these are at stake, the Security Council (SC) can make binding decisions.

Aside from issues of peace and security, states still depend a great deal on reciprocity and insist on determining the significance of reciprocity in each case for themselves. Institutionalization of mutual agreement imposing constraints on this freedom may not be assumed but should be laid down explicitly. This situation gave rise to the principle of 'substitution', which entails that what can be, should be left to lower organizational levels. The use of such a principle depends on the organizational and financial capacities of the higher level to assume the powers and duties of lower levels temporarily or otherwise, if the need arises.

Organizational Substitution

The UN cannot as yet compete with its member states on an organizational level. The organization is based on the principle of the sovereign equality of all its members. Nothing in the Charter authorizes the UN to intervene in the internal affairs of any state, member or not, or requires that members submit such matters to settlement under the Charter. The only exception is the application of enforcement measures of the SC with respect to threats to the peace, breaches of the peace and acts of aggression. In that respect the maintenance of international peace and security is a more truly international concern than the maintenance of human rights.

The SC is the only UN organ that may adopt binding decisions against members and even against non-member states. However, these binding decisions may only be concerned with the maintenance of international peace and security. In view of this, the SC is organized in such a way that it functions continuously. Nevertheless it is not an executive committee, for it is not concerned with the whole range of the organization but only the maintenance of international peace and security for which it has primary responsibility. The SC has no specific powers with respect to the supervision and enforcement of human rights. This is just as well, because the lack of democratic control on the decision-making process within the SC would hardly be compatible with the principles of non-selectivity, impartiality and objectivity. This holds particularly for the right of veto of the permanent members.

The SC is not obligated to give account of its decisions to the UNGA as the representative body of all members. The end of the Cold War has not made the UN a more democratic institution. Permanent members of the SC may back out of their treaty obligations simply by manipulating the SC in such a way that a binding decision is made under Chapter VII assigning them rights. Western powers are in a position to do so because of the dependence of the poor(er) non-permanent members of the SC upon the rich(er) countries.

No other UN organ, not even the International Court of Justice (ICJ), can prevent such a manipulation of the Third World by the First World in the SC. The UN Charter does not provide for a constitutional review of binding decisions of the SC. Such decisions may even frustrate the judicial process, for, according to the Court, the obligations of parties under the UN Charter prevail over their obligations under any other international agreement (Libya *vs.* USA and Britain, ICJ Reports 1992, 126).

Financial Substitution

The UN cannot compete with its member states on a financial level. The regular budgets of the UN and its specialized agencies are too modest to enable any functionalist intervention by these organizations in member states (Harrod, 131-32). In 1975 a group of high level experts stated in their report on *A New United Nations Structure for Global Economic Co-operation*

> We mentioned at the outset that four fifths of the $1.5 billion a year spent by the United Nations system is devoted to economic and social activities. But it is useful to record that the expenditures of the United Nations system during the past three decades have amounted to only 0.4 per cent of the total gross national product of member States in the single year of 1974 and that the

> Current United Nations expenditures barely equal the sum spent on armaments by Members in only 36 hours. (Doc E/AC.62/9 of 28 May 1975, 3)[6]

With their proposals for structural change the experts hoped to enhance the credibility of the UN system. However, the implementation of the proposals did not have this effect: member states apparently were not really interested in improving the efficiency of the UN system for fear of creating a competing world government.

The UN's financial circumstances have become substantially worse. Thirteen peace-keeping operations have been established since the end of the Cold War in 1987, i.e., equivalent to the number established in the entire period between 1945 and 1987.

> The costs of these operations have aggregated some $8.3 billion till 1992. The unpaid arrears towards them stand over $800 million, which represents a debt owed by the Organization to the troop-contributing countries. Peace-keeping operations approved at present are estimated to cost close to $3 billion in the current 12-month period, while patterns of payment are unacceptably slow. Against this, global defence expenditures at the end of the last decade approach $1 trillion a year or $2 million per minute. (Boutros-Ghali, 1992a, 28-29)

Quite understandably, the Agenda for Peace stated that the

> contrast between the costs of the United Nations peace-keeping and the costs of the alternative, war - between the demands of the Organization and the means provided to meet them - would be farcical were the consequences not so damaging to global stability and to the credibility of the Organization.(*ibid.*)

Thus a chasm has developed between the tasks entrusted to the UN and the financial means provided for it. Even if proposals to increase the annual budget are fully realized, the financial basis of the UN will remain quite narrow. It will not support its effective role in promoting good governance, let alone in its active prevention of bad governance. The latter responsibility would require that the UN be in a position to replace civil administration temporarily in a member state where bad governance had obviously become the real root of a state of emergency, threatening the life of the nation concerned.

---

[6] The amount of US$ 1.5 billion covers the UN system as a whole, exclusive of its financial institutions. In addition, the World Bank and the International Monetary Fund at the same time made over US$ 5 billion available in medium-term and long-term loans to member states. The total amount of US$ 6.5 billion was less than a third of, for instance, the 1975 annual budget of the Netherlands. The 1992 regular UN budget is US$ 1.3 billion.

Perspective

Good governance in the UN requires consultation, participation and engagement of its constituent members, i.e., all states, large and small, but also non-governmental organizations, academic institutions, parliamentarians, business and professional communities, the media and the public at large:

> The social stability needed for productive growth is nurtured by conditions in which people can readily express their will. For this, strong domestic institutions of participation are essential. Promoting such institutions means promoting the empowerment of the unorganized, the poor, the marginalized. To this end, the focus of the United Nations should be on the "field", the locations where economic, social and political decisions take effect. (Boutros-Ghali, 1992a, 46-47, 48)

If the Cold War prevented the UN from implementing the framework for good governance, its end may now help to bring it into existence. The annual World Development Reports of the World Bank and Human development Reports of the UN Development programme (UNDP) are of great value in that respect. Impressively, the World Bank is quantifying absolute poverty resulting from malfunctioning global commercial and financial markets. The most degrading consequence of the lack of freedom in the international market in general and the labour market in particular is hunger among a large part of the world population (Fischer, 152-55).

UNDP is developing indicators for measuring human development in general and human freedom as well as political freedom in particular. The 1992 *Human Development Report* contains an illustrative checklist of political freedom which was published after being approved by the UNDP Governing Council as a professional basis for a constructive policy dialogue (see Appendix I). The commendable achievement of a political freedom checklist should be made complete by the presentation of an illustrative checklist of social freedom in the shortest possible term (see Appendix II). The resulting comprehensive system for measuring human development is essential for any objective assessment of the implementation of civil and political rights as well as economic, social and cultural rights. Only such an assessment may result in a truly constructive dialogue without unwanted pillorying side-effects. Legally, such a dialogue will provide the only effective basis for an interpretation and justification of the inherent dignity of the human person from within religious traditions as the 'common core' of a universal morality between these traditions from which, according to the International Bill, human rights are derived.

BIBLIOGRAPHY

Arzt, D.E. "The Application of International Human Rights Law in Islamic State." 202-30.

Bernhardt, R. (ed.). *Encyclopedia of Public International Law*. Vol. 1-12. Amsterdam, 1980-90.

Berting, J. *et al.* (eds.). *Human Rights in a Pluralist World*. Westport, 1990.

Brohi, A.K. "Nature of Islamic Law and the Concept of Human Rights." In: International Commission of Jurists, Human Rights in Islam. Geneva, 1982. Pp. 41-60.

Brölmann, C. *et al.* (eds.). *Peoples and Minorities in International Law*. Dordrecht, 1993.

Boutros-Ghali, B., *An Agenda for Peace*. New York, 1992a.

——. *Report on the Work of the Organization from the Forty-sixth to the Forty-seventh Session of the General Assembly*. New York, 1992.

Cassese, A. "The Self-determination of Peoples." in L. Henkin (ed.). *The International Bill of Human Rights: The Covenant on Civil and Political Rights*. New York, 1981. Pp. 92-113.

Chowdhury, S.R. *Rule of Law in a State of Emergency: The Paris Minimum Standards of Human Rights Norms in a State of Emergency*. London, 1989.

——. *et al.* (eds.). *The Right to Development in International Law*. Dordrecht, 1992.

Delissen, A.J.M. and G.J. Tanja. (eds.). *Humanitarian Law of Armed Conflict: Challenges Ahead*. Dordrecht, 1991.

De Vattel, E. *Le droit des gens ou principes de la loi naturelle appliqués à la conduite & aux affaires des Nations & des Souverains*. Leiden, 1758.

De Waart, P.J.I.M. "Subscribing to the 'Law of Geneva' as Manifestation of Self-determination: The Case of Palestine." In: A.J.M. Delissen and G.J. Tanja, (eds.). *Humanitarian Law of Armed Conflict: Challenges Ahead*. Dordrecht, 1991. Pp. 465-94.

——. "Statehood and International Protection of Peoples in Armed Conflicts in the 'Brave New World': Palestine as UN Source of Concern." *Leiden Journal of International Law* 5 (1990): 3-31.

——. "Implementing the Right to Development: The Perfection of Democracy." In: S.R. Chowdhury *et al.*, (eds.). *The Right to Development in International Law*. Dordrecht, 1992. Pp. 191-211.

——. "Implementing Human Rights: Good Governance as a UN Concern." In: K. Ahuja *et al.* eds). New Delhi, 1993. Chapter 22 (New Delhi 1993).

Donnelly, J. "Postmodern Tribalism and the Right to Secession." In: C. Brölmann *et al.* (eds.). *Peoples and Minorities in International Law*. Dordrecht, 1993. Pp. 119-150.

Fawcett, J.E.S., *The Application of the European Convention on Human Rights*. Oxford, 1987.

Fischer, G. *et al. Hunger: Beyond the Reach of the Invisible Hand*. Luxenburg, 1991.

Franck, T.M., "Postmodern Tribalism and the Right to Secession." In: C. Brölmann *et al.* (eds.). *Peoples and Minorities in International Law*. Dordrecht, 1993. Pp. 3-27.

Ginther, K. "The Domestic Policy Function of a Right of Peoples to Development: Popular Participation a New Hope for Development and a Challenge for the Discipline." In: S.R. Chowdhury *et al.* (eds.). *The Right to Development in International Law*. Dordrecht, 1992. Pp. 61-83.

Hannum, H.. "Synthesis of Discussions." In: C. Brölmann *et al.* (eds.). *Peoples and Minorities in International Law*. Dordrecht, 1993. Pp. 331-39.

Harrod, J. and N. Schrijver. *The UN under Attack*. Aldershot, 1988.

Henkin, L. (ed.). *The International Bill of Human Rights: The Covenant on Civil and Political Rights*. New York, 1981.

——. *Human rights*. In: R. Bernhardt, (ed.). *Encyclopedia of Public International Law*. Vol. 8. Amsterdam, 1985. Pp. 268-74.

Higgins, R. "Postmodern Tribalism and the Right to Secession." In: C. Brölmann *et al.* (eds.). *Peoples and Minorities in International Law*. Dordrecht, 1993. Pp. 29-35.

Humphrey, P. "Political and Related Rights." In: T. Meron, (ed.). *Human Rights in International Law: Legal and Policy Issues*. Oxford, 1985. Pp. 171-203.

International Commission of Jurists, Human Rights in Islam. Geneva, 1982.

Khadduri, M. "International Law, Islamic." In: R. Bernhardt, (ed.). *Encyclopedia of Public International Law*. Vol. 6. Amsterdam, 1983. Pp. 227-33.

Klabbers, J. and R. Lefeber. "Africa: Lost between Self-determination and *Uti Possidetis*." In: C. Brölman *et al.*, (eds.). *Peoples and Minorities in International Law*. Dordrecht, 1993. Pp. 37-76.

Lapeyre, A. *et al. Les dimensions universelles de droits de l'homme*, Vol. I. Brussels, 1990.

Meron, T. (ed.). *Human Rights in International Law: Legal and Policy Issues* . Oxford, 1985.

Remec, P.P. *The Position of the Individual in International Law according to Grotius and Vattel*. The Hague, 1960.

Thornberry, P. *International Law and the Rights of Minorities*. Oxford, 1991.

UN Development Program (UNDP). *Human Development Report 1990*. Oxford, 1990.

——. *Human Development Report 1991*. Oxford, 1991.

——. *Human Development Report 1992*. Oxford, 1992.

Vasak, K. "Les différentes catégories des droits de l'homme." In: A. Lapeyre *et al.*, (eds.). *Les dimensions universelles de droits de l'homme*, Vol. I. Brussels, 1990. Pp. 297-309

Wolfrum, R., "The Emergence of 'New Minorities' as a Result of Migration." In: C. Brölman *et al.*, (eds.). *Peoples and Minorities in International Law*. Dordrecht, 1993. Pp. 153-166.

World Bank. *World Development Report: Poverty*. Oxford, 1990.

Zayas, A.-M. de, "Westphalia, Peace of (1648)." In: R. Bernhardt, (ed.). *Encyclopedia of Public International Law*. Vol. 7. Amsterdam, 1984. Pp. 537-39.

——. "The International Judicial protection of Peoples and Minorities." In: C. Brölman *et al.*, (eds.). *Peoples and Minorities in International Law*. Dordrecht, 1993. Pp. 253-287 (1993).

CHAPTER IV

Human Rights, Entitlement Systems and the Problem of Cultural Receptivity

Bas de Gaay Fortman

There are great cultural differences but there are also great universals.
The Economist, January 9, 1993

INTRODUCTION

Power, as we all know, is often abused. Hence, in human history there have been continuous attempts to bind the execution of power to certain norms. Where such norms state the rights and freedoms of every human being on the grounds of simple human dignity, based on the general principles of freedom, equality and solidarity, we speak of *human rights*. These rights are sometimes further typified as universal, absolute and inalienable, of which only the last is undisputed. If human rights do exist, then these rights are inherently inalienable and hence also untransferable. But they can be absolute only insofar as the underlying moral idea or principle can be regarded as absolute. One consideration is, for instance, how far one person's freedom affects the freedom of others since freedom may well imply power in the sense of limiting other people's possibilities. The freedom of big fish to eat small fish is not supposed to have its parallel in the human world. The protection of other people's freedom against the use of private power may take the form of specifying public interests in such a compelling manner that even certain human rights may have to take second place. There is a growing conviction, however, that the norms behind human rights are of such a strong nature that they should ordinarily 'trump' private and public interests not based on such rights (Dworkin), although this view is generally confined to the so-called civil and political rights. Human rights, one might say, are *prima facie* rights intended to provide a general protection against abuse of power.

Human rights have been authoritatively defined in the *Universal Declaration of Human Rights* as well as various covenants, protocols and conventions of the United Nations. Legally, their universality is almost undisputed, although a supra-national process to guarantee certain specified human rights to individuals effectively exists only in Europe. It is true that states are under a general obligation to respect and promote human rights - particularly in regard to certain core rights whose implementation is regarded as *obligationes erga omnes*[1] - but procedures to enforce their realisation by unwilling governments are of a political rather than judicial nature. In politics, as we know, *de lo dicho a lo hecho hay gran trecho*. This process from words to deeds will also depend on the moral strength of the human rights idea within a particular society. Thus the question of *cultural receptivity* to human rights confronts us with the moral foundations of the concept of human rights in regard to cultural differences. This is a rather complicated matter.

Do human rights "have their roots in many different nations and cultures" or were they rather adopted by "a small clique of lawyers, bureaucrats and intellectuals who are highly westernized and most of whom have absolutely nothing to do with the cultures in which ... their fellow nationals live" (Meron, 17)? These are two different questions; the first one refers to basic ideas and the second to formulations. Let us look first briefly at the underlying ideas. An American minisyllabus for teaching human rights suggests starting with the question "What are human rights?" along the following lines:

> Here the student should be exposed to the difficulties of the definitional and justificatory process. The following questions could be the focus for this discussion.
> 1. Is it needless to determine what is morally right?
> 2. Is it impossible to justify a supreme moral principle?
> 3. How should one determine which rights are universal and inalienable?

In regard to the above questions, there is an ongoing debate between legal theorists arguing on the basis of a universalist position and social anthropologists defending cultural relativism. A primary theoretical problem is that the concept of *human rights* is not a homogeneous one, subject to a single interpretation. While historically, for example, the notion of human rights is definitely connected with the attempt to restrain sovereignty, the American liberal view on this particular relationship is not generally accepted. Meron describes this view as follows: "Upon entering society, the autonomy of each individual is combined with that of other individuals, and transformed into sovereignty of the people" (Meron, 29). Thus, individuals would retain some autonomy in the form of rights that protect them against the State they themselves created. (It should be noted that in this view without the self-created State the community would have no say over individuals whatsoever.) Thus, human rights becomes a *protective*

---

[1] See Case of the International Court of Justice Concerning the *Barcelona Traction, Light and Power Company Limited (New Application: 1962) (Second Phase) Belgium v. Spain*, ICJ 1970, Rep. 3.

concept based on *individual autonomy*. This interpretation is by no means globally accepted and in terms of cultural receptivity it is problematic in connection with those rights that follow from *freedom from want*.[2] We may note here already that the problem of cultural receptivity is not unrelated to different ways of interpreting human rights.

Cultural relativists "reject the possibility that there can be universal moral standards because no justification [of human rights] can avoid being culturally based and thus limited in scope" (Dundes Renteln, 9). This view, however, conflicts with an apparently universal moral intuition that certain actions are *obviously* wrong (e.g. to kill another human being because one does not like the person). Nevertheless, anthropologists cause a great deal of difficulty for themselves through the cross-cultural approach in empirical investigations of norms and values. Thus, in an analysis of retribution (recompense for evil done) tied to proportionality, it was empirically found that disproportional violence is universally rejected (Dundes Renteln). In regard to the norm employed (proportional, disproportional), such findings do not come as a great surprise. As for certain core rights, legal universality would not make it unreasonable to *assume* moral universality, although not in the form of universally identical formulations.

One should distinguish formulations from underlying principles. If, for example, Moslems approach poverty from the perspective of responsibilities (the responsibility of the rich to the poor) while humanists adopt a position based on the perspective of rights (the rights of the poor vis-à-vis the rich), the outcome may still be the same. Hence, there seems to be good reason to approach the problem of human rights and cultural receptivity not so much from the viewpoint of setting standards but focusing rather on *implementation*.

In this paper I shall discuss the operation of human rights from one particular angle: *the political economy of jurisprudence*. Human rights play their part in the interrelationship between the economic, political, social and legal aspects of ordering a society. It is in this context that we shall touch upon the problem of cultural receptivity. But first it is necessary to understand processes of transforming rights into accepted claims.

---

[2] In his famous address of 1941 President Franklin D. Roosevelt summarised human rights in the four freedoms: freedom of speech and expression, freedom of every person to worship God in his own way, freedom from want and freedom from fear. To each of these freedoms he added the universalist clause "everywhere in the world". See "Address of the President of the United States," January 6, 1941, *Congressional Record*, Vol. 87, part 1, 46-47.

IMPLEMENTATION OF RIGHTS

Rights enable us, among other things, to participate in processes of production, distribution and consumption of goods and services. Economic rights represent "the abstract acknowledgement of the legitimacy of claims to income and to participation in resource allocation" (Samuels, 1974, 118). But the problem with rights is their relativity. One individual's rights are limited by another's rights. Ownership, for example, is not to be regarded today as an absolute right "to use and abuse" property but rather as a general presumption of entitlement on the part of the owner. Whether the owner's claims, indeed, will be realised, depends also on other people's interests and the possible protection of these interests through rights.

Behind different rights are different interests. Rights legitimise claims only insofar as there are corresponding obligations on the part of others to respect these rights. This depends on the relative strengths of the respective rights. In a society that tries to settle conflict through law, the conflicting interests are weighed against one another, on the basis of norms, by some institution or person not part of the conflict.

Because of the general uncertainty as to the acceptance of a person's claims, Samuels argues that rights cannot be regarded as pre-existing: "The economic reality is that rights which are protected are rights only because they are protected; they are not protected because they are pre-existing" (*ibid.*, 118-19). He confuses rights and effectuated claims here, as becomes clear in the sentence: "Each present right is only one successful claim or expectation among others which did not materialize ...." If, however, a claim does not materialise, this does not mean that the person (A) had no (pre-existing) right. It only means that there was something lacking in the conditions necessary for the materialisation of his claim. The problem may have been the existence of a conflicting claim by another individual (B) whose right had to take precedence.[3]

In actuality, law is a process rather than a product; it is a process of continuous change in the way in which human behaviour is ordered through making and applying rules and settling disputes. Inevitably, legal rules are imprecise, requiring a non-mechanical application, which makes it impossible to determine in a normative and predictable manner which types of loss or injury to private

---

[3] Samuels' view comes down to the belief that all subjective rights are merely fictions. Bentham also took this view: "The word right is the name of a fictitious entity: one of those objects, the existence of which is feigned for the purpose of discourse, by a fiction so necessary that without it human discourse could not be carried on. A man is said to have it, to hold it, to possess it, to acquire it, to lose it. It is thus spoken of as if it were a portion of matter such as a man may take into his hand, keep it for a time and let it go again" (quoted in Oliver, 50). Today this view is taken by legal positivists, who refuse to discuss law in normative terms.

persons should be compensated. The problem of compensation, in other words, is theoretically insoluble (Samuels 1974, 1978, 1980).

Legal anthropologists have gone to great lengths in attempting to describe real types of legal order in terms of different distributions of rights and duties among individuals and groups. Such attempts are, however, bound to be frustrated by the radical indeterminacy of any type of legal order. The actuality of pre-existing rights does not imply a pre-existing legality since, as was pointed out above, one person's rights may conflict with another person's rights or with public interests. Sally Falk Moore has therefore proposed a conceptual framework that takes indeterminacy as the theoretical basis of social, cultural and legal relationships, an indeterminacy that individuals attempt either to exploit through "processes of situational adjustment" or to combat through "processes of regularisation" (Falk Moore, CH. 7).

It is in such undetermined social fields with different power relations, as based on divergent private and public interests and different degrees of legal protection, that human rights may play their part as well. Binding the execution of power to certain morally compelling standards constitutes their essence. Wherever power is executed and disputes arise, human rights may influence such processes and thus their outcome. It is not without reason that a great deal of attention is paid to the setting of standards. "The language of human rights", Bhagwati has rightly observed, "carries great rhetorical force .... At the level of rhetoric, human rights have an image which is both morally compelling and attractively uncompromising" (Bhagwati, 1). Yet, we must be aware of substantial differences in cultural receptivity to human rights discourse. "Often the most blatant transgressors of human rights have the best records in terms of acceptances of human rights instruments" (Dinstein as quoted by Meron, 19). The problems of implementing human rights relate to the dialectics of law and power. This may become clear if we analyze different types of entitlement systems as mechanisms for the transformation of rights into realised claims.

ENTITLEMENT SYSTEMS

Entitlement is the possibility of making legitimate claims, i.e. claims based on rights. It is a function of both law and power. Power means opportunity, actual command. Law legitimises and hence protects this power in case of dispute.

It is the combination of law and power that makes entitlement such a precious affair. Even more than the occasional claim, the entitlement situation as such is an object of desire. People continuously try to improve their entitlement situation. Hence, more than a given state of affairs, entitlement too, is a *process*. It is part of social processes in society. Indeed, there is always an interrelationship between rights and obligations within a socio-cultural context.

Three main types of entitlement systems can be distinguished: direct resource-connected entitlement, institutional entitlement and state-arranged entitlement. We shall briefly review the operation of each different type of entitlement system while paying specific attention to possibilities and constraints in the realisation of human rights. This may also give us some insight into problems of cultural receptivity in regard to the implementation of human rights.

Direct Resource-Connected Entitlement

Sen's book on entitlement and deprivation focussed specifically on entitlement based on direct access to resources. The field of socio-economic relations as governed by private law (principally property and contract) is described as follows:

> In an economy with private ownership and exchange in the form of trade (exchange with others) and production (exchange with nature), E_i [the entitlement set of person i in a given society, in a given situation] can be characterised as depending on two parameters, viz. the *endowment* of the person (the ownership bundle) and the *exchange entitlement mapping* (the function that specifies the set of alternative commodity bundles that the person can command respectively for each endowment bundle).For example, a peasant has his land, labour power, and a few other resources, which together make up his endowment. Starting from that endowment he can produce a bundle of food that will be his. Or, by selling his labour power, he can get a wage and with that buy commodities, including food. Or he can grow some cash crops and sell them to buy food and other commodities. There are many possibilities.... (Sen, 45-46)

Thus the key-word in entitlement positions based on direct access to resources is the adjective *own*: his own land, her own labour, his own shop, her own knowledge, etc. Such ownership enables people to engage in transactions with others on the basis of rights and obligations. Indeed, property and contract constitute the juridical basis of such entitlement positions.

Here it is private law, as guaranteed by the state that is to provide security in the sense of "the predictive states of mind, the *expectations*, that result from assurances given by the law of property and contracts" (Karst and Rosenn, 637). Thus a person who owns some land may expect to be able to use its produce because society protects property, and a person who sells something under contract may expect payment because organised society has provided a regularised means of enforcing contracts. It is the law that enables individuals to make legitimate claims.

Unlike institutions with a 'real' existence, i.e., forming part of reality whatever their legal status may be, property and contract are legal constructions, conceptions created by law. As Bentham has put it, "Property and law are born together and die together. Before laws were made there was no property; take away laws and property ceases" (quoted in De Gaay Fortman, 1982b, 79).

Private law is based on individual freedom coupled with individual responsibility. It has developed mechanisms for weighing different interests against one another on the basis of universal rules which ought to be applied equally in equal cases. Thus it constructed a law of torts. Where other people's interests are harmed, even an owner may act unlawfully and hence be condemned to restoration or at least compensation. Yet there remain many cases of damages without compensation because the action concerned was not considered to be unlawful (*damnum absque injuria*).

A private system of law is well suited for the implementation of fundamental human freedoms (freedom of conscience and religion, freedom of expression, freedom of assembly and association, etc.), provided it operates within the framework of the rule of law. This implies government by law, which means that even the state itself can be summoned for unlawful action. A certain amount of human rights activism on the part of the judiciary is also required. Indeed, judges may play a prominent part in translating the rhetoric of human rights into normative decisions. They tend to reason in an *evaluative* manner, not so much oriented towards goals as towards norms (Graver, 60). While evaluating different interests in the light of norms, judges may pay specific attention to human rights. Thus, Justice Bhagwati has cited several cases in which human rights have been put into law by the Indian judiciary (e.g. free legal aid for criminal defendants, as a result of interpreting Articles 2 (3)(a) juncto 14 (3)(d) of the International Covenant on Civil and Political Rights).

Judicial activism in putting human rights into law is possible only where the judiciary is independent, creative and committed to human rights. But even when all those conditions obtain, human rights will not be transformed into actual entitlement if law does not rule. It appeared to be difficult, for example, to implement the Indian Supreme Court's condemnation of bonded labour in outlying areas where feudal lords rather than the law were in control.

Direct resource-connected entitlement plays a major part in market economies based on freedom of enterprise and consumption and free exchange through systems of markets and prices. Such an economic order is conducive to continuous change from which individual A, through the use of her rights, may benefit more than individual B. Thus, it can happen that some people experience an increase in their wealth while the wealth of others is decreased, leading them into poverty. Private law is not an appropriate mechanism to correct this, whereas criminal law, its sister system in providing the legal foundations for a market economy, protects property against unauthorised attempts to correct the distribution of wealth.

It is true that private law also recognises equality as a fundamental legal principle, besides freedom, but this primarily takes a formal character (freely negotiating citizens are equal before the law). Yet, through concepts such as *abuse of law* and *undue influence*, attention to material inequality in the sense of inequality following from unequal distribution of power has been increasing.

Principally, however, private law is not particularly well equipped to prevent substantial socio-economic inequality, nor to tackle the relative poverty resulting from such conditions. Private law, in other words, is not the right system for the protection of economic and social rights. It is noteworthy in this connection that Sen's entitlement analysis was highly inspired by the Great Bengal famine of 1943 when people were starving on the pavement in front of well-stocked food shops (Sen, CH. 6). Police protection was used here to prevent rather than promote a realisation of the right to food. It is the majestic equality before the law, Anatole France has observed, which prohibits the rich and the poor alike to sleep under bridges, to beg on the streets and to steal bread (Peters, 17).

The debate in the British Parliament in the early nineteenth century on the abolition of slavery presents an interesting example of the dichotomy between private law and public justice. While some members maintained that the masters had to be compensated for the loss of their slaves Benjamin Pearson argued that "he had thought it was the slaves who should have been compensated". Samuels, who discusses this example within the framework of his analysis of the compensation principle, sees it as an indication "of the need, in advocating public policy, of an ethical system, of a concept of justice" (Samuels, 1974, 126 n. 29). Although to some extent a *socialisation* of private law may well take place (De Gaay Fortman, 1982a, 477-78), this type of law remains rather unrelated to social justice. Its essence lies in the old Justinian precept *suum cuique tribuere* in the sense of respecting existing rights rather than guaranteeing people the entitlement that morally should be theirs.

Still, in relations between individuals economic and social rights may play a role, for instance, through an application of the old adage, *Quod est illicitum lege, necessitas facit licitum*. Thus, in nineteenth-century France Judge Malinvaud ('le bon juge') used to accept *force majeure* whenever it was evident that a person accused of theft of food had been in a state of hunger (De Monchy, 1905).

Roman law contains a specification of an economic right in the rule, *Nemo de domo sua extrahi debet*. Acceptance of the right of squatters to occupy empty houses or office buildings, as has happened in Dutch law, goes a great deal further in realising a right to housing. Thus, economic and social rights may have an impact on the social and economic relations between people as protected by private and criminal law. This is termed their *horizontal operation*. For this horizontal functioning of economic and social rights, those whose claims find their basis in these rights obviously have to take action. Through action first, and acquiescence in the new situation later, a pre-existing illegality may be made legal. Illustratively, Karst and Rosenn's discussion of Bolivian land reform in 1952-53 is entitled, *Land Reform First, Then Law*: "Effective land reform in Bolivia occurred when the *campesinos* occupied the great estates, ejecting both owners and administrative foremen" (Karst and Rosenn, 650). This action was followed by a great deal of legal activity arising out of the peasants' desire to stabilise the new situation by acquiring proper titles.

The reverse, a process of turning apparent legality into illegality may also occur, as events in Eastern Europe have recently demonstrated. This is bound to happen some day when positive law is connected with a regime that lacks legitimacy based on representative, participatory and accountable government. The persistent violation of human rights by such regimes may act as a catalyst for resurrection. Obviously, the implementation of human rights does not just depend on existing legal arrangements. What has also become clear is that human rights by their very nature are *action-oriented*.

Institutional Entitlement

As sources of entitlement, institutions may be seen as "semi-autonomous social fields". An institution is autonomous in the sense that it possesses its own rule-making capacities, and the means to induce or coerce compliance. It is only *semi*-autonomous since it is part of a larger social matrix which may invade into its autonomy (Falk Moore, 55-56).

An obvious example of such a semi-autonomous social field is the tribe which allocates access to the land together with entitlement to the fruits of its exploitation - usually under the chief's authority - at the same time expecting the fulfilment of various obligations. But modern society is full of such institutions as well. In terms of social relations the modern enterprise, for example, is much more than just an employer while a job implies more than merely a number of fixed working hours in exchange for a wage.

Other institutional entitlement systems are the family (nuclear and/or extended), political parties, trade unions, schools, universities, sports clubs, churches and other religious organisations. People derive their security - the desire to prevent threats and minimise risks - from belonging to such institutions. Compared to entitlement systems regulating relations based on direct individual access to resources, institutional entitlement systems tend to be better tuned towards a realisation of *positive freedom* or opportunity: freedom *to*. But in terms of *negative freedom* or liberty (the freedom *from* (interference by the other powers)), institutional entitlement systems may be more problematic. Thus, within such institutions even freedom of thought, conscience and religion may be suppressed. Violation of women's rights and child rights, for example, particularly occurs within an institutional context as well. Since the larger social matrix of which semi-autonomous institutions are part includes supervision mechanisms for the implementation of human rights, they are certainly not sacrosanct. But it is important to note that the root causes of violations of fundamental freedoms and equality rights lie in the internal organisation of certain institutions. Indeed, the human rights' cause is intimately connected to the struggle for *democracy* in the sense of representative, participatory and accountable execution of power.

Here we touch upon the problem of the cultural receptivity of specific institutions. It is particularly religious institutions such as the Roman Catholic Church that are known for their lack of internal democracy. It is also in this connection that we may find answers to such difficult questions as the massive violations of the right to life in Sri Lanka which occurred at the instigation of Buddhist monks, even though Buddhism is a religion of tolerance. Institutional culture is not the same as the normative system on which the institution is formally based.

The entitlement basis of an institution as such depends on its relative power vis-à-vis the state and other institutions. Remarkably, there has been little analysis of such entitlement positions in connection with institutional cultures. An exception to this *lacuna* is the work of Sally Falk Moore. In her paper *Law and Social Change: The Semi-autonomous Social Field as an Appropriate Subject of Study* she presents an entitlement analysis of a particular part of the dress industry in New York. The analysis focuses on the allocators of scarce resources in relation to both written and customary rules. Her conclusion is that "...neither effective sanctions nor the capacity to generate binding rules are the monopoly of the state" (Falk-Moore, 79).

Thus, an analysis of institutions as bases of entitlement and commitment should focus not so much on rules *per se* but rather on the systems within which the rules are applied and on the sources of effective inducement, coercion and claims. One institution which might have a much more prominent place in research in most countries is the political party that regularly participates in government. This applies not only to Eastern Europe - where analysis of political parties in relation to entitlement systems and institutional culture could not easily be carried out - but also to Italy, where the total collapse of the public credibility of political parties in power came as a remarkable surprise.

State-Arranged Entitlement

Today, access to health care, education, police protection and other collective goods is largely regulated by the state. State law produced for this purpose tends to be of an instrumental character in the sense that it is intended to support and promote policies for collective action. The process of socio-economic collectivisation is based on interdependence in modern economies (De Swaan, 13).

The state gives through collective action and takes through taxation, thus rearranging entitlement. Policies for this purpose are, however, not always easily accepted. People may try to circumvent laws by changing the situation on which their treatment by the state is supposed to be based. In reaction to taxation, for example, they may increase their deductible costs. One might call this *fiscalisation* of behaviour. It results in 'side law' (*ius obliquum*) in the sense that *unintended* - rather than the intended - effects of instrumental law predominate. A similar situation may arise in cases of subsidisation. People may try to fall into the category that would entitle them to a subsidy, even though this subsidy was clearly not intended for people such as them. As an example of this, we could mention subsidised housing from which persons in higher income brackets manage to benefit. The opposite occurs when people having a lower income do not succeed in acquiring subsidies intended for their aid. Indeed, the problem of not availing oneself of benefits is well known in the literature on social welfare.[4]

Instrumentalist policies tend to be faced not only with side effects and attempts to circumvent intended entitlement reductions by the state but also with a simple reluctance to obey the law. Thus, apart from a formal (official) sector and an informal (circumventing) sector, an evading sector (black market) emerges. As a result, it becomes rather difficult to analyze, let alone direct, processes of entitlement.

State-arranged entitlement is particularly important for the realisation of economic and social rights. It is often stated that a realisation of those rights requires the state to take affirmative action while implementation of civil and political rights would imply a restraint on state power. This is not generally true. Promotion of civil and political rights requires positive measures to create a socio-economic and political context that is conducive to the observance of human rights whereas violation of, for example, the right to food may be the result of agricultural policies tuned to the production of foodstuffs for the world market while destroying domestic food security.

Where the state takes positive measures to implement social and economic rights, there is good reason to focus on improvement of existing entitlement positions rather than creating an alternative entitlement mechanism based on state bureaucracies. Generally, *primary entitlement* is to be preferred to *subsidiary entitlement* in the sense that people have access to resources and rights to goods and services on the basis of their integration into the community rather than as compensation for their marginalisation. In India, for example, the introduction of green revolution technology seriously affected the entitlement position of the weaker groups in the rural areas. Subsidiary entitlement in the form of

---

[4] A citizen who wishes to make use of her rights to a subsidy or welfare allowance has to cross at least five different barriers:

1. She should know that there is such aid in place.
2. She should know where to get information about that aid.
3. She should overcome any embarassment in collecting the information.
4. She should be able to understand the information (the brochure) and to apply that to her own situation.
5. She should fill in the forms while going through the whole bureaucratic procedure.

One particular cause of trouble arises during the moment of application. In a study of benefits being taken up in the Netherlands, Filet found that no less than 30% of the respondents were of the opinion that they had submitted a formal request for social welfare while the civil servants concerned felt they had merely supplied information (quoted in Van Oorschot, 9).

food coupons distributed by the state could not be regarded as a satisfactory compensation (cf. Ramprasad).

Subsidiary entitlement may be easily affected by the socio-political culture as expressed in the spirit of the times (*der Zeitgeist*). In practice there are no 'acquired rights' in the sense of a permanent and standing guarantee of entitlement by the state. New concepts such as 'no-nonsense', 'deregulation', 'privatisation', and 'structural adjustment' may result in new policies with direct effects on the entitlement situation of certain categories of people. Indeed, state-arranged entitlement makes people dependent upon those in political power. This becomes particularly exacting in situations of a *corruptive* nature in the sense that the whole process of declaring and enforcing state law and settling disputes is misused for purposes other than their public political aims. Where the existing distribution and organisation of state power is of a highly personalised nature - networks of patron/client relationships - the introduction of new authority for public officials may merely promote the misuse of office, i.e. corruption.

To prevent corruption or, worse, tyranny, state power needs to be depersonalised. Here we are back at the principles of the *Rechtsstaat*, the Rule of Law. Since the fall of the Berlin Wall the illusion that human rights could be realised with any type of political regime has disappeared.

THE PROBLEM OF CULTURAL RECEPTIVITY

The problems of cultural receptivity to human rights are not confined to non-Western peoples. Apart from implementation in Western societies themselves - which is not unproblematic - the very idea of universality also signifies Western responsibility for the realisation of human rights for people in other parts of the world. Global inequality illustrates, however, the lack of global mechanisms to correct injustice. (One billion people at the top of the world's income scale receive 150 times the income of the one billion people at the bottom.) The phrase "everywhere in the world" used by Roosevelt in his *Four Freedoms Address* and subsequently endorsed in the *Universal Declaration of Human Rights* still primarily requires implementation rather than setting standards. Whatever view one takes on the question of the universality of human rights norms, there is definitely a universal problem with respect to cultural receptivity.

It should also be realised that cultural receptivity is not a one-way process from existing and unchanging human rights norms to certain specific cultures. Since the Universal Declaration of Human Rights non-Western cultures have had a growing influence on formulations in new charters and covenants. This has meant a shift in emphasis towards duties, also in regard to communities, positive freedom rights (economic, social and cultural rights) and collective rights. In further attempts to realise human rights, non-Western views may play an increasing role. We may think here, for example, of the Islamic concept of *Shura* or the Hindu notion of *Dharma*. The latter entails that, in whatever situation a human being finds himself, he should always be aware of his limits. This provides a significant moral input into human rights thinking, provided such thinking is receptive to nonliberal cultures. Although an individual-centred and rights-oriented view lies at the roots of the historical process of formulating international human rights standards, a growing moral universality will require receptivity to alternative approaches to justice. In regard to economic and social rights a predominance of non-Western (communitarian) thinking is already noticeable. As Virginia Leary has concluded:

> Despite its Western origin, the concept of human rights must now be recognised as a universal term accepted through the world. But the concept is a dynamic and evolutionary one that has recently been extended to cover many aspects of human dignity not contemplated under the traditional Western rubric of human rights. Western influence, dominant in the origin of the development of international human rights norms, is now only one of a number of cultural influences on the development of international human rights standards. Its contribution to the development of human rights has been great, but it has not been unique, and other cultures have made and are making significant contributions to our collective conception of human dignity. (Leary, 29-30)

Cultural justifications for continuing violations of human rights in developing countries do not usually come from non-Western academics. The late Senator Diokno of the Philippines once summarised the arguments as follows:

> One is that Asian societies are authoritarian and paternalistic and so need governments that are also authoritarian and paternalistic; that Asia's hungry masses are too concerned with providing their families with food, clothing and shelter to concern themselves with civil liberties and political freedoms; that the Asian conception of freedom differs from that of the West; that in short, Asians are not fit for democracy.
>
> Another is that developing countries must sacrifice freedom temporarily to achieve the rapid economic development that exploding populations and rising expectations demand; that in short, government must be authoritarian to promote development.
>
> The first justification is racist nonsense. The second is a lie; authoritarianism is not needed for developing, it is needed to perpetuate the status quo. (Quoted in Surendra, 3-4)

In our review of human rights in relation to different entitlement systems we have focussed on problems of implementation rather than those of setting standards. Indeed, the processes of acculturation of the great world religions themselves among peoples who had not exercised any influence whatsoever on the formulations in the holy books which they later accepted as the basis of their faith, is proof of the possibilities of cultural receptivity in regard to alien texts.

The real challenge in the implementation of human rights is their full integration into existing entitlement systems. In developing countries - but also today in Eastern Europe - a complication is that these countries find themselves in processes of rapid transition from institution-based and/or state-arranged entitlement to direct resource-connected entitlement systems. Such processes tend to be tuned to financial/economic parameters rather than focussed on the creation of institutions conducive to the realisation of human rights. The question then arises as to how far international human rights standards and supervision mechanisms can set corrective processes of political and social change in motion. To use Sen's terminology, what happens in cases of *entitlement failure*?

It is noteworthy that while in their Western historical context human rights developed as a protective concept - to defend the autonomy of individual citizens against particular threats from sovereigns (states) that wished to extend their power into the citizens' own realm - in the cultural context of Africa, Asia, South and Central America the idea of human rights is of a much more *emancipatory* character: a struggle for the rights of the have-nots. While our analysis has already revealed that human rights are highly *action-oriented*, this applies particularly to the situation in developing countries. "Human rights," Surendra has noted from an anonymous observer,

> have often been functioning as the rights of the privileged both at the world level and also in national and local societies. But the dispossessed, the underprivileged, and that is the majority of the world, they regard human rights as instruments of liberation and emancipation. (Surendra, 3)

In such a context human rights are used as a legal resource for social change while playing a particular part in the struggles of social movements.

Essential in such struggles for social change is the *conscientisation* of those who have to fight for their own rights so that apathy and resignation to the status quo may be overcome. Hence the challenge of cultural receptivity is to get the human rights idea integrated into their hearts. As Judge Learned Hand once put it:

> I wonder whether we do not rest our hopes too much upon the Constitution, upon laws and upon Courts. These are false hopes. Liberty lies in the hearts of men and women. When it dies there, no Constitution, no laws, no Courts can do much to help it. While it lives there, it needs no Constitution, no law, no Court to save it. (Quoted in Bhagwati, 10)

To find its root in the hearts of people the idea of human rights would have to be supported rather than obstructed by existing cultural identities. Here we touch upon the role of religion. One relevant factor, for example, is how people look at the course of events, whether as 'the Will of God' or as the result of human action. Another element concerns people's approach to power, in full submission or critically demanding accountability. One might also mention attitudes towards plurality, religious zeal based on fundamentalism (*compelle intrare*) over against tolerance and acceptance of other people's fundamental freedoms.

I shall resist the temptation to go further into these questions since they should be left, primarily, to religious anthropologists and students of comparative religion.

BIBLIOGRAPHY

An-Na'im, A.A. and F.M. Deng (eds.). *Human Rights in Africa: Cross-Cultural Perspectives*. Washington, D.C.: The Brookings Institution, 1990.

Bhagwati, P.N. *Address to the Caribbean Human Rights Seminar*. Jamaica, 1989. (unpublished).

Biesheuvel, M.B.W. and C. Flinterman (eds.). *De rechten van de mens*. Amsterdam, 1983.

De Gaay Fortman, B. "Parlement en hercodificatie." *Weekblad voor Privaatrecht, Notarisambt en Registratie*. No 5617 (1982): 474-78.

——. "You Cannot Develop by Act of Parliament: Rethinking Development from the Legal Viewpoint." in B. de Gaay Fortman (ed.). *Rethinking Development*. The Hague: Institute of Social Studies, 1982.

De Monchy, S.J.R. *De Nederlandsche Wetgever tegenover de armoede*. 1905.

De Swaan, A. *In Care of the State: Health Care, Education and Welfare in Europe and the USA in the Modern Era*. Cambridge: Polity Press, 1988.

Dundes Renteln, A. *International Human Rights: Universalism versus Relativism*. Newbury Park: Sage, 1990.

Dworkin, R. *Taking Rights Seriously*. London: Duckworth, 1977.

Falk Moore, S. *"Law as Process": An Anthropological Approach*. London: Routledge and Kegan Paul, 1983.

Graver, H.P. "Norms and Decisions." in *Scandinavian Studies in Law* 32 (1988): 49-67.

Karst, K.L. and K.S. Rosenn. *Law and Development in Latin America: A Case Book*. London, 1975.

Leary, V.A.. "The Effect of Western Perspectives on International Human Rights." In: A.A. An-Na'im and F.M. Deng (eds.). *Human Rights in Africa: Cross-Cultural Perspectives*. Washington, D.C.: The Brookings Institution, 1990.

Meron, T. (ed.). *Human Rights in International Law: Legal and Policy Issues*. Oxford: Clarendon Press, 1985.

Olivier, P.J.J. *Legal Fictions: An Analysis and Evaluation*. Diss. Leyden: Beugelsdijk, 1973.

Peters, A.A.G. De emancipatie van de mens, In: M.B.W.Biesheuvel and C. Flinterman (eds.). *De rechten van de mens*. Amsterdam, 1983.

Ramprasad, V. *The Hidden Hunger: Food Policy in India and its Impact on Entitlement*, Penang, Malaysia: Third World Network, 1990.

Samuels, W.J. "An Economic Perspective on the Compensation Problem." *Wayne Law Review* 21 (1974): 113-34.

—— and N. Mercuro. "The Role of the Compensation Principle in Society." *Research in Law and Economics* 1 (1977): 210-45.

——. "The Role and Resolution of the Compensation Principle in Society: Part Two - The Resolution." *Research in Law and Economics* 2 (1980): 103-28.

Sen, A. *Poverty and Famines: An Essay on Entitlement and Deprivation*. Oxford: Oxford University Press, 1981.

Surendra, L. "Human Rights in the Context of Asian Cultural Tradition." *Human Rights Forum* 4 (1985): 3-8.

Van Oorschot, W. and P. Kolkhuis Tanke. *Niet gebruik van sociale zekerheid: feiten, theoriën, onderzoeksmethoden*. The Hague: Rapport voor Ministerie van Sociale Zaken en Werkgelegenheid, Commissie Onderzoek Sociale Zekerheid, N0 16A, 1989.

CHAPTER V

Cultural Relativism and Universal Human Rights?*

André Droogers

INTRODUCTION

In their study of culture, cultural anthropologists have, often implicitly, moved between the extremes of uniqueness and universality and the built-in contradiction has led to a state of mind bordering on schizophrenia. On the one hand, anthropologists have defended the (human) right to the idiosyncracy of the cultures and peoples they studied. On the other hand, unhindered by the prospect of contradiction, they also have shown a deep interest in a universal definition of 'the' human being. Interestingly, the word 'culture' has been used for both the specific and general understandings.

The concept of religion carries the same double significance. Like 'culture', 'religion' can be used in the singular, stressing the universal phenomenon. But it can also be used to indicate concrete forms of religion, and in that case the term has both singular and plural uses. Again, the uniqueness of a specific religion puts general definitions of religion and on generalizations of a phenomenological nature into question. In fact, anthropologists have been among the most active critics of phenomenology, drawing attention to the cultural context of phenomena. Moreover, it is argued that religions are based on experiences that lie beyond words. As one culture may already have difficulty in expressing this experience, it is all the more difficult to establish cross-cultural communication. Nonetheless, efforts at interreligious dialogue are continually being made.

The apparent contradictions between universality and specificity have contributed to important debates in two ways. First of all, the concept of cultural relativism has come under attack. Second, the question has been raised whether rationality can be said to be a universal characteristic of humankind and should be defined accordingly. Interestingly, this second debate began with a discussion on the religious phenomenon of witchcraft among the Sudanese Azande (cf. Ev-

* I am grateful to Sander Griffioen, Hans Tennekes and the participants in the research program on Encounter of Religions at the Free University for their stimulating comments on an earlier version of this paper.

ans-Pritchard). In fact, cultural relativism has been presented as the opposite of the claim that rationality is a universal phenomenon. In both debates the methodological issue of whether elements of one culture can be translated into another has been raised.

Both problems are relevant to the question of human rights and to the central question of this volume: can human rights be interpreted and justified from within religious traditions, such that they are supported, rather than undermined, as the 'common core' of a universal morality between these traditions? The acceptance of cultural relativism implies a rejection of the possibility that universal human rights can be rationally formulated. If human rights are nevertheless imposed but fail to be respected, a cultural relativist has no difficulty in explaining the failure. Similarly, when cultural relativism denies the existence of a universal rationality, the framework needed to formulate human rights appears to be absent. Conversely, human rights presuppose a minimum of communality, and a minimal intercultural communication.

In this article I will summarize the debates about relativism (sections 1 and 2) and rationality (section 3). Then I will investigate the applicability of the anthropological discussion to that on religions and human rights (section 4).

THE SOURCES OF RELATIVISM

Cultural relativism has several origins. A short overview of these sources can help in understanding the phenomenon.

First of all, relativism is part of the cultural anthropologist's basic fieldwork experience. The dramatic impact that thorough contact with a foreign culture has on the fieldworker convinces him or her of the uniqueness of the experience. While research proposals are overloaded with theoretical considerations, presupposing the possibility of generalization, statements or paradigms disappear as soon as the idiosyncratic complexity of the field has made itself felt. Even when the fieldworker has been warned against exotism, he or she will have difficulty in maintaining the right balance between the specific and the universal. When the (often outspoken but otherwise tacit) idiosyncracy of the fieldworker's personality is added to that of the field, cultural relativism is a logical result.

There are other sources that nurture the idea of cultural relativism. Its origin is closely linked to a critique of evolutionism, especially where Western culture has been seen as the apogee and ultimate criterion of the other cultures in the world. The cultures located high on this scale were thought to merit the predicate 'civilized'. Interestingly, almost all these civilizations coincided with what are now called the 'world religions'. In the course of the evolutionist phase of cultural anthropology tribal cultures were called barbaric, savage, or primitive. That racist arguments reinforced this kind of evolutionism needs no elucidation. Cultural relativism contested the validity of value judgements across cultural boundaries, arguing that all knowledge, including moral criteria, is culturally determined (Tennekes, 185-86).

The rehabilitation of the so-called primitive cultures had a clear political-ethical dimension and thus cultural relativism also had a political source. It was a weapon in the struggle against growing Western influence. Even though anthropologists were part of Western expansionism and served the interests of colonial authorities, there was - and still is - a tendency to protect indigenous peoples against modernizing influences. This does not exclude the possibility that cultural relativism has served a colonial conservatism, directed against supra-tribal independence movements (Lemaire, 175). Though lacking such a colonial context, American anthropologists sought to protect what was left of the Amerindian cultures. Especially when anthropological theorists presented tribal societies as harmonious and in equilibrium, external influence - political, economic, religious - was viewed as harmful (Kloos, 56-57). Interestingly, an essential part of the current efforts to defend human rights is concerned with indigenous peoples.

The roots of cultural relativism also include the discussion centring around hermeneutics, through which the relativity of the construction of knowledge was emphasized. The fundamental question became whether reality could actually be represented and if so how (Ormiston and Schrift, 4). Postmodernism has revived cultural relativism by emphasizing contexuality and fragmentation and by proclaiming the end of paradigmatic discourse (Marcus and Fischer, 7-16).

THE CRITIQUE OF RELATIVISM

Despite these arguments, cultural relativism has come under criticism. Though still present in cultural anthropology, it was at its peak in the 1930's, associated especially with the names of Franz Boas, Melville Herskovits and Ruth Benedict. The course of events, however, soon proved the complexity of the cultural relativist stance: it would have been absurd to justify the atrocities committed during World War II on the basis of the idiosyncracies of the cultures of those who committed them. The question could be raised whether a cultural relativist point of view really excludes value judgements on one culture from within another, even if those outside the speaker's culture do not share this judgement.

In the period after the Second World War the former colonies were replaced by independent states. A new supra-tribal framework was put into place. In the post-colonial situation, tribal cultures continued to be integrated into larger units in some way. The 'primitive isolate' no longer existed. Development as guided modernization became a goal, and many anthropologists were employed as experts whose task it was to facilitate this process (Kloos, 58-59).

But this process had wider consequences. Many worlds were merging into one world. The symmetry between societies that cultural relativism presupposed became an illusion, since one expansionist culture dominated what happens in the rest of the world, creating a fundamental asymmetry. Even though Western ethnocentrism might be wrong, nevertheless, it is the global reality. What seemed theoretically impossible has become the standard practice. Economic and political events have overruled cultural relativism.

In this 'one' world people increasingly migrate across cultural boundaries. Some do so on a voluntary basis, but the majority are compelled to do so in order to survive. Intercultural contacts have also been promoted where religions defend universal pretensions and strive to be a worldwide presence (Tennekes, 191). While encounter between religions has become common so has conflict. Even if one would prefer to avoid value judgments, this is utterly impossible (Gellner, 71, Tennekes, 187-88). Ethnic minorities, each with its own culture, are present in modern plural societies. Their presence creates the necessity of an ethical discussion. Peoples are living apart together. If the earlier discussion took place in the colonies and concerned head hunting and the burning of widows, the current discussion is in the West's own backyard and concern female circumcision, gender relations, education and ritual sacrifice. Reappraising classic monographic studies of cultures, scholars have become conscious of the ever-present differences between subcultures within one - seemingly homogeneous - culture. Even such a culture has included value judgements on subcultures (Tennekes, 189-190). Cultural relativists cannot escape the inevitable human tendency to distinguish between good and evil: they cannot suspend that part of their human nature (*ibid.*, 191).

It was not only history, however, that eroded the notion of cultural relativism. There were also theoretical reasons. First of all, universal rationality was emphasized in the debate over rationality. Since I will discuss this debate in more detail in the next section, it will suffice here to mention this position. Cultural relativism has provoked an epistemological philosophical debate.

Secondly, the question arises as to how the above-mentioned fieldworker could even have the dramatic experience of uniqueness if there were not some form of intercultural communication. Knowledge about a different culture presupposes some common basis for understanding. Would it not be better therefore to find some mediating point along the spectrum between universality and uniqueness? Equally, cultural relativism inevitably leads to the conclusion that all cultural anthropological knowledge is limited and that total understanding will never occur. But how can anthropology then be the thriving science that it is? In other words, anthropology would be impossible if cultural relativism, at least in its absolute forms, obtains (Lemaire, 157-59).

The criticism could be posed in a different way, in the sense that the defense of any foreign culture implicitly entailed admiration for that culture and a comparison with the fieldworker's culture. Certain values that Western culture had marginalized were very much present in tribal cultures: sociality, emotion, ludicity, wholeness, etc. Thus cultural relativism, intended to guarantee an objective approach, indirectly stimulated the fieldworker's bias and provoked a methodological debate (Tennekes, 186).

Thirdly, cultural relativism led to an emphasis on moral values as tolerance, modesty, and mutual respect: Were these values universal or part of a Western (sub)culture? How could a relativist defend these values as universal and as absolute rules (cf. Lemaire, 158)? Or should one allow for the possibility that a culturally determined value judgement might be true, either objectively factual or fundamentally human, so that in practice - notwithstanding various inherent epistemological and ethical problems - cultures can be compared with respect to the evidence of their truthfulness and inherent humanity (Tennekes, 192)? Since the validity of judgements does not depend on their - in this case internal cultural - genesis (Lemaire, 157), this is perfectly viable. Could tolerance, modesty and mutual respect then be true and human in that sense (Tennekes, 199)? Moreover, respect does not exclude value judgement and might even demand such a judgement (*ibid.*, 199). Again, what can Western culture learn from other cultures? Cultural relativism has provoked an ethical debate that has relevance for the human rights issue.

RATIONALITY

The debate over rationality took its starting-point in Evans-Pritchard's classical study of Sudan Azande witchcraft, where he analyses accusations of witchcraft as a way of dealing with and expressing social tensions. This function of witchcraft is one of the reasons why people, though considered "capable of rationality persist in practices deriving from mystical beliefs about non-existent entities", i.e., witches (Hirst and Woolley, 85). Ironically, the way Evans-Pritchard, no doubt capable of rationality, described his own attitudes during his fieldwork shows that he then adopted the Azande way of thinking with regard to accusations of witchcraft and the corresponding ordeal by poison; accordingly, in his approach there is a significant ambiguity (*ibid.*). In the end, however, Evans-Pritchard contrasts Azande thought to Western scientific thought. Inspired by the hermeneutical discussion and Wittgenstein, Winch, in his 1964 article on "Understanding a Primitive Society" (republished in Wilson, cf. bibliography), criticized this point of view and thus the so-called rationality debate began. The problem, according to Hirst and Woolley's summary (92), is that Western scientific thought has become less useful in evaluating 'primitive' cosmologies. Science was also shown to start from unverifiable presuppositions and intuitions. Moreover, as soon as mutually exclusive paradigms, each with its own presuppositions, dispute the 'ultimate' truth, it becomes less ultimate. If the criteria of rationality are internal to a certain culture, it is useless to speak of witches as non-existent entities. Whereas Evans-Pritchard's presupposition is that reality is in itself intelligible, independent of the knower (Hirst and Woolley, 94; Winch, 81), the hermeneutical problem is, as we saw, whether it is possible to know reality, and what the nature of the link between a paradigm's discourse and reality is (Hirst and Woolley, 94). Those who like Winch do not share Evans-Pritchard's presuppositions must necessarily come to the conclusion that Western scientific discourse cannot be used to judge Azande witchcraft. The question is "whether or not there are alternative standards of rationality" (Lukes, 194).

In response, MacIntyre (1979ab) attacked Winch's supposed relativism, arguing on the basis of the idea of a cumulative development of humankind's knowledge. He used the asymmetry argument that we already encountered when discussing criticisms of cultural relativism. Rationality is understood as having developed in the course of human history, in a dialectical process, and Western society cannot but use and apply that rationality (Hirst and Woolley, 96). Similarly, in criticizing cultural relativism, Gellner (80 ff.) recommends what he calls a "rationalist fundamentalism". Hirst and Woolley comment that indigenous peoples unfortunately did not draw much advantage from this highly developed form of rationality: "Western civilization came as a calamity" (97). How effective were Western science and technology? In other words: what is the moral surplus value of Western rationality?

On the other hand, complete relativism would lead to the petrifaction of tradition and to the elimination of any rational criticism of irrationality, however they are defined. Cultural relativism would then produce the same ethnocentrism it was meant to combat (Lemaire, 161). Thus, even if rationality was not in itself something of which one could be proud, it could not easily be discounted.

Lukes opts for the compromise solution "that some criteria of rationality are universal, i.e. relevantly applicable to all beliefs, in any context, while others are context-dependent, i.e. are to be discovered by investigating the context and are only relevantly applicable to beliefs in that context" (208). This view is similar to Tennekes' above-mentioned plea for a culturally determined value judgement on the evidence of truth and inherent humanity of cultures (Tennekes, 192).

Bernstein (97 ff.) has criticized an over-schematic presentation of the debate. In his view, Winch did not want to adopt a relativist stance. Besides, according to Bernstein, even though Winch insists on the different standards of rationality, he does not exclude common characteristics between Azande and scientists: "there are patterns of logical inference that we share with the Azande ... there is a range of common objects that both the Azande and we identify in similar ways" (100). Bernstein presents Winch's central concern as the question of what genres or language games scientists use to classify what Azande are doing: symbolics, theology, technology, magic, myth (103)? Winch's message was that science, with its standards of rationality, does not seem to be the right genre for understanding Azande witchcraft. As Ulin summarizes Winch's view:

> it is not empirical verification that establishes what is in agreement with reality but, on the contrary, the uses of language, or language games, through which a particular speech community constitutes reality intersubjectively ... Winch's

> contribution is important because it brings into question the relation between methodology and epistemology in the social sciences by arguing that there is an indissoluble relationship between language as discourse and what is regarded as real. (xii)

Bernstein suggests that the "task of understanding an alien culture may require the imaginative elaboration of new genres, or the stretching of familiar genres, in order to compare what may be incommensurable" (103). New language games can be invented. Moreover, his point is that incommensurable forms can be rationally compared (107). This can also be taken as an answer to cultural relativism: even cultural relativists make comparisons and are not able to stress the differences without some common ground, some common language game, that makes comparison possible (Kloos, 108).

This leads me to a final remark on rationality. The definition of rationality is in itself problematic. It is, for example, not clear where the rational stops and the irrational begins, or whether there is a diffuse field between the two. Rationality sometimes seems identical to Western scientific positivism and technological reasoning, but it has wider connotations that may ultimately make it a general human characteristic that takes local forms. When a developmental cumulative dimension is included it comprises a human capacity, even if its potential is not yet fully realized. Thus, the Azande were considered "capable of rationality", even though they believed in witches. If rationality as a concept thus lacks a clear definition, its vague limits necessarily exclude sharp boundaries like those common in dichotomic reasoning. It is moreover significant that examples from tribal religions, e.g. witchcraft, seem to be preferred to those from the so-called world religions, as if the latter were closer to rationality. Again this suggests that tribal religions fit dichotomous thinking (primitive/civilized). Nevertheless the opposition empirical/religious is also present in the debate. The two debates on cultural relativism and rationality seem to have stagnated because of the central role given to these and other dichotomies. In actuality, once one is aware of the roots in the movement in recent Western thinking from positivism to constructivism (cf. Guba), the two debates are revealed as a commentary not on tribal cultures but on Western culture - more specifically, science and its bias toward dichotomies.

RELATIVISM, RATIONALITY, HUMAN RIGHTS, RELIGION

From the debates on cultural relativism and rationality it has become clear first of all that the construction of oppositions between extremes - such as the pairs universal/local, rational/irrational, science/religion, tribal religions/world religions - has to be replaced somehow by a relativizing exploration of each spectrum that goes beyond such dichotomies. Comparison then becomes possible. This conclusion has been reached in part on theoretical grounds, in part under the pressure of recent history. If the focus is on the whole spectrum rather than on the extremes a model must be found that leaves room for differences as well as common characteristics. Lukes' distinction between universal and contextual criteria of rationality move in that direction, as does Tennekes' advice to maintain the possibility of a value judgement despite cultural differences.

In the second place, what seems to be fundamental is to rediscover the dynamics. Instead of concentrating on the opposition between seemingly static and closed views on relativism and rationality and particular cultures as well, research should focus on the processes involved. This also leads away from extremes and dichotomies towards what occurs on the spectrum between them. If views and cultures are less static than their proponents may believe, then changes become interesting.

The central problem of this volume is very similar to the one discussed in an earlier volume on sharing religious experience. Cultural relativism was as much present there as it is here. The present theme could be reformulated as 'on sharing human rights'. As I did then (cf. bibliography), I will also indicate here a constructivist perspective, defined in terms of human meaning-making and power. The inclusion of the power dimension will help in avoiding a simplistic idealism. At any rate, in the context of a discussion on human rights the power dimension cannot be ignored.

Guba's description of the presuppositions of constructivism is relevant here (cf. Guba, 27). The ontology of constructivism refers not to one reality but to realities that "exist in the form of multiple mental constructions, socially and experientially based, local and specific, dependent for their form and content on the persons who hold them". This may be read as a cultural relativist creed, but it must be complemented by Guba's description of constructivism's epistemology: "inquirer and inquired into are fused into a single (monistic) entity. Findings are literally the creation of the process of interaction between the two." The same process approach, which includes power relations, characterizes constructivism's methodology: "individual constructions are elicited and refined hermeneutically, and compared and contrasted dialectically, with the aim of generating one or a few constructions on which there is substantial consensus." It seems that interreligious dialogue has some constructivist characteristics.

The constructivist approach moves beyond sterile dichotomies without denying their value. It allows for a universal as well as a culturally specific dimension. In addition, it makes room for continuity as well as change, the static as well as the dynamic. It applies to religion as well as to science, to rational as well as irrational dimensions. It helps in discovering the common, without denying conflict and contrast. One might say that constructivism is culturally determined, a Western way of rationality, but the alternative is silence, abstention. And constructivism perhaps comes close to a model of culture that allows for universal application. This view will now be presented.

The central idea of the model is that human beings can be defined by their capacity to produce signification, to give meaning to the world they live in and to the events that happen to them or that they help to bring forward. This capacity, as a universal phenomenon, can be called culture in the sense of the exclusive singular. It comes close to the more amply formulated definitions of rationality (see e.g. Horton). Though meaning-making suggests an active and creative role of the subject, it is obvious that the subject does not start from scratch and is not entirely free in his or her options. Through education society transmits a huge stock of meanings that is often reproduced but can also be reproduced, reinterpreted and changed. Subject and society are dialectically related, as are culture and social structure. Culture is subject to a hermeneutical process. Especially in religion, people experience the imposing presence of a tradition of meanings. The possiblity to use the gift of culture has been proposed as a fundamental human right, basic to many others. Its local manifestations are also called culture, including a plural use of the word. Yet since culture, in either of the two senses, is morally neutral, it can be used for good and for bad. As such, the right to culture can also be used against humanity. When it is proposed, as in the defence of indigenous peoples, it refers to a right to identity, not to immorality. The ambiguity of human beings as signifiers points to the tension between the moral and the universal.

Culture and cultures use symbols or tropes, of which the metaphor is the most frequently used. Metaphors are based on the comparison of two seemingly unrelated domains, one known and familiar, the other new and open to signification. The first domain furnishes the meanings that can be applied in order to understand the second domain. Through metaphors phenomena are classified, categories are created, and order is established. Thus, religions use supernatural worlds to understand the world in which people live. But science too makes use of signification through metaphor. The infinite possibilities of creating, manipulating and transforming meanings opens the perspective on the eternal, the transcendent, the utopian. One should add the irrational, because the choice of a determinate metaphor is often arbitrary and axiomatic. What in reality seems impossible becomes viable, interestingly so in religion as well as science.

The concept of power is a necessary complement to this view. Power and meaning-making are dialectically related. Like culture, power is morally neutral and can be used both ways. It can be defined as the capacity to influence another person's behaviour. This includes controlling signification processes, the definition of what is normal and what not, what is good and what is evil. The limits of the imagination are circumscribed. Power can be used to defend an established order. As a consequence, obeying commandments, laws and rules is a way of 'economizing' in the process of meaning-making, whether in the scientific or religious signification process. On the other hand, power itself is subject to meaning-making and can therefore be used to promote an alternative order. It can be controlled and made explicit, as a topic of reflection, in order to come to a common point of view in a climate that is *herrschaftsfrei* (Habermas). Human rights declarations are meant to curb and control the exercise of power. One might think that power is always contrary to human rights interests, but within the definition used here, power can be put to a morally good use, as e.g. in the activities of the United Nations.

The notion of power draws attention to a certain asymmetry. Societies and religions differ as far as the degree of asymmetry is concerned. Since meaning-making is an ongoing process, despite constraints, the model is not static but dynamic, yet allowing for the possibility of reproduction (often in fact re-production) of tradition. Individuals, not seldom marginal to current interests, can play an innovative role and challenge prevailing power relations. The global encounter between cultures and religions that is characteristic of the modern world has brought extra stimulation to the process of meaning-making. Power relations orient that encounter. The discussion on human rights must be understood within this context. This is not only an exchange of established views, but the encounter takes people beyond these, creating a new discourse, a new order, but always subject to the mechanisms of the power game.

In the religious context, power operates at three levels (Droogers, 1992, 51; Droogers and Siebers). The first might be called supernatural and involves God, gods and/or spirits on the one hand and believers on the other. Both sides exert power. The second level can be termed internal. Meaning-making, though generally human, is claimed by those who present themselves as religious specialists and often claim to control access to supernatural resources. Their position is generally legitimized by a process of meaning-making. Believers, however, negotiate space for their own meaning-making, as occurs in popular religion. On the third level, the external, the power relations are between believers and non-believers. Some forms of religion may seek to influence what happens in the society in which they occur, e.g. by introducing certain laws, seeking political influence, or recruiting new believers. Of course, the promotion of moral values, sometimes viewed as human rights and sometimes as their opposite, is another example of the exercise of a religion's power on the external level. The relations with other religions, whether they be dialogical or combative, can be located here. It is the level of the one world in which we live, despite the many worlds from which we come. The first two levels are characterised by the relativism of a closed culture or religion, while the third opens the window to the universal.

The first level, the supernatural, seems to be the most fundamental, in that meaning-making and power relations on that level orient and may even determine what happens on the other two levels. Together, therefore, the three levels form a specific constellation, typical of the religion under discussion. An important aspect of the ideas produced on the first and second levels is the view of the human being, an anthropology. The world view includes a 'person view'. It is here that the essentials of what can be considered human rights are formulated.

Whereas the signification and power processes on the first two levels seem to confirm cultural relativist ideas, the third level poses the problem of the universality of cultural elements like rationality and human rights. The contemporary world has increasingly emphasized this external level. The 'paradigm communities' formed at the first two levels meet at the third level and negotiate their positions. Becoming a part takes the place of being apart. Therefore, as was observed above, value judgements that once were the prerogative at the first and second levels can no longer be avoided at the third level. While intercultural communication has its difficulties, it also represents a challenge that may require, as we already quoted from Bernstein, "the imaginative elaboration of new genres, or the stretching of familiar genres." If the concept of language game is not viewed as static and closed but as dynamic, it offers the possibility of understanding how new genres can be elaborated, i.e., through the human capacity of meaning-making. It is this same capacity of playing and experimenting with meanings that makes interreligious dialogue possible. By extension, it serves as a basis for a discussion on human rights, their viability and their content.

It is only realistic, however, to recognize the power dimension of this discussion. The partners in dialogue seek to influence each other's behaviour and will do so under the legitimation that was defined at the first and second level. One must not expect rapid consensus. The religions' interaction often entails violence, war and death. The negotiation that is proper to power processes depends on the human capacity of meaning-making. This can be used for the purpose of the reproduction of established values, but it can also be creative.

CONCLUSION

Let us return to the central question of this volume: Can human rights be interpreted and justified from within religious traditions, such that they are supported rather than undermined as the 'common core' of a universal morality among these traditions? We can now reply with a hesitant affirmative, because the human capacity of culture as meaning-making, though in itself morally neutral and exercized within the constraints posed by power relations, allows for the construction of a bridge between the unique and the universal. This leads to a delicate and sometimes painful endeavour, because the instrumentally possible is not always the morally permissable; one has to reckon with the ever-shifting results of signification and power processes. On the other hand, it also is a promising enterprise, since the unity in diversity can be discovered.

There is a link with human beings' fundamental existential condition: to be part of the cosmos and outside it simultaneously (cf. Van Baal). In the modern world this tension is assuming new forms, on the one hand through the struggle against relativism and regionalism in favour of some form of rationality and universality, on the other through the promotion of ethnicity and religious superiority. These new forms represent challenges as well as hopes. Religions have always shown how to live with the fundamental human condition to which Van Baal pointed. Their experience will therefore also help to solve the modern forms this fundamental tension takes when the human rights issue is discussed between believers of different religions.

BIBLIOGRAPHY

Bernstein, Richard J. *Beyond Objectivism and Relativism: Science, Hermeneutics, and Praxis*. Oxford: Basil Blackwell, 1983.

Droogers, André. "Meaning, Power and the Sharing of Religious Experience: An An thropology of Religion Point of View." In: Jerald D. Gort *et al.* (eds.). *On Sharing Religious Experience: Possibilities of Interfaith Mutuality*. Amsterdam/Grand Rapids: Rodopi/Wm. B. Eerdmans, 1992. Pp. 45-54.

—— and Hans Siebers. "Popular Religion and Power in Latin America." In: André Droogers*et al.* (eds.), *Popular Power in Latin American Religions*. Saarbrücken/Fort Lauderdale: Breitenbach, 1991. Pp. 1-25.

Evans-Pritchard, E.E. *Witchcraft, Oracles and Magic among the Azande*. Cambridge: Clarendon Press, 1937.

Gellner, Ernest. *Postmodernism, Reason and Religion*. London/New York: Routledge, 1992.

Guba, Egon G. "The Alternative Paradigm Dialog." In: Egon C. Guba (ed.). *The Paradigm Dialog*. Newbury Park: Sage, 1990. Pp. 17-27.

Hirst, P., and P. Woolley. "Witchcraft, Rationality and Other Cultures." In: Robert Bocock and Kenneth Thompson (eds.). *Religion and Ideology*. Manchester: Manchester University Press, 1985. Pp. 84-109.

Horton, Robin. "African Traditional Thought and Western Science." In: Bryan R. Wilson (ed.). *Rationality*. Oxford: Basil Blackwell, 1979. Pp. 131-71.

Kloos, P. *Filosofie van de antropologie*. Leiden: Martinus Nijhoff, 1987.

Lemaire, Ton. *Over de waarde van kulturen: Een inleiding in de kultuurfilosofie, tussen europacentrisme en relativisme*. Baarn: Basisboeken Ambo, 1976.

Lukes, Steven. "Some Problems about Rationality." In: Bryan R. Wilson (ed.). *Rationality*. Oxford: Basil Blackwell, 1979. Pp. 194-213.

MacIntyre, Alasdair. "The Idea of a Social Science." In: Bryan R. Wilson (ed.). *Rationality*. Oxford: Basil Blackwell, 1979. Pp. 112-130.

——. "Is Understanding Religion Compatible with Believing." In: Bryan R. Wilson (ed.). *Rationality*. Oxford: Basil Blackwell, 1979. Pp. 62-77.

Marcus, George E., and Michael J. Fischer. *Anthropology as Cultural Critique: An Experimental Moment in the Human Sciences*. Chicago: University of Chicago Press, 1986.

Ormiston, Gayle L., and Alan D. Schrift (eds.). *The Hermeneutic Tradition: From Ast to Ricoeur*. New York: State University of New York Press, 1990.

Tennekes, J. *De onbekende dimensie: Over cultuur, cultuurverschillen en macht*. Leuven/Apeldoorn: Garant, 1990.

Ulin, Robert C. *Understanding Cultures: Perspectives in Anthropology and Social Theory*. Austin: University of Texas Press, 1988.

Van Baal, J. *Man's Quest for Partnership: The Anthropological Foundations of Ethics and Religion*. Assen: Van Gorcum, 1981.
Wilson, Bryan R. (ed.). *Rationality*. Oxford: Basil Blackwell, 1979.
Winch, Peter. "Understanding a Primitive Society." In: Wilson, Bryan R. (ed.). *Rationality*. Oxford: Basil Blackwell, 1979. Pp. 78-111.

Part 3

Case Studies from Religious Traditions

CHAPTER VI

Raja Rammohun Roy's Thought and its Relevance for Human Rights

Victor A. van Bijlert

WHAT ARE HUMAN RIGHTS?

The twentieth century has seen the rise of totalitarian, anti-human ideologies such as fascism, Leninist and Stalinist socialism, colonialism, imperialism, nazism, and rabid nationalism,[1] all of which have had a global impact. The list is perhaps not exhaustive, and in certain cases the movements have coalesced. Their adherents have often defended the absolutism of these ideologies on the grounds that they constituted the apex of historical necessity and human destiny and therefore needed to be ruthlessly put into practice.[2] Thus these 'isms' became the modern scourge of the earth. One of the main reasons for their ultimate moral failure lies in their contempt for human life, which manifests itself, for example, in the pursuit and extermination of so-called enemies of the state, of a superior race, of the proletariat, or of one's own people.

A powerful moral (and even to a certain extent ideological/political) weapon against such outrages (which are mainly perpetrated by governments or political organizations) is the concept of human rights and the consequent democratic temperament. Especially during the last decade the question of human rights has become increasingly pertinent. The most widely known modern formulation of human rights is the *Universal Declaration of Human Rights* adopted by the UN in 1948. The horrendous magnitude of the Nazi war crimes stimulated a rapid

---

[1] Nationalism dates from the late eighteenth century. It acquired its most ugly manifestations in this century, rather unexpectedly after the near demise of the other ideologies. All of these ideologies probably derive their initial success from their populist rhetoric giving a fixed direction to otherwise diffuse mass aggression. From the last decade onwards, militant nationalism, which together with fascism is the most irrational ideology, is apparently raising its head again.

[2] Because of their brutal claims, it is possible to regard these ideologies as secular fundamentalist religions.

formulation of human rights as a universal moral code. Since then, the *Declaration* has gained more and more recognition as a charter for moral human conduct. In almost every nation non-government groups have sprung up which report and investigate abuses of human rights including torture, rape, murder, unlawful detention, disappearances, genocide, etc. This *Declaration* was the first globally acknowledged basic instrument[3] intended to fight such abuses.

The *Declaration* serves as the source of inspiration for a large number of international instruments in which it is explicitly invoked, some of which are: the International Covenant on Civil and Political Rights, the International Covenant on Economic, Social and Cultural Rights, the Convention Relating to the Status of Refugees, the International Convention on the Elimination of All Forms of Racial Discrimination, the Convention against Torture and other cruel, inhuman or degrading Treatment or Punishment, the Declaration on the Elimination of all Forms of Intolerance and of Discrimination based on Religion or Belief.[4] In the final analysis the *Declaration* is a moral rather than a legal document: it constitutes a global moral appeal and the rights it proclaims could be interpreted as deriving from the idea of the sacredness of life as well as a few moral precepts that flow from this idea.

In order to relate the modern discussions on human rights to moral questions raised by religious traditions, we will first try to highlight the moral precepts underlying the *Declaration*. They and the concept of the sacredness of life constitute the parameters within which the discussion on present-day religion and human rights ought to take place. Then we will look at the history of these precepts in connection with formulations of civil and human rights in the eighteenth-century European 'Enlightenment'. Can it be said that these precepts and their underlying idea of the sacredness of life are a Eurocentrist moral project or do they indeed have universal validity? We will try to answer this important question by showing how this idea and such precepts were set down and discussed in the beginning of the nineteenth century by the Bengali Hindu philosopher, social and religious reformer and humanist Raja Rammohun Roy. Although Roy was not the only proponent of Hindu humanism, he was certainly one of the earliest in modern India. His position is especially interesting, since it strongly resembles the ethos behind the *Declaration*. At the same time we will show Rammohun Roy's influence on the idea of the civil rights (in stature and impact similar to human rights) embodied in the Constitution of independent India.

---

[3] Though without the status of binding international law! Cf. P. Davies (ed.), *Human Rights* 36, 37.

[4] The texts of these instruments can be found in Van Dijk *et al.*, 5-16, 20-26, 32-43, 47-55, 68-76, 96-98 respectively.

ETHICAL PRECEPTS OF THE UNIVERSAL DECLARATION

The bulk of the text of the *Declaration* formulates different civil, cultural and social rights including the right to life, liberty and security of person (art. 3), right to a fair trial (art. 10), right to a nationality (art. 15), the right to freedom of thought, conscience and religion, and the right to change one's religion (art. 18), the right to an adequate standard of living (art. 25), and education (art. 26). The moral goals and imperatives that underlie these rights can be found in the Preamble and articles 1 and 2. The Preamble states:

> Whereas recognition of the inherent dignity and of the equal and inalienable rights of all members of the human family is the foundation of freedom, justice and peace in the world, Whereas disregard and contempt for human rights have resulted in barbarous acts which have outraged the conscience of mankind, and the advent of a world in which human beings shall enjoy freedom of speech and belief and freedom from fear and want has been proclaimed as the highest aspiration of the common people.

The Preamble seems to assume the sacredness of all human life tacitly as its leading moral principle and, on this basis, outlines the ideals and aspirations behind the rights to be proclaimed in the sequel: each "member of the human family" ought to recognize the inherent equality and dignity of every other human being. Every human being ought to be able to live in freedom, every human being ought to respect the dignity and worth of every other human being.

This is again repeated as a principle in article 1: "All human beings are born free and equal in dignity and rights. They are endowed with reason and conscience and *should* act towards one another in a spirit of brotherhood." Clearly, the *whole of humankind*, without any conceivable exception, ought to be regarded and respected as being as intimately related as members of the same family would be: all human beings are brothers and sisters of one another. For this reason the Preamble speaks of the "human family". Such a conception of humankind seems to imply brotherly and sisterly love of all humans for one another or, if not love, then at least sympathy and compassion, and at the very least mutual respect and tolerance, such as members of a family would feel for one another.

This feeling of brotherhood and sisterhood is further intensified by insisting on the equality, the equal worth, of all humans. This means that no human being can claim superior worth or greater human value than all his or her fellow humans. This denies any validity to racism, discrimination, gender pride, ethnic pride (certainly ethnic or communal cleansing!), for all these old vices deny the worth and the brotherhood and sisterhood of all humans.

If we should not maltreat our brothers and sisters, it quite naturally follows that we should leave them in peace, as long as their exercise of freedom does not harm us positively. Such freedom can never mean a license to kill, for then it would destroy the freedom of the victim and violate the family solidarity that is expected to obtain among all humans. Freedom thus defined comprises the freedom to practice, propagate and change one's religion. But religion remains a matter of one's own conscience. We could imagine a religious organization invoking the freedom of religion as a basis for persecuting, torturing and burning heretics at the stake, but such an abuse of freedom could never be condoned. Taking the ethics of the *Declaration* seriously, as well as all the articles contained in it, entails that certain limits to freedom are necessary in order to preserve intact the intentions and the spirit of the *Declaration* as a whole. But who would object to limiting the freedom of evildoers to continue in their wickedness?

Enlightenment and Civil Rights

The concept of human rights, as ethical precepts in the political sphere and social life, did not begin in 1948. Attempts to define human rights were certainly also inspired by the 'Enlightenment', i.e., the intellectual project of seventeenth and eighteenth-century rationalism that involved the great progress made in the natural sciences, religious scepticism and anti-clericalism. In the revolutionary period of the late eighteenth century, both in America and Europe, human or civil rights more or less constituted the political credo of the 'Enlightenment'.

Civil rights were advanced in terms of the equality of all humans, freedom from tyranny and oppression, and the freedom of opinion and conscience. From the eighteenth century onwards they play an increasingly important role in political life. Nurtured by the dissatisfaction of the urban middle classes with royal absolutism, they became political demands for constitutional checks on the almost unchecked dominance of the aristocracy, the Church and (often absolute) monarchs. In the nineteenth century this led to the ultimate victory of the democratic constitutional republic as the most desirable form of the nation-state.

Significantly enough, in connection with India, one of the earlier formulations of human rights was advanced by another British colony, a colony prepared to throw off the yoke of British domination. We refer here, of course, to the American *Declaration of Independence* of 4 July 1776:

> We hold these truths to be self-evident: that all men are created equal; that they are endowed by their Creator with certain inalienable rights; that among these are life, liberty, and the pursuit of happiness. That to secure these rights, governments are instituted among men, deriving their just powers from the consent of the governed .... (quoted in Asbeck, 37)

In 1789 revolutionary France adopted a declaration consisting of seventeen articles that stated the rights of human beings and citizens - the famous *Déclaration des Droits de l'Homme et du Citoyen*. The first articles, which state the ethical principles on which the rights rest, will give a good impression of liberal ethos of the *Déclaration*:

> 1. Men are born and remain free and equal in rights. Social distinctions may not be based on anything but public utility.
> 2. The goal of every political association is to preserve the natural and imprescriptible rights of man. These rights are liberty, property, security and resistance to oppression ....
> 4. Liberty consists in being able to do everything that does no injury to others. Hence the only limitations on any one's exercise of natural rights are those which ensure the enjoyment of these same rights to all other members of society .... (this translation is my own from the French version found in Asbeck, 48-49)

Enlightenment outside Europe and Anti-Colonial Struggle

However we evaluate the eighteenth-century 'Enlightenment', we cannot escape the fact that the concept of human rights associated with it has in one way or another influenced political thought all over the world. Some good examples of this influence were the different indigenous struggles for political and economic independence within the regions colonized by European powers. This is not to suggest that these non-European struggles for political independence were ultimately an enterprise inspired by European culture as a whole.

With regard to India, one can make a plausible case that nineteenth- and twentieth-century British colonialism undertook few means to establish genuine parliamentary democracy based on universal suffrage and the equality of all citizens there (cf. Mittal, 12-107). British paramountcy in India hardly promoted the ethical values of universal human rights that we associate with the 'Enlightenment'. British rule usually endorsed the cause of conservatism (local and at home), and, at its best, presented itself as benevolent paternalism (cf. Sarkar, 13-14, 20-24; *Oxford History of India*, 662-70, 683-92). Mainly due to indigenous struggles for independence, the decolonization process, modestly begun in 1885 by the Indian National Congress, got into full swing between the two world wars and culminated in full independence in 1947. This set the pace somewhat for similar processes in Indonesia, Indo-China, and the African colonies, most of which became independent states in the decades after the second world war. The prime moving force and ethical imperative behind the Indian struggle and decolonization, as well as behind these similar movements elsewhere, was the intrinsic value of political freedom, equality, democracy and the right of self-determination of all peoples, values surely consistent with the 'Enlightenment' ethos outlined above. Another significant example of 'Enlightenment' influence is the *Universal Declaration of Human Rights* itself.

It could be argued that the notion of human rights is a purely European concept, for its philosophical justification was laid down in the works of the eighteenth-century French philosophers Rousseau, Diderot and Voltaire, as well as others. In the English-speaking world Thomas Paine (1737-1809) was a famous propagandist of civil rights, enlightenment and rationalism.

In colonial India, many progressive Indians, among whom Rammohun was one of the earliest, regarded human or civil rights as the ground for demanding concessions from the British rulers.[5] This brings us to the question of whether the enlightened, humanist ethos behind the idea of human rights constitute a typically (politically progressive) European/Western idea. First of all, posing this question appears to give too much credit to European culture as the sole repository of humanism. Further, we should remain aware of the fact that the Enlightenment itself constituted only one of many European cultural and political discourses in the past and that its cultural/religious anthropology was heavily contested until recent times in Europe itself. Investigating the particularity of humanism as a European construction will entail a discussion of the influence of one's own culture on one's perceptions of other civilizations. This could also invite a lengthy debate on 'orientalism' and 'antiracism', but space does not permit us to delve deeper into these exciting matters.[6] For the present, all we can say is that if we believe that all humans on earth share the same humanity and therefore deserve to be treated with respect, even with love, then differences of culture and civilization do not constitute absolute barriers to mutual understanding. As we will presently see, the human rights ethos, whether partly a product of (European) Enlightenment or not, did and continues to have numerous advocates outside Europe and America, one of whom was Rammohun Roy.

RAMMOHUN THE FIRST MODERN REFORMER

The beginning of the nineteenth century was an important period for eastern India, since, from its commercial and political metropolis, Calcutta, the East India Company gradually established its territorial paramountcy over the subcontinent (cf. Marshall and Bayly). At the same time Calcutta became the cradle of nascent Indian nationalism and (mainly Hindu) reformist consciousness among the urban Hindu elite. The first able spokesman of modern reformist Hindu enlightenment was Rammohun Roy (1772?-1833) (on the somewhat contested date of his birth, cf. Dobson Collet, 1-2, 9-15). His intellectual and social activity heralded an indigenous movement of cultural, political and social modernization

---

[5] Already in 1823 Rammohun pleaded for greater freedom of the press in then British India. Cf. his famous 55-point "Appeal to the King in Council," in: Racanavali, 508-28. Cf. also Desai, 221-40, 320-80.

[6] For an elaborate treatment of western orientalism in connexion with India see Inden. On Indian views on nationalism and the somewhat strained relationship between Indian nationalism and its European models with regard to the Indian political developments of the last 100 years, see Chatterjee.

among the Bengali Hindu middle class elite (among whom the Tagore family figured very prominently). This movement was later called the 'Bengal Renaissance' as well as the 'Indian Renaissance', since from the end of the nineteenth century onwards it provided inspiration and role models for the progressive independence movement.[7]

Rammohun is honourably remembered by posterity for at least two public actions which have a bearing on human rights. First, he agitated continually against the practice of burning widows - suttee or *sati* - alive. Although the Anglicized misspelling suttee actually signifies the person, the term is often used to refer to the practice itself. Secondly, in 1828 he founded the so-called *Brahmo Samaj*, "Society (*Samaj*) of [believers] in the Deity (*Brahmo*)", a theistic, unitarian religious body open to all. The prime Hindu scriptural sources of inspiration for the Brahmo's of that time were the Upanishads and the Vedanta Sutra (on the foundation of the *Samaj*, see Dobson Collet, 222, 236-38).

Rammohun was also a redoubtable disputant and pamphleteer. During his lifetime he published numerous tracts: an early pamphlet in Persian on the one God who could be known independently of religious traditions, more than twenty minor and major tracts in both English and his native Bengali on religious, legal and social topics, as well as a few theological and philosophical works only in Sanskrit. Moreover, he edited the Sanskrit texts of five Upanishads along with his own translations in English and Bengali. Nothing of this sort had been done with respect to English and the Indian vernaculars, although quite a number of Persian translations of some Hindu scriptures had been in existence from the times of the Mughals and were still being read in Rammohun's time. Besides Sanskrit, Bengali, English, and Persian, Rammohun knew Arabic, and in his later life also learned Latin, Greek and Hebrew in order to be able to read the Christian and Jewish scriptures in the original languages.[8] His study of Christianity resulted in two major theological works on the ethical teachings of Jesus. A full list of the titles of his works is to be found in Racanavali, 606-11.

Thus, Rammohun was well qualified to accomplish what he believed to be his task, namely, reforming Hinduism on a more spiritual and philosophical basis and doing the same for religion on a wider basis.[9] Reform movements in India have been in existence since the beginning of recorded history, the earliest

[7] Here one should think primarily of the Indian National Congress along with Mahatma Gandhi and Jawaharlal Nehru and his family.

[8] A good survey of the different aspects of Rammohun's thought on various subjects and discussions on his position within Bengali culture of nineteenth-century Calcutta, can be found in Niharranjan Ray.

[9] For a useful summary of Rammohun's ideas on religion, see Ajit Kumar Ray, 1976. A briefer summary is given in Dilip Kumar Biswas, 1976, 97-112.

of which could include the mystical/philosophical revolution of the Upanishads and, of course, early Buddhism and Jainism (both fifth century BC). In the Indian Middle Ages the greatest socio-religious reformers, both men and women, who criticized Brahmanic arrogance and pride of caste and taught the unity and easy accessibility of God through love and the equality of God's devotees, were followers of the Bhakti movement. In this way Rammohun's reformist zeal does not radically differ from these older movements. His uniqueness and modernity lie in the fact that he recognized the universal political implications of such religious ethics. To a large extent, his activities set the trend for later socio-religious reform movements in British India (cf. Jones, 1989).

Against the Practice of Sati

In India *sati* (suttee) had been practiced for ages among high-caste Hindus mostly of royal extraction. Suttee means the self-immolation by a widow on the pyre of her deceased husband. It was said that the widow would thus reach heaven (*svarga*) or could be regarded as a divine being, because of her unflinching devotion to her husband. Although the practice may not have been extremely widespread in eastern India, Dobson Collet (87-88) does report figures totalling 2365 recorded instances for the Bengal Presidency alone between 1815-1818.[10] The British government of this region, then still in the hands of the East India Company, did nothing to stop it on the grounds of non-interference with the religious customs of the peoples of the land. An official letter from W. Bayley, acting registrar on behalf of the *Sudder Adalat* (court of law) dated 5 June, 1805 stated that

> ...the court apprehend that it would be impracticable at the present time, consistently with the principle invariably observed by the British government, of manifesting every possible indulgence to the religious opinions and prejudices of the natives, to abolish the custom in question [ie widow-burning]; whilst such a measure [ie banning this custom] would, in all probability, excite a considerable degree of alarm and dissatisfaction in the minds of the Hindoo inhabitants of the provinces. The courts are accordingly of opinion, that the immediate adoption of a measure of the above nature would be highly inexpedient. (quoted in Majumdar, 98)

---

[10] One should not conclude that these figures can be used to demonstrate the immoral nature of Hinduism, for they seem small compared to the millions of human beings that have been burned at the stake as heretics by institutionalized Christianity, especially during the Inquisition. The latter's record of cruelty, persecution, torture and mass extinction in the name of religion is probably unparalleled in history. And then we have not even mentioned the deeds of other Christian Churches, nor, for example, the role of the Church in and after the conquest of America, etc. At present, however, the Churches have "repented from this their wickedness".

However, the police were permitted to investigate whether or not the widow had been drugged, was pregnant, or too young, in which cases the Hindu priests (*pandits*) claimed the Hindu lawbooks (*dharma-shastra*'s) did not allow self-immolation (cf. *ibid.*, 104-05 for directions issued to the police to this effect).

Rammohun had witnessed a suttee in his own family in 1812.[11] His eldest brother had died and the widow was forced by her orthodox in-laws and the Brahmans present to mount the pyre. Rammohun wanted to save her but arrived too late at the cremation ground. Then and there he vowed to have the practice abolished, and later began to write pamphlets against it. Between 1818-1820 he published three such tracts in both Bengali and English (Dobson Collet, 40, 69, 514, 517, 521 ff.). These tracts derived their power of conviction by their appeal to reason, humanity, and because they set out to demolish orthodox arguments by showing them to be inconsistent with the ultimate values of the best Hindu scriptures. Here Rammohun used his exegetical skills to the utmost in order to show that the custom was not sanctioned by the scriptures. In his own English translation (1818) of his first dialogue against the practice he has the opponent of it say:

> It is every way improper to persuade to self-destruction by citing passages of inadmissible authority. In the second place it is evident from your (i.e. the defender's) own authorities, and the Sankalpa [intention] recited in conformity with them, that the widow would voluntarily quit life, ascending the flaming pile of her husband. But, on the contrary, you first bind down the widow along with the corpse of her husband, and then heap over her such a quantity of wood that she cannot rise. At the time too of setting fire to the pile, you press her down with large bamboos. In what passage of Harita [a late dharma shastra, quoted by the defender] or the rest do you find authority for thus binding the woman according to your practice? This then is, in fact, deliberate female murder ... It never was the case that the practice of fastening down widows on the pile was prevalent throughout Hindustan: for it is but of late years that this mode has been followed, and that only in Bengal ... No one besides who has the fear of God and man before him, will assert that male or female murder, theft, &c., from having been long practiced, cease to be vices. ... The Shastras, and the reasonings connected with them, enable us to discriminate right and wrong. In those Shastras such female murder is altogether forbidden. And reason also declares, that to bind down a woman for her destruction holding out to her the inducement of heavenly rewards, is a most sinful act. (Racanavali, 573-74; English Works, III, 95-96)

Mainly due to Rammohun's propaganda against suttee, Lord William Bentinck, who had only recently become governor-general, issued a regulation on 9 De-

[11] An interesting discussion of the psychology behind Rammohun's campaigns against the practice of suttee can be found in Nandy, 168-94.

cember 1829 declaring suttee to be culpable homicide punishable by the Criminal Courts. (See Majumdar, 139-55 for many of the relevant documents pertaining to the abolition of suttee and Rammohun's role in it.)

The beneficial influence of these and subsequent reforms pressed by other enlightened Indians can be seen in the present Indian Constitution adopted in 1949. This constitution grants freedom of religion but at the same time tries to ban "deleterious" religious practices, i.e., practices which under the cloak of religion involve mutilation, torture or murder. Article 25 (1) of the Constitution says: "Subject to public order, morality and health ... all persons are equally entitled to freedom of conscience and the right freely to profess, practice and propagate religion." The commentary on p. 199 states: "These words have the power of a competent Legislature to prohibit deleterious practices, such as the sacrifice of human beings in the name of religion." The crucial words in the article of the Constitution itself are "public order, morality and health," for this triad, especially the last term "health", can be invoked to blunt the claws and fangs of deleterious religion.

If the constitution by itself does not suffice to expose religious crimes, there is the Indian Penal Code to persecute capital offences. Article 306 states: "If any person commits suicide, whoever abets the commission of such suicide, shall be punished with imprisonment of either description for a term which may extend to ten years, and shall also be liable to fine." The commentary (p. 305) mentions the possibility of a voluntary act of self-immolation by a widow. Any person who helps her is punishable according to the above article. If the act of self-immolation would not be voluntary, we would be faced with an evident instance of culpable homicide, i.e., murder.

The Foundation of the Brahmo Samaj

Rammohun had never been fully satisfied with any of the religious traditions known to him. His major moral criticism of religious traditions was directed against orthodox and strict Brahmanic Hinduism (although later on he also argued against trinitarian Christianity on rational grounds as being a form of polytheism). This is understandable, given the fact that he campaigned against the Hindu practice of suttee. Rammohun thought his fellow Hindus, who followed rites in which the various Hindu deities were being worshipped with the help of consecrated images, and different ritual utensils, were misguided in this, especially if the rites included the destruction of living beings. He found that his contemporary fellow Hindus hardly possessed any knowledge of the ancient Sanskrit texts that belonged to the most sacred sections of the canon, texts which - in his view - taught an enlightened and intelligible theism. Among these texts were the Upanishads,[12] the philosophical/mystical writings of the Vedas. The Upanishads form the primary basis of the Vedanta school of philosophy, whose first systematic schooltext is the Vedanta Sutra (2nd century AD?). Subsequently, a monistic school of exegesis of the Upanishads sprang up, the Advaita Vedanta, of which the most famous ancient exponent was Shankara (8th cent. AD).

Rammohun took the Upanishads, the Vedanta Sutra, along with the exegetical commentaries on them by Shankara, to be the genuine scriptures of Hinduism. He made it one of his aims in life to propagate this body of literature among the educated Hindus of his day. In a letter written in 1828 to John Digby he explained his intentions thus:

> I ... with a view of making them (ie the Hindus) happy and comfortable both here and hereafter, not only employed verbal arguments against the absurdities of the idolatry practiced by them, but also translated their most revered theological work, namely, Vedant, into Bengali and Hindustani and also several chapters of the Veda, in order to convince them that the unity, of God, and absurdity of idolatry are evidently pointed out by their own scriptures .... (Racanavali, 461)

Elsewhere, in the introduction to his translation of the Ishopanishad, Rammohun outlined his program of religious and moral regeneration of Hinduism through rationality, humanity and factual knowledge of the real content of some of the great Hindu religious classics. He asserts:

> I have never ceased to contemplate with the strongest feelings of regret, the obstinate adherence of my countrymen to their fatal system of idolatry, inducing, for the sake of propitiating their supposed Deities the violation of every humane and social feeling ... more especially in the dreadful acts of self-destruction and the immolation of the nearest relations under the delusion of conforming to sacred religious rites ... I, have never ceased ... to view in them the moral debasement of a race who, I cannot help thinking, are capable of better things, whose susceptibility, patience, and mildness of character, render them worthy of a better destiny. Under these impressions, therefore, I have been impelled to lay before them genuine translations of parts of their Scripture, which inculcates not only the enlightened worship of one God, but the purest principles of morality, accompanied with such notices as I deemed re-

---

[12] Incidentally these are the same texts that roused the admiration of the Mughal crown prince, Dara Shikoh (1615-1659), who even regarded the Upanishads as revelations of God on a par with the Koran. With the help of Brahmanic *pandits*, Dara Shikoh translated the Upanishads into Persian. On Dara Shikoh's views on religion and his writings, see Hasrat, and on Dara Shikoh's translation of the Upanishads, *ibid.*, 254 ff. I would submit as a hypothesis that Dara Shikoh's translations and writings may initially have inspired Rammohun, but this is uncertain.

> quisite to oppose the arguments employed by the Brahmins in defense of their beloved system. Most earnestly do I pray that the whole may ... prove efficient in producing in the minds of the Hindus in general, a conviction of the rationality of believing in and adoring the Supreme Being only together with a complete perception and practice of that grand and comprehensive moral principle - Do unto others as ye would be done by. (Dobson Collet, 75; English Works, II, 52)

Initially, Rammohun seems to have contemplated establishing a theistic church that would propagate humanistic, rational, monotheistic religion in association with English Unitarians, and consequently organized a "British Indian Unitarian Association" in 1827 (Dobson Collet, 219). Since he wished to reach his fellow Hindu countrymen as well, he and some friends, including Prince Dvarakanath Tagore, grandfather of the poet Rabindranath Tagore, tried to set up an auxiliary branch of this association as a Hindu theistic church (cf. *ibid.*, 220-22). On 20 August 1828, this Hindu theistic church of modern India took shape under the name of *Brahmo Samaj* (see *ibid.*, 222, 236-38 on the name of the church). On that day the first Brahmo service was held. It consisted of chanting from the Vedas and the Upanishads in Sanskrit, singing hymns in Sanskrit and Bengali, and a sermon in Bengali on these texts (*ibid.*, 223-24).

Rammohun and his friends drafted a Trust Deed in 1830 which, although a legal document, more or less contains the first public statement of the *Brahmo* creed. Even though there were several signatories, the wording of the text itself is generally believed to be largely the work of Rammohun himself. The relevant passage of the rather lengthy Deed states that the premises of the *Brahmo Samaj* are to be used as a:

> place of public meeting of all sorts and descriptions of people without distinction as shall behave and conduct themselves in an orderly sober religious and devout manner for the worship and adoration of the Eternal Unsearchable and Immutable Being who is the Author and Preserver of the Universe but not under or by any other name designation ... used for ... any particular Being or Beings by any man or set of men whatsoever and that no graven image ... or the likeness of anything shall be admitted ... and that no sacrifice offering or oblation ... shall ever be permitted therein and that no animal or living creature shall ... be deprived of life either for religious purposes or for food. (Dobson Collet, 435)[13]

Furthermore, the worship performed in these premises should lead to the "promotion of charity, morality, piety, benevolence, virtue and the strengthening of the bonds of union Between men of all religious persuasions and creeds ..." (*ibid.*, 436).

---

[13] For the complete text, see Dobson Collet, 432-41.

Importance of the Trust Deed for the Constitution

We can derive several basic tenets from this text. First of all, the place of worship is open to all regardless of their social status (and their gender, one would assume, but the active participation of women came much later). The object of worship is the one Deity of the universe, but not particularized under any anthropomorphic conceptualization. No culturally determined, specific religious imagery is allowed, in order to assure the universality of the worship to be performed. Every person should be able to feel at home and not be alienated by specific symbols. This universality already foreshadows the universality of the later Indian Constitution which guarantees equal respect for all the different religions practiced in independent India.

No blood may be shed on the premises. This rule probably refers both to Hindu and Moslem forms of animal sacrifice. As far as Hinduism is concerned, this rule probably applied to goats being sacrificed to the goddess Kali or any other 'deleterious' religious acts. With regard to Islam, the only form of animal sacrifice that Moslems occasionally perform, is the Qurban. The Trust Deed tries to ban all acts of violence or cruelty regarded as inconsistent with pure spiritual worship of a singular Divinity. This rule is clearly inspired by the age-old Indian ideal of non-violence (*ahimsa*), an ideal held by almost all forms of Indian spirituality (cf. Schmidt, 625-55). Finally, the spirit in which the religious activities of the Samaj are to take place, ought to be one of high morality and the belief in the universal brotherhood of the different religious communities.

Thus, we could probably regard the Trust Deed not only as a document relating to the foundation of a religion, but also as a very early modern Indian attempt to formulate ethics consistent with universally valid human rights. The least that can be said is that the ethics behind this passage of the Trust Deed is one of human rights, of a sense of equality, brotherhood and respect for life. In this sense the Trust Deed foreshadows the Indian Constitution.

The Spirit of the Indian Constitution

In 1949 the Indian constitution established India as a secular republic, not as a religious state. The constitution cannot be read as endorsing any interference on the part of the area in the other, for, according to the constitution, the practice of religion remains a private matter, except in cases of criminal offences or a breakdown of public peace and order. This means that the Constitution's view of the Indian citizen cannot be understood to be directly legitimized by Hinduism. Nonetheless, because it is the religion of the majority of Indians, one can recognize - India being a parliamentary democracy - that the Constitution's anthropology is indirectly inspired by the most humane norms and values in Indian spiritual traditions, among which is Hinduism (cf. Swarup, 69-72).

The liberal, egalitarian and humane spirit of the Constitution can easily be seen in the Preamble of the same:

> We, the people of India, having solemnly resolved to constitute India into a sovereign socialist secular democratic republic and to secure to its citizens:
> Justice, social, economic and political;
> Liberty of thought, expression, belief, faith and worship;
> Equality of status and opportunity;
> and to promote among them all
> Fraternity assuring the dignity of the individual and the unity and integrity of the Nation ... do hereby adopt, enact and give to ourselves this constitution.

These words embody the highest moral and social ideals the founding fathers of the Indian Republic wished India to represent after it achieved independence.[14] In intention they reflect the same spirit as found in the works of Rammohun quoted above.

A RELIGIOUS PERSPECTIVE

At the beginning of this article we stated that the underlying idea of the Preamble of the *Universal Declaration* could be interpreted as the idea of the sacredness of life. This idea was expressed time and again in Hindu texts, of which the classical Upanishads figure among the earliest and best known. The Isha Upanishad which Rammohun translated into English offers a good example of this idea. This Upanishad presents the totality of life as enveloped by the Divine (God). Since we are discussing Rammohun's thought, it is only fitting that we quote the relevant passage from this Upanishad in his own English translation, thus showing his understanding of the text:

> All the material extension in this world, whatsoever it may be, should be considered as clothed with the existence of the Supreme regulating spirit: by thus abstracting thy mind from worldly thoughts, preserve thyself from self-sufficiency, and entertain not a covetous regard for the property belonging to any individual. (Isha Upanishad 1, English Works, II, 53)

The whole universe, including every living being, is to be regarded as filled with the Divine, and regulated by the Divine. This is the sacredness of life, for life originates from the Divine spirit. From this universal vision of divinity, the same Upanishad derives - according to the interpretation of Rammohun - a deeply moral attitude, the kind of attitude from which the concern for human rights can rise:

---

[14] For a good summary view on the civil rights embodied in the Indian Constitution and their relation to universal human rights, as well as to the present-day situation of human rights in India, see Iyer.

> He, who perceives the whole universe in the Supreme Being (that is, he who perceives that the material existence is merely dependent upon the existence of the Supreme Spirit); and who also perceives the Supreme Being in the whole universe (that is, he who perceives that the Supreme Spirit extends over all material extension); does not feel contempt towards any creature whatsoever. (Isha Upanishad 6, *ibid.*, 53)

On the basis of these words alone we can already argue plausibly that Rammohun Roy has been the first modern Hindu to reinterpret for his contemporaries the humane ethical values to be found in ancient Indian spirituality, while at the same time giving them civil and political relevance.

Applying the spiritual vision of the divinity of life offered by this Upanishad and Rammohun's understanding of the best in Hindu religion to the concept of human rights would give the latter a deep universal religious meaning, for we are enjoined to regard the whole universe and all it contains as sacred. It does not take many words to verbalise such a vision, but to acquire it as a living experience is quite something else. It would mean a complete change of heart, a shedding of one's limited former self. A first step towards such a deeply religious goal could be the fostering of the ethics of human rights in their fullest measure, which, seen in this light, seem no more than a vague shadow of the spiritual vision.

BIBLIOGRAPHY

Bayly, C.A. *Indian Society and the Making of the British Empire*. The New Cambridge History of India II.1, Cambridge, 1988.

Biswas, Dilip Kumar. "Rammohun as a Social and Religious Reformer." In: Niharranjan, (ed.). *Rammohun Roy: A Bi-Centenary Tribute*. New Delhi: National Book Trust, 19[illegible]. Pp. 97-112.

Chatterjee, Partha. *Nationalist Thought and the Colonial World: A Derivative Discourse?* Zed Books Ltd. (The United Nations University), 1986.

Davies, P. (ed.). *Human Rights*. London/New York: Routledge, 1988.

Desai, A.R. *Social Background of Indian Nationalism*. Bombay: Popular Prakashan, repr. 1991[5].

Dobson Collet, Sophia. *The Life and Letters of Raja Rammohun Roy*. Dilip Kumanr Biswas and Prabhat Chadra Ganguli. Calcutta: Sadharan Brahmo Samaj, 1988[4].

Granthavali. *Ramamohana Granthavali*. Prathama - saptama khanda. Vrajendranatha Vandyopadhyaya Sajanikanta Dasa sampadita. Vangiya Sahitya Parisat, Calcutta Bengali era 1362-1380 (in 7 parts but bound together in a single volume).

Hisrat, Bikrama Jit. *Dara Shikuh: Life and Works*. Calcutta: Visvabharati Publishing Department, 1953.

Inden, Ronald. *Imagining India*. Cambridge MA/Oxford: Blackwell's, 1992.

Indian Constitution: Shorter Constitution of India. New Delhi: Durga Das Basu, Prentice-Hall of India, Private Ltd., 1988[10].

Indian Penal Code: The Indian Penal Code. By Ratanlal Ranchhoddas and Dhirajlal Keshavlal Thakore, 1987[26]. Reprint, 1990 by Hon'ble Mr. Justice M. Hidayatullah in collaboration with R. Deb, Wadhwa and Company Pvt. Ltd. Nagpur 440 012 India.

Iyer, V.R. Krishna. *Human Rights and Inhuman Wrongs*. Delhi: B.R. Publishing Company, 1990.

Jones, Kenneth W. *Socio-Religious Reform Movements in British India*. The New Cambridge History of India, III.1. Cambridge: Cambridge University Press, 1989.

Majumdar, J.K. *Raja Rammohun Roy and Progressive Movements in India*. Vol.I. A Selection from Records (1775-1845). J.K. Majumdar (ed.). Calcutta: Brahmo Mission Press, 1983. (repr.).

Marshall, P.J. *Bengal: The British Bridgehead, Eastern India 1740-1828*. The New Cambridge History of India, Vol. II.2. Cambridge, 1987.

Mittal, J.K. *Indian Legal and Constitutional History*. Allahabad: Allahabad Law Agency, 1990.

Nandy, Ashis. "Sati: A Nineteenth Century Tale of Women, Violence and Protest." In: V.C. Joshi (ed.). *Rammohun Roy and the Process of Modernization in India*. Delhi: Vikas Publishing House, 1975.

The Oxford History of India. Delhi: Oxford University Press, 1992[4].

Racanavali. *Ramamohana Racanavali*. Pradhana sampadaka Dr. Ajitakumara Ghosa, Harapha Prakasani, Calcutta, 1973.

Rammohun Roy, *The English Works of Raja Rammohun Roy*. Ed. Kalidas Nag and Debajyoti Burman. Vol. I-V. Calcutta: Sadharan Brahmo Samaj, 1947-1951.

Ray, Ajit Kumar. *The Religious Ideas of Rammohun Roy: A Survey of his Writings on Religion Particularly in Persian, Sanskrit and Bengali*. New Delhi: Kanak Publications, Books India, 1976.

Ray, Niharranjan, (ed.). *Rammohun Roy: A Bi-Centenary Tribute*. New Delhi: National Book Trust, 1974.

Sarkar, Sumit. *Modern India 1885-1947*. MacMillan India, 1983.

Schmidt, Hanns-Peter. *The Origin of Ahimsa*. Mélanges d'Indianisme A La Mémoire de Louis Renou. Paris: Publications de l'Institut de Civilisation Indienne, 1968.

Swarup. V. *The Protection of Civil Rights Act and Rules*. Revised K.K. Singh, Allahabad: The Law Book Company (P) Ltd., 1989[3].

Van Asbeck, F.M. (ed.). *The Universal Declaration of Human Rights*. Leiden: Brill, 1949.

Van Dijk, P. *et al.* (eds.). *Internationale Regelingen, Mensenrechten*. Lelystad: Koninkklijke Vermande B.V., 1987.

CHAPTER VII

Traditional Hindu Values and Human Rights: Two Worlds Apart?

Corstiaan J.G. van der Burg

INTRODUCTION

In recent years, two issues concerning human rights have in particular dominated Indian politics. First, the implementation of the recommendations of the Report of the Mandal Commission, which asked for more jobs to be reserved for the so-called Other Backward Classes (OBC's), unleashed a general outcry of indignation among the lower middle classes, who feared increasing competition in an already tight labour market. Second, the issue of the *Babari Mashid Ram Janam Bhumi* in Ayodhya revealed strong anti-secularist and anti-Islamic sentiments, particularly on the part of the most orthodox, fundamentalist Hindus.

Both instances are extreme reactions to a government policy which, since India's independence, has been characterised by the promotion of the peaceful coexistence of social, ethnic and religious groups, and the guarantee of fundamental democratic rights to all its citizens, irrespective of their status. This policy has been legitimised by the Constitution which has been demonstrably influenced by enlightened humanism, the Virginia Declaration of Human Rights, the Constitution of the United States, the Universal Declaration of Human Rights, and even by the Constitution of the former Soviet Union. Although, generally speaking, a difference between constitutional ideals and everyday practice is not uncommon, the extreme reactions cited above require more clarification.

Since the Founding Fathers of independent India were inspired to such an extent by the humanist ideals laid down in these Western documents, they obviously did not find it hard to make these ideals the basis of the new India's secular polity. In this connection we are confronted with the question as to why they were not motivated by a more obvious source of inspiration, namely Hinduism - India's cultural tradition. Or, more in keeping with the theme of this volume, would it not have been possible to provide 'Human Rights' - as a norm for India's multi-cultural society - with a religious underpinning from a generally accepted, mainstream Hindu view of life, without having to go to the extremes of, for example, either secularism (as is the official government policy) or fundamentalism (as some sections of society advocate)?

'HINDU' RELIGIOUS ANTHROPOLOGY AND HUMAN RIGHTS

One suggestion which can be derived from the issue under discussion in this volume would be to look for those aspects which Hinduism has in common with other religious traditions regarding ideals of human existence and the fulfilment of 'true humanity'. However, it is the merest truism to say that it is far from easy to label Hinduism 'a' religious tradition, because the very term is no more than an umbrella denominator for an extremely complex, pluriform, diversified, but long-standing cultural tradition, within which a bewildering plethora of religions and creeds can be distinguished. This implies that to look for common aspects of human rights within 'Hinduism' will, in itself, be an enterprise that is almost doomed from the start.

One can, however, go beyond such general remarks. In an article on religious change Mark Holmström states that existing Hindu societies and Hindu history can only be understood in terms of the interplay between two radically different kinds of religion, associated with two kinds of morality and social relations (Holmström, 28). On the one hand, there is a religion that sanctifies the existing social order, values of submission and hierarchy, and a relativist morality of closed groups. On the other hand, Holmström indicates a devotional religion that encompasses values of choice and equality, and a tendency towards a universalist 'open' morality. In his opinion these two types of religion coexist in an unstable combination in every Hindu community, traditional as well as modern. They correspond to the values of heteronomy and autonomy that coexist in every social morality. He continues with the argument that moral innovation, influenced but not directly determined by (changing) circumstances, upsets the equilibrium between the two types of religion, which in turn involves a change in the nature of the social relations concerned.

In broad terms Holmström refers to the views of Louis Dumont, who in his famous 1960 article on the renunciation of the world in Indian religions distinguished between two types of religion: 'group religion' and 'religion of choice'. The latter is, according to Dumont, associated with - and, on the whole, even derived from - the thinking of the *sannyasin*, the renouncer who has broken his ties with society in an attempt to reach *moksha* or liberation from rebirth. Thus Dumont sees the polarity between 'group religion' and 'religion of choice' in Hinduism as an extension of the polarity between the ideas of the heteronomous 'man-in-the-world' over against the autonomous renouncer.

Apart from Holmström, others, such as Richard Burghart and Timothy Fitzgerald, have also elaborated on and improved Dumont's typology. Basically, they distinguish between (type I) the ever-present moral order of the universe, a *dharma* to which all beings are subject, a religious outlook that stresses ritual order and hierarchy, and (type II) a soteriological religion that emphasises the path of salvation. Type I stands for the traditional "mainstream" Hinduism, which is "group-tied". This latter term simply means that this form is embedded in the social relations of a group or a set of groups. Its ideology is that of a "hierarchy or ritual order that embraces the whole mythical cosmos, but which is manifested to the observer most evidently in 'caste'" (Fitzgerald, 112ff.), based on the principle of relative purity. *Dharma*, as the fundamental unifying principle of traditional Hinduism, defines the status and obligations of all beings in the cosmos, from the gods to inanimate matter. It could also be called "karmatic" Hinduism, because "the importance of correct ritual action [*karma*] in the fulfilment and maintenance of cosmic order is paramount". Type I is not a 'World Religion' and is not to be exported; it is neither a soteriology nor a system of meaning of which non-Hindus can avail themselves. Analytically speaking, it is the "centre of gravity, the context within which the other phenomena, the sectarian soteriologies, the potential 'religions' for export, are rooted".

The other kind of Hinduism, type II, comprises the ideologies which are generally centred around a personal soteriology. It is sectarian rather than based on caste and concerns more a free choice of personal devotion [*bhakti*] rather than a prescribed status and duties; it is 'other-worldly' rather than 'this-worldly' and tends towards egalitarianism and individualism, rather than hierarchy (*ibid.*, 113). Authority does not lie with the Brahmin, the traditional religious specialist, but with the ascetic who has achieved some personal realisation of the transcendent deity.

Historically, these two ideal types have been interwoven and dynamically related. Since empirical Hindu reality is a mixture of these types, neither one can be presented as 'Hinduism' *tout court*, "as if [these doctrines] existed in abstraction from the wider ritual context in which they are anchored" (*ibid.*, 114). The influence emanating from type II Hinduism can hardly be underrated. This more or less 'abstract', extra-cultural, form of Hinduism seems to correspond most to the Western and Christian conceptions of religion, and therefore, since Svami Vivekananda's famous speech at the 1893 Parliament of the World's Religions in Chicago, appeals to non-Hindu Westerners as an equivalent alternative. There seems to be a constant interest in and a growing acquaintance with whatever this form of 'universal' Hinduism has to offer, even though this is not reflected in the actual numbers of adherents from non-Hindu backgrounds that it attracts. As a result, this kind of Hinduism has gradually become the measuring rod with which type I Hinduism is judged - not only by non-Hindus but also by educated Hindus themselves.

What is clear from this typology is that type I Hindu traditions, because of their closed worldviews and anthropologies, will not provide the sought after religious justification for general human rights. In the traditional type I Hindu worldviews, religious and social equality is generally never seen as universal but rather as limited to certain religious and social groups, classes and castes.

Likewise, devotional Hinduism (type II), which in (Western) scholarly circles is generally assumed to go hand in hand with a tendency towards religious egalitarianism, seems to fit easily with any value orientation, either hierarchical or egalitarian, depending on the historical situation (Van der Veer, 682). However, the very same type II Hinduism, the autonomous renouncer's religion of choice, can offer points of departure for ethical change, because its worldview is open enough to allow ideological change. This is illustrated in an exemplary way by M.K. Gandhi's denunciation of untouchability. Gandhi's profound religious experience can be seen as one of the "critical moments" in the development of Hinduism, "setting into motion one of the most liberalizing forces in human religious history" (Rao, 152). Gandhi can indeed be viewed here as an "agent of change" and "a creator of values" in Dumont's sense (Dumont, 46). This seems also the case with Raja Rammohan Roy, who provided his moral innovation ("All men are equal because the whole universe is filled with the Divine") with an Advaita Vedantic justification (cf. Van Bijlert's article in this volume).

In our opinion, therefore, the idea that more information can be derived from lofty theoretical speculations about 'Hinduism' in general should be abandoned - if one does not wish to fall victim to an unjustified form of essentialism - and the more down-to-earth realities concerning human rights in a given situation in contemporary India, exemplified in the two cases cited above, should receive central place. Thus the question of representativeness and universality of a given religious worldview will be put aside in order to avoid encouraging the need for a normative view of Hinduism. In our view, the latter, because of the complexity of the issue, cannot be provided. A better strategy, therefore, would be to position the two cases we want to highlight at the extremes of a continuum of Hindu culture, thereby indicating its dynamic nature.

THE COMMON BACKGROUND OF THE CASES

If the two cases are viewed from a historical point of view, one discovers that the ideologies behind them, *viz.* secularism and fundamentalism, are the outcome of one and the same historical process.

From the perspective of its historical context, the arrival of the British as the new colonial power meant - particularly in the north of India - the end of six centuries of Moslem rule over the Hindus. However, since the Western colonialists and their missionary zeal formed a constant threat to Hindu culture and religion, some of the intelligentsia became defensive, which resulted in a religious renaissance and revivalism as expressions of the search for a new identity.

> This revival was simultaneous both among Hindus and Muslims, and became part of the freedom movement from the beginning of the century. Politicisation of religion, both by the British and some Indian leaders, resulted in the end of the colonial era in the partition of the subcontinent into India and Pakistan. Hindu-Muslim tension thus became part of the search for identity of the new

> countries. A large number of the religious leaders to be (for example, L. K. Advani, the present BJP leader) came from groups displaced by the Partition. (Fernandes, 3)

The British utilised not only religion but also the caste-system in their policy of divide-and-conquer. For example, until 1931 the decennial census included a person's caste, motivated in part by the desire to show that India was a conglomerate of castes, religions, languages and ethnic groups which could only be held together by a foreign power. Because of this colonial legitimation, the freedom fighters opposed the inclusion of caste in the census. It was therefore discontinued as of 1941. Caste-consciousness as a source of power, however, had already been recognised and used.

Moreover, many movements of the lower castes, tribals and other marginalised classes had gained strength already in the mid-nineteenth century. These movements were coopted by the upper-class freedom fighters. Unlike the those of the elite who had become defensive, others responded to these movements as well as to colonial and missionary threats to their society and culture by developing an attitude favourable to social reform.

Thus, religious revival and the promise of social reform were the most important factors in turning the freedom struggle into a mass movement. At the same time, however, the movement was split between religious revivalists and social reformers (Fernandes, 3).

SECULARISM AND HUMAN RIGHTS: THE MANDAL COMMISSION REPORT

We have placed secularism at one extreme of the cultural continuum. That secularism has become so important in independent India is due to these early social reformers. In order to get a better understanding of this concept in the Indian context one must realise that it is of Western origin and for some time was viewed as an alien element in Indian culture. Nevertheless, since independence it has been widely accepted in Indian politics, together with the ideals of liberty, equality and respect for human dignity: the 42nd Constitutional Amendment in 1976 made India a "Sovereign, Socialist, Secular Democratic Republic", which it still is.

> Thus, the secular provisions of the Constitution are explicit. Article 14, for example, gives equal protection of the law to all citizens, while Article 15 forbids the state to discriminate against any citizen on grounds of religion, race, caste, sex, or place of birth in employment or any other matter. Article 25 guarantees freedom of conscience to all, and equal rights to profess, practice and propagate religion, subject only to public order, health and morality. Article 26 gives each religious denomination the right to establish and maintain institutions, to own and acquire property, and to administer its affairs itself in

> accordance with the law. Articles 27 and 28 prohibit the state from levying taxes in support of religion or making religious instruction compulsory in state schools. Article 30 gives all religious and linguistic minorities the right to establish and administer educational institutions which may qualify for grants from the state without discrimination. These constitutional provisions are part of the chapter on fundamental rights and therefore justifiable. Equally important is the fact that political participation is open to all citizens. Adult suffrage is the basis of elections, unqualified by separate electorates, proportional representation, religious or caste identity, or property. In sum, no legal or constitutional connection exists between the Indian state and any particular religion. (Björkman, 185)

However, the constitutionally guaranteed secularism has still not been successful in shaping India into a secular state, for there are several other factors that obstruct the development of this secular ideal of no preference for and no interference in religious matters. Therefore, India remains characterised by a lack of separation between religion and politics and for that matter, between religion and human rights. The case of the so-called Mandal Commission Report offers an appropriate illustration.

On 5 August 1990, V.P. Singh, the National Front Prime Minister (November 1989 to November 1990) implemented the recommendations of the Mandal Commission Report on the Backward Classes, in order to prevent a possible overthrow of his government (Fasana, 3). To understand why the implementation of these recommendations, which had been shelved since the Report's publication in 1980, generated so much upheaval, one must take its genesis into consideration. Therefore we must go back to the first years of India's independence.

> The group which took power at that time was dominated by those who thought of secularism as the separation between religion and the state in the Western sense. Besides, it saw the need for social reform. They therefore introduced in the Constitution positive discrimination in favour of the most marginalised, i.e. the Untouchables and tribals and reserved for them 22.5% of the seats in Parliament, Government and Public Sector jobs and seats in State run schools and colleges. The 1950 Constitution mentioned such reservations also for the so-called 'other backward classes' (OBC's), but no follow up action was taken on it till 1977. Then, a commission headed by J. P. Mandal was appointed to look into the matter and make recommendations. Its report (Mandal, 1991) given in 1979, stated that the backward classes formed 52% of the population but held fewer than 20% of the government jobs. Therefore, the Commission recommended a quota of jobs amounting to 27% for the social groups classified as Backward Classes. (Fernandes, 4)

Added to the quotas already allocated to the Scheduled Castes and Tribes, the recommended figure became 52%, implying that the jobs available on an intense competitive basis were now the minority.

Till 1990 no party dared (nor felt the need) to take a stand on the Report, even though they had all had accepted it. After the 1979 elections it was forgotten. Fierce reactions followed the implementation of the Report, and until 21 September, when the Supreme Court decided to block the Recommendations, hundreds of young people died in street riots or committed suicide.

If the Mandal Report and its consequences is viewed within the framework of India's professed secularism, we see that the motivations behind the report were in line with the secular ideology of promoting human rights. However, in terms of these same human rights, it was completely counter-productive in its implementation, because it actually reinforced the economic and social inequality it sought to undermine.

Thus, the report attacked the inequalities brought about by the caste system, which was presented as

> having weakened the unity of India and as bearing the main responsibility for the social and educational inequalities which the Commission was set up to remove. Having determined 'caste' to be the main culprit for the existence of the Backward Classes, the Commission could offer no other source for the enumeration of these Classes than the 1931 Census Report, the last report to officially present the castes as having their own individual identity. According to the Commission, no significant changes had occurred between 1931 and 1980, apparently. The same number of castes and posts follows progressively the natural demographic growth, as if the castes of 1931 had not been modified or integrated, or become extinct. The main aim which emerges from the report is that of raising the classes defined as backward. (The word 'class' in the Report has the same meaning as 'caste'). The caste roles sanctified by tradition are totally rejected and the major group held responsible for legitimising the system through an extensive set of scriptures, ritual and mythology are the Brahmans. (Fasana, 11)

This accounted, according to the Commission, even for the current discrimination between higher and lower castes, while low ritual status was closely linked to social and educational backwardness.

Taking the facts into consideration, the Mandal Commission could not deny that the world of 1980 had little to do with the traditions of the past. Even what remained of these traditions had been deeply modified by the new institutions and reformist movements. Moreover, 'casteism' (i.e. the caste system in its negative effects), which was then rampant, was already the outcome of the fragmentation of the system. The Brahmans had been the first to change with the times, while those who remained attached to their traditional roles certainly could not be considered as either powerful or advanced. The Report still settled on the caste system as the factor which most hindered the social and educational improvement of the Backward Classes the most.

However, some anthropologists, such as Dumont, are much more cautious about the negative influence of the caste system. They have often observed that the stability of the Indian social system was due to its caste system. Many historians, for their part, stress that the social changes brought about by the economic and social reforms introduced during the British colonial period actually aided casteism to a greater extent, because they helped to crystallise the groups into self-sufficient entities with specific characteristics. This, of course, is in striking contrast to the organic whole into which the caste system had evolved, in which each caste had a different function, and was strongly linked to the other groups, on the basis of certain forms of social exchange, which were also legitimised religiously as well. The recently formed caste groups, however, became the new individual entities, set on entering the political arena (Fasana, 16).

In sum, by this untimely implementation of constitutional provisions, inspired by a secularist ideology, the government was not only unsuccessful in checking the ongoing process of the politicisation of the caste system, but even paved the way for an outburst of social unrest, which eventually led to what we see as another extreme example of a clash between religion and human rights: the issue of the *Babari Mashid Ram Janam Bhumi* in Ayodhya.

FUNDAMENTALISM AND HUMAN RIGHTS: THE ETHOS OF *HINDUTVA*

In line with the attempted implementation of the Mandal Report recommendations lies the issue of the *Babari Mashid Ram Janam Bhumi* in Ayodhya, which culminated in the destruction of the mosque and the subsequent series of massacres that continued until recently.

> One of the consequences of the Backward Classes policy was, that another political party, labelled as Hindu fundamentalist, the Bharatiya Janata Party (BJP) fearful of losing its electoral Hindu basis, and decidedly opposed to whatever resulted from a split of caste groups, seen as the break-up of the Hindu nation, tried to divert attention from the controversial Mandal issue to the Ayodhya Mandir (i.e. Hindu temple). The Hindu temples having been destroyed or desecrated by Muslim rulers, re-occupation or rebuilding of the holy Hindu places was stressed. V.P. Singh declared himself opposed to the temple issue and when the opposition (BJP and allied movements) started pressing for occupying the holy site of Ayodhya, he had L. K. Advani, the BJP leader arrested. In its turn the BJP withdrew its 'benevolent neutrality' towards the government, there was a breakaway of the ruling party, and finally the government of V.P. Singh toppled. (Fasana, 6)

This, in short, was what happened in October 1990 and it was only a forerunner of the storm of anti-Islamism that would sweep the country in the subsequent years. From a historical perspective, even the massacres that took place on 4 December 1992 are no more than the logical consequences of a fundamentalist anthropology in India as old as secularism itself. People such as Vir Savarkar (who published *Hindutva* in 1923), Hedgewar (the founder of the Rashtriya Svayamsevak Sangh in 1925), and Golwarkar (the publisher of the 1939 'We or Our Nationhood Defined') cleared the way for such extremist excesses.

Partly on the basis of their publications a general consensus has emerged within the milieu of fundamentalist parties and institutions concerning a definition of a Hindu ideology. It involves a certain "interpretation of the past, an analysis of the present and a set of precepts and imperatives for future conduct" (Banerjee, 97). In general, Hindu fundamentalism - multi-faceted as it is - derives its inspiration from an alleged glorious past, prior to the arrival of Islam, while on the other hand it is directed against all 'alien' elements in Indian society, particularly Muslims. Vir Savarkar's *Hindutva* ('Hindudom') is said to refer to a people united by a common country, blood, history, culture and language. He was also the first to use the term *Hindu Rashtra*, 'Hindu Nation', an oft-repeated notion in the ideology of Hindu communalism. In an atmosphere of mounting tension between Hindus and Muslims, the Hindus were said to constitute a 'nation', while the Muslims were only a 'community' (D'Cruz, 23). For these reasons, we see the fundamentalist movement as a religiously based nationalist social reform movement rather than another type of Hinduism.

Concerning morality and human rights, one can say that the fundamentalist ideology has developed a powerful and extensive image of the 'enemy', primarily directed against Muslim citizens. The recurring fundamentalist theme in this respect is "that the Hindus are the only ones upholding India, while the other communities, who have been given all kinds of guarantees and protection by the Indian Constitution, are bent on breaking it up" (Gupta, 573). Hindu interests should therefore prevail and at some stage India should be declared a Hindu Rashtra, for Hindus are, after all, the majority, accounting for 85% of the population, according to the census. In attempting to unify Hindus, they are seeking a model of social harmony with pronounced authoritarian implications without addressing actual social and economic conflicts within the Hindu community. This is meant to serve as a moral and ethical basis for individual sacrifice and surrender to the leaders at the top.

The fundamentalists carry their arguments for unifying Hindus to their logical conclusion while redefining Indian 'nationalism'. As for the Hindu community, so also for the country 'unity and integrity' mean a specific pattern of authority and precedence. Being the majority, the Hindus should have precedence, and they are therefore entitled to exercise authority, precedence and domination over others. Anyone can be an Indian - even a Muslim - provided he or she accepts Rama as the omnipotent and denounces Babar and his descendants as foreigners. The recurring note in the fundamentalist propaganda is that the supremacy of Hinduism is being threatened by Muslims. It is therefore essential to reduce the Muslim individual to a stereotype: habitual traitor, Pakistani spy, a religious bigot, a committed killer who needs to be kept under perpetual vigilance by Hindu society.

Having created this image, the fundamentalist ideologues then pose the question: 'Should this undeserving Muslim be pampered and protected by the state?' By granting him minority rights and special privileges, the state is resorting to 'pseudo-secularism'. The proponents of *Hindutva*, on the other hand, claim to possess the superior nostrum of 'positive secularism'. Hinduism is projected as a secular and tolerant philosophy since it embraces within its fold different cults and sects (all of which, however, swear by the common Hindu divinities). Similarly, 'positive secularism' envisages the coming together of all the religious communities bound by a uniform code of conduct, rights and responsibilities. This is presented as the ideal democratic solution to communal conflicts. However, a uniform code based on so-called 'positive secularism' will invariably be heavily weighted in favour of the Hindu concepts of rights and responsibilities. The distinct identity of other minorities - whether religious or cultural - is bound to be submerged in the larger hegemony determined by the majority community.

In brief, then, one should realise that the play of forces in Hindu-Muslim relations is taking place today in a society which is marked by sheer inequalities of power (Banerjee, 99).

CONCLUSIONS

This article was intended to show what possibilities 'Hinduism' offers for a religious underpinning of human rights and to what degree these possibilities are feasible. From the examples given one cannot help but conclude that Hinduism in its most dominant form is not really favourably constituted towards universal human rights. Viewed historically, the whole concept of universal human rights has been introduced as an alien element into Indian culture, as was the case with Western culture. The concept has been incorporated in India's legislative system, however, and has consequences - for Hinduism as well.

On the one hand, the Government appears to be unable to steer a straight course between the Scylla of distributive justice and the Charybdis of unintended casteism. On the other hand, the Hindu majority seems to be uninterested or unwilling to extend minority rights to those who deserve them as human beings, and fundamentalist Hinduism pretends, for the most part, to be ignorant of them.

The general case is clear: as a 'group religion' Hinduism offers no basis for *universal* human rights. Even fundamentalist group Hinduism, with its inclination towards inclusivisim, extends those rights only to those belonging within its own sphere of influence. Only the kind of Hinduism characterised as a 'religion of choice' appears to leave room for a religious interpretation of the ideal of universal human rights: from the normative texts Hindus such as Raja Rammohun Roy conclude that Hinduism does offer support for universal human rights. However, this does not alter the fact that, if Hindusim is viewed as an ongoing hermeneutical process, other interpretations are possible. The latter, as shown in our discussion of the two cases, could lead to an entirely different view of human rights.

BIBLIOGRAPHY

Banerjee, Sumanta. "'Hindutva' - Ideology and Social Psychology." *Economic and Political Weekly* (January 19, 1991): 97-101.

Björkman, James Warner (ed.). *Fundamentalism, Revivalists and Violence in South Asia.* New Delhi: Manohar, 1988.

Burghart, Richard (ed.). *Hinduism in Great Britain: the Perpetuation of Religion in an Alien Cultural Milieu.* London/New York: Tavistock Publications, 1987.

D'Cruz, Emil. *Indian Secularism: A Fragile Myth.* Indian Social Institute Monograph Series 30. Walter Fernandes (Series ed.). New Delhi: Indian Social Institute, 1988.

Dumont, L. "World Renunciation in Indian Religions." *Contributions to Indian Sociology* 4 (1960): 33-62.

Fasana, Enrico. "A New Definition in Search of an Identity: The Backward Classes." Unpublished paper read at the Twelfth European Conference on Modern South Asian Studies, Berlin, 1992.

Fitzgerald, T. "Hinduism and the 'World Religion' Fallacy." *Religion* 20 (1990): 101-18.

Fernandes, Walter. "India at the Crossroads: The Historical Background." Cyclostyled copy. S.L. 1990.

Gupta, Dipankar. "Communalism and Fundamentalism: Some Notes on the Nature of Ethnic Politics in India." *Economic and Political Weekly* (Annual Number, March 1991): 573-82.

Holmström, M.N. "Religious Change in an Industrial City of South India." *Journal of the Royal Asiatic Society* 1 (1971): 28-40.

Mandal, J.P. *Reservations for Backward Classes: Mandal Commission Report.* The Backward Classes Commissions, 1980. New Delhi: Akalank Publications, 1991.

Rao, K.L. Sheshagiri. "Mahatma Gandhi and Christianity." In: Arvind Sharma (ed.). *Neo-Hindu Views of Christianity.* Leiden: Brill, 1988. Pp. 143-55.

Van der Veer, Peter. "Taming the Ascetic: Devotionalism in a Hindu Monastic Order." *Man* (N.S.) 22 (1987): 680-95.

CHAPTER VIII

Combatting The Enemy

The Use of Scripture in Gandhi and Godse

Rein Fernhout

INTRODUCTION

Mohandas Karamchand Gandhi was murdered 30 January 1948. In that same year, on 10 December, the Universal Declaration of Human Rights was accepted. Although Gandhi's death preceded the formal acceptance of this Declaration by some ten months, his views nonetheless contain ideas that are still relevant for the discussion on human rights. This obtains especially for the relation between these rights as *universal* rights and religions. Gandhi believed that a universal morality, 'fed' by the different religions, was possible. He based this view on one of the Sacred Scriptures of Hinduism, the Bhagavadgita. In his opinion, the Gita provided "a complete reasoned moral code" (CW. 34, 395), which he considered to be the synthesis not only of Hinduism but of all religions. According to Gandhi, therefore, the Gita does not exclude any adherent of any religion whatsoever (Jordens, 93, 100).

The precariousness of this appeal to the Gita can be demonstrated by its consequences for fundamental human rights such as the right to life (art. 3 of the Declaration). As a general rule, this right may encounter no opposition, but what is one to do with a political enemy who constitutes a serious threat to society? Gandhi held that one should indeed combat such an enemy - but in a nonviolent way. One should even be prepared to make the sacrifices necessary for this nonviolent struggle. He writes: "Individuals or nations who would practice nonviolence must be prepared to sacrifice (nations to the last man) their all except honour" (Gandhi, 1936, 236). He felt he could find a basis for this view as well in the Gita. We are, however, confronted by the baffling fact that Gandhi's murderer, Nathuram Vinayak Godse, also appealed to the Gita for support. Thus the Scripture in which Gandhi found a universal 'moral code' was used to justify two diametrically opposite positions with respect to the right to life: nonviolent struggle against a political enemy and murder of such a person.

In this contribution we will attempt to investigate how the same Scripture could give rise to two such opposite opinions and how we should view this.[1] First, we will consider what it was in the Gita that fascinated Gandhi and the problem that he encountered here. Next, we will discuss his hermeneutics. We will then turn to Godse: what was the source of his interpretation of the Gita and was his action consistent with this interpretation? Finally, a number of conclusions will be drawn.

NONATTACHMENT AND VIOLENCE

One can scarcely exaggerate the role the Gita played in Gandhi's life. For him it was, in his own words, "the book *par excellence* for the knowledge of Truth". Gandhi continues: "It has afforded me invaluable help in my moments of gloom" (1983, 59). Prayer meetings in his ashrams were closed by reciting a part of the Gita. Initially, the complete recitation of the Gita was distributed over two weeks, but this was later changed to one week in order to have a fixed reading for each day of the week (CW 44, 320-322). Gandhi himself translated this Scripture into the language of his native state, Gujarat, and supplied his translation with a commentary. His gifted secretary, Mahadev Desai (d. 1942) translated this work into English and added both an extensive introduction as well as elaborate notes. This English translation was published only after Desai's death (Desai, 1946). The parts representing Gandhi's original work have been included in Gandhi's Collected Works under the title "Anāsaktiyoga", i.e., "Yoga of Nonattachment" (CW 41, 90-133).

According to Gandhi, the Gita calls people to *karmayoga*, i.e., the practice of asceticism. This asceticism, however, is not practised by retiring from the world but precisely in the activity of one's daily life. It consists of *anasakti*, "nonattachment", that is, not allowing oneself to be governed by feelings of desire, hatred, anger, yearning for success or fear of failure. In Gandhi's opinion, this nonattachment is extolled particularly in the last nineteen stanzas of the second canto of the Gita. We will quote one of these stanzas from Desai's translation: "The man who sheds all longings and moves without concern, free from all the sense of 'I' and 'Mine' - he attains peace" (BhG. 2, 71). For Gandhi, the corollary of such nonattachment could only be *ahimsa*, 'nonviolence'. These three motives, 'asceticism *in* worldly practice (*karmayoga*)', 'nonattachment' (*anasakti*) and 'nonviolence' (*ahimsa*), are the ingredients of Gandhi's struggle against the English whose occupation of India he considered to be illegal. Gandhi believed that all three were to be found in the Gita and thus V. Mehta is right to argue

[1] A succinct treatment of this question can be found in my "Autoriserende hermeneuse als interreligieus fenomeen," *Nederlands Theologisch Tijdschrift* 39 (1985): 276-94.

that this Scripture is the basis of Gandhi's political activity as a whole (Mehta, 172).

It is the most impressive aspect of Gandhi's politics - 'nonviolence' - that at the same time poses the most serious problem here. The issue of nonviolence does come up a few times in the Gita but in contexts that have nothing to do with political or military struggle (Sharma, 101). In contrast to nonviolence, the Gita as a whole is of a distinctly violent character. A short outline of its contents may help to clarify this.

The Bhagavadgita forms part of the voluminous heroic epic, the Mahabharata, which tells the story of the conflict between two related ruling clans, the Pandavas and the Kauravas. Through devious means the Kauravas had usurped the right of succession to the throne from the Pandavas. The Bhagavadgita opens in the final hour before the last and decisive battle and comprises the dialogue between Prince Arjuna, one of the leaders of the Pandavas and his charioteer Krishna, who appears to be a manifestation of the god Vishnu. Arjuna sees not only hostile relatives among his enemies but beloved ones as well. Moreover, he sees as their commander-in-chief the noble teacher, Bhishma, whom he also esteemed highly. It seems completely wrong to attempt to kill them in battle. Utterly confused, he lets the bow drop from his hands and decides to withdraw from the battle completely.

Krishna urges him to abandon this decision, arguing that Arjuna is a *kshatriya*, a 'nobleman' and it is the 'duty (*dharma*)' of a nobleman to maintain justice - by force if necessary. The sight of beloved persons and Bhishma among his enemies should not prevent Arjuna from fulfilling his duty. On the contrary he should be prepared to kill Bhishma and others of his foes whom Krishna mentions by name (BhG. 11, 34). However, he is to fight this battle with a sense of 'nonattachment', without feelings of hatred, hope for reward or fear of punishment. This battle is to be fought for the sole reason that it is Arjuna's duty. Then he can be certain that this battle will not entail any disastrous consequences for him in the hereafter. Arjuna allows himself to be persuaded by Krishna's argument and abandons his initial decision. Here the Bhagavadgita ends. The section of the Mahabharata that immediately follows bears the significant title "The Slaying of Bhishma (*Bīṣmavadha*)."[2] In accordance with Krishna's summons, it is Arjuna himself who applies the final, deadly blows to Bhishma.[3] Nonetheless, he does not fail to show the dying Bhishma his respect.

In view of all this, one can imagine that Gandhi was continually questioned about his understanding of the Bhagavadgita. This occurred for the first time in 1919 when Gandhi advised his followers to fast and to read the Gita in prepara-

---

[2] Van Buitenen, 3, even holds that within the framework of the epic as a whole the aim of the Bhagavadgita was to justify the killing of the high-principled Bhishma.

[3] I will leave aside here the question of Shikhandin's role as 'middleman'.

tion for a certain activity. Some protested because they were of the opinion that the Gita taught precisely the opposite of nonviolent struggle (Jordens, 89).

GANDHI'S HERMENEUTICS

In Western Europe the hermeneutical discussion concerning literary texts from the past had just begun during Gandhi's lifetime. As is well-known, this discussion has deeply influenced reflection on the understanding of the Bible. It would be preposterous, however, to suppose that Gandhi was aware of even the first rustlings of this discussion. Thus it is even more remarkable that the motifs present in this discussion can be clearly seen in Gandhi's understanding of the Bhagavadgita. One might say that analogous problems have led to analogous solutions. We will review some of these motifs to show that Gandhi sought to demonstrate with their help that the Gita, if understood correctly in the present time, does not only call one to a nonattached struggle but to a nonviolent one as well.

The first motif is that of the core and periphery of a literary text. According to Gandhi, as we stated above, the central message of the Gita is found in the last nineteen stanzas of the second canto. The whole Gita should be interpreted from the perspective of these stanzas. As Gandhi himself stated, he would even go so far as to advise that those statements in the Gita which could not be reconciled with this central message should be rejected or at least dropped (CW. 28, 16). With respect to his own understanding of the Gita this resulted in completely overlooking the special role of Krishna in the Gita as the all-encompassing God who guided all things. This role culminates in the well-known 'stanza of refuge', in which Krishna invites Arjuna to cast all his obligations aside and to take refuge solely in Him, who will deliver Arjuna from all his sins (BhG. 18, 66). This stanza is to Hindus the best known text of the entire Bhagavadgita. Gandhi, however, omitted it both in his translation and in his commentary.

A second motif is that of contextuality. To understand Holy Scripture, Gandhi says, "one should not stick to its letter, but try to understand its spirit, its meaning in the total context" (CW. 28, 318). By 'total context' he appears to have in mind the dialectic between the core message of a Holy Scripture, which remains unaffected by circumstances, and the historically determined religious and cultural idiom in which this message is expressed. Under this idiom he categorizes several things that others see as quite essential, such as new paths to 'ultimate salvation (*moksha*)', 'loving surrender to a personal God (*bhakti*)', and the repeated appearances of *avataras* ('incarnations') of the highest God to save humanity from destruction. According to Gandhi, none of this belongs to the essential message of the Gita (Jordens, 104). This obtains for war in the Gita as well. Gandhi maintained that people believed firmly in nonviolence at the time the Gita was written, but it did not occur to anyone that nonviolence and war were mutually exclusive (CW. 41, 99). Thus, the author could use the battle between the Pandavas and the Kauravas as an opportunity to address the issue of nonattachment (CW. 28, 318). At present, however, in Gandhi's opinion, we know that it is impossible to combine armed struggle with nonattachment in any way. Interpretation of the Gita should thus follow this hermeneutical key, possibly even contradicting the author's intention: "I believe that the teaching of the Gita does not justify war, even if the author of the Gita had intended otherwise" (CW. 45, 96-97). In other words, the message of the Gita is such that it even transcends the intentions of its own author. In view of this, one cannot come to any other conclusion, according to Gandhi, than that "under the guise of physical warfare, it [the Gita] described the duel that perpetually went on in the hearts of mankind" (CW. 41, 93).

The most surprising correspondence with modern hermeneutical perspectives is found in Gandhi's emphasis on practice and experience as hermeneutical principles. According to him, the interpreter's real task does not consist in investigating the exact meaning of the words and sentences but in applying the ethical code of the Gita in one's personal life (Jordens, 105). It was in this way as well that Gandhi himself had learned to understand the Gita. Forty years of continuous effort to put the teachings of the Gita into practice led him to see that the required nonattachment can never be achieved without nonviolence "in every shape and form" (CW. 41, 100). He is quite convinced that he is essentially in agreement with the author of Gita in this, however much this author had expressed his message in the language of physical warfare. Thus the experience acquired in the practical application of the Gita determines the understanding of its message in different circumstances. This approach could entail, according to Gandhi, that what is lawful for one person is unlawful for another and what is permitted in a specific time and place is not permitted at another time and place (CW. 41, 100). To conclude that Gandhi thus opened the door to ethical arbitrariness would be a mistake. It is neither the principle of nonattachment nor, as a matter of fact, the combination of nonattachment with nonviolence that are under discussion.

GODSE AND TILAK

Gandhi's murderer was Nathuram Vinayak Godse, about whom a great deal of information can be found in a book by G.D. Khosla, one of the judges in his trial (Khosla, 1963). In his mid-thirties when he murdered Gandhi, Godse had moved some ten years earlier from rural India to Poona (now Pune), where he became involved in the Hindu nationalist movement. He became secretary of the local chapter of the Hindu Mahasabha, a group whose slogan, 'Undivided India!' is fully representative of its aims. With this slogan they protested the threatened secession of predominantly Moslem territories from India. Godse participated in an act of civil disobedience against the Moslem ruler of nearby Hyderabad, who had been accused of depriving his Hindu subjects of their rights and Godse was sentenced to prison for some time. Godse decided to remain unmarried in order to be better able to dedicate himself to the Hindu cause and also thoroughly familiarized himself with the history and sociology of India. In Pune he made the acquaintance of Narayan Dattatraya Apte, whose nationalist fervour was equal to his and together they began a newspaper that eventually became the *Hindu Rashtra* ("The Hindu State"), after being published for a while under a different name. Because of its subversive articles this newspaper repeatedly came into conflict with the political authorities.

Godse wrote several articles in the *Hindu Rashtra* criticizing Gandhi's appeasement policy with respect to the Moslems and lenient attitude towards their leader Mohammed Ali Jinnah. Godse had already been involved in a failed attempt on Gandhi's life ten days before he actually did kill him. Although this attempt caused quite a stir, the authorities were unable to gather enough facts to take appropriate action. Godse dedicated an editorial to it in the *Hindu Rashtra* entitled "Representative Action shown by Hindu Refugees against the Appeasement Policy of Gandhiji" (Khosla, 217-218). I suppose that the term 'refugees' was intended to refer to the Hindu people who had fled from Pakistan.

Godse had made a thorough study of the Bhagavadgita and knew large parts of it by heart. In contrast to Gandhi, however, Godse would recite stanzas from the Gita to defend violent action undertaken for what in his view was a just cause (Khosla, 218). According to his own statement at his trial, one of the writers who had influenced him was Bal Gangadhar Tilak (d. 1920), who had also lived in Pune. Tilak's influence can still be felt in Pune. He was an erudite and energetic person who played a very important role in India's struggle for independence and has been called "the father of Indian unrest" (Stevenson, 48). Which of Tilak's works had Godse read? In view of his interest in the Bhagavadgita we may in any case assume that he had read Tilak's *Gītā Rahasya*, ("The Hidden Meaning of the Gita"). This work contains a number of essays on the Gita, the text of the Gita, and a commentary. It was very popular and by the time Godse took up residence in Pune five editions had already been published in Marathi, the language of the region, as well fourteen editions in other Indian languages. Almost ready for publication in Pune at the time was an English translation, which included the pregnant heading "The Hindu Philosophy of Life, Ethics and Religion" above the title, *Gītā Rahasya*. This work has been characterized as a peculiar mixture of traditional interpretation and modern scholarship (Stevenson, 49). Gandhi found it interesting but did not consider himself competent to judge it. However, for him that was not an issue since, according to him, scholarship was not necessary to understand the Gita: "The Gita was not composed as a learned treatise" (CW. 34, 89).

Tilak's commentary on a stanza from the eighteenth canto is quite important for our topic. The English translation of this stanza runs as follows: "Who does not possess the belief that "I am doer", and whose Reason is unattached, such a person, even destroying others persons, cannot be said to have killed them; and that (Action) does not bind him" (BhG. 18, 17). That Gandhi omits this stanza completely from his translation and commentary is not at all surprising, considering his point of view. Tilak, however, discusses it at length. In short, his opinion amounts to the thesis that a nonattached person is no longer an acting person and therefore cannot be held responsible even for killing another man. Tilak writes, "It, therefore, necessarily follows, that, even if a man, (whose Reason has first been proved to be pure and clean), does something, which may appear improper from the worldly point of view, yet, the seed of that action must be pure; and stanza 17 says that such a pure-minded person cannot be responsible for such Action" (II, 1183). The convoluted prose here betrays some caution, but Tilak's meaning is beyond all doubt: where a just cause is concerned, a nonattached person has the authority to go beyond the limits of ordinary ethics - even to commit an atrocity such as manslaughter or murder.

Completely in line with this principle, Tilak defended the actions of Sivaji against his Moslem enemies. Sivaji (d. 1680) was a Hindu prince who had resided in Pune and, using it as his base, had successfully fought against the Moslem rulers of the Mogul empire. He is considered to be the outstanding example for the struggle against non-Hindu rule. According to Tilak, such people were not to be measured by standards applied to ordinary mortals: great men were above the principles of conventional morality. Did Krishna not teach in the Gita that we could even kill our *guru* and relatives? In Tilak's view, one should abandon the Penal Code in order to take delight in the teachings of the Gita and to heed the actions of great men (Stevenson, 58).

We may conclude that the script for Godse's act had already been written in Pune, even though Tilak had not intended it to be interpreted in that way.

GODSE'S APPLICATION

Godse and his comrades considered Gandhi's liberal attitude towards the Moslems to be responsible for the division of what in their view was one India into two states, India and (East and West) Pakistan. Moreover, they held Gandhi to blame for seeking reconciliation with the Moslems after they had, according to them, committed the most heinous cruelties against Hindus. At his trial Godse said that Gandhi had even dared to have the Koran recited in a Hindu temple, in spite of protests from Hindus. Of course, Godse continued, Gandhi would never have dared read the Gita in a mosque "between the teeth of the Muslim opposition". Gandhi's general behaviour, culminating in his last pro-Moslem hunger strike, had brought Godse to the conclusion "that the existence of Ganghiji should be brought to an end immediately" (Khosla, 239-40).

In spite of everything for which he blamed Gandhi, Godse nonetheless looked upon Gandhi as a noble adversary. He explicitly stated that he abhorred Gandhi's behaviour but did not want to judge him harshly as a person. He was, according to Godse, an impressive mixture of egotism and greatness: "...childish inanities and obstinacies coupled with a most severe austerity of life, ceaseless work and lofty character made Ghandhiji formidable and irresistible" (Khosla, 241). Richard

Attenborough's film on Gandhi reminds us that Godse indicated his respect for Gandhi by the well-known gesture of two hands pressed flat against each other and only then did he fire the three deadly bullets. I do not know whether this scene fits the actual facts, but it does in any case illustrate the *mysterium fascinans* which Gandhi, in spite of everything, represented for Godse as well as for so many others. It invokes Arjuna's act of showing respect to Bhishma just before the latter dies from the wounds inflicted by Arjuna.

Godse's line of action clearly shows the influence of Tilak's interpretation of the Bhagavadgita with respect to the 'nonattached' person. The murder was planned by a small group of people, among whom was Apte, Godse's co-publisher of the *Hindu Rashtra*. It would be Godse, however, who would carry out the deed and take all responsibility for it. With Apte and another member of the group he went to the spot where Gandhi would be shot. Afterwards, while his two friends escaped in the general confusion, Godse himself made no attempt to flee. Bystanders seized him and a police officer had to rescue him from them. Later on Apte and some other suspects were arrested as well and tried with Godse. Both Godse and Apte were sentenced to death, while five others received life imprisonment. All of them appealed and Godse's arguments for the appeal were very unusual, perhaps even unique, in criminal procedure. He did not deny his guilt nor did he challenge the death sentence. Instead, he pleaded that he alone be held responsible: a plot would have been out of the question (Khosla, 210-11). The court judged otherwise. Two of the life sentences were repealed, but the other sentences remained unchanged.

The high point of the trial was a speech by Godse lasting several hours, in which he explained his action. In this speech he followed, broadly speaking, the line of argument contained in a previously written statement, from which we quote the following passage:

> Briefly speaking, I thought for myself and foresaw that I shall be totally ruined and the only thing that I could expect from the people would be nothing but hatred and that I shall have lost all my honour, even more valuable than my life, if I were to kill Gandhiji. But at the same time I felt that the Indian politics in the absence of Gandhiji would surely be practical, able to retaliate, and would be powerful with armed forces. No doubt, my own future would be totally ruined but the nation would be saved from the inroads of Pakistan. People may even call me and dub me as devoid of any sense or foolish, but the nation would be free to follow the course founded on reason which I consider to be necessary for sound nation-building. (Khosla, 242)

Echoes of Tilak's view concerning the extraordinary rights to which great men are entitled, according to the Gita, can be heard in the following words: "I fully and confidently believe that if there be any other Court of justice beyond the one founded by the mortals, my act will not be taken unjust" (Khosla, 242). Godse concluded by quoting some stanzas from the Gita (Khosla, 243). I do not know which these were, but we may perhaps think of Krishna's order to Arjuna to kill Bhishma (BhG. 11, 34) or of the assurance that a nonattached person engaged in fulfilling his duties cannot be held responsible for killing other people (BhG. 18, 17). Khosla reports that Godse's plea made a deep impression on the public. He was convinced that if the audience present on that day had constituted a jury, Godse would have been declared innocent "by an overwhelming majority" (Khosla, 243).

WHICH INTERPRETATION WAS CORRECT?

It challenges the limits of reason when two people like Gandhi and his murderer, with such opposite views, could both appeal with some justification to the Bhagavadgita for support of their views. Therefore we will try to determine whether Gandhi or Godse - or perhaps neither - was in the right.

Gandhi's appeal to the Gita concerning the combination of the ascetic concept of 'nonattachment' with political action and struggle seems to be quite justifiable. This combination, however, was not the issue in the differing interpretations of Gandhi on the one hand and Tilak and Godse on the other. On the contrary, both Gandhi and Godse tried to put this combination into practice. But Gandhi's view that such action and struggle can only be undertaken in a nonviolent way, if the Gita is correctly understood, is rather problematic. A. Sharma speaks of an "obvious gap" between what seems to be the explicit meaning of the Gita here and the implicit meaning for which Gandhi argues (Sharma, 98). One cannot avoid the impression that Gandhi's hermeneutical arguments are based too much on a conviction that he already had. He does not succeed in demonstrating convincingly that the Gita means exactly the reverse of what it says explicitly.

This problem with Gandhi's interpretation emerged quite painfully in a conversation with Toyohiko Kagawa (d. 1960). Kagawa was a Japanese Christian who, with great personal sacrifice, had devoted himself to social reform in his country and was a confirmed believer in pacifism. After he had attended the missions conference in Tambaram (1938), he visited Gandhi in January, 1939 and Desai recorded their conversation verbatim (CW. 68, 295-98). Gandhi reproached Kagawa for not making an open stand against Japanese militarism and the cruelties committed by Japanese soldiers in China. Kagawa responded with the question of how Gandhi could appeal to the Bhagavadgita, which still proclaimed a violent struggle. Gandhi went to great lengths to convince Kagawa that the real issue was a spiritual battle. Kagawa, however, remarked matter-of-factly: "To the common mind it sounds as though it was actual fighting". He even stated his preference for Arjuna whose view (the refusal to take part in the battle) seemed superior to that of Krishna. Gandhi answered that one could not prefer the disciple to the master. But who, we ask in the spirit of Kagawa, is the real master: Krishna or Gandhi himself?

Kagawa could not but consider Gandhi's interpretation of the Gita as purely subjective. This is of course, in Gandhi's view, a misunderstanding, for if such were the case, his interpretation would have no authority for others. It is not a subjective but "a reasonable interpretation". In my opinion, however, Kagawa has indicated precisely where the weak point of Gandhi's interpretation lay: the interpretation was not decided by what the Gita itself stated but by what Gandhi himself had experienced, as he explicitly stated elsewhere. That this personal experience would produce a 'reasonable interpretation' for others as well appears to be asking too much. Arguing for nonviolent struggle by appealing to the Bhagavadgita is hermeneutical ventriloquism.

The conclusion seems inevitable that the interpretation of Tilak and Godse is more adequate than Gandhi's. Of course this does not mean that Gandhi's murder could be justified by an appeal to the Gita. One could ask oneself whether Godse and his friends did not identify Gandhi and the Moslems too quickly with Bhishma and the Kauravas. This is a difficult question and in any case it requires more space than is available here. On the other hand, it is relatively simple to demonstrate that Godse could not appeal to the Gita for support for his action, even if his interpretation was correct.

One of the most famous rules of the Gita is that known as the *svadharma*, the observation of one's "own duty', i.e., the duties of one's own caste. One is not to attempt to fulfil the duties of other castes. Engaging in armed battle belongs to the duties of the *kshatriyas*, the 'nobility'. As Khosla mentions, however, Godse belonged to the caste of the brahmins (Khosla, 208) and thus could not have taken upon himself the task of killing Gandhi through the use of weapons - however dangerous Gandhi might have been for Hindu society. The *svadharma* rule is so generally known in India that Godse could not fail to have noticed his infraction of this rule, even if he had not studied the Gita. What justification could he have had for this?

We will consult Tilak again. In the English translation of his work, the most famous phrasing of the *svadharma* rule in the Gita is as follows:

> Even if it may be easier to follow the religion of another, yet, one's own religion (that is, according to the religion of the four castes) is more meritorious, though it might be '*viguna*' (that is, full of faults); though death results (while acting) according to one's own religion, there is bliss in that; (but) the religion of another is risky. (BhG. 3, 35; cf. 2, 31)

The term translated by 'religion' is *dharma* and Tilak defines one's own 'religion' as the "code of duties prescribed for every one (...) according to the arrangement of the four castes (...)" (II, 934). In my opinion, this is correct and in accordance with the teaching of the Gita. However, Tilak comments on an alternative wording of the rule (BhG. 18, 47) thus: "When once one has accepted a particular Action as one's own, for whatever reason one may have done so, one must perform it, unattachedly, however difficult or undesirable it may be" (II, 1198). Here one's *dharma* is no longer determined by one's caste but by one's own choice (Stevenson, 59). Tilak's translator even adds a footnote to this, stating that it is difficult to understand: according to the translator, one may only undertake one kind of 'Action', namely that which corresponds to the duties of one's own caste.

How Tilak arrived at this view becomes clear at the end of the series of essays on the Gita that precedes his commentary and translation (II, 697-98). He brings the reader back to the glorious past of the Maharashtra state with its former capital of Pune. The actual authority of the descendants of the great warrior Sivaji has been taken over by peshvas, 'major-domos', among whom Madhav Rao (d. 1772) was the most famous and competent. Madhav Rao was a brahmin but had chosen a career as a soldier and a sage had confirmed this choice, assuring him that it was the defense of society that mattered at the time. Madhav Rao was a brilliant strategist who succeeded in inflicting a decisive defeat upon Haider Ali of Mysore, his formidable Moslem foe (Kulke/Rothermund, 253-54). Tilak mentions Madhav Rao as the outstanding example of a person for whom an obligation taken upon himself - not because of caste but through his own choice - became a "moral duty". It is significant that Tilak himself belonged to the same (sub)caste as the former peshvas, the Chitpavan brahmins.

For his infraction of the *svadharma* rule, Godse could appeal to Tilak and even draw his inspiration from him. Tilak's work on the Gita, however, is not the Gita itself and Tilak's interpretation here is very much open to debate. The cautious criticism of his translator seems fully justified. When Tilak interprets *svadharma* as the *dharma* of one's own choice he contradicts the obvious meaning of the Gita - no less than Gandhi did with his nonviolence. In short, according to the Scripture to which he himself appeals, Godse was not qualified for the task of killing Gandhi. An unbiased interpretation of the Gita can no more confirm Godse's view than it can Gandhi's. On the contrary, Godse's act fully bears the *odium* that the Bhagavadgita lays on any transgression of the *svadharma* rule: "(fulfilling) the *dharma* of another is terrifying (*bhayavaha*)" (BhG. 3, 35)[4].

CONCLUSIONS

Gandhi's own experience forms the existential counterargument against his thesis that the Bhagavadgita contains a "complete reasoned moral code" that could serve as a source of inspiration for people of all religions. He did not succeed in convincing his fellow pacifist, the Christian Kagawa, that his appeal to the Gita was correct. His fellow Hindus, Tilak and Godse, derive a 'moral code' from the Gita that is at odds with Gandhi's and, in the case of Godse, even leads to Gandhi's murder. Of course this *casus* does not prove that other Sacred Scriptures do not

[4] The translation of this term as "risky" is too weak.

contain such a 'complete reasoned moral code' either. However, it seems wise to maintain that the particular messages of, for example, the Bible and the Koran as well cannot be translated into the language of 'universal morality', without employing some hermeneutical sleight-of-hand.

Should we then conclude that the appeal to a Sacred Scripture is authoritative only for those who already adhere to its teachings and does not have any connection to a common rationality? It does not appear to be limited to just this. One can demonstrate, by means of rational arguments, that the Scripture to which Godse appeals did not give him the right to kill Gandhi. Even Tilak's translator provides support here. The process of interpreting a Sacred Scripture is not the same as that of solving a mathematical problem, but neither is it a question of sheer religious subjectivity. Here lies the possibility for dialogue with those who are prepared to violate human rights by appealing to a Sacred Scripture. One does not necessarily have to be an adherent to ask: "Is your appeal to the Scripture to which you adhere correct?" It is a secondary issue as to whether the other will be convinced by one's argument, in any case the attempt is worthwhile.

What would have been the case if Godse had belonged to the caste of the *kshatriyas* and reasonable arguments could have been adduced to identify Gandhi and the Moslems with Bhishma and the Kauravas? In this case there might be a conflict between the Universal Declaration of Human Rights which decries murder and the Bhagavadgita which maintains that the duty of a nobleman includes the killing of Bhishma (Gandhi). Here the choice cannot be evaded: either we are 'converted' to the teaching of the Bhagavadgita in this respect, or we hold to the universal right to life, at least where murder is concerned. The latter option, however, is possible only through the restriction of another fundamental human right, the freedom of religion (art. 18). But then we have arrived at the exact opposite of what Gandhi intended: instead of being 'fed' by religion, human rights would restrict the free expression of religion. Even though the case is hypothetical, it does bear, unfortunately, on current reality.

BIBLIOGRAPHY

Desai, M. *The Gospel of Selfless Action or The Gita according to Gandhi*. Ahmedabad: Navajivan, 1946.

Fernhout, R. "Autoriserende hermeneuse als interreligieus fenomeen," *Nederlands Theologisch Tijdschrift* 39 (1985): 276-94.

Gandhi, M.K. *Autobiography: The Story of My Experiments with Truth*. New York: Dover, 1983; Republication of the edition of 1948.

Collected Works. Ahmedabad: Navajivan, 1958-. (CW).

"God of Love, not War." *Harijan* (September 5, 1936).

Jordens, J.T.F. "Gandhi and the *Bhagavadgita*." In R. Minor (ed.). *Modern Indian Interpreters of the Bhagavadgita*. Pp. 88-109

Khosla, G.D. *The Murder of the Mahatma and Other Cases from a Judge's Note-book*. London: Chatto & Windus, 1963.

Kulke, H. and D. Rothermund. *Geschichte Indiens*. Stuttgart: Kohlhammer, 1982.
Mehta, V. *Mahatma Gandhi and His Apostles*. London: Deutsch, 1977.
Minor, R. (ed.). *Modern Indian Interpreters of the Bhagavadgita*. Delhi: Indian Books, 1986.
Sharma, A. "The Gandhian Hermeneutical Approach to the Gītā: A Case-study of Ahiṃsā." In *Indian Philosophy and Culture* 19 (1974): 98-106.
Stevenson, R.W. "Tilak and the *Bhagavadgita*'s Doctrine of Karmayoga." In R. Minor (ed.). *Modern Indian Interpeters of the Bhagavadgita*. Pp. 44-60.
Tilak, B.G., *Śrīmad Bhagavadgītā Rahasya or Karma-Yoga-Śāstra*. Tr. Bh.S. Sukthankar, 2 Vols. Poona: Tilak Bros. 1857/1936.
Van Buitenen, J.A.B. (ed. and tr.). *The Bhagavadgītā in the Mahābhārata*. Chicago: Chicago University Press, 1981.

CHAPTER IX

Human Rights in Buddhist Perspective

Padmasiri de Silva

THE PROBLEM

A central concern of this volume is whether the different conceptions of the good life provided by the world's greatest living faiths leave room for neutral norms and values independent of such traditions. "Given the fact of pluralism and the necessity of coexistence, traditions will have to pass the test of some sort of universal code."[1] Do human rights provide such a neutral standard and what are the resources in the different religious traditions to appropriate the norms of the discourse on human rights? The question is obviously presented in terms of the *Universal Declaration of Human Rights* of 1948 and I am specifically concerned with the resources in the Buddhist tradition.

When we talk of resources in the Buddhist tradition we are first of all concerned with the primary discourses in the form of available texts, secondary sources and current discussions. But there is also a historical as well as socio-economic and socio-political adjustment that religions make as a response to the changing tides of human rights discourse. Thus, even the intellectual responses of scholars in different religious traditions come within the purview of social activists. Theravada Buddhist scholars in countries like Thailand and Sri Lanka do show a concern with the need to modernize the Buddhist worldview and to interpret their religious tradition in terms relevant to the new challenges in the socio-economic and political world. Hence, even the 1948 *Declaration* has over the years been updated, supplemented, expanded, and reinterpreted. If the very UN charter of human rights has been alert to these changing tides of human concerns, the religious traditions should be concerned about these challenges as well. Thus a specific focus of my paper is whether the ethical norms and moral discourse in the Buddhist tradition are *applicable* in current contextual situations in terms of human rights discourse.

It is thus not merely the availability of norms, precepts and ethical values in Buddhist texts but *also* the need to *apply* and *interpret* them with imagination

[1] Cf. the position paper in the preface to this volume, p. viii.

and flexibility to the challenging forms of human rights discourse today. It is also a current concern for all religious traditions in the search for a neutral language to talk about religion and human rights.

RELIGIOUS DIALOGUE ON HUMAN RIGHTS: ISSUES AND RESPONSES

I shall now briefly raise several issues of a challenging nature which may stand in the way of using the human rights charter as a neutrally formulated common ground for religions, and then take these issues separately for discussion.

1. First is the issue of the *diversity* and ramifications of the items (30 articles) listed as *human rights* in the 1948 UN declaration. To cover all these items would be too unwieldy in determining a neutral medium for interreligious dialogue. It may be possible to search for more basic values that constitute the background of the human rights declaration, such as the sanctity of life, which are common to the religions, the law, and the human rights declarations.

2. The next issue emerges from certain intrinsic qualities of the nature of *morality*. The distinction between the 'narrow' morality of constraint which considers ethics in terms of rules and rights and the 'broad' morality which focusses on the development of virtues and character, point towards certain limitations with respect to the formulations of human rights. There are other distinctions regarding divergent moral perspectives, like the 'ethics of care' and the 'ethics of rights', the ethics of virtues and vices and the ethics of will and decision-making, etc. These distinctions are not the same, but there is a great deal of overlapping and generally they seem to contrast the legalistic and the more humanistic sources of our moral life. This gap has to be closed in one way or another if one is to integrate human rights discourse into religions.

3. The third issue arises in relation to the multiplicity of the religious traditions, their logic, metaphysics and cultural embodiment. In spite of the claim that there is a certain commonality in the ethical codes of the different religious traditions, the alternative religious visions may stand in the way of finding a common frontier in human rights. How can we blend the need to preserve the distinctiveness of each religious tradition and yet discover commonalities through human rights discourse.

4. While the first issue deals with the variety of 'articles' in the list of human rights, the second with the divergence of moral perspectives, the third with the plurality of religions, the fourth is concerned with the issue of *contextuality*: the new challenges for human rights perceptions and interreligious perspectives. This paper will devote the majority of its discussion to this issue. Religious traditions are thus subject to great stress: they have to combine their distinctive religious visions with the need of finding a neutral language for human rights, as well as keeping an eye out for the contextualization of issues that emerge in relation to each tradition.

THE VARIETY AND DIVERSITY OF HUMAN RIGHTS

The variety and diversity of human rights as embodied in the *Universal Declaration of Human Rights* need not present a problem in connection with the need for a common language of human rights in a pluralist society. A multi-religious effort to look closely at the perception of human rights in Sri Lanka coinciding with the 40th anniversary of the adoption of the Universal Declaration does show that *at the conceptual level* a common language independent of religion, race, language, culture, and caste may be achieved (cf. Perera). The problem, of course, is that in *actual practice* the multi-religious resources were not effective in preventing some of the tragic consequences of *group conflicts* that were dramatically manifest in Sri Lanka. Of course, it is to the credit of the multi-religious context of this country that *religious conflicts* of any importance are absent or very minimal. Whatever possibility there was, however, for discourse on neutral human rights did not result in precepts for action and praxis.

At a conceptual level, the Buddhist tradition has a rich resource with respect to issues of equality, rights and freedoms with reference to race, sex, language, religion, political opinion, social origin, property, birth, or any such status. It is a richness which may be shared to a great extent with other religious traditions.

I have discussed the main strands in the Buddhist concept of equality in detail elsewhere (de Silva, 1987) and will sum up its main features:

(i) rejection of artificial and arbitrary distinctions among human beings, rejection of caste distinctions based on birth, and emphasis on character.

(ii) common human potentialities (spirituality and moral transformation, rationality, ability to sympathize with the suffering of others, free will, possession of secular skills).

(iii) All beings (including animals) are subject to the common predicament, described as a state of unsatisfactoriness (*dukkha*). This is the great leveller.

(iv) The great cosmic order which rules all beings in terms of *kamma* and rebirth. The Buddhist notion of equality is coloured by this moral order, *dhamma* as a righteous order. The king is referred to as a 'wheel-turning monarch' who attempts to insure that this *dhamma* is manifest in the rule of his kingdom. This is what gives a moral footing to the Buddhist perspectives on equality, even before it is legally enshrined by the state.

(v) The concept of human dignity and equal respect for all (*samanatata*): this describes Buddha's attitude to Ambapali (a moral outcast), Angulimala (a criminal), Rukkhas (a social outcast), the diversity of personality types and the diversity of vocations from which his adherents came.

(vi) Basic needs and the conditions for self-development, common to all.

(vii) The Buddhist notion of benevolence and compassion shows that equality as a human rights orientation in Buddhism rests on a humanistic rather than a legalistic conscience.

Apart from the moral basis and the humanistic flavour in the Buddhist perspectives on equality (which may be shared by other religions). there is an additional variable which may not be shared by religions dominated by the undercurrents of Western culture. This is important since differences among religions which may affect our attempts to find a neutral language of human rights may not be *metaphysical* and *doctrinal* but emerge out of the *cultural* frame in which the religions were originally clothed.

A major variable in the Buddhist discussion on equality is the notion of 'reciprocity' which brings duties and obligations into certain specific kinds of relationships. The *Signalovada Sutta* (Dialogues of the Buddha, Sermon 33) discusses the way in which man, as husband, father and master, and woman, as wife, mother and mistress, perform diverse functions which are reciprocated. Instead of raising questions of equality, the reciprocal duties and obligations supplement each other. It is a similar type of ethic of reciprocity which is manifest in the traditional Chinese moral life and the Confucian discourse about the rules of proper conduct.

In terms of these variables it has been observed that the notion of human rights is too much a product of the West and needs more flexible integration in terms of religious traditions much more rooted in the Orient. A recent study comments: "It is becoming increasingly evident that the Western political philosophy upon which the (UN) Charter and Declaration (of Human Rights) are based provides only one particular interpretation of human rights, and that this Western notion may not be successfully applicable to non-Western areas ..." (Polis and Schwab). The notion of *kamma* too is more than a mere point of doctrine: it is a cultural framework by which Buddhists and Hindus order their personal, social and cultural lives.

It appears that the presence of a variety of human rights as found in the thirty articles may not be a great obstacle to the development of a common human rights language. One can see within the declaration that, clarified and presented in a variety of ways, they embody basic norms and values that have a universal appeal: equality, rights concerning life, liberty, security, and property; freedom of thought, expression, conscience and the political rights of selecting and participating in a government; the right to belong to a nation and enjoy the fruits of marriage, right to work and employment, education and health, legal protection and equality before the law. I have categorized them broadly in five groups and their universal appeal is accepted. Along with other religions, Buddhism has the textual and conceptual resources to integrate them into the religious perspectives of the adherents.

Though there is an appeal to them as basic values and norms, human rights discourse in a narrow legalistic frame may not penetrate the distinctive ethos of the different traditions. Thus the flesh and blood of the articulation of these values in the different religious anthropologies may not always be captured by the focus on the anatomy of the declaration itself. Such a plurality of sources of inspiration and the ethos of the different traditions need not always be a liability in achieving a common platform - it may be an asset that could enrich a more authentic approximation of a framework for mutual co-existence. Due to the constraints on a lengthy discussion of the five groups of values and norms listed above, I have only taken equality as an example for discussion. If one looks at life, liberty, security and property, one would see them having a central place in the ethical codes of all the major religions (cf. de Silva, 1985, 140-42).

These different styles of appropriating the meaning of the human rights discourse may become a liability if and only if each tradition becomes frozen in its distinctive outlook, as if there were no other roads to the same goal. This is the contribution of the comparative study of religions: helping students of other religions than their own to understand the logic of discourse in these traditions. One has to take religious differences seriously and this is clearly the case in the context of Buddhism, when one individually seeks liberation from the cycle of existence. Such discourse centred on individual liberation, however, is always supplemented by more socially accepted modes of interaction with other individuals.

At the level of social ethics there is legitimate room for a Buddhist to work with others (of different religions) for the realization of common goals, whether it be social services, social justice or alleviation of poverty. Human rights often provide a negative field of constraint, but it is necessary to work for more positive goals. Even at the level of discourse on liberation, the Buddha said that there could be degrees of spiritual growth outside Buddhism: "The early Buddhist conception of the nature and destiny of man in the universe is, therefore, not in basic conflict with the beliefs and values of the founders of the great religions so long as they assert some sort of survival, moral values, freedom and responsibility and the non-inevitability of salvation" (Jayatilleke).

NARROW MORALITY AND BROAD MORALITY

The position paper for this volume, included in the preface, distinguishes between narrow and broad moralities. The former focusses on the rules and principles that make social co-existence possible, having duties, obligations and rights as its central categories, whereas the latter is an ethics of virtue and character. It is claimed that the doctrine of human rights seems only possible within narrow morality, concerned as it is with the existence of a common core between different traditions.

While this distinction is rooted in the history of the development of ethical systems, the language of rules and rights may not always be the best to adopt even in situations of resolving human rights conflicts. Perhaps we need new distinctions that will help us to penetrate narrow morality from the bases of broad morality. Carrol Gilligan points towards an interesting approach to situations dominated by the ethic of rules and rights. A man named Heinz has to decide whether or not to steal a drug (which he cannot afford to buy) in order to save his wife's life. Jake, an eleven year old boy, sees the problem in clear logical terms as a conflict between the value of property and the value of life. He upholds the value and priority of *life* over *property*. On the other hand, Amy, an eleven year old girl, responds differently: "Well, I do not think so, I think there might be other ways besides stealing it, like, if he should borrow the money or make a loan or something but he should not steal the drug - but his wife should not die either." Both children recognize the need for agreement, but it is mediated in different ways: *in Jake it is mediated through the impersonal systems of logic and law, while in Amy it occurs personally through communication in relationships*. Gilligan points out that the construction of the moral problem in this context is one of care and responsibility rather than one of rights and rules (cf. also de Silva, 1984).

This example shows that there is a limitation to using human rights discourse as the sole paradigm for dealing with human problems of an ethical nature. Thus we need a more flexible approach to deal with moral situations generating human rights claims. Human rights discourse has an important function (as will be clarified in the last section of this paper) but it has to be mediated by other perspectives on morality, depending on each context.

The social ethos of Buddhism leaves room for both the 'ethic of care' and the 'ethic of rights', but, as we mentioned earlier, the latter is tempered by duties and obligations based on reciprocity and a concept of righteousness based on the moral order (*dhamma*) and the concept of moral causation (*kamma*). Buddhist ethics is a blend of humanistic altruism (resting on the philosophy of the four sublime states) and the notion of a *righteous* social, moral and political order (see de Silva, 1991). Although the ethical path of Buddhism may be described as leading towards a consequentialist ideal, Buddhism has a tempered and culturally-coloured deontological strand. The vibratory base of Buddhist ethics is the doctrine of compassion (de Silva, 1992) and it brings into play a wide variety of virtues. To some extent, Buddhist ethics is an ethics of virtues and vices (de Silva, 1991).

As an ethics concerned with the moral development of human beings, Buddhist ethics deals with both the nature of evil states which darken the mind as well as the wholesome mental states which illuminate the mind. The discourse on the *Simile of the Cloth* (Middle Length Sayings I, Discourse 7) mentions sixteen states that may interfere with positive and wholesome morality: greed, covetousness, malevolence, anger, malice, hypocrisy, spite, envy, miserliness, deceit, treachery, obstinacy, impetuosity, arrogance, pride, and conceit. The management, control and eradication of evil psychological states and the growth of wholesome states provides the deeper basis of moral development in Buddhism and this ethics of virtue and character (broad morality) have both a personal and social dimension. The virtues recommended fall into three groups: (i) virtues of conscientiousness (veracity, truthfulness, and righteousness); (ii) virtues of benevolence (lovingkindness, compassion, sympathetic joy and equanimity); (iii) virtues of self-restraint (self-control, abstinence, contentment, patience, celibacy, chastity, purity.

From the perspectives of Buddhist ethics as briefly described, the lasting base for the preservation of human rights and their natural flowering in human society will be broad morality, but both types of morality (the narrow and the broad) need to penetrate each other. Does this strong strand of broad morality in Buddhist ethics stand in the way of the development of a neutral language of human rights discourse across religions?

If we concentrate on praxis rather than the theoretical vocabulary of moral emotions, 'compassion', whether it is Buddhist, Christian, Hindu or Islamic, should certainly prepare the way for the preservation of human rights. If we look at compassion across religions - not merely as discourse oriented towards liberation but as socially manifest patterns of interaction among peoples - it provides one of the lasting bases for the preservation of human rights and their neutral vocabulary. Of course, the need for human rights emerges either because the great faiths and their adherents do not always reflect the message of their teachers in what they do and think *or* if religious identities, lacking authenticity and good communication, are not strong enough to penetrate other identities (such as political, ethnic, economic, linguistic, etc.) which cause problems.

The real world, however, the world of practice, is always a mixture of the best and the worst. All this seems to suggest, perhaps, is that narrow morality *has* to rest on broad morality, and the fact that religious traditions are heavily immersed in morality need not stand in the way of the development of a neutral language of human rights discourse. On the contrary, broad morality in the religions may provide a rich basis for its preservation. The problems that arise are not conceptual but issues of praxis and contextuality (cf. below).

MULTIPLICITY OF RELIGIOUS TRADITIONS

The very fact that there is a multiplicity of religious traditions and that their followers go to the temple, church, kovil, and mosque also implies that they also meet each other in business, at the office, play, courts of law, police stations and theatres. If issues of religious discrimination emerge, freedom of conscience as a human right has to mediate between conflicting religious identities, which are strongly affirmed and protected. In such situations, human rights discourse itself is summoned to preserve the very survival of religions, but it is also possible, as at the Colombo multi-religious conference (de Silva, 1985, 137), that a strong body of opinion across religious communities can take a stand against the very misuse of religion to justify prejudice, hatred and warfare.

Metaphysical differences among religious traditions stand in the way of the development of a neutral vocabulary of human rights, only if the religious tradition as a group has developed harmful and even pathological 'identity profiles'. Collective identities, if viable and wholesome, have an impact on individuals. It is thus my contention that the issues pertaining to religious traditions, their metaphysical variety and their attempts to develop human rights discourse is encouraged by the development of the correct type of identity profile and obstructed by the wrong type. As Bardwell Smith observes,

> At the heart of identity always is what it means to be a person, a community, which is a religious more than it is a social or political or ethnic issue. In fact, it is significantly religious to the very degree that it not only takes seriously these other aspects of personhood (i.e., one's communal, national and cultural roots) *but does not bestow ultimate status upon them.* (Bardwell L. Smith, 1976)

As the identity of persons is both individual and corporate, Bardwell Smith adds that continuous self-criticism is necessary to develop the correct kind of identity profile.

The teachings of the Buddha present a sustained analysis and critique of the issue of personal identity, although its logical implications for collective identity concepts have not been greatly explored by Buddhist scholars. But the extensions are useful and provide the Buddhist with a tool for authentic self-criticism (de Silva, 1988). The fivefold identification emerging from corporeality, feeling, perception, dispositions, and consciousness manifests itself in a number of ways, generating as many as twenty types of wrong personality beliefs. On the one hand, both personal identity and group identity is not seen as simply a grand illusion; on the other hand, personal identity is not just a shapeless protoplasm with no sense of direction. Within the debris of the illusion, we have to generate a lifestyle withough falling into the traps of false identity. The dissolution of the ego does not necessarily mean a dimunition of one's coordinating powers. Thus, as I have stated elsewhere (de Silva, 1988), one has to balance on the razor's edge of the middle ground between utter chaos and the paths of identity illusions. We have to find a realm of critical and interim identities, dissolving them as we cross them and transcending them as we cut across their inner dialectic: "The reality of personal and group identities all flounder on this narrow ridge, and to steer clear of the traps is the greatest challenge" (de Silva, 1988, 17).

This is the Buddhist conceptual framework for understanding the nature of religious identities, and it is from this vantage point that one has to probe the issue of the possibility of a variety of religious anthropologies appropriating a neutral discourse of human rights. I have done a case study of a Buddhist predicament in the context of ethnic and religious identities in the article cited above.

ISSUES OF CONTEXTUALITY

In the previous sections I have looked at human rights as a relatively stable and relevant concept for ordering our lives. Although this appears to be a workable assumption, even while it is being updated and even reinterpreted, there are certain emerging contexts where its relevance is being questioned. Due to the constraints of space here, I shall select one specific issue for discussion and raise some questions. I have been very much interested in the place occupied by human rights in the context of environmental issues. This is, of course, a question that has not been probed very deeply by experts on human rights. The interest has mainly emerged in the work of moral philosophers looking at the ethical issues of environmentalism.

Some have observed that the 'language of rights' is out of vogue among environmental philosophers. It may be that not only is such language merely out of vogue but that, because the rights approach is heavily focussed on individual desires and preferences, the ecological notions of 'relatedness' and 'compatibility' sound out of place in a language concerned with the adjudication of rights claims between humans. As William Aiken writes, "Maybe ... we need a more relational or communitarian, albeit humanistic, moral theory which recognizes responsibilities without requiring a reduction to right claims" (pp. 196-97).

The rights approach has also been found to deficient in the development of a holistic conception of the environment. In 1982, when the United Nations issued its *World Charter for Nature*, there was a shift from the language of rights to the language of responsibility. This is an important change of perspective, but this has been countered by a swing back to the language of rights and thus, when the Brundtland report was released, the most important right was that concerning the environment: "All human beings have the fundamental right to an environment adequate for their health and well-being" (*Our Common Future*, 1982, 4). Critics feel that the commission has merely inserted the vocabulary of rights into their statement but not integrated it very well into the report as a whole. While such attempts were made during recent times to invoke the human rights discourse to include claims to a proper environment, the Rio conference witnessed the voice of Third World countries that sustainable development has to converge with social justice and the alleviation of poverty. They spoke of the violence of the green movement and thus the voice of economic equality emerged.

This short commentary on human rights and environmentalism indicates that both the ethic of rights and the ethic of care are perenially rooted in the moral perspectives developed over the years and they emerge in novel ways. Buddhism is quite at ease with the ethics of the new environmentalism (de Silva, 1993). In both its environmental philosophy and its environmental ethics Buddhism is not very dependent on human rights discourse, although some of its very important strands, like the *concern* for future generations may be described in terms of the vocabulary of *rights*. In the way that Buddhist ethics emphasizes the reciprocal duties and obligations between husband and wife, parents and children or student and teacher, the principal of reciprocity based on the principle of 'interdependence of all living beings' offers the framework for the relations between humans and nature and humans and non-human creatures.

The principle of reciprocity and interdependence call for an ethic of responsibility rather than one of rights. The Buddhist concept of dependent origination shows that a living entity cannot isolate itself from the vast causal network around it. The notion of environmental holism emphasizes that a system is more than the sum of its parts. While right-centred environmental norms may find some place in Buddhist ethics, the global attitude it contains, the concern for the non-human world, the focus on the eco-system and the concern for future generations does not lead us to a 'rights-centred' morality in environmental concerns.

There are trends, perhaps, that could make environmentalism very visionary and then a rights approach to environmental protection may be a needed corrective. It has even been said that the only realistic and feasible approach to ecological and political reform is through the society that respects human rights (cf. McClosky). There is some political weight when one uses the familiar human rights discourse, which has become a familiar international language, to uphold the protection of the environment as well as the enforcement of necessary rules. The human rights approach can contribute to environmental issues. As Aiken has pointed out, if a spiritually green communitarian era arrives in the world, the human rights approach may not be needed for the protection of the environment, but until then it has to be only one of the approaches for dealing with the environment. Buddhist ethics takes more naturally to a communitarian approach to environmentalism, but it certainly leaves room for a rights approach - when it is tied contextually to a much needed praxis.

I have taken this question on human rights in an ecological era to emphasize that when we look at human rights discourse from the perspectives of the major religions, the issue can not be decided merely by looking at religious texts *only*, even though they provide a goldmine of insights. It is necessary to be aware that the very framework of human rights has been put to the test by these changing conditions of the human situation. From 1948 (Declaration of the UN Charter of Human Rights) to 1987 (The Brundtland Report, *Our Common Future*) the changes that have emerged can be seen in the number of charters and commission reports that have been published.

Any commentary on the place of human rights discourse in the religious traditions has to take account of these changing perspectives on human rights. Environmental ethics in a pluralist world will try to combine the different moral perspectives - an even broader task than using the language of moral rights as a neutral discourse common to the different religious traditions. Human rights discourse may not exhaust the potential common frontiers among religions.

BIBLIOGRAPHY

Aiken, W. "Human Rights in an Ecological Era." *Environmental Values* I (1992): 191-203.

De Silva. Padmasiri. *The Ethics of Moral Indignation and the Logic of Violence*. V.F. Gunaratne Memorial Lecture. Colombo: Public Trustee Department, 1984.

———. "Religious Pluralism: A Buddhist Perspective." In: J. Hick and Hasan Askari (eds.). *The Experience of Religious Diversity* Hampshire: Gover Publishers, 1985.

———. "The Concept of Equality in the Theravada Buddhist Tradition." In: R. Siriwardena (ed.). *Equality and the Religious Traditions of Asia*. London: Francis Pinter, 1987.

———. "The Logic of Identity Profiles and the Ethic of Communal Violence." In: K.M. de Silva (ed.). *Ethnic Conflict in Buddhist Societies*. London: Pinter Publishers, 1988.

———. "Buddhist Ethics." In: Peter Singer (ed.). *A Companion to Ethics*. Oxford: Basil Blackwell, 1991.

———. *Twin Peaks: Compassion and Insight*. Singapore: Buddhist Reasearch Society, 1992.

———. *Environmental Ethics in Buddhism*. Paris: UNESCO, forthcoming.

Gilligan, Carrol. *In a Different Voice: Psychological Theory and Women's Development*. New York, 1982

Jayatilleke, K.N. *The Principles of International Law in Buddhist Doctrine*. Extracts from *Recuil de Cours*, Vol. II. Leiden, 1967. Circulated privately.

———. *The Buddhist Attitude to Other Religions*. Kandy: Buddhist Publication Society, 1970.

McCosky, H.J. *Ecological Ethics and Politics*. Totowa: Rowman and Littlefield, 1983.

Perera, Horace, (ed.). *Human Rights and Religions in Sri Lanka*. Colombo: Sri Lanka Foundation, 1988

Polis, Adamantia and Peter Schwab, (eds.). *Human Rights*. New York, 1979.

Smith, Bardwell L. *Religion and Social Conflict in South Asia*. Leiden: Brill, 1976.

World Commission on Environment and Development. *Our Common Future*. The Brundtland Report. Oxford: Oxford University Press, 1987.

CHAPTER X

The Buddhist View of Human Rights

Masao Abe

The Buddhist view of 'human rights' is significantly different from that found in Western tradition. Strictly speaking, the exact equivalent of the phrase 'human rights' in the Western sense cannot be found anywhere in Buddhist literature. In the Western notion of human rights, 'rights' are understood as pertaining only to humans; nonhuman creatures are either excluded or at least regarded as peripheral or secondary. Human rights are understood not from the nonhuman or wider-than-human point of view but only from the human point of view - an anthropocentric view of human rights. In marked contrast, in Buddhism a human being is grasped not only from the human point of view, that is, not simply on an anthropocentric basis, but on a much broader transhomocentric, cosmological basis. More concretely, in Buddhism human beings are grasped as one part of all sentient beings or even as one part of all beings, sentient and nonsentient, because both human and nonhuman beings are equally subject to transiency or impermanency. (A basic principle of Buddhism is that nothing is permanent.) If this universal impermanency that is common to both human and nonhuman beings is not dealt with, the problem of life and death peculiar to human existence cannot be properly resolved. Both the Buddhist understanding of human suffering and its way of salvation are rooted in this transanthropocentric, cosmological dimension.

This is in sharp contrast to Judaism, Christianity, and Islam, in which the understanding of human suffering and its way of salvation are based primarily on the personal relationship between the human being and God, a relationship which Martin Buber rightly described in terms of the "I-Thou relationship". That the Buddhist understanding of human suffering and its way of salvation are based on the transanthropocentric, cosmological dimension, however, does not indicate that Buddhism disregards the special significance of human beings in the universe. On the contrary, Buddhism clearly esteems the special distinctiveness of human beings in the universe, as seen in the following verse which is usually recited by Buddhists as a preamble to the Gatha, "The Threefold Refuge":

> Hard it is to be born into human life.
> We now live it.
> Difficult it is to hear the teaching of the Buddha.
> We now hear it.
> If we do not deliver ourselves in this present life,
> No hope is there ever to cross the sea of birth and death,
> Let us all together, with the truest heart,
> Take refuge in the three treasures!

I have commented on this verse elsewhere as follows:

> The first and second lines express the joy of being born in human form during the infinite series of varied transmigrations. The third and fourth lines reveal gratitude for being blessed with the opportunity of meeting with the teaching of the Buddha - something which very rarely happens even among men. Finally the fifth and sixth lines confess to a realization that so long as one exists as a man one can and must awaken to one's own Buddha-nature by practising the teachings of the Buddha; otherwise one may transmigrate on through *samsara* endlessly. Herein it can be seen that Buddhism takes human existence in its positive and unique aspect most seriously into consideration. (Abe, 1982, 152)

As a religion, Buddhism naturally is primarily concerned with human salvation. In this sense Buddhism is not different from Semitic religions. Both Buddhism and Semitic religions are anthropocentric in that they are equally concerned with this issue. The difference between them lies in the fact that while the *basis* for human salvation in Semitic religions is the personal relationship between humans and God, in Buddhism that *basis* is the transpersonal, cosmological dimension common to human beings and to nature: the *Dharma*, that is, the 'suchness' ('as-it-is-ness') of everything in the universe. In Buddhism, the human problem is grasped not only from the human point of view within the human realm but also from the much wider transhuman, cosmological point of view that extends far beyond the human dimension. Yet it is human beings who, alone in the universe, have self-consciousness and can thus transcend their own realm and reach the universal, cosmological dimension.

In Buddhism, "human rights" are to be understood in this transanthropocentric, universal dimension. If "human rights" are understood as indicating these rights as grasped only from an anthropocentric point of view - as is the case in the West - we cannot find its counterpart in Buddhist literature. In order to understand the Buddhist view of "human rights" properly we should consider the problem of "self", since in any religion, particularly in Buddhism, human rights and human freedom cannot be legitimately grasped without a proper understanding of the problem of self.

Self is not an absolute but a relative entity. As soon as one talks about self one already presupposes the existence of the other. There can be no self apart from the other and vice versa. Self and the other are entirely interdependent and relational. Self is not an independent, self-existing, enduring, substantial entity. Nevertheless, because we human beings have self-consciousness and a strong disposition toward self-love and self-attachment, we often reify it as if it were an independent, enduring substantial entity. Self-centeredness is simply an outcome of this reification or substantialization of the self. Buddhism emphasizes that this reification of the self and its resultant self-centeredness are the root-source of evil and human suffering. Accordingly, as a way of salvation, Buddhism teaches the necessity of realizing the nonsubstantiality of the self, that is, of realizing nonself or *anatman*.

The Buddhist notion of nonself, however, does not preclude human selfhood in the *relative* sense. It is undeniable that we come to a realization of the "self-identity" of ourselves through memories from our childhood and through interaction with friends and other fellow beings. I am I and not you; you are you and not me. Hence, there is a clear distinction between self and other and, thereby, a clear realization of self-identity or selfhood. The question in this regard, however, is whether this self-identity or selfhood is *absolutely* independent, enduring, and substantial. The answer must be 'no'. For there is no 'I' apart from 'you', just as there is no 'you' apart from 'I'. As soon as we talk about 'I', we already and categorically presuppose the existence of 'you', and vice versa. Accordingly, although we have self-identity in a relative sense, we do not have it in the absolute sense. I am I in the relative sense, but I am not I in the absolute sense. The notion of absolute self-identity or substantial, enduring selfhood is an unreal, conceptual construction created by human self-consciousness. Buddhism calls it *maya*, or illusion, and emphasizes the importance of awakening to nonself by doing away with this illusory understanding of the self.

Once we awaken to our own nonselfhood, we also awaken to the nonselfhood of everything and everyone in the universe. In other words, we awaken to the fact that, just like ourselves, nothing in the universe has any fixed, substantial selfhood, even while maintaining relative selfhood. So, on the relative level, all of us have our distinct selfhood; yet, on the absolute level, we have no fixed, substantial selfhood but, rather, equality and solidarity in terms of the realization of nonself. Accordingly, from an absolute standpoint, we can say that, because of the absence of substantial selfhood, I am not I, and you are not you; thereby, I am you, and you are me. We are different relatively but equal absolutely, interfusing with one another, even while retaining our distinct identity. The same is true with the self and nature, and with the self and the divine. The self and nature are different from one another on the relative level, but on the absolute level they are equal and interfuse with one another because of the lack of any fixed, substantial selfhood. Consequently, nature is not merely a resource for the human self; it is grasped in sympathetic relationship with the self. Finally, and most importantly, the self and the divine - whether one calls it God, *das Heilige*, *Brahman*, or *Nirvana* - are, relatively speaking, essentially different from one another. Speaking in an absolute sense, however, the self and the divine are not different but equal, interfusing and interpenetrating one another. This is the case because even the divine is understood here without independent, enduring, substantial selfhood.

Clearly Buddhism and monotheistic religions are radically different on this point, and this difference has important ramifications when we come to the crucial point of the problem of religious tolerance. In Judaism, Christianity, and Islam the divine is the One Absolute God who, being the ruler of the universe, possesses a free will and is self-affirmative and essentially transcendent to human beings and nature. The self-affirmative character of Yahweh is clearly seen when Yahweh's "self" is revealed to Moses at Mount Horeb by saying, "I am that I am" (Ex. 3:14; according to certain interpretations the original Hebrew of this phrase, *'ehyeh 'asher 'ehyeh*, means "I am that I am" or "I will be what I will be"). Further, in the Ten Commandments he gave to Moses Yahweh emphasizes, "You shall have no other gods before me" (Ex. 20:3).

In religions in the Israelite tradition this strongly monotheistic commandment comes first among the Ten Commandments. Buddhism has a Decalogue very similar to that of the Israelite tradition, emphasizing that, "You shall not kill, shall not steal, shall not lie, shall not commit adultery," and so forth. In the Buddhist Ten Commandments, however, there is no equivalent to the first commandment of the Decalogue, "You shall have no other gods before me." Instead, the first of the Buddhist Ten Commandments is: "Do not destroy life", and this commandment refers not only to human life but also to the life of all sentient beings. In the Judeo-Christian tradition the problem of human rights and human duties to others must be considered in relation to the exclusive commandment of the supreme God, whereas in Buddhism the same problem should be grasped in relation to all living beings in the universe. This difference entails that in Buddhism the conflict between human rights and religious freedom becomes much less serious than in the Judeo-Christian traditions. It also leads to a different attitude toward the problem of the environment, another burning issue of our time. Under the commandment "Do not destroy life", the rights of animals and plants are as equally recognized as are human rights. Not only is nature subordinate to human beings, but human beings are also subordinate to nature.

How can Buddhism contribute to the issue of "religious tolerance and human rights"? I would like to offer Buddhist solutions to this problem in three ways:

1. Elimination of the attachment to doctrine and dogma. No religion is without doctrine, but the attitudes toward doctrine are not the same. When doctrine is regarded as authoritative and binding upon all the faithful, it turns into 'dogma'. Dogma is a fixed form of belief formulated in creeds and articles by religious institutional authority for acceptance by its followers. Within Christianity, the Roman Catholic Church still promulgates dogmas, while Protestant

churches have 'confessions' in which the faithful confess what they believe from the heart rather than submit to an imposed, external doctrinal statement (dogma) - although the Protestant 'confessions' are also interpreted 'dogmatically' by some. When dogma is emphasized, schism often takes place within a religion, and opposition among other religions occurs. Conflict - even religious war - erupts. Religions which are based on divine revelation and emphasize exclusive faith in the revealed truth are frequently liable to the intolerance generated by fixed forms of belief.

By contrast, Buddhism, which is not based on divine relationship but on self-awakening, has no dogma. Although Buddhism has various forms of doctrine - such as the Four Noble Truths, the Eightfold Path, and the twelve-link chain of causation - doctrines are not regarded in Buddhism as something essential. The Buddha himself said: "My teaching is like a raft to cross the stream of life and death so as to reach the other shore of enlightenment. Once you reach the other shore there is no need to carry the raft" (*The Dhammapada*). From the Buddhist standpoint, it is not doctrine (to say nothing of dogma) that is important to religion but one's existential commitment to the religious truth underlying the doctrinal formulation. If we eliminate attachment to dogma and return to the religious truth as the root-source of doctrine, we can overcome schisms and religious wars for the most part and become more tolerant, not only within our own religion but also towards other religions.

2. Emphasis on wisdom rather than justice. In the Judeo-Christian tradition, God, as a judge, is believed to have the attributes of justice or righteousness, and, as the one who forgives, those of love or mercy. Because God is the fountain of justice, one may trust that everything God does is just. Since God's verdict is absolutely just, human righteousness may be defined in terms of God's judgment.

The notion of justice or righteousness is a double-edged sword, however. On the one hand, it aids in maintaining right order, but, on the other, it can easily lead to the establishment of clear-cut distinctions between the righteous and the unrighteous, promising eternal happiness to the former but condemning the latter to eternal punishment. Accordingly, if justice or righteousness is the sole principle of judgment or is too strongly emphasized, it creates serious disunity and schism among people. This disunity cannot then be healed, for on this construal of things it is the result of divine judgment.

Although his religious background was Jewish, Jesus went beyond such a strong emphasis on divine justice and preached the impartiality of God's love. Speaking of God the Father he said: "He makes his sun rise on the evil and the good, and sends rain on the just and on the unjust" (Mt. 5:45). Thus, he emphasized, "Love your enemies and pray for those who persecute you, so that you may be sons of your Father who is in heaven" (Mt. 5:44). Nevertheless, in the Judeo-Christian tradition the notion of narrowly confined divine election has been evident among some influential commentators. In their view the Old Testament teaches God's choice of Israel from among all the nations of the earth to be God's people in the possession of a covenant of privilege and blessing (Dt. 4:37, 7:6; 1 Kg. 3:8; Is. 44:1-2). In the New Testament divine election is a gracious and merciful election. Traditionally, however, this election has often been seen on the basis of certain New Testaments texts to be of a rather restricted nature: "Many are called, but few are chosen" (Mt. 22:14). Thus "the terms [election or elect] always imply differentiation, whether viewed on God's part or as a privilege on the part of men" (Harrison, 179). In Christianity the notion of the "Elect of God" has often overshadowed the "impartiality of God's love". If I am not mistaken, this is largely related to a onesided emphasis on justice or righteousness.

Whereas Christianity talks much about love, Buddhism stresses compassion. In Christianity, however, love is accompanied by justice. Love without justice is not regarded as true love. In Buddhism, compassion always goes with wisdom. Compassion without wisdom is not understood to be true compassion. Unlike the Christian notion of justice referred to above, however, the Buddhist notion of wisdom does not entail judgment or election. Buddhist wisdom implies the affirmation or recognition of everything and everyone in their distinctiveness or in their 'suchness'. Further, as already noted, the particular notion of justice in Christianity outlined in the foregoing[1] creates an irreparable split between the just and the unjust, the righteous and the unrighteous, whereas the Buddhist notion of wisdom evokes the sense of equality and solidarity. Again, justice, when carried to its final conclusion, often results in punishment, conflict, revenge, and even war, whereas wisdom entails rapprochement, conciliation, harmony, and peace. Love and justice are like water and fire: although both are necessary, they go together with difficulty. Compassion and wisdom are like heat and light: although different, they work together complementarily.

The Judeo-Christian tradition does not lack the notion of wisdom. Wisdom literature (Job, Proverbs, Ecclesiastes, etc.) which make frequent use of the term *hokmah* (wisdom), constitutes a significant part of the Hebrew Bible. *Hokmah* refers both to human knowledge and to divine wisdom. In the latter case, as wisdom given by God it enables humans to lead a good, true, and satisfying life by helping them to keep God's commandments. In the New Testament, *sophia* is understood to be an attribute of God (Lk. 11:49), the revelation of the divine will to people (1 Cor. 2:4-7). But, most remarkably, Jesus as the Christ is identified with the wisdom of God because he is confessed as the ultimate source of all Christian wisdom (1 Cor. 1:30). Nevertheless, in the Judeo-Christian tradition as a whole, the wisdom aspect of God has been neglected in favor

---

[1] Other modern interpretations emphasize that divine justice and righteousness are always *salvific* and therefore that there is no separation or contradiction between God's love and God's justice.

of the justice aspect. Is it not important and terribly necessary now to emphasize the wisdom aspect of God with a view to solving the conflict within a religion as well as among religions?

3. A new understanding of monotheism. Above, I criticized monotheistic religion in that, due to its strong emphasis on the One Absolute God, it is apt to be exclusive and intolerant. To any religion, however, the realization of the oneness of ultimate reality is important, because religion is expected to offer an integral and total - rather than fragmentary or partial - salvation from human suffering. Even so-called polytheistic religions do not believe in various deities without any order but often worship a certain supreme deity as a ruler over a hierarchy of innumerable gods. Further, the three major deities often constitute a trinity - as exemplified by the Hindu notion of *trimurti*, the threefold deity of *Brahman*, *Vishnu*, and *Shiva*. Such a notion of trinity in polytheism also implies a tendency toward a unity in diversity - a tendency toward oneness.

This means that in any religion, especially in higher religions, the realization of the Oneness of ultimate reality is crucial. Yet, the realization of Oneness necessarily entails exclusiveness, intolerance, and religious imperialism, which cause schism within a given religion and conflict among the various religions. This is a very serious dilemma which no higher religion can escape. How can we believe in the Oneness of the ultimate reality in our own religion without falling into exclusive intolerance and religious imperialism toward other faiths? What kind of Oneness of ultimate reality can solve that dilemma and open up a dimension in which positive tolerance and peaceful coexistence are possible among religions, each of which is based on One Absolute reality?

In this connection I would like to distinguish two kinds of oneness: the first monistic; the second, nondualistic. It is my contention that only nondualistic oneness or unity, not monistic oneness or unity, can provide a real common basis for the contemporary pluralistic situation of world religions. How are monistic and nondualistic oneness different from one another? I would like to clarify their differences by making the following four points:

First, monistic oneness is realized by distinguishing itself and setting itself apart from dualistic twoness and pluralistic multiplicity; it is thus still dualistically related to them. Monism excludes dualism and pluralism and, therefore, stands in opposition to them. Accordingly, monistic oneness is neither truly monistic nor true oneness. In order to realize true oneness we must go not only beyond dualism and pluralism but also beyond monistic oneness itself. *Then* we can realize nondualistic oneness, because at that point we are completely free from any form of duality, including both the duality between monism and dualism and the duality between monism and pluralism.

Second, monistic oneness is realized as the goal or end to be reached from the side of duality or plurality. It is somewhat 'over there', not right here. It is conceived and objectified from the outside. Contrary to this, nondualistic oneness is the ground or root-source realized here and now, from which our lives and activities can properly begin. When we overcome monistic oneness we come to a point which is neither one nor two nor many but which is appropriately referred to as 'zero' or 'nonsubstantial emptiness'. Since the 'zero' is free from any form of duality (and plurality), true oneness can be achieved through the realization of 'zero'. My use of the term 'zero' in this regard may be misleading, however, because it often indicates something negative. But here in this context, I use 'zero' to indicate the principle which is positive and creative as the source from which the one, two, many, and systematic whole itself can emerge. Since I use the term 'zero' in a positive and creative sense, I may call it 'great zero'. Monistic oneness is a kind of oneness which lacks the realization of 'great zero', whereas nondualistic oneness is a kind of oneness which is based on the realization of 'great zero'.

Third, the true Oneness which can be achieved through the realization of 'great zero' should not be objectively conceived. If it is objectified or conceptualized in any way, it is not the real Oneness. An objectified oneness is merely something named 'oneness'. To reach and realize the true Oneness fully, it is necessary to overcome conceptualization and objectification completely. True Oneness is realized only in a nonobjective way by overcoming even 'great zero' objectified as the end. Accordingly, overcoming 'great zero' as the end is a turning point from the objective, aim-seeking approach to the nonobjective, immediate approach, from monistic oneness to nondualistic oneness. Monistic oneness is oneness before the realization of 'great zero', whereas nondualistic oneness is oneness through and beyond the realization of 'great zero'.

Fourth, monistic oneness, being somewhat 'over there', does not immediately include two, many, and the whole. Even though it can be all-inclusive, it is more or less separated from the particularity and multiplicity of actual entities in the world. This is because monistic oneness is usually substantial. However, nondualistic oneness, which is based on the realization of 'great zero', includes all individual things, just as they are, without any modification. This is because in nondualistic oneness conceptualization and objectification are completely overcome. There is no separation between nondualistic oneness and individual things. At this point the one and the many are nondual. Though we should not confuse monism with monotheism, problems involved in monistic oneness in relation to dualistic twoness and pluralistic multiplicity may be applied to monotheism as well.

Buddhism often emphasizes the oneness of body and mind, the oneness of life and death, the oneness of good and evil, and the identity of *samsara* and *nirvana*, Buddha and sentient beings. It also talks about *ekacitta* (one dharma Mind), *ekalapsana* (one Nature), *ekayana* (one Vehicle), and the like. It appears to be quite monistic or 'mono-theistic' from a surface perspective. In view of the difference between monistic oneness and nondualistic oneness as described in the above four points, however, it is clear that the Buddhist notion of oneness is not monistic but nondualistic. As stated before, Gautama Buddha rejected the age-old Vedantic notion of *Brahman* as the sole and enduring reality underlying the universe. Instead, he advocated the law of "dependent co-origination" and the nonselfhood and nonsubstantiality of everything in the universe, including the divine and the human. Even the notion of Buddha is nonsubstantial without enduring, fixed selfhood. Rather, one who awakens to the nonsubstantiality and nonselfhood of everything is called a Buddha.

Nirvana, which is often regarded as the goal of Buddhist life, is not really the goal to be reached at the end of life. Mahayana Buddhism emphasizes, "Do not abide in *samara* or *nirvana*." One should not abide in *samsara*, the endless process of transmigration, but, through the realization of wisdom, should attain *nirvana*, the blissful freedom from transmigration. However, if one remains in *nirvana*, one may enjoy the bliss but forget the suffering of his or her fellow beings who are still involved in the process of *samsara*. Thus it is necessary "not to abide in *nirvana*" by overcoming the attachment to *nirvana*. One should not become attached to *nirvana* as if it were a substantial, fixed entity. In order to fulfil compassion toward one's fellow beings, one should not abide in *nirvana* but return to *samsara*. This means that true *nirvana* in Mahayana Buddhism does not lie in *samsara* or in *nirvana* in a fixed sense of the terms but in a dynamic movement between *samsara* and *nirvana* without any attachment to either, without any reification of either. Accordingly, Mahayana Sutras, particularly in the *Prajnaparamita Sutra*, emphasize detachment from the sacred realm. In a sense this *Sutra* places greater emphasis on the harmfulness of attachment to the sacred realm than that of attachment to the secular realm. It stresses the necessity of detachment from the 'religious' life. This is simply because the attachment to the divine as something substantial is a hindrance for true salvation and because the divine which is substantialized and objectified cannot be the true divine. Yet, Buddhism talks about one Mind, one Nature, and one Dharma. This oneness, however, is not oneness before the realization of 'great zero' but oneness beyond or through the realization of 'great zero'. In short, it is not monistic oneness but nondualistic oneness. In the long history of Buddhism we have encountered difficulties from time to time when we deviated from this nondualistic oneness in our faith.

When the divine, God or Buddha, is believed to be self-affirmative, self-existing, enduring, and substantial, the divine becomes authoritative, commanding, and intolerant. On the contrary, when the divine, God or Buddha, is believed to be self-negating, relational, and nonsubstantial, the divine becomes compassionate, all-loving, and tolerant. I believe all three monotheistic religions (Judaism, Christianity, and Islam) preach the love of God while emphasizing the Absolute Oneness of God. If our friends of these religions place more emphasis on the self-negating, nonsubstantial aspect of their 'God' than on God's self-affirmative authoritative aspect, that is, if the Oneness of God in these monotheistic religions is grasped not as one before the realization of 'great zero', but as one beyond the realization of 'great zero', while thoroughly maintaining their faith in the One Absolute God, they may then overcome serious conflicts with other faiths. In this case, as a correlative attribute of God's love and mercy, the wisdom aspect of God must be more emphasized than the justice aspect of God.

This is my humble proposal to this conference as a Buddhist remedy to the problem of the religious intolerance and human rights. In conclusion, I quote the following words of Buddha:

> Not by hatred is hatred appeased:
> Hatred is appeased by the renouncing of hatred.
> It is so conquered only by love
> This is the law eternal.[2]

BIBLIOGRAPHY

Abe, Masao. "Man and Nature in Christianity and Buddhism," In: Frederick Franck, (ed.). *The Buddha Eye: An Anthology of the Kyoto School*. New York: Crossroad, 1982.

The Dhammapada: The Path of Perfection. Tr. Juan Mascaro. Harmondsworth: Penguin, 1973.

"Elect, Election." In: Everett F. Harrison (ed.). *Baker's Dictionary of Theology* (Grand Rapids, MI: Baker Book House, 1960)

Note: This essay is largely based on Abe's paper "Religious Tolerance and Human Rights, A Buddhist Perspective." In: Leonard Swidler (ed.). *Religious Liberty and Human Rights in Nations and in Religions*. Philadelphia: Ecumenical Press, 1986. Pp. 193-211.

---

[2] *Maha-Vagga*.

CHAPTER XI

Shinkoku (Divine Country) and the Violation of Human Rights

Jacques H. Kamstra

INTRODUCTION

I would like to advance the following thesis about human rights:

> That which is considered most sacred in this world can lead to the most extreme forms of violations of human rights and even to the complete deprivation of all human rights.

It is not difficult to prove this thesis. One might, for example, refer to the idea of sacred or holy land in various cultures and historical periods. The behaviour of colonial powers in their former colonies and that of Serbia at present demonstrate that the emphasis on the sanctity of one's own land leads, for the most part, to the violation of the rights of others: in the past the victims were the slaves and oppressed peoples, today they are raped Bosnian women and uprooted Bosnian Moslems.

In this paper I propose to examine briefly the religious principles of the sacredness of hearth and home, the mother/fatherland, the *heimat*. This will be followed by an examination of some sacred Buddhist principles closely connected with the sacredness of the country. And finally, I will discuss more extensively the idea of *shinkoku* (divine country) as it took shape through many centuries and which led (and still leads) to the violation of human rights and nature outside of the divine country.

HUMAN RIGHTS AND THE HOLY LAND

The current situation in Yugoslavia, where people have not only been uprooted from their own property and the homeland where they were born and have lived but are also deprived of their dignity and right to life, reminds us of the fundamental human right which can be defined as the right to live in one's own country. Every people and every nation claims the right to a country of its own.

Since Israel came into existence, the Jewish people have made their claim to live in the holy country clear. At the same time, the realization of this claim has resulted in depriving many Palestinians of locations and land which they consider to be sacred and to be their own. Thus, the implementation of this sacred claim seems to involve an alliance of the violation of the human rights of others, on the one hand, and the right to live in one's own country, on the other. The arguments on both sides do not only refer to historical claims to the holy land but also to several other religious aspects of this land. Many texts - indeed, the whole theme of the Exodus in the Old Testament - support the claims of the Jewish people to the holy land. God is considered to be the King of his people who guided them people to the promised land. The kingdom of God encompasses the whole world and Jerusalem is the city of the Great King (Mt. 5:34 f.). For Amos, God is sovereign over the Philistines and Aramaeans as well (Amos 9:7). This Exodus theme has become a model of liberation and salvation for the oppressed everywhere in the world: blacks in South Africa, American Indians in Canada and the USA, as well as the poor in Western countries.

It is curious that even the most recent encyclopedias of religion - not to mention other books on comparative religion - do not examine and discuss the topic of holy land in relation to human rights. The research ends with Eliade's investigation of the sacredness of space (Eliade, 20-67). Yet the theme of sacred land as the dwelling place of humans and gods alike is present in the mythology of Africa and the world in general and in many sacred texts. Joel P. Brereton points out that in traditional societies

> the whole land of a culture is normally sacred, and this sacredness is often communicated in the narratives of its foundation. Sometimes the land is uniquely created. The *Kojiki* and *Nihongi* record the traditions of the age of the *kami* when Japan and its way of life were established. According to these texts, the divine pair, Izanagi and Izanami, looked down upon the waters of the yet unformed earth and dipped a jeweled spear into the ocean. From the brine that dripped from the spear the first island of Japan was formed. The divine couple later gave birth to other deities, among them the sun goddess, Amaterasu, whose descendants rule over Japan. Thus Japan is different from all other places: it is the first land, and the land whose way of life is established by the gods. Or a land may become sacred because it is given by a god, like the land of Israel. Or again a land may be established by ritual. According to an early Indian tradition in the Satapatha Brahmana, the land lying to the east of the Sadanira River was unfit for habitation by brahmans. It became fit when the sacrificial fire was carried across the river and established in the land. (Brereton, 526-27)

The land is sometimes considered to be sacred because it conceived to be heaven on earth. The gods dwell in the land together with the human beings created by them. Eliade refers several times in his books to the view that the centre of the land is the *axis mundi* connecting heaven and earth. As the centre of the world, the land is sacred and is very near to heaven. Thus Jerusalem is the *axis mundi* for both Jews and Moslems. The arguments with respect to the former are well-known and, concerning the latter, Brereton draws attention to the fact that

> Jerusalem from the time of Muhammad, has been a holy place for Islam. Although various traditions were attached to the city, it was above all the Prophet's journey there that established its sanctity. One night Muhammad was brought to Jerusalem and to the rock on the Temple mount, and from there he ascended through the heavens to the very presence of God. The mosque of the Dome of the Rock and the establishment of Jerusalem as a place of pilgrimage both expressed and intensified the sanctity of the city. That sanctity was heightened by the discovery of the tokens of Muhammad's journey: his footprints on the rock, the imprint made by his saddle, and even the place where the angel Gabriel flattened the rock before the Prophet's ascent. And it was further intensified by bringing other religiously significant events into connection with it. The stories of Abraham and Isaac, of Melchizedek, king of Salem, and of Jacob's ladder were among the other biblical and non-biblical narratives set there. (Brereton, 527)

With respect to China and Japan, the gods designed the foundations of their capital cities: the administration of the country depended on the accuracy of the geomantic techniques and rituals performed in a city's foundation.[1] In these countries the city became the centre of the country, which in turn was said to be *chung kuo*, the country in the centre of the world. To some Chinese it is "that place where the heavenly and earthly forces of heat, cold, light, dark, etc., were most perfectly harmonized and balanced" (Meyer, 142-43).[2]

When the gods created different peoples in the same country, they also created sacred barriers to separate these peoples from one another and the gods from the common people. Thus, special sacred barriers were created in this holy land to separate the places of the gods from those of the common people just as thresholds in houses and temples separate profane and sacred space. Sometimes the nation or land is sacred because it is the site where the people originated. Thus Kosovo is considered to be sacred Serbian country even though its current population is entirely made up of Albanians to the exclusion of any Serbian inhabitants at all.

---

[1] In China (Sian) and Japan (Kyoto) this was done by Feng-shui, the technique of wind and water. Cf. Meyer, 138-55.

[2] Eliade presents his conclusions about the *axis mundi* as a general human characteristic, not admitting of any exceptions. Japan, with its own concept of 'inwardness', is an exception to this rule. See Kamstra, 1983, 230-41.

BUDDHISM AND THE SACRED COUNTRY

Buddhism includes some very sacred principles which to some extent contribute to the notion of sacredness of the land and the nation. Thus, these very noble principles in Buddhism might lead to violation of human rights.

1.The principle of *ahimsa* is the Buddhist principle of respect for all forms of life and indirectly respect of the land where they live.[3] In China and Japan however, *ahimsa* became limited to only a few animals, for which the ritualiza-

---

[3] Caillat, 152-53, writes that one can deduce from the more ancient texts that the Vedic Indians believed in an inverted "world beyond", where one must suffer from that which one previously inflicted on other beings. While the Vedic brahmans succeeded in devising elaborate rituals in order to escape the consequences of one's (cruel) deeds, they still thought it important that one not injure other creatures (thus that one practise *ahimsa*) in order to avoid retaliation.

He also points out that "... magico-ritualistic attitudes subsided in favour of ethical and mystical values: thus the Upanishadic sages point to the identity of *atman* and *brahman* and praise the man who 'sees the Self in self, sees the Self in everything ....' In this way the traditional, magical fear of retaliation was replaced by a sense of fellow feeling towards all that lives; *ahimsa*, endowed with an indubitably positive value, was expanded into such concepts as 'compassion' (*daya*), a virtue that is required particularly of those who strive after liberation, regardless of the community to which they belong."

Ahimsa is the first Buddhist vow and entails that one avoid eating meat. In a more extreme view, plants that are cultivated and then cut and destroyed for food are also forbidden. The ideal diet, then, consists of fruits, which fall naturally from the trees. *Ahimsa* is thus closely connected to vegetarianism. See Caillat, 152-53. It is well known that for Gandhi *ahimsa* entailed nonviolence.

Nakamura, 1, points out that *ahimsa* was mentioned for the first time in the *Upanishads* (*Chandogya Up.*); it is fourth in the eightfold path and, forbidding killing, the first of the five interdictions. The development of *ahimsa* can be traced back to the time of the rock inscriptions of king Ashoka. Cf. Bloch, 91-93 on the first rock inscription:

> Ici il est défendu de sacrifier en tuant un vivant quelconque. Il est même défendu d'y tenir assemblée; car le roi ami des dieux au regard amical voit un grand mal dans les assemblées. Il y a pourtant des assemblées spéciales que le roi ami des dieux au regard amical considère comme bonnes.
>
> Auparavant, dans la cuisine du roi ami des dieux au regard amical, chaque jour plusieurs centaines de milliers d'animaux étaient tués pour le repas; mais maintenant, au moment où l'on grave ce texte de la Loi, on ne tue (pour le repas) que trois animaux: deux paons, une gazelle; et cette gazelle même, pas constamment. Même ces trois animaux ne seront plus tués désormais.

See further 165-66 for the interdiction against killing animals in the fifth rock inscription.

tion of *hojôe* (the festival of the release of life, i.e., that of fish and birds, celebrated in the eighth month of the lunar calendar) became the symbol (or concession?) for all living creatures. On the precincts of Shinto shrines and Buddhist temples special ponds, the *hojo-ike* (ponds for the release of living creatures) were dug for fish. *Ahimsa* is fundamental not only for human and animal welfare but also for a healthy environment. In Japan this principle is combined with the feeling of purity and respect for the cleanliness of nature. This is a basic belief in Shinto, which in Japan - as is well known - has always been closely intertwined with Buddhism. This double principle looks at every living being in nature as a *kami* (god) and endowed with Buddha-nature. Japan, the country that offers shelter to these sacred beings, is viewed as a holy land. This sacred principle, however, can lead to serious violations of human rights if it entails that those who, because of their occupations, must kill animals or deal in animal carcasses are not only considered to be impure but are discriminated against and deprived of their basic rights.

2. A second principle is that of *anatta*.[4] This doctrine applied only to those who practise meditation and not to the laity who were completely dependent on the religious practices of the monks. Conze points out that this underwent a different development in China:

> The anatta-doctrine implies an extension to the universe. So Tao-an (314-385) once wrote: the plane of the practitioner of Yoga is the mysterious hall in which are assembled those who are attuned to the truth. It is the secret chamber of the immortals who prepare themselves to ascend to Heaven. Hard to climb is this expanse of Non-production, because it is so sublime; hard to cross is this rampart of Non-action, because it is so immense. Through the tiny door, through the mystic opening, the inner court can barely be seen at all. The absolute truth is like the ocean; each day you may bowl out some water, and yet you can never exhaust it. Even so, although countless efforts are made to cause the essence to return to its source, no one can ever fully succeed in doing so. This absolute truth contains the infinite, it is calm, it seems to exist, but cannot be expressed in words. After he has realized it the saint expounds a teaching without words, he dispenses peace, and reveals insight. (pp. 12-13)

---

4 "By realizing *anatta* and its liberation from false individuality, a state is achieved in which all things are Buddha nature." In Mahayana Buddhism this statement applies to all. In Theravada Buddhism, however, this doctrine is quite different, valid only for those who practice meditation and attain Buddhist gnosis. Only the monks "tell of the good they have achieved without invoking their own ego (*atta*) (*Anguttara Nikaya*, iii, 359). Cf. Conze, 11-12: "Nowhere is there any permanence in becoming, and there is no eternity about conditioned things. The skandhas rise, and then dissolve again. Now I know that this is a reason to feel perturbed. No longer do I seek for further becoming. Freed am I of the objects of sense. All my blemishes are now extinct."

Quite often the ruler, as *cakravartin* (who turns the wheel of rebirth) is worshipped as a great saint and virtuous human being. He is the sacred axis of his country and the country's sanctity depends on him. He decides who belongs to this holy land and who does not. It is quite obvious that this can lead to a variety of human rights violations.

3. A third principle closely associated with the preceding is the doctrine of the equality between the enlightened and the so-called *icchantika*, i.e., 'sentient beings who are prevented from attaining enlightenment'.[5] Like the 'taoist' cosmic principle of the superman, Buddha is innate, not only in every Chinese but in every human being, including Indians and the barbarian tyrants who oppressed the Chinese people for many centuries. The Chinese translation of the *Mahaparinirvana sutra* by Fah-hsien and Buddhabhadra in 417-418 A.D.[6] led Tao-sheng (360-432), who livedin the same Lung-kuang-su monastery as Fah-hsien, to proclaim that Buddha nature was also innate in the *icchantika* and not only in the Chinese. This doctrine was formulated and confirmed in another translation of the *Mahaparinirvana sutra* by Dharmaksema in 421 A.D. and in the final (and generally accepted) translation of this sutra by Hsieh Ling-yün (385-433) and his friends Hui-yen and Hui-kuan. Since then this doctrine, claiming that everyone, even heretics and barbarians, are endowed with Buddha nature, has become widely accepted in China. Hence, for centuries Chinese Buddhism never made any distinction between Chinese and non-Chinese, between the faithful and heretics. The refusal of the Chinese communists to grant the Tibetan people the right to live in their own country is in flagrant contradiction of this centuries-old principle.

None of these three sacred Buddhist principles obtained in Europe - it is hardly necessary here to mention the persecution of Jews and Gypsies during the Holocaust. But what is sacrosanct, even in Buddhism, can turn into the most serious violations of human rights. The ideas in Japanese Buddhism concerning the holy land, therefore, can lead to serious discriminations against those who were assumed not to belong to this country. What are these principles?

BUDDHISM AND JAPAN AS THE SACRED COUNTRY

As I have pointed out elsewhere, Buddhism was accepted in Japan only when the role played by Korean immigrants, including those related to the imperial family, was obscured in the official chronicles (1991, 219-47). At the end of the eighth century the writings that described their influence in Japanese society

---

[5] The term *icchantika* means "sentient beings, who being inherently unreceptive to the teachings of the Buddha, will never attain enlightenment". See Blyth/Huntington, 132.

[6] Demiéville, 435-36, points out that this translation led to a "bruit considérable".

were burned.[7] In 815 other writings were also affected. For instance, the *shojiroku*, 'the register of noble families', which dated from 659, was changed to *shinsen-shojiroku*, 'the register of noble families according to a new selection', from which the names of the Korean immigrants were removed (cf. Kamstra, 1967, 222).

These developments had their source in nationalistic considerations that had been formulated some decades earlier during the reign of emperor Shomu (724-749). During this period, the Japanese empire was believed to be endowed with two wings like a phoenix: the law of the rulers (*obo*, raja-dharma), which puts the divine descent of the emperors and the law of Buddha (*buppo*) on the same level. The unity of the state is dependent on both wings and the building of temples and the opening of the eyes of huge Buddha statues had a national interest that would determine the well-being of the state and emperor (cf. McMullin, 13-15). This ideal of the two wings of the state explains why the first step towards introducing Buddhism into Japan had to be taken by the emperor and not by a foreigner.

Since that time the emperor himself became superior to all other human beings in Buddhism. Between 1068 and 1847, by means of a special Buddhist ordination ceremony and ascent of the throne while reciting special Buddhist mantras, all emperors became the Japanese manifestation of Dainichi, the highest Buddha, who in turn is considered to be equal to the Shinto sun goddess Amaterasu. The emperor thus became a kind of Japanese Dalai Lama. Since 1868 and the abolition of this Buddhist ritual, only the divine nature of the emperor in Shinto has been emphasized and his relation to Amaterasu intensified. In spite of Dainichi's relationship to Amaterasu, Shinto nationalists did not wish to accept Buddhism since it was a foreign religion.[8]

Elsewhere I have dealt with Shinto developments up to the present which led to the idea of Japan as the holy land with a divine emperor (cf. Kamstra, 1991), so here I will focus on Buddhism's role in the constitution of Japan as *shinkoku*. Aside from what I described so far, i.e., the ideology of the two wings and the ordination of the emperor as the Japanese equivalent of the Dalai Lama, Japan became a Buddhist *shinkoku*, holy land, particularly in certain writ-

---

[7] During the reign of emperor Kammu in particular several documents on Korean influence were burned. Kitabatake Chikafusa (1293-1354) confirms this in his book *Jinnoshotoki* (The History of the Succession of the Divine Monarchs), when he writes, "The documents which established that Japan belonged in ancient times to the three Han-states (Ma-han, Chin-han and Pyon-han [present-day Korea]) were burned under emperor Kammu." See Kamstra, 1967, 222.

[8] This Buddhist ordination explains why the Shinto ordination turning the emperor into a Shinto god did not occur for many centuries. For more details concerning the Buddhist ordination of the emperor (*sokui kanjo*) see Kamikawa, 243-80.

ings and the ideology of some Buddhist sects. The theme in these writings is the mandalization of Japan's space (particularly mountains) on the one hand and on the other the idea of Japan being the only proper place of salvation and utmost purity.

The Mandalization of Japan's Space

In 1982 Grapard described how Japan had become a Buddhist mandalized country over the course of the centuries. The whole process started with the sacralization of mountains on the one hand and the description in Buddhist sutras of holy and often distant lands on the other. Grapard gives a simple explanation of the former:

> Human activity belonged to the plains, where people lived; mountains were untouched and were areas of nonactivity. Corpses were abandoned or buried on mountains; hence the mountain was seen as a space whose nature was Other (not belonging to common categories of experience within the profane). (Grapard, 200)

Japanese agricultural and ancestral festivals, therefore, consist in dramatic processions to and from mountains (Kamstra, 1983, 231). The oldest history of Buddhism in Japan on the other hand testifies to the belief in several kinds of holy and hence distant lands, of which the oldest representation is an embroidery showing the dwelling-place of *hijiri* in the 'land of heavenly long life', the *tenjukoku-mandara*. This is a mixture of Taoist belief in long life and a Buddhist heaven of sorts. Soon, i.e., in the sixth and seventh centuries, the Tusita heaven of Maitreya and the Pure Land became (and continue to be) quite popular (Kamstra, 1967, 168, 169 n. 5, 1). Both the Chinese and the Japanese, unlike most Christians, view these heavens as a distant place on earth, lying mostly to the West. Hence Amitabha's *sukhavati* or Pure Land is also called the Western Paradise (Abegg, 35-36). In Japanese Buddhism these two ideas of the holy mountain and of the Buddhist Pure Land were united in the idea of Japan as the mandalized country. Grapard refers to Kukai who once wrote: "Who is within illusion resides in a polluted space; he who awakens resides in a pure space, which is also called Pure Land."(cf. Grapard, 208) Those who practice Shingon or Tendai Tantrism need a mandala in order to reach enlightenment.

> A practitioner of Esoteric Buddhism 'enters' a mandala through its gate, invokes the divinities which are represented, and identifies with them one after the other until reaching the center, in which there is a representation of the cosmic Buddha from which all other Buddhas and their lands emanate. The practitioner goes from the manifestation to the source, from the form to the essence, and finally reaches the realization that form and essence are two-but-not-two. (Grapard, 209).

Through meditation the absolute becomes integrated with the relative, the metaphysical with the physical, and the eternal ideal with transitory reality.

This concept did not lead to the Buddhist differentiation between relative and absolute truth, between *samvrti* and *paramartha*, but to their identification, that is, to a sacralization of different areas: sacred mountains were turned into huge mandalas. This was also extended to other sacred mountains, particularly those in Shinto[9] until finally Japan as a whole came to be viewed as a sacred space. Thus Japan became a divine country (*shinkoku*) for Japanese Buddhism as well. A good example of this process is the text *Hachiman* ('lord of the country') *Gudokun* written between 1301 and 1304:

> This land Akitsushima (i.e., Japan) is the noble space of the manifestation of more than three thousand divinities; it is the superior space of the spreading of the saintly teachings of the greater and lesser vehicles, true and temporary alike ... Since this country is by nature the Original Country of the Great Sun [Mahavairocana, or Dainichi no honkoku/Dai nipponkoku, but also the Shinto goddess Amaterasu], the eight Provinces of Bando correspond to the eight petals of the lotus in the Whomb mandala, and the Nine Regions (Kyushu) of the Western Sea correspond to the nine parts of the Diamond mandala; the yin and yang aspects correspond to the mandalas in their aspect of Principle and Wisdom. Those who inhabit this country are the descendants of Izanami and Izanagi, and are the heirs of the original nature, the Tathata in its body of essence. (Grapard, 214)

This text demonstrates that already in the fourteenth century the idea of Japan as a holy country was firmly established and confirmed by other sacred Shinto texts such as the *Kokiki* and the *Nihonshoki*. The sacredness of the country included Buddhist monasteries and temples as well as Shinto shrines.

The text *Jinnoshotoki* shows that in 1338 the idea of Japan as a divine country was generally accepted. Japan was now a country where even sacred places and mountains in other parts of the world by a "manipulation of space" "had come flying in and landed with all the pomp that one can imagine accompanying such an event" (*ibid.*, 218). Thus, Omine is in fact the southwestern area of the Diamond cavern (= Vulture's Peak), located in the southeast of the country where Buddha was born. A long time ago, Kimpusen was a mountain in China and the residence of the bodhisattva Vajragarbha (Zao). "Kumano, the Pure Land of Avalokitesvara (Kannon), flew in from India, making stops in

[9] Grapard, 210, describes some other details of this development. Kukai (774-835), the founder of the Shingon sect, considered Mt. Futara to be the cosmic center, while Shobo (839-909), founder of the Shugendo sect, developed the doctrine that sacred space began at Mt. Yoshino. In the eleventh century, this mountain was considered to be the site of Maitreya's appearance. In 1180 the *Shozan engi* described Mt. Yoshino as the Vajradhatu and Garbhadatu mandalas.

China, Kyushu (at Hikosan), and Shikoku, before reaching the Kii peninsula, where it landed and remained" (*ibid.*, 218). As such, Japan is the very Lotus sutra and contains more temples than there are words in this sutra (cf. *ibid.*, 218 ff.).

Japan as the only Place of Salvation: Nichiren

In spite of its renunciation of its Korean roots, Buddhism has always been viewed as a foreign religion. During the Kamakura period the great founders of new sects went to China in order to become inspired with new ideas, particularly during the thirteenth century. Some monks discovered new ways of salvation which they exemplified to such an extent that they became popular among the common people.[10]

During this period, a monk, who called himself Nichiren, 'the sun lotus', (1222-1282),[11] believed that he had discovered the elements of a genuine Japanese Buddhism in Japan itself. Nichiren did not think it necessary to travel to China in order to broaden his knowledge of Buddhism in general and of the Lotus sutra in particular, for, as we have pointed out, Japan itself was believed to be equal to the Lotus sutra. Nichiren taught that Buddha's doctrine had been revealed to humankind via two lines: 1) an exoteric tradition originating in India and China, taught by many masters in Japan, and 2) an esoteric, intrinsic and direct line that depended on the immediate revelation of Buddha in his (Nichiren's) own heart.[12] His preaching was therefore superior to that of his contemporaries who had acquired their extensive Buddhist knowledge with great difficulty in China.

Nichiren's direct knowledge of Buddha's teachings made Japan independent of foreign influence with regard to the doctrine of Buddha. He tied his doctrine to what he called the *Guzu no goko*, the five ropes of the propagation (of Buddhism). These are as follows:

1. *kyo* (doctrine). The best doctrine to lead people to happiness is the Lotus sutra.
2. *ki* (capacity of the mind). This sutra was explained to the people living under the worst conditions.

[10] This is called Kamakura Buddhism, after the period (1185-1333) in which it came into being. Cf. Kamstra, 1988, 72-93.

[11] The sun refers to his country, *Nihon* (the origin of the sun) and Lotus refers to the Buddhist sutra that he considered to be Buddhism's highest expression: the Lotus sutra. For Nichiren's biography cf. Kamstra, 1988, 87-89.

[12] More precisely, in the heart of Visista-Caritra (described in the Lotus sutra as the leader of the bodhisattvas) with whom Nichiren identified himself.

3. *ji* (time). The appropriate time for spreading this teaching is now, during the decay of the Law (*mappo*).
4. *koku* (country). Japan is the most suitable place for such propagation.
5. *jo* (order, arrangement). The popularity of the provisional Mahayana paves the way to the true Mahayana.[13]
During Nichiren's lifetime these five ropes, which shortened the road to paradise considerably, appealed chiefly to common people. The true doctrine preached by a Japanese in a country considered to be the earthly paradise at a time believed to be the fulfilment of all times are all elements which can be recalled in evil times.

Buddhism since 1945

The above, in fact, has been occurring, *inter alia*, since 1945 when MacArthur, in destroying State Shinto, created new room for Nichiren's *shinkoku* ideas. Especially Toda Josei, the cofounder of the Soka Gakkai, a new Nichiren movement, emphasized those elements in Nichiren's teaching that concerned Japan as the most suitable place for salvation. An immense temple in the proximity of Mt. Fuji was be the symbol of Japan as the only holy place on earth. This temple would replace the grand shrine of Isé. As he wrote in his *obutsumyogoron*:

> The purpose of our national policy is the foundation of a great national temple, a national monument of political and religious importance. Policy and religion belong together and have to unite the emperor and his people in the belief in the teachings of Nichiren. Hence politicians by all means and in name of the emperor should do their very best for the general spread of the true Buddhist doctrine. They will have to construct a temple on grounds determined by them which will be the largest and the most beautiful of the world. It will have to be built for all peoples of the world who out of respect for the teachings of Nichiren will pilgrimage to Japan. (Kamstra, 1960, 102-03)

The effects of Toda's writings are well known: between 1952 and 1960 the movement gained more than seven million members. Since 1960 the Soka Gakkai has tried to connect its Lotus sutra with the first deity of State Shinto: the sungoddess Amaterasu. The movement's manual reads:

---

[13] For more details see the *Shakubuku kyoten*, 1954, 118-24; 1969, 95-98. For the *kyohan* of Nichiren see Taya, 127c; Blyth, 92. Nichiren's contemporaries employed similar criteria as well. Shinran (1173-1262) mentions three of these identifying marks, but he was opposed to the interference of the state in monastic rules and excluded nationalism from his teachings. What he calls sacred and Pure Land have nothing in common with Nichiren's identifying mark of *koku*. Cf. Marra, 289.

> Now during the last war Japan did raise the nation as a whole in reverence to Amaterasu Omikami (i.e. the Great Goddess Amaterasu) and fought against America which reveres the philosophy of Western Europe. This resulted in a ruthless defeat of the war. Why did Amaterasu Omikami, though as *ujigami* she was the general, not protect Japan? To answer this question in short: "because Amaterasu Omikami did not stay anymore in Japan." After having referred to Nichiren's sayings the text continues: "This means that Amaterasu Omikami is the tutelary deity of the *Lotus sutra*. She does not live in a country where the dharma is reviled. Now, because there was no taste of the flavour of the dharma, all the immortals and good gods not to mention Amaterasu left Japan. Consequently there are here no *kami* in the shrines and in the *kamifuda*. On the contrary devils and evil spirits who ruin the people inhabit them. Japan had to experience the unprecedented heavy defeat of the war. Even if one agrees on this point, Amaterasu is not to blame for it. If the whole nation of Japan loses no time in becoming converted to the true Law (i.e. the *Lotus sutra*), Amaterasu Omikami will be delighted. It is our duty to speed up the propagation and dissemination (of the true Law) and to pray for the return of Amaterasu Omikami and the other gods. (Kamstra, 1989; cf. *Shakubuku kyoten*, 190)

Thus, in this "Buddhist" defense of Amaterasu the *Lotus sutra* became the modern *shintai*, i.e., the divine body of Amaterasu and all the other gods.

It is clear that Nichiren was not the only one who was convinced that Japan is heaven, the Pure Land, and the dwelling place of gods, Buddhas and Bodhisattvas. The idea of Japan as a *shinkoku* is as old as the *Kojiki*, which describes this holy land as originating from the sexual union of the divine couple Izanami and Izanagi. It became reinforced mainly through Neo-Confucian developments in Shinto as well as by the Buddhist doctrines described here. The Buddhist idea of Japan as the holy land gave added impetus to Shinto in its development into State Shinto. This idea continues to claim adherents: many recent religions in Japan teach that only Japan as *shinkoku*, the only paradise on earth, is where salvation and even freedom of environmental pollution can be realized and guaranteed (Kamstra, 1991, 191).

THE HOLY LAND VERSUS THE UNHOLY: FOREIGNERS AND FOREIGN COUNTRIES

The idea of Japan as divine country evokes the idea that foreign countries and foreigners themselves are believed to be unholy, and do not merit any form of ethical treatment in war or in economics. In Japan therefore, there are many people, such as the Eta and the Koreans, who are despised and deprived of their human rights because they do not belong to the holy land. Eta was the former name for descendants of Korean and Chinese foreigners who introduced Buddhism into Japan from abroad. In Japan their fate has been comparable to that of many oppressed minorities throughout history and at present in the world.

They were deprived of all their civil rights through special measures and now number about two and a half million outcasts. Written in Chinese characters, the word Eta means 'dung' and currently they are referred to as *burakumin* or *shinheimin* i.e. 'outcasts' or 'new civilians'.[14] During the period between 1603 and 1868 particularly, but even at present, these people were designated in the Japanese language by animal words and counters: they are not dignified with the status of human beings. Hence, they are also called *hinin*, nonhumans.

In addition to these 'new civilians', Japan has a Korean population numbering about 600,000, the remainder of the 2.4 million Koreans deported to Japan as slaves during the Japanese occupation of Korea. This group, however, does not enjoy the same rights as the Japanese. They are forced to abandon their Korean identity by adopting Japanese names and are refused homes. Their children may not be educated in their own Korean language and they are forced to register by means of the taking of hated fingerprints.[15]

The holiness of the country implies that respect for nature and human solidarity with nature ends at Japan's borders. On the one hand, Japan is closed to foreign enterprise and industries and on the other hand, the acts committed by the Japanese during World War II against foreigners and their countries seems to be legitimized by this idea. Their actions have often been glossed over: e.g., the bombing of Nanching, the cruelties in the Japanese concentration camps, the chemical experiments with Western prisoners of war in Manchuria. The same idea also legitimizes the 'crimes' against the environment, e.g., overfishing in the Pacific Ocean, whaling, logging in the Philippines, Malaysia and in South America, which endangers even the living conditions in these countries. All this could be called violations of human rights due to a lack of respect for foreign countries.

The same can also be said with respect to the dishonest industrial competition and dumping of industrial goods in Western countries. The ideology behind the cut-throat competition over European video recorders with Phillips, European cars, the microchip producers of the Silicon Valley, etc., does not seem to differ much from that of the kamikaze pilots of World War II: those who inhabit an unholy world do not merit human treatment and human rights.[16]

Is there a way out? The radical Nicheren Buddhist emphasis on Japan as the only holy country of the world is not shared by many other Buddhist sects such

[14] For more details see Shigeaki Ninomiya, 47-153.

[15] For a short and systematic recapitulation of the oppression of Koreans during Japan's history see Terazono, 54-59.

[16] For a detailed description of this competitive warfare since 1945, planned and organized by the Japanese Ministry of Trade and Industry see Wolf, 1983 and Van Marion, 1992.

as Tendai, Shingon, Jodo, and Zen Buddhism in particular. These extend the mandalization of space to include the whole universe, including any 'sentient being' which is intrinsically able to acquire full Buddhahood. This is in accordance with the Buddhist saying: *issai mina ku*, i.e., all sentient beings are "Emptiness' or are endowed with Buddha nature. This universal principle which guarantees the preservation of human rights in Buddhist countries includes Eta, Koreans, members of foreign nations and companies and Christians, even though the latter are believed to be endowed with the *anima naturaliter christiana*, the soul that by nature is not Buddhist but Christian.

BIBLIOGRAPHY

Abegg, E. "Der Buddha Maitreya." In: *Mitteilungen der Schweizerischen Gesellschaft der Freunde Ostasiatischer Kultur*, VII. (1945). Pp. 7-37.

Bloch, J. *Les Inscriptions d'Asoka*. Paris, 1950.

Blyth, R.H. and Huntington R. *Japanese-English Buddhist Dictionary*. Tokyo, 1965.

Brereton, P. "Sacred Space." In: M. Eliade and V. Turner (eds.). *The Encyclopedia of Religion*, Vol. 12. New York, 1987. Pp. 526-35.

Caillat, C. "Ahimsa." In: M. Eliade and V. Turner (eds.). *The Encyclopedia of Religion*, Vol. 1. New York, 1987. Pp. 152-53.

Conze, E. *Buddhist Meditation*. London, 1959.

Demiéville, P. *L'Inde Classique*. Paris, 1953.

Eliade, M. *The Sacred and the Profane: The Nature of Religion*. New York, 1959. Pp. 20-67.

Grapard, A.G. "Flying Mountains and Walkers of Emptiness: Toward a Definition of Sacred Space in Japanese Religions." *History of Religions* 21 (1982): 195-221.

Kamikawa, M. "Accession Rituals and Buddhism in Medieval Japan." *Japanese Journal of Religious Studies* 17 (1990): 243-80.

Kamstra, J.H. "Japans grösste Gefahr - die Sokagakkai." *Zeitschrift für Missionswissenschaft und Religionswissenschaft* 44 (1960): 41-51; 98-106.

——. *Encounter or Syncretism?* Leiden, 1967.

——. "Between Inwardness and Axis Mundi: Analysis of some Japanese Rituals and their Background." N.T.T. 37 (1983): 230-41.

——. *De Japanse religie: Een fenomenale godsdienst*. Hilversum, 1988.

——. "Changes in Buddhist Attitudes towards Other Religions: The Case of the Soka Gakkai." *Zeitschrift für Missionswissenschaft und Religionswissenschaft* 73 (1989): 28-61.

——. "Religion in the Era of Environmental Pollution: The New New-religions in Japan." *Zeitschrift für Missionswissenschaft und Religionswissenschaft* 74 (1990): 176-92.

——. "Japans Fundamentalisme." In: P. Boele van Hensbroek, (ed.). *Naar de Letter: Beschouwingen over Fundamentalisme*. Utrecht, 1991.

Marra, M. "The Development of Mappo Thought in Japan (II)." *Japanese Journal of Religious Studies* 15 (1988): 287-305.

McMullin, N. "Historical and Historiographical Issues in the Study of Pre-modern Japanese Religions." *Japanese Journal of Religious Studies* 16 (1989): 1-40.

Meyer, J.F. "Feng-shui of the Chinese City." *History of Religions* 18 (1978): 138-55.
Nakamura, H. *Bukkyôgo Daijiten*, Vol. 1. Tokyo, 1975.
Ninomiya, S. "An Inquiry Concerning the Origin, Development, and Present Situation of the Eta in relation to the History of Social Classes in Japan." In: *The Transactions of the Asiatic Society*. Second Series, Vol. X. 1933: 47-153.
Shakubuku Kyoten. Soka Gakkai, under supervision of J. Toda. Tokyo, 1954; under supervision of D. Ikeda. Tokyo, 1969.
Taya, R. *Bukkyo-gaku Jiten*. Tokyo, 1957.
Terazono, Y. *et al.* (eds.). *Brennpunkte in Kirche und Theologie Japans*. Neukirchen, 1988.
Van Marion, M.F. *Liberal Trade and Japan: The Incompatibility Issue in Electronics*. Groningen, 1992.
Wolf, M. *The Japanese Conspiracy*. London, 1983.

CHAPTER XII

Restricted Freedom in Europe

The Case of Religious Sects

Reender Kranenborg

INTRODUCTION

Since 1971, when the movement Free the Children of God[1] was founded, the attitude towards sects (new religious movements) has become increasingly negative. In some circles these groups were considered to be very dangerous and government measures were thought to be necessary. Several governments investigated the options available to them. In Europe the European Parliament and the Council of Europe were asked to take action and they have addressed the issue.

The question that arose when such measures were sought was whether taking action against sects was a violation of the right to freedom of religion. Since every citizen has the right to confess and practise his belief in freedom, any restriction of this fundamental right conflicts with human rights. Thus taking measures against sects does indeed present problems in relation to the issue of human rights. In this article we will consider the proclamations of the European Parliament and Council of Europe and ask if such measures do conflict with the right to freedom of religion (which these institutions also profess) or constitutes a violation of human rights.

In this context we need to refer to three important texts:

1) Art. 18 of the United Nations Universal Declaration of Human Rights:

> everyone has the right to freedom of thought, conscience and religion; this right includes freedom to change his religion or belief, and freedom, either alone or in community with others and in public or private, to manifest his religion or belief in teaching, practice, worship and observance.

[1] This was the first parents' organisation against sects, founded by Ted Patrick in the USA.

2) Art. 9 of the European Convention for the Protection of Human Rights and Fundamental Freedoms:

a) Cf. art. 18 of the UN Declaration.
b) Freedom to manifest one's religion or beliefs shall be subject only to such limitations as are prescribed by law and are necessary in a democratic society in the interests of public safety, for the protection of public order, health or morals, or for the protection of the rights and freedoms of others.

3) Art. 18 of the United Nations International Covenant on Civil and Political Rights:

a) Part 1 and 3 are the same as in art. 9 of the European Convention.
b) Part 2: No one shall be subject to coercion which would impair his freedom to have or to adopt a religion or belief of his choice. (cf. Laqueur and Rubin)

SECTS VIOLATE HUMAN RIGHTS

The decade of the sixties witnessed the rise of several new religious movements, called 'sects' by many,[2] in the Western world. Whereas in the beginning this phenomenon was only noted and not considered to be dangerous, this attitude has been changing since 1971. More and more, parents and friends of members of sects encountered difficulties with their child's or friend's membership in such a group; the process of becoming a member and his/her treatment once inside the group were very important points of discussion. It was also discovered that ex-members were disoriented or psychologically damaged. Thus both in Europe and the USA several parents' organisations were founded, known as 'anti-cult movements'. The collective suicide that occurred in Guyana in 1978 reinforced the negative image of sects as 'dangerous and destructive' and affirmed the anti-cult movements' view of sects. As a result, the appeal for governments to take action became much more intense. In many countries governments established committees to study the necessity of such measures.

The criticism made by anti-cult groups was fierce. The fundamental idea was (and is) that sects are dangerous and undemocratic. Their presentation of themselves is misleading: they pretend to offer something different from what they actually do (in many cases omitting the name of the group from such a presentation). Future members are subjected to deceptive techniques and new members are not allowed to go or to have any contact with their parents. Sects, it is claimed, employ continuous brainwashing; the member is exploited and has a

---

[2] The word 'sect' has negative connotations and I therefore prefer the term 'new religious movement'. I use the term in this article only because it is the term employed by anti-cult movements and its use here is not intended in any pejorative sense.

very difficult life within the group. Ex-members are psychologically damaged to such a degree that they can no longer function in society. As formulated in the Declaration of Paris,[3]

> It was noted that these new movements' religious claims often defend them from criticism by a public which believes all religion to be good. In fact, with their elitist and totalitarian claims, some of them are a threat to freedom.
> Religious freedom has traditionally protected the individual from oppressive institutions, but these movements use the term "religious freedom" to attack the individuals who criticise them.
> For the sake of their own closed communities they destroy normal family relationships.
> In the name of loyalty, they preach and enforce an absolute surrender to a "Fuehrer" figure, who is the characteristic center of such groups. In the name of liberty, they enslave their recruits.
> Under the pretext of developing consciousness, they suppress the conscience, intelligence and the wills of their converts.

The Dutch parents' organisation, *Samenwerkende Ouders Sekteleden*,[4] agreed with this view; their pamphlets charged sects with "deceptive propaganda", "manipulation", "depersonalisation" (members undergo a radical change of life-style, receive new names, move to foreign countries, etc.). These pamphlets state further that sects inflict psychological damage on their members (through the use of meditation techniques and other methods), issue intolerable instructions ("people are sometimes compelled to commit suicide") and make members completely dependent on the group or leader. Ex-members are disoriented and require extensive treatment after leaving such groups.[5]

It is quite clear, these organisations claim, that sects violate the individual right of people to be free, including the freedom to choose a religion. Moreover, sects infringe on the laws of several countries. Thus, measures to restrict or even to prohibit such dangerous groups are necessary. According to the anti-cult movement, such measures do not conflict with the right to freedom of religion. First of all, they make an important distinction between sects and religions. Sects are seen as 'pseudo-religious' or suspected of using religion as a cover for illegal or dubious practices (as can be seen in the Paris declaration). Sects can-

---

[3] In December 1980 the first international meeting of parents' organisations was held. They intended to found a permanent international body but this did not emerge. At the end of the meeting, however, they did formulate a declaration.

[4] This organisation (*SOS* = "Parents of Members of Sects Working Together") was founded in 1979.

[5] On the *Samenwerkende Ouders Sekteleden* see Kranenborg, 1993.

not, therefore, claim the same legitimacy and thus the same rights as churches and other religions. Secondly, when the religious claims of sects are taken seriously, a distinction is made between belief and practice. There can, according to the anti-cult movement, be no discussion on a cult's articles of faith - their content and value cannot be evaluated by outsiders. The practices in which cults engage, however, are clear enough and need to be restrained. Restraint on such practices will not conflict with the freedom of religion. Thirdly, a distinction is made between old and new religious movements. Under the former category belong the churches and religions that enjoy a long history and societal acceptance in society; the latter category is comprised of the sects and their importance and value is as yet unclear. It is not enough simply to accept all groups and movements that call themselves religious and to take them seriously. A fundamental investigation is necessary. Since many governments did not want to take action against sects, some of the anti-cult movements took the initiative themselves and began the so-called 'deprogramming' treatment.

This view requires some response. First, one should note that their view of sects is unclear. They have neglected to give an adequate definition of the term 'sect' and to indicate which groups are to be seen as sects. Secondly, the pamphlets betray a dominant unjustified generalisation. Research has shown that the charges concern, for the most part, a limited number of movements (mainly the Unification Church); nevertheless, these charges are seen as applying to all sects.[6] Thirdly, one can see that the one-sided negative interpretation is based exclusively on the views of members of the anti-cult movements. This raises the following question: do the problems to which they refer exist in fact or only in the perception of some people? To cite an example, if somebody joins a sect and quits his studies, does he do so because he has been brainwashed or because he is attracted by a religious ideal and thus chooses a different way of life? Either choice would be painful for parents, but the fact that it is painful does not provide grounds for judging sects or religious movements as definitely negative. Fourthly, not everybody experiences the membership of relatives and friends in sects as negative. This is true only of a minority, although that minority is very active.

Thus, the statement that sects conflict with the right of religious freedom by their existence and activities is open to question. It is rather the case that this conflict is found in the anti-cult movements themselves. Not to qualify a sect as a religion is untenable. To the outsider, some ideas and activities may seem strange, but that fact does not disqualify an organisation from being called a religion. Sects are religious movements and should be respected as such. Not

---

[6] In most cases, these charges can be limited to the following groups: the Unification Church, Hare Krishna Movement, Scientology, Children of God and some small independent groups. Cf. Kranenborg, 1984.

viewing sects as religions and consequently denying them the freedom granted to religions conflicts with the human right to choose and propagate one's own convictions. It is possible that this conflicts with art. 11 and 12 of the *Universal Declaration of Human Rights* as well.

It is incorrect to differentiate between beliefs and ideas on the one hand and practices on the other, arguing that the former are to be considered free on the basis of freedom of religion and the latter to lie outside the domain of such freedom and need to be restricted. It is essential to a conviction that it be put into practice; belief does not only concern thought but also - and even more so - action. The enactment of legal measures against practices, based on such a separation, gives rise to a conflict with the freedom of religion. For the *Universal Declaration of Human Rights* clearly states that people are allowed to practise their belief. This does not mean that religious practices are beyond criticism or that religious practices are always good and healthy - they are subject to scrutiny as well. Moreover, religious practices are also limited by their possible threat to other human rights. Finally, it is also possible that some practices can conflict with existing national laws. Nevertheless, it is unjustified to exclude religious practices from freedom of religion or to prejudge them.

Furthermore, it is clear that one cannot argue on the basis of the difference between old and new religions: old religions began as new ones. In addition, several of the 'new' groups are not new at all but are continuations of older elements or traditions.[7] The 'newness' of something does not constitute sufficient grounds to launch an investigation; conversely, 'old' is no guarantee of truth and reliability. Finally, deprogramming, which includes kidnapping, isolation and pressure, is an obvious violation of the fundamental human right of freedom (art. 4 and 5). Of course, it is equally clear that the 'indoctrination' (called 'programming' by the anti-cult movement) that takes place in many groups (not only religious ones) may also conflict with human rights.

THE RESOLUTION OF THE EUROPEAN PARLIAMENT

According to the anti-cult movement, it is important that governments investigate sects and their practices and take legal measures to control their activities, in order to protect citizens. Governments have carried out such investigations in many countries, including the Netherlands. Alarmed by the *Samenwerkende Ouders Sekteleden*, the Dutch government asked a parliamentary commission to carry out a thorough investigation. A report prepared in 1984 concluded that

---

[7] The Hare Krishna Movement, while new in the West, has a tradition extending back to the fifteenth century in India. Many evangelical groups may be new, but they claim to be a legitimate and true continuation of the old truth, closer, in fact, to the latter than the official churches, in their view, are.

there was no need for special laws concerning sects in relation to public mental health (cf. Witteveen). The existing laws were sufficient in case transgressions occurred or sects engaged in strange practices. More laws could entail a restriction of the freedom of religion. Although sects encountered stronger opposition in other countries and problems related to sects and their members were recognised, for the most part no legal action was taken against these groups, except occasionally.[8]

Supporters of legal measures against sects also approached the European Parliament, since the importance of regulating sects required an international body for such measures. From the European Parliament the issue received the attention that had been lacking in the case of the national parliaments. The former not only recognised the problems relating to sects but also pleaded for legal measures to be taken. No government had done so up until that point and this state of affairs continues at present.

On 19 August 1983 R. Cottrell presented his "Motion for a Resolution on the Activity of certain[9] new Religious Movements within the European Community" and on 22 May 1984 the proposed resolution was accepted, with several amendments but essentially unchanged.[10] Cottrell's motivation and argumentation stems from the views of the anti-cult movements. Although he does point out that the reason for the resolution resulted from "the distress caused by Sun Myung Moon's Unification Church" and its activities and in the explanation mentions some other groups (Children of God, Hare Krishna Movement, Movement of Bhagwan Shri Rajneesh, Scientology) in a negative way, he nevertheless speaks of sects in a very general way. The resolution repeatedly speaks of "these" or "such movements", without any specification. Cottrell mentions the collective suicide in Guyana, cases of fraud and other crimes of a financial nature (he mentions Moon's financial problems in the USA and his relations with the Central Intelligence Agency) and relates how sects cause family grief and psychologically damage their members. Cottrell further criticises the "love-

---

[8] In some countries the Scientology Church was judged to be illegal and in many cases it was required to pay heavy fines for the nonpayment of taxes.

[9] In the Dutch text the word "certain" is missing; without this word the motion gets a much wider influence!

[10] Cottrell's report is known as a "Motion for a Resolution", Code PE 82.322/rev. The resolution is coded as PE 90/562. For the text of the resolution, see Appendix III at the end of this volume.

bombing" (i.e., brainwashing)[11] recruitment methods and draws attention to the fact that young people who become members abandon their studies and work, break with their families and parents, are required to live and work in foreign countries, cannot leave the group, are exploited, undergo radical mental changes, are no longer fit to re-enter normal society, etc. Cottrell is acquainted with other views on sects, such as those that were published in E. Barker's studies of the Unification Church but nevertheless fails to take these into account.[12]

Although Cottrell argues for legal measures, he clearly states that it is not his intention to interfere with the right to religious freedom, even in the case of very extreme beliefs. He maintains, however, that attention should be paid to the practices in which these sects engage, that they should be investigated, analyzed, restricted or prohibited, if necessary. As it states in the resolution:

> ... having regard to the concern felt by individuals and families in the Community at the activities of certain organisations described as 'new religious movements' insofar as their practices infringe on human and civil rights and are detrimental to the position in society of those affected;
> stressing that full freedom of religion and opinion is a principle in the Member States and that the Community Institutions therefore have no right to judge the value of either religious beliefs in general or individual religious practices;
> convinced that in this instance, the validity of religious beliefs is not in question, but rather the lawfulness of the practices used to recruit new members and the treatment they receive ....[13]

Cottrell requests that governments make an inventory of and evaluate the activities of the new religious movements in order to protect the citizens of these countries. He thinks it is necessary that the countries of Europe should work together, so that "the Council of Europe ... will guarantee the individual effective protection from the machinations of these movements and their physical and moral coercion."

The resolution of the European Parliament offers some criteria that European governments can use when investigating sects:

[11] Here he is referring to the recruitment method employed by the Moonies and Children of God in some situations: they receive future members very kindly and since these mostly young people are unable to leave the group, they become members against their wishes.

[12] Cf. E. Barker, *The Making of the Moonie* and other studies on new religious movements.

[13] Here the resolution fails to indicate which groups and/or activities are intended.

a) persons under the age of majority should not be induced on becoming a member of a movement to make a solemn long-term commitment that will determine the course of their lives;
b) there should be an adequate period of reflection on the financial or personal commitment involved;
c) after joining an organisation contacts must be allowed time with family and friends;
d) members who have already commenced a course of education must not be prevented from completing it;
e) the following rights of the individual must be respected:
- the right to leave a movement unhindered;
- the right to contact family and friends in person or by letter and telephone;
- the right to seek independent advice, legal or otherwise;
- the right to seek medical attention at any time;
f) no one may be incited to break any law, particularly with regard to fund-raising, for example by begging or prostitution;[14]
g) movements may not extract permanent commitments from potential recruits, for example students or tourists, who are visitors to a country in which they are not resident;[15]
h) during recruitment, the name and principles of the movement should always be made immediately clear;[16]
i) such movements must inform the competent authorities on request of the address or whereabouts of individual members;
j) new religious movements must ensure that individuals dependent on them and working on their behalf receive the social security benefits provided in the Member States in which they live or work;

---

[14] "Begging" refers to the selling of books and leaflets that are free; but it is possible to give a donation - as is the case with groups other than sects. "Prostitution" refers to the "flirty fishing" method of the Children of God: the women of the group were to recruit male members by means of their bodies. This is, indeed, a kind of prostitution.

[15] Cottrell has in mind here the so-called 'backpack tourists', young people from Europe travelling in the U.S.A. and meeting some members of the Unification Church who approach them in a very friendly way and invite them to participate in a free weekend somewhere far from the city. Once present in that situation, it is said, it is impossible for them to escape the Moonie atmosphere and thus after some time they become members of the Church. Indeed, such situations have happened but only exceptionally and not as a rule.

[16] This concerns those groups that work through cover organisations. The Unification Church has many of these and the Church of Scientology also works through them. Sometimes groups change their names: the Children of God became the Family of Love and the Divine Light Mission became Elan Vital, etc..

k) if a member travels abroad in pursuit of the interests of a movement, it must accept responsibility for bringing the individual home, especially in the event of illness;
l) telephone calls and letters from members' families must be immediately passed on to them;
m) where recruits have children, movements must do their utmost to further their education and health, and avoid any circumstances in which the children's well-being might be at risk.

These criteria make clear that the resolution is based on the anti-sect ideology of the anti-cult movements. This resolution encountered protests from many different sides before it was passed. Although the Unification Church, which felt itself threatened by it, was very heavily engaged in stimulating protest (several letters are very similar in terminology and formulation), it was not alone. Other organisations reacted as well, since they viewed it as a potential threat to the freedom of religion and because the resolution was very one-sided. These organisations included churches, Councils of Churches (from the Netherlands, France, Great Britain), universities, political organisations. Many of the protests were formulated in the following ways: "an unprecedented assault on religious freedom in Europe"; "the threat to all religions created by the proposal pending before the European Parliament"; "...which would deny to new religious movements rights which no one would dare to deny to the mainline churches and religions"; "...will interfere with the religious freedom of individuals in European countries"; "any religion or ideology can have 'negative consequences' for the person in question and the social system. Why should new religions be an exception?"; "which basically seeks to restrict the freedom to worship of 'certain new religious movements' in the European Community"; "setting out guidelines to restrict the religious freedom of certain new religious movements".[17] People everywhere considered the possible passing of the resolution to be a threat to the freedom of religion. Nevertheless, the resolution was passed by the European Parliament.

Can this resolution be seen as conflicting with the freedom of religion? Did the European Parliament proceed illegitimately in undemocratic fashion? The Parliament has clearly declared itself fully in support of the *Universal Declaration of Human Rights*, but when it states that sects cannot be treated on the same level as religions and churches, that belief systems can be separated from practices, and when it interprets 'new' as 'not serious', it is unjust to sects,

[17] Reactions of the Evangelische Fachhochschule (Weinschenk), Mansfield Council of Churches (Williams), 20 November Union (Kopenhagen), Mozano Bisco Christo Church (London), A.T. Peperzak (Nijmegen), J.M. van de Lans (Nijmegen), K. Dobbelaere (Louvain), national Councils of Churches.

denies their existence as a religion, and thus threatens freedom of religion by invoking these proposed measures.

This becomes clear if we apply the same criteria to the churches, which are considered to be religions, whose practices are not separated from their belief, and for which the adjective 'old' is seen as a guarantee of reliability.

Ad a) Applied consistently, this would mean that minors could not be confirmed in churches, nor would they be allowed to convert and to adopt a different life-style. They would also be prohibited from entering a monastery or religious order. The resolution uses the word "induced" (the Dutch text uses the word for "forced"), but it is very difficult to discern whether one's choice is actually free or compelled by circumstances. It is also questionable whether sects engage in such practices. In short, this criterion can violate the freedom of religion.[18]

Ad b) It is impossible to grant someone sufficient time to reflect, if that person wishes of his own free will to join a new church or change his beliefs. If somebody makes a choice, that is the choice he wishes to make and he is prepared to live with the consequences. Such choices are not usually spur-of-the-moment decisions but the result of a lengthy period of reflection. It is also not clear how such a process can be controlled. This criterion entails a violation of the belief of the individual believer.

Ad c) A reasonable demand with respect to minors (insofar as the children have not been officially removed from the parents), it is not clear why adults would be obligated to maintain such contacts. Adults have the right and freedom to choose and maintain relationships of their own making and are not obligated to maintain any. Without any foundation, however, the criterion suggests that adult people are estranged from their parents and friends against their will.

Ad d) People abandon their studies or quit their jobs all the time, sometimes simply because of circumstances. There is no reason to make an exception with respect to religious circumstances. The problem here, however, arises from the word "prevented" (the Dutch text renders this as "hindered"): as a rule, sects do not prohibit their members from studying. It is rather the case that the members themselves voluntarily give up their studies after some time, as they have found meaning for their lives in the sect.

Ad e) Sects do not deny these recently formulated "human rights', but it is difficult to realise them. Everyone has the right to leave a group, but it is not feasible to demand that this happen unimpeded: no group likes to see its members leaving. Neither do they deny people the right to have contact with others, but they can attempt to dissuade them on religious grounds (e.g., if they believe

[18] If this were in fact accepted, it would result in a situation very similar to that in the former communist countries, where the church was denied access to young people between the ages of 14 and 18 and young people were not allowed to choose a church.

that parents or friends will try to persuade the member to leave or cause difficulties). Members also retain the right to legal advice, but it is possible they will not make use of it. As a rule, the right to medical help is also not denied, even if some groups, because of specific views on health, attempt to dissuade their members from using the official healthcare in existence and advise them to employ their own medical principles.[19]

Ad f) The situation is complicated here. Indeed, it can be said that the laws of a country should not be broken, but there are situations in which a religious organisation can ask its members to break laws, e.g., in cases of objection to military service, civil disobedience, or in the neglect of public pronouncements. Governments, perhaps, do not approve of such views, but it can be part of one's belief to violate some rules. Sects have this 'right' as well.

Ad g) If applied to churches, which also include members of foreign extraction, this recommendation can restrict freedom of religion. All over the world people are permitted choose their own religion or church; all over the world religions and churches have the right to convert people, irrespective of their backgrounds. Restricting this can violate human rights.

Ad i) If applied consistently, this can be a violation of the right to privacy and confidentiality. For whatever reason, people may seek refuge with a church or religion for protection. Furthermore, a church takes the responsibility for its membership itself and memberships lists are confidential. In principle, it is possible here again to violate a fundamental right.

If recommendations a, b, g and i are consistently applied to all religions (and sects can be considered as religions), the danger exists that human rights will be violated. Nevertheless, because the European Parliament is not a government, it cannot be accused of such violations. Those governments which belong to the European Parliament are invited to reflect on the issue and possibly adjust their own laws to take account of some of the criteria. The resolution has not had any effect on the laws of individual countries. No member state of the European Parliament has implemented this resolution. It is still alarming, however, that the European Parliament could be so influenced by a small, non-representative entity like the anti-cult movement.

THE RECOMMENDATION OF THE COUNCIL OF EUROPE

It looked as if the question of sects had been put to rest within Europe. In some countries there were occasional problems with some extremist groups who violated national laws, but the call for governmental measures seemed past. Many

[19] There are some groups with specific views on health (Jehovah Witnesses, Christian Science, etc.), but for the most part the views on medical healthcare are no different than in mainstream society.

people were therefore surprised when a report was presented in the Council of Europe on 25 November 1991 called *On Sects and New Religious Movements.* The basis of the report was that "The activities of certain sects disrupt public order" and the question was: "Is there a need for legislation to curb the freedom of sects or even prohibit them? Or, on the contrary, is there a need for a framework within which sects can pursue their activities freely, provided that these match certain objective criteria?" The report asked the Council to do the following: "Consider the introduction of legislation to require the registration of all sects and new religious movements" and "Provide the public - and particularly adolescents - with maximum information on the nature, activities and aims of sects". The report endorsed the Cottrell report of the European Parliament and on 5 February 1992 the Council passed the report and its considerations with few amendments.[20]

In the explanation of the report Hunt seems to agree with Cottrell's report, not only historically but also materially. He expresses his concern about the activities of some sects, and also mentions that the creation of the report was stimulated by the questions raised by parents' organisations. In the end, however, it is clear that Hunt is much more perceptive than Cottrell and sharply notes which problems, possibilities and impossibilities arise if measures against sects are enacted. He refuses to distinguish between sect and religion[21] and between old and new religions. He acknowledges that the term 'sect' is very difficult to define and also observes that practices and beliefs cannot so easily be separated from each other. He sees that it necessarily remains a possibility that activities on the part of the world religions will conflict with governments or public order. It is clear that a sect, as a religion, has the right to claim all the freedom any religion or church can claim. He comes to the conclusion that special measures against the sects are not necessary and undesirable. In such cases a conflict with human rights is possible.[22] Moreover, the existing legislation is sufficient to deal with abuses and to punish violations in almost all cases. There are two final

---

[20] *Report on Sects and New Religious Movements*, by John Hunt of the Council of Europe to the Parliamentary Assembly. Code ADOC6535, Recommendation 1178.

[21] "It must be said that some of the constituents of religion recur in any attempt to define a sect and some people who are fond of pithy formulas even say that religions are merely sects which have succeeded."

[22] "Should the risk be taken of interfering with the freedom of conscience or religion of a large number of people for the sake of protecting a minority?"; "... since rights and freedoms cannot be protected by suppressing or limiting other rights and freedoms"; "This means that in a democracy the freedom of all religious, cultural or other groups must be respected, as long as they do not threaten the personal, professional and cultural relationships, nor of course the security of their property or their rights as workers."

matters of importance which which are stressed in the advice to the member states of the Council of Europe: to register sects and to provide good information on them. The Council advises:

> I. The basic educational curriculum should include objective factual information concerning established religions and their major variants, concerning the principles of comparative religion and concerning ethics and personal rights;
> II. Supplementary information of a similar nature, and in particular on the nature and activities of sects and new religious movements, should also be widely circulated to the general public. Independent bodies should be set up to collect and circulate this information;
> III. Consideration should be given to introducing legislation, if it does not already exist, which grants corporate status to all sects and new religious movements which have been registered, together with all offshoots of the mother sect;
> IV. To protect minors and prevent abductions and transfers abroad, member states which have not yet done so should ratify the European Convention in Recognition and Enforcement of Decisions of Custody of Children (1980) and adopt legislation making it possible to implement it;
> V. Existing legislation concerning the protection of children should be more rigorously applied. Additionally, those belonging to a sect must be informed that they have the right to leave;
> VI. Persons working for sects should be registered with social welfare bodies and guaranteed social welfare coverage, and such social welfare provision should also be available to those who decide to leave the sects.

The report did not invoke many reactions either within or outside the Council. Only the Unification Church responded, but it met with no support this time. In the assembly itself no fundamental criticism was expressed; on the contrary, the proposal was passed almost unaminously. And rightly so, one might add, for the proposed measures do not go too far and do not conflict with freedom of religion. At the same time, it is clear the Council dissociates itself from the ideas of the anti-cult movements. In some cases there may be some objections against sects, but there is no basis to take legal measures against sects or to treat them differently than religions.

Concerning the proposals, a great deal of what is suggested already exists in several countries. The educational programs of several member states includes 'information on religion', which deals with the world religions as well as sects. The independent organisations for providing information, as proposed by the Council, do exist in some countries: INFORM (Great Britain); the 'Evangelische Zentralstelle für Weltanschauungsfragen' (Germany) , etc. The proposed registration (which is required if the organisation is to be treated as a legal person) is not quite clear: does it require a sect be registered as a 'sect', making its character as a religious organisation explicit? Or is it sufficient, in order to acquire the legal status of person, to be registered at the Chamber of Commerce as a foundation, in which case the religious character is not important? The Council seems to want a register of 'sects'. Some countries still require religious organisations are to be registered, while others (e.g., the Netherlands) no longer do. Recommendations IV and V are not problematic. It is clear that minors are intended here, for which the existing legislation is sufficient. Adults are not, of course, covered - to the disappointment, one supposes, of the anti-cult movements. The last recommendation depends on the situation in each separate country.

In short, the Council of Europe has, on the one hand, taken up the line of the European Parliament but, on the other, has elaborated on it so much that the Council's proposal is justified. We hope that it has now come to an end. This proposal has made it clear that no special measures against sects are needed, since these groups belong to the religious climate of the West and should be regarded as religions that have the right to exist.

BIBLIOGRAPHY

Kranenborg, R. "The anticult movement in the Netherlands." In: A. Shupe and D. Bromley (eds.). *Anti-cult Movements in Comparative Perspective*. 1993.

——. *Een nieuw licht op de kerk?* Den Haag, 1984.

Laqueur, W. and B. Rubin. *Human Rights Reader*. New York, 1993.

Schnabel, P. *Tussen stigma en charisma*. Deventer, 1982.

Witteveen, T.A.M. *Overheid en nieuwe religieuze bewegingen*. Den Haag, 1984.

CHAPTER XIII

The Pursuit of Full Humanity

An Asian Christian View of Human Rights

Arnulf Camps OFM

Christian theologians in Asia often take up the topic of human rights. They do so because they feel the need to restore contact between the Christian faith and Asian realities. Their study of human rights is thus related to the process of contextualizing the Christian faith. In this article I will discuss the following four points:

1) What is the Asian understanding of contextualization?
2) What are the Asian realities?
3) The criticism of Asian theologians with regard to human rights.
4. The contributions of Asian Christians to the development of the concept of human rights.

WHAT IS THE ASIAN UNDERSTANDING OF CONTEXTUALIZATION?

There is a general tendency among Asian theologians to prefer the term 'contextualization' to 'inculturation', of which a widely accepted definition can be found in Arie Roest Crollius: "The integration of the christian experience of a local church into the culture of a given people, and in such a way that this experience is expressed not only in the elements of that culture but that it becomes a force giving this culture life, direction and renewal" (15-16; cf. also Standaert). According to Asian theologians, in most cases "the christian experience of a local church" in Asia is *not* a Christian experience of a local church in Asia. A local church in Asia is a foreign entity and not the result of a dialogical meeting between the religious experience of Asians and Christian experience. Inculturation is considered to be a one-sided movement of a foreign form of Christianity toward another culture and religion. It is seen as rather paternalistic and colonial. Moreover, Asian theologians are asking whether their own cultures and religions await such an input of life, direction and renewal (Pieris, 1988, 36).

Contextualization entails a different process. Asian theologians have come to understand that the text of the Christian memoria or tradition will remain irrelevant without a prior analysis of and internal relation to the context into which the tradition enters. This context needs to be viewed in as broad a sense as possible: the history, culture, and religion of a people as well as the struggle for justice and liberation and the changes resulting from the process of modernization. The contextual analysis by Asian theologians is not restricted to sociological or economic/political realities but includes the anthropological, cultural, historical and theological realities as well. It is the theological analysis that is most important.

This theological analysis could be called a theological rehabilitation of Asian cultures and religions, implying a new understanding of salvation history, of the real meaning of religion, of tradition or memoria, of scriptures and the founders, seers or sages of all religions, and of dialogue. Salvation history should not be restricted to the Judeo-Christian history, as the Supreme Being is the creator of all human beings - all have been created in his image. The Supreme Being continues his efforts to restore the relationship of mutual love: he unceasingly invites humans to enter into a covenant with him and this invitation is open to all. People respond to this invitation as members of a community living in a given culture and with a given religion. Culture and religion are the human societal responses to God's invitation to accompany him on the way of life in history. All religions cherish this memoria, the memory of this history, in doctrine, ways of life and celebrations. It is no longer possible to refer to other religions as idolatry, natural religions or efforts at self-justification. The holy scriptures and the founders, seers, or sages who played an essential role in bringing forth these religions should be given their rightful place in the history of God's dealings with all people. This is the reason why the encounter between religions should never be polemical or destructive: through dialogue the various gifts of God to the different groups of humans should be brought together for mutual enrichment and correction.

When religions meet, they should first of all discover God's presence within the culture and religion of the other and the riches contained in the social human responses, the religions and cultures of the world. Asian theologians stress the need for this as the deepest theological meaning of dialogue. Conversion and building up the kingdom of God constitute the goals of such meetings. Contextualization looks forward to a period at the end of history when God will be all in all and prepares for this final situation when all human beings together with their cultures and religions will be in harmony and will have found the fulness of God. Religions are servants who are to build up the kingdom of God in harmony and cooperation. It is this that Asian theologians have in mind when they speak or write about full humanity. A human being in isolation from others can never be fully human, can never be whole and move towards the fulness of God. Thus, these theologians have invited Asian churches to make a new start by discovering God's presence in the cultures in which they live and the religions to which they belong. It is only after this process of learning and discovering that the reality of God's presence in Jesus of Nazareth and the way of life he initiated can be understood and made to bear fruit (Camps, 1992, 53-54; 1993, 85-89).

WHAT ARE THE ASIAN REALITIES?

Asian theologians are realists: they refuse to glorify the past as if everything was good and beautiful prior to the arrival of colonial powers. Neither do they offer typical Asian values as uncontaminated, entailing harmony, tolerance and wholeness. Their realism consists in stressing both Asian values and their lack of proper application.

Asian reality poses a threefold challenge to the Asian peoples. The first is the challenge of the poor. With the exception of a few affluent islands (Japan, Taiwan, Hong Kong, Singapore) and South Korea, Asia is a poor continent. It is burdened by internal and international structures of injustice and oppression and economic and social justice is sorely needed. Asia includes a variety of democracies and totalitarian systems as well as capitalistic and socialist ideologies. In all Asian countries linguistic, ethnic, cultural and religious pluralism give rise to several problems. Minority groups are oppressed; material poverty is rampant, but cultural and religious poverty imposed by majority groups is also widespread. Michael Amaladoss has described the various kinds of action groups operating on unofficial levels:

> Some are involved in radical forms of social protest and struggle. Among these one can identify two sorts of groups: while one sort is collaborating fully with various marxist parties and movements, another sort tries to be independent, offering critical collaboration in particular programmes. Some others are committed to socialist projects, engaging in conscientisation, non-formal education and community organisation, and are inspired by an ideology of active non-violence. Among these one finds sometimes efforts to integrate a revolutionary ideology with the Christian faith and they would encourage basic Christian communities. Others still try to combine some conscientizing techniques with development and educational programmes both formal and non-formal. (1986, 327)

The challenge of poverty needs to be linked with the challenge of religions. According to Aloysius Pieris, the Asian reality is a complex structure constituted by the religiosity of the poor and the poverty of the religious masses. Effective collaboration of the socio-economic and political levels in a multi-religious society is hardly possible in a situation where there is no mutual acceptance and respect and no openness for dialogue. Here both Amaladoss and Pieris agree. Religions can be liberating if the mammon within one's inner self is renounced and a world order built on mammonistic values is denounced. At their best, all religions are aware that the Divine Being is a liberative agent, opposed to mammon and accumulation of wealth as the source of human enslavement. There is a great need for basic human communities or societies, in which members of various religions live and work together in order to reach the goal of full humanity for all human beings. Members of various religions should learn a double loyalty by discovering the common ideal of their strivings: full humanity or freedom from any enslavement through the liberating power of a liberated religion. Monastic people should return to their original calling (charism): voluntary poverty as a symbol of the struggle against mammon and the accumulation of wealth with the intention to create a situation in which full humanity can be achieved, in which the goods of this world are shared and destructive egocentrism is controlled. The Christian contribution here is unique: the Bible teaches that God has made a pact - a covenant - with the poor against the agents of mammon, so that the struggle of the poor for their liberation coincides with God's own salvific action (Pieris, 1987, 17-38).

A third challenge is that of culture. Again, Amaladoss is able to give an exact description of the situation:

> In a given culture there will be an ongoing dialectic between elite and folk elements. The elite groups are well versed in traditional literature and the arts and familiar with philosophical and theological reflection. They would also have been more quick to profit by contemporary contacts with the outside world and with the modern sciences. They control the cultural institutions. Their culture is developed, refined. By the side of this 'high' culture and in a sort of osmosis with it are the local, folk cultures. They have a popular base with geographically localized myths and festivals and carried by local languages. There is a constant interaction between the elite and folk levels of a culture. Upward cultural mobility would be seen in terms of moving from the popular to the elite level. Alongside this main stream are the tribal cultures, isolated geographically and self-contained, often relating to the main cultural traditions as the oppressed to the oppressor. This complex whole has been facing two sorts of challenges in recent years. The colonial past of most of the Asian countries has forced on them an unequal dialogue with European/American cultures. I think this has been basically a love-hate relationship: a secret admiration of and consequent acculturation to the dominant partner on the one hand and on the other hand a search for roots and freedom, catalyzed, however, by the challenges of the other. I think that in Asia this second reaction has on the whole predominated, especially in the post-colonial era. The second challenge comes from modern science and technology, often mixed with commercial colonialism, leading to situations linked to industrialization - urbanization. There has been a certain secularization. There is an ongoing tension between tradition and modernity, made more acute by the rapidity of the process of change. It has also created vast slums of culturally uprooted people. (1986, 335-36)

Asian reality thus has three dimensions: poverty, religion and culture dominate the continent; Asia is poor, religious and cultured. These characteristics, however, are strongly interrelated. Asian theologians want this highly complex reality to be their starting point when reflecting on the meaning of the Christian faith. It is in this context that the ideal of 'full humanity' for which members of various cultures and religions are to strive in basic human communities is formulated. It is also in this context that the proposals for a double loyalty are made. It now becomes possible to understand the criticism of human rights made by Asian theologians.

THE CRITICISM OF ASIAN THEOLOGIANS RE HUMAN RIGHTS

Felix Wilfred, who holds the chair of Christianity at the University of Madras, has written extensively on this issues and introduces the problem in this way:

> The emerging global unity and the consciousness of belonging to one human family are symbolized today by the progressive recognition of human rights. The ideals they represent have found place, in one way or other, in most constitutions of the family of nations and in their legal systems. The charter of human rights proclaimed by the United Nations in 1948, however, has its own limitations and conditionings, moulded and shaped as they were in particular historical and cultural contexts. They stand in need of not only being complemented through the contribution of other peoples and cultures, but also of being re-thought and re-oriented. This is the message, or rather challenge, that comes to us from the struggles of liberation today, particularly from the grassroots experiences in Asia. (Wilfred, 1991)

We will examine here Wilfred's proposals with regard to a reorientation and rethinking of human rights.

Wilfred is well aware of the fact that the universality of human rights is challenged today. In fact, human rights were formulated in a Western context and Western culture, history and philosophy constitute the matrix for the emergence of the tradition of human rights. The cultures and religions of the Third World, however, have their own worldviews and presuppositions: the 'human' and the 'rational' are perceived differently. The main problem, therefore, is not the universality of human rights but the reality of pluralism:

> One such vital issue is ethnicity and the progressive awareness of collective identities - religious, regional, linguistic, etc. The critique then, is not so much that the human rights in their conception and philosophy are not universal or comprehensive, for its failure to take into account other cultural worlds, patterns of thought, but that they are, in their present form, inadequate to respond to the contemporary Third World experiences - experiences in which not simply theoretical conceptions but social and political forces are in complex interaction. This is not a motive to abandon the language of human rights, which

> has become in a way part of the common consciousness of humanity. Rather, we are challenged to re-cast them from out of new historical experiences and socio-political struggles. (*ibid.*, 48, 52-53)

By collective identities and ethnicity Wilfred primarily understands nonprivileged groups, such as the until now faceless peoples, classes, castes, etc. In the conception of human rights, based mainly on the rights of the individual, the rights of these oppressed groups and collectivities are denied by the power of oppressive states and other dominant groups. Human rights should, therefore, be reformulated in order to restore collective rights to these groups.

Another reason for a reorientation of human rights is to be found in their lack of internal coherence. In case of a conflict between two or more human rights, no solution is possible since all are human rights. There are no criteria or principles by which priority can be determined. Thus human rights can easily be exploited by those in power: in the name of human rights other human rights are violated. Again the nonprivileged suffer. It is not Wilfred's intention to set individual human rights and collective rights over against each other. Individual rights have sometimes proved to be very effective in contexts charged with communalism and interreligious conflicts. Wilfred does not opt for the language of human rights over against the language of liberation. By opting in favour of the oppressed and the poor he wants to mould human rights so that they support the cause of liberation. He concludes:

> In the light of what we have reflected above, it should be clear how we cannot found human rights on a 'common ground', unaffected by the concrete processes and struggles of life. Rather each group has to find its own motives for the praxis of the ideals of human rights on the basis of its history, culture and religion. This is no isolationism. On the contrary this is an invitation for permanent dialogue and exchange of experiences among various people. If we can speak of anything common, it is the universal and imperative necessity of practising and reformulating human rights through option for the poor and solidarity with them. It could be seen as the directive principle for any serious talk about human rights in our world today. (*ibid.*, 63)

It is in this context that Wilfred asserts that the peoples' movements play a crucial role in this process. These movements help us to rediscover the *humanum* in this context. Full humanity can never be found by practising individual human rights in an exclusive way. A final quote:

> Such an approach to human rights would call for liberating alternatives to the present pattern of governance, to the system of economy to the general culture of mega-science and high technology. The discourse about human rights and the practice of them cannot be separated from these. It is a package. And that makes our task very challenging. (*ibid.*, 64)

THE CONTRIBUTIONS OF ASIAN CHRISTIANS

In order to contribute to a reformulation of the concept of human rights Asian theologians have developed some interesting proposals for reforming the presence of Christianity in Asia. They will be treated here only briefly. One should not forget that all these proposals are very closely related to the Asian concept of contextualization. Contextualization has a different starting point in Asia: the theological evaluation of the Asian reality. These theologians have discovered both the enslaving and the liberating aspects of religions and cultures, intending to do away with the first and to promote the latter. At their best, all religions are well aware of their mission to set human beings free and thus offer ways and paths that lead pilgrims from darkness to light, from oppression to liberty, from partial happiness to fulness. Their goal is full humanity and one should not understand this as humanism.

Religions and cultures are authentic ways and paths developed by an interplay between the Supreme Being and groups of human beings. From a theological point of view, they should be considered valid and therefore their identity should be discovered and accepted. Asian religions do not consider themselves as limited only to the spiritual or purely religious aspect of human life. They have never accepted a dichotomy between the material, social, economic or political on the one hand and the spiritual on the other. They stress the interconnection or wholeness of all these aspects. There is no place for Western secularization or individualism. Modernization is certainly not rejected, but it is subordinate to this wholeness. Therefore, capitalism in its Western form cannot be an ideal for Asians. This is true as well in respect to power struggles and the imposition of a world culture. Religions teach humans to oppose mammon and the human tendency to accumulate more and more material possessions and power. Asian theologians strive for a balance by teaching the practice of voluntary poverty so that sharing becomes possible and that all human beings are equally provided with the goods of this earth. They preach and practise non-violence as an effective way to overcome domination and oppression and do not imitate Western democracies and their system of elections, parties and the rule of a majority over a minority. Asian spirituality prefers a system of consultations and deliberations so that all involved can come to an agreement.

Asian theologians know very well that these ideals are always in danger of being obliterated in the struggles of life, but they want to help Asian religions to return to their original vision of a full and therefore human life. Most important here is the fact that these theologians request a reform of Asian Christianity, a reform which they term the third reformation. This implies a return to their own religious and cultural context. Christianity should not exist in Asia separate from the Asian context, but should take its place among and not against other religions: it should seek to be a pilgrim on the road that all religions wish to travel. According to these theologians basic ecclesial communities are needed in order to find and preserve a Christian identity, but these communities should never become isolated from other communities. They should join with other religious and cultural communities and together with them build up basic human societies. Within the latter a common spirituality should be developed and a new practice of cooperation, dialogue, correction and rehabilitation put into effect. The third reformation seeks the primacy of lay people, who will not indulge in abstract dialogues or purely intellectual speculations. They are conscious of the problems of life and they prefer to begin with a dialogue of life. The third reformation allows plenty of opportunity for interfaith action groups, which should have specific goals and programmes of action in political and social areas. Christians should actively participate in activities and programmes operating on behalf of workers, peasants, for the dignity and rights of women, tribes, dalits and minorities. The spirit and the tradition of each religion could be brought to bear for joint actions and deeper motivations (Amaladoss, 1990, 112-13; Pieris, 1987, 37-38; Wilfred, 1992, 192-214).

We will give the last word to Aloysius Pieris of Sri Lanka:

> We pray that here in Asia this new method of theology will be respected or at least tolerated by those who have the power to frustrate it. The first step in this method is the building up of 'Kingdom communities' or 'basic human communities' wherein Christian and non-Christian members strive together for the dawn of a Full humanity. 'Full humanity' is not only the common ideal of their strivings, but also the Christological title by which the Christian members of such communities recognise and confess the One whose disciples they boldly claim to be. (1987, 38)

BIBLIOGRAPHY

Amaladoss, M. SJ. "The local churches in Asia: problems and prospects." *Verbum* 27 (1986).

——. *Making all Things New: Dialogue, Pluralism and Evangelization in Asia*. Maryknoll, 1990.

Camps, A. OFM. "Missiology and secularization or a new evangelization in the light of worldwide human and religious experiences." *Exchange 21* (1992).

——. "Uniciteit en universaliteit van Christus: overwegingen ter bevordering van een gelovige en zinvolle discussie." In: *Missie: einde of begin?* Louvain, 1993.

Crollius, A. Roest, SJ. "What is so ^New about Inculturation?" In: A. Roest Crollius SJ and T. Nkéramihigo (eds.). *What is so New about Inculturation?* Rome, 1984. Pp. 15-16.

Pieris, A. SJ. "A Theology of Liberation in Asian Churches?" In: S. Arokiasamy SJ and G. Gispert-Sauch SJ (eds.). *Liberation in Asia: Theological Perspectives*. Delhi: Anand, 1987.

——. *An Asian Theology of Liberation*. Maryknoll, 1988.

Standaert, N. SJ. *Inculturatie, evangelie en cultuur*. Mechelen, 1990.

Wilfred, Felix. *Sunset in the East? Asian Challenges and Christian Involvement*. Madras, 1991.

———. "The Language of Human Rights: An Ethical Esperanto? Reflections on the Universal Human Rights from an Indian/Third World Context." *Vidyajyoti* 56 (1992): 194-214.

CHAPTER XIV

Calvinist Thought and Human Rights

Aad van Egmond

INTRODUCTION

The Free University, Amsterdam, where the papers in this volume were discussed, has a very special – religious – tradition. It was founded more than a century ago by a group of Christians of Calvinist background. Peculiarly enough, this tradition has, as a matter of fact, criticized the idea of 'human rights' fiercely. I refer deliberately to the *idea* of 'human rights' and not to 'human rights' as such because, as will be seen, it is precisely where the idea of human rights is hailed with enthusiasm that the content of these rights are under discussion. In his most important work, significantly entitled *Unbelief and Revolution* (1847), Groen van Prinsterer, who can be seen as a precursor of the tradition at this Calvinist university, quoted De Bonald's statement, "The revolution began with the declaration of the rights of man. It will end only with the declaration of the rights of God," with great approval (1924, 5). Abraham Kuyper, the founder of this university, one of its first professors and later Prime Minister of the Netherlands, wrote in one of his most well-known works, *De gemeene gratie* ("Common Grace"), of the "false considerations of the French Revolution, which derives all rights and liberties from man as such, and which therefore speaks about *Droits de l'homme*, that is, about *Human Rights*, and chooses these as its starting-point" (II, 75).[1] In 1934, at the Second International Congress of Calvinists held at this university, one of the most highly esteemed jurists of his time, Dr. A. Anema, spoke about "the absolute repudiation of all sovereignty of man as the ultimate source of authority and liberty" and emphasized that "no human authority is ever justified in itself but always needs the justification of the will of God as revealed to us in Holy Scripture and in history" (p. 62).

---

[1] For the majority of the Dutch works quoted here, no English translations exist. The translations that are found here are my own (AvE). English translations of quotations from Lecerf are provided by Henry Jansen.

Of course, in 1847, 1880, and 1934 it was the 'old' liberal, political rights that were at stake and not the social and cultural rights of a later period. In all fairness, however, it must be admitted that the idea of human rights was treated with some suspicion for a long time yet after the proclamation of the Universal Rights of Man in 1948, however the rights themselves merited support and sympathy. The reason why the idea of 'human rights' encountered such suspicion in the Calvinist tradition is directly connected to the theme of this volume: the religious anthropology of Calvinism rejects this idea in principle. In the next section of this paper I will explain why this is so. I will subsequently show that Groen, Kuyper en Anema were not opposed to human rights as such but to their foundation, and that they even defend the rights themselves. Following this, I will show that the thought of Calvin himself provides some very important arguments in favour of human rights. Finally, I will demonstrate that, even according to the Calvinist tradition itself, the usual foundation of human rights, though perhaps not the correct one in the view of this tradition, nevertheless cannot be considered as entirely inadequate.

CALVINIST ANTHROPOLOGY

In the Reformed (Calvinist) tradition human rights as rights established and decided by human beings themselves and founded in humanity itself seem at first glance to be impossible. The primary reason for this is that human beings were created by the sovereign God, who remains sovereign over human beings after their creation as well. This God is not only the creator, but also the governor of this world: he directs the whole world according to his sovereign will. It is for this purpose that he appoints governments to serve Him, for it is particularly through them that he exercises his providential power. For this reason governments are to be obeyed – although there are a few exceptions. This absolute sovereignty of God does not mean that God – as in late medieval nominalism – is *ex lex*, not even limited by his own nature. According to Calvin, God does not possess a *potestas absoluta* but a *potestas ordinata* (cf. Lecerf, 25ff.). Nevertheless, being God, he reigns in absolute sovereignty.

The primary goal of living creatures is to know and serve this God, that is, to live in accordance with his commandments. In all human activity, the honour of God has priority. The whole creation is a *theatrum gloriae dei*, a theatre of the glory of God, where God glorifies himself through his merciful condescension and accommodation to human beings and lets himself be glorified by them (Kolfhaus, 515). This glorification of God by humans consists in the fact that everything demonstrates that human beings are not their own but belong to God and that they are aware of this. Calvin provides a good example of this when he writes:

> Now the great thing is this: we are consecrated and dedicated to God in order that we may thereafter think, speak, meditate and do, nothing except to his glory ....
>
> If we, then, are not our own but the Lord's, it is clear what error we must flee, and whither we must direct all the acts of our life.
>
> We are not our own: let not our reason nor our will, therefore, sway our plans and deeds ... We are not our own: in so far as we can, let us therefore forget ourselves and all that is ours.
>
> Conversely, we are God's: let us therefore live for him and die for him. We are God's: let his wisdom and will therefore rule all our actions ... so the sole haven of salvation is to be wise in nothing and to will nothing through ourselves but to follow the leading of the Lord alone. (*Inst.* III.7.1)

Calvin explicitly turns against those who "set up reason alone as the ruling principle in man, and think that it alone should be listened to" and declares that the Christian "bids reason give way to, submit and subject itself to, the Holy Spirit so that the man himself may no longer live but hear Christ living and reigning within him" (*ibid.*).

This sovereignty of God has been a central theme in the entire Calvinist tradition. Kuyper called it "the fundamental conception of religion as maintained by Calvinism" (1931, 46). The Second International Congress of Calvinists mentioned above was completely devoted to the concept of the sovereignty of God. In his opening address, the professor of Christian dogmatics at the Free University at the time, Valentijn Hepp, stated that "the dogma of the sovereignty of God is not to be considered the essence or basic principle of Calvinism" (p. 20). He did so, however, only to declare later that Calvinism surpasses all other forms of Christianity in all aspects that were of any consequence. He was also convinced that it was the privilege of Calvinism to interpret this sovereignty as absolutely as possible (*ibid.*, 13). At the same conference, an equally famous French Calvinist theologian, Lecerf, stressed "the courage and steadfastness of thought that Calvinism has in its passionate and rigorous affirmation of the *sovereignty of God*" (p. 25).

It is clear that in this quite strongly theocentric tradition the idea that human beings, because of their own reason, might be able to establish rights for themselves, to decide these on the basis of their own authority and to ground these in their own humanity, would not meet with any support. It is impossible to reflect on human beings for the slightest moment apart from God, apart from his authority. If human beings have rights, these can only be granted to him by God: the very thought of humans claiming those rights is absolutely alien to Calvinism. The Bible, the most important source for Calvinism, does have passages where people ask to be treated with justice by God, but Calvin's explanation of these passages (probably correct) is that God's intervention is sought in a struggle with one's own adversaries and not that any rights are being claimed here over against God. God and humans do stand in a covenantal relationship with each other, but this is a relationship based on grace, so it does not provide any grounds for claiming one's rights. If it is possible to speak of 'human rights' by means of this covenant, the nature of this covenant makes clear that they are only granted and not innate. They are, in other words, gifts.

It is not only this relationship between God and human beings as creator and creatures, ruler and subjects, that rules out any talk of 'human rights'. Humans are not only creatures over against a sovereign God; they are also sinners in the presence of the holy God. This absolutely excludes any talk of human rights. The sinful creature has no rights to assert but is totally dependent on grace. One might even say that the very fact that human beings award rights to themselves is positive proof *par excellence* of their sinfulness, as the biblical story of Paradise shows. The person who justifies himself and refuses to depend on grace, who does not want to exist in absolute dependence on God, is the chief example of the sinful person.

On this point the Protestant traditions are profoundly different from Roman Catholicism. In the view of the latter, only the supernatural gifts are lost by sin and human nature still bears its original integrity or does so only in a slightly lesser degree. The Lutheran and Calvinist traditions, in contrast, teach a 'total depravity'. The relationship with God, that is, living for and serving God, is the very essence of humanity. The distortion of this relationship by humankind means a *corruptio totalis*, a total corruption. If it was already dubious whether humankind's 'being created' or even 'being created in God's image' constituted a basis for speaking about 'human rights', this is now completely out of the question, since it is clear that this involves humankind not only as created but also as sinful.

Since the notion of human rights arose in history (in the American and French Revolutions), the Reformed tradition, particularly Calvin's, dating back to the Reformation and ultimately rooted in Augustine, has distrusted any talk of human rights as allocated by humankind to itself on the basis of humanity and whatever philosophical or religious foundation is at hand. Of course, one should distinguish between the declarations of American origin (where the rights were still founded on God as creator) and those of French origin (where such a foundation is definitely missing). Particularly the latter was subject to criticism from a Calvinist perspective. Calvinism includes a 'religious anthropology' that apparently excludes 'human rights' as an idea, as an ideology.

A BETTER FOUNDATION

It is remarkable that this criticism is directed against the founding human rights in humankind itself. The criticism does not arise from the fact that there may be much wrong with these rights (as rights or liberties of the people - the writers apparently have first-generation rights in mind) themselves but from the fact that this foundation is so *unstable*. This can easily be discerned in the writings of

Groen, Kuyper and Anema. One can almost hear them sighing: if only these rights had been founded in God and not in humankind, in God's eternal commandments and ordinances and not in human arbitrariness, in God's sovereignty and not that of the people.

The real background of Groen's opposition to 'human rights' is his fear of the absolutism of the state, as can be seen in the following citations: "These rights, as it is said, beyond the reach of the administration, are at the mercy of each government: always insofar as it suits the State, the collective despot" (p. 220); "Freedom, total freedom as far as your sovereign, the State, allows it" (p. 221); "... the ground of my complaint is that, defined and confirmed by the immutable laws and institutions of God in earlier times, they now are dependent on the consent of the state, of the will of changeable men ..." (p. 221). In brief, true freedom and actual rights are guaranteed only by God, not by human beings. As mentioned above, in 1847 Groen was referring to those 'human rights' now usually termed political and liberal rights: equality, property, freedom of religion, freedom of speech. To root these in a sovereignty of the people is eventually to abolish them; to root them in God's sovereign commands and ordinances is to guarantee them.

In Kuyper it is approximately the same: it is not the liberties (the 'human rights') as such that are under discussion but their foundation. If these rights are founded in God, his commandments and ordinances guarantee the boundaries between government and subjects *and* the rights and liberties of the people, which are to be defended at all costs against every abuse of power of the government (*Gemeene gratie*, II, 77). This can be noted in the following quotation:

> Whoever pleads the cause of the people's rights and liberties because his spirit is opposed to subjection or because he himself likes to wield the power he denies the government and might preferably see the government as his own agent, thus rejects the principle of authority placed over us. On the contrary whoever ... begins with God, upholds his sovereignty and both people and prince submit to that high sovereignty of the Lord, does not undermine authority, but honours and strengthens it. ... Everyone to whom rights and liberties are granted, is thus under obligation to watch over these rights and liberties and to plead their cause with all possible means. The people that abandons its rights and liberties is guilty. (*ibid.*, II, 83f.)

Only when 'human rights' are seen as rooted in God's ordinances can they be defended in his name.

When Anema spoke of "the absolute repudiation of all sovereignty of man as the ultimate source of authority and liberty", he did so to illustrate what he called the negative side of the idea of God's absolute sovereignty: if God is sovereign, then humans are not. But this divine sovereignty also has a positive side: "Seen from the positive side the doctrine has a double signification: every legally existing government ought to be acknowledged and obeyed, not because the government has any claim to this, derived from its own being ... but only because it is God's will" (Anema, 62). Secondly, "the power of the government is limited ... also by the rights belonging to the people. Those rights of the people are in their turn also derived from the sovereignty of God" (*ibid.*). Again, "So the dogmatic significance of the sovereignty of God for political relations implies that degrading the government to a mandatary of sovereign man and the debasement of man to a object of an arbitrary and omnipotent state without any rights is forbidden" (p. 63). Both government and people have their "own duties and their own independent rights, which God as the sovereign of both granted to each of them for the glorification of his name" (*ibid.*).

It is clear once more that, if humankind does possess rights, they are, according to Calvinist teaching, granted by God. At the same time, however, it is also clear that, if the rights of governments and people are rooted not in the sovereignty of government or people but in the sovereignty of God himself, this suddenly creates room to speak of the rights of governments and subjects and thus of 'human rights': those rights of the people are in turn also derived from the sovereignty of God. The so-called Calvinistic rejection of 'human rights' appears to be far from simple: it is due to their origin within a humanist frame of thought in which humankind itself sovereignly allocates these rights to itself. As far as the rights themselves are concerned, as opposed to the question of their foundation, Calvinists have no objection. Rather, they oppose the idea of human rights for sake of human rights. The Calvinist tradition itself even provides quite strong arguments in favour of human rights, whether this involves the first, second or third generation.

HUMANITY'S OWN FLESH AND BLOOD – AND THE IMAGE OF GOD

It is astonishing that the very same tradition that is so opposed to the *idea* of 'human rights' so strongly pleads their case. Of course, some rights are emphasised more than others and the right to freedom of religion sometimes conflicts with others that derive more from humanist traditions. But this need not be a major problem since contemporary thought acknowledges that because of the different historical contexts of the various rights some may conflict with others. What are the arguments on the basis of which Calvinists support human rights and which, in their eyes, are more suited to that purpose than the arguments usually brought to the fore in their defense, rooted as they are in human autonomy?

The Calvinist view is not limited to the fundamental anthropological principle of sinful creatureliness outlined above. It does not endorse a static anthropology, explaining the constitution of human beings, but endorses a view of humankind as existing in a relationship, in a history. It is a dynamic religious anthropology.

God, for whom and with whom human beings live in a reciprocal covenantal relationship and whom to know, serve and obey is the highest aim of human life, takes pity on his sinful creatures in an act of sovereign grace. He overlooks their sinfulness and accepts them in spite of everything. At the centre of this activity stands Jesus Christ, who came from God as his eternal Word made flesh and who partakes in both divine and human nature. As a human being, he fulfils the requirement of perfect obedience (*oboedientia passiva*) and bears the divine judgement on the apostate sinfulness of humankind. His divine nature enables him to complete this task. This obedience of this one and only man is imputed to all human beings. God thus honours his own justice that cannot endure sin and his love (the ground of all that is) by which he surrounds his creatures from the beginning. Humans are now invited to put their trust – again – in God's goodness, love and faithfulness. This 'putting trust in' or 'relying on' is called 'faith'. Through this faith human beings appropriate salvation: not only this undeserved pardon, but also being able to stand once more in proper relationship to God and to live out of this relationship. This faith not only clarifies what life is intended to be, but the spirit of God, who is also the spirit of Jesus Christ, enables human beings, although never perfectly so,[2] to act according to this relationship. The divine commandments, proclaimed to him by the Holy Scripture - which also informs human beings about their creatureliness and being pardoned sinners -serve this purpose. These commandments cover all of life, not only its private dimensions but the social and political dimensions as well.

To understand what ideal relations between people should look like and the principles of such relationships, according to the Calvinist view, we will look once more at Calvin. We then find the following:

a. Just as we are not our own but the Lord's, all human goods, gifts and qualities are God's as well. This means in the first place that we are to honour these divine gifts in others:

> we are bidden so to esteem and regard whatever gifts of God we see in other men that we may honour those men in whom they reside. For it would be a great depravity on our part to deprive them of that honour which the Lord has bestowed upon them. (*Inst.* III.7.4)

The converse of this is that "the lawful use of all benefits consists in a liberal and kindly sharing of them with others" (*Inst.* II.7.5). It is striking that here Calvin uses the word 'right' without any difficulty: we must be led by the hand "to yield willingly what is ours by right and resign it to another" (*ibid.*).

b. Calvin states emphatically that by the will of God people form communities in which the principles of identification, empathy and solidarity ought to be maintained: "They must put themselves in the place of him whom they see in need of their assistance, and pity his ill fortune as if they themselves experi-

---

[2] It should be remembered that this point is debated within the tradition itself.

enced and bore it ..." (*Inst.* III.7.7). It is important that one "not despise his needy brother or enslave him as one indebted to himself" and "... will so consider with himself that ... he is a debtor to his neighbors ..." (*ibid.*). Commenting on Luke 10:30 Calvin writes,

> The primary character of the social order created by God is the solidarity that unites all beings one with another. The human race is conjoined together by a sacred bond of community. All are neighbors one of another. ... We must never wipe out our common nature. (quoted in Wolterstorff, 254)

Elsewhere we read, "We cannot but behold our own faces as it were in a glass in the person that is poor and despised ..., though he were the furthest stranger in the world (*ibid.*, 256).

c. Calvin bases this unity of the human race, however, emphatically on the idea that every person is created in God's image. Through this idea of 'man as God's icon', the first principle of honouring God's goods and gifts in others and therefore of these others themselves, is strengthened considerably. For even if no divine gifts can be discerned in others, the gift of God's image is always present:

> ... we are not to consider what men merit of themselves but to look upon the image of God in all men, to which we owe all honour and love ... the Lord has given him a mark that ought to be familiar to you ... the Lord shows him to be one to whom he has deigned to give the beauty of his image ... God, as it were, has put him in his own place .... (*Inst.* III.7.6)

Wolterstorff has shown that this last statement, which points to a radical identification of God with humankind, is no exception in Calvin. He writes, for example, in his commentary on Genesis that, because of the fact that humans "bear the image of God engraven on them, He deems himself violated in their person .... This doctrine ... is to be carefully observed, that no one can be injurious to his brother without wounding God himself" (quoted in Wolterstorff, 257). And in his commentary on Habakkuk Calvin even writes about the human cry over injustice: "It is then the same as though God heard himself, when he hears the cries and groanings of those who cannot bear injustice' (*ibid.*).

In short, any injury to people, their dignity or welfare is neglect of the solidarity in which the human race was created, contempt of the image of God they bear and finally an attack on God himself. One could speak here of 'human rights', if one takes into account that it is not a question of people claiming their rights autonomously, solely on the basis of their own humanity, but only of rights founded on God's ordinances and God's commandments. In addition, it is remarkable that Calvin again and again speaks of rights that *others* may claim and much less about claims *I myself* might have (cf. Wolterstorff, 256). Finally, the duty of the government, deriving as it does its authority from God's sovereignty, appears in a special light. Its task, in obedience to God's commands, is to maintain the order discussed above. Calvin's demand that the government should be obeyed as God's servant here receives a special slant.

One may now have a slight notion of the aversion the Calvinist tradition had towards the 'idea' of human rights that are founded in humanity itself and depend on a government which is itself solely dependent on the sovereignty of the people. We will now turn to the question of whether – in the light of its own tradition – this Calvinist aversion is entirely justified.

COMMON GRACE

The knowledge of God's order and commandments – and the will to act in conformity to this order and these commandments - is first of all the privilege of human beings who are reconciled with God and now live in proper relationship with him. They are the fruits of faith by which humans embrace the proclamation of their being pardoned by the sovereign creator. Our discussion has shown, however, that the divine grace by which God takes pity on sinful humanity is not confined to their acceptance in love and election to eternal life. Even from the task implied by the divine commandments for believers it appears that all people are objects of God's pity and grace: he sustains them and issues his commandments precisely for their welfare. It therefore appears that a second type of grace exists, a second way by which God's pity and mercy are manifested and which extends far beyond the imputation of Christ's righteousness and the gift of the Spirit. In the Reformed tradition this second type is usually called 'common grace' in distinction from 'special grace'. The latter grants eternal life; the first guards humanity from disaster.

There has been much debate within the Calvinist tradition on the correct relationship between these two types of grace. Some have gone so far as to see 'common grace' as only serving 'special grace': if God wants to pardon people and grant them eternal life, the existence of these people is presupposed. Total depravity and sin, however, would destroy all of humanity and all human life if God did not mitigate the consequences of sin through "common grace', so that there would always be those who could hear the proclamation of divine grace and mercy and have the opportunity to put their trust in this message, i.e., believe. Others have seen the relationship as almost diametrically opposite: God's aim is the salvation of the world, and the believers' faith in his mercy serves this great salvation. Thus 'special grace' serves 'common grace'. However this is viewed, the warning arises time and again that both types of grace are not to be treated in isolation from each other and this is true especially of 'common grace' with respect to the atoning death of Jesus Christ.

This doctrine of 'common grace', taught above all by Kuyper but supported by Herman Bavinck as well and rooted in Calvin, is of the greatest importance for reflecting on the relationship between Calvinist anthropology and human rights. 'Common grace' is active because God has granted to every person – not only to believers – an interior, subjective sense of the truth, even under conditions of total depravity and has left exterior, objective evidence of this truth in the world. As far as the knowledge of God is concerned, this sense and this evidence are very weak, but with respect to morality and ethics, this 'common grace' is of wider significance. Human beings not only have a sense of right and wrong, of justice and injustice (implanted in the heart by God; cf. Wolterstorff), but they are also able, albeit only partially, to create the necessary political, social, and cultural institutions. It is precisely there that the consequences of sin are mitigated and these institutions are therefore gifts of God. This entails that all people have some knowledge of rights and the responsibilities of governments and subjects and thus of human rights, despite the fact that these are wrongly founded in the autonomy of human beings rather than God.

Good Calvinist might see – and often they do see – in human rights at least the fruits of 'common grace' through which people know of the justice they are required to bestow on others and which others are required to bestow on them. If human beings, though having no knowledge of the foundation of human rights in God himself, nevertheless appear to have a some idea of what 'human rights' are, then Calvinists ought to ascribe this fact to common grace, rather than rejecting them because they lack an adequate foundation. To quote Calvin yet again: "For how comes it that all, being touched with weariness, cry out, How long? except that they know that this confusion of order and equity is not to be endured? And this feeling, is it not implanted in us by the Lord?" (quoted in Wolterstorff, 257).

CONCLUSION

The Calvinist recoil from the 'idea' of 'human rights' is to be understood as resistance to their wrong foundation which ironically finally undermines them. Insofar as human rights are intended to create a just order, they meet with the full support of Calvin and Calvinists. One might, of course, ask (for Calvin and Calvinists an impossible question) whether this foundation in God is perhaps nothing else than another way of founding these rights - and even a dangerous one at that. Nevertheless, it should be said that Groen's conviction *cum suis* that these rights are in better hands with God than with a government that is totally dependent on the arbitrariness of the sovereignty of the people is not entirely uncongenial and certainly testifies to a certain amount of realism. The long tradition of 'common grace' provides Calvinists with the simple possibility of being grateful for all insights that exist outside the light of special grace in the issue of human rights, and nevertheless to maintain the sovereignty of God.

BIBLIOGRAPHY

Anema, A. "The Sovereignty of God and Political Relations." In: *Tweede Internationale Congres van Gereformeerden (Calvinisten) (Second International Conference of Calvinists)* (Reports). 's-Gravenhage, 1935.

Calvin, J. *Institutes of the Christian Religion*, Vol. 1-2. Ed. J.T. McNeill. Tr. F.L. Battles. Philadelphia, 1960.

Groen van Prinsterer, G. *Ongeloof en Revolutie: Eene reeks van historische voorlezingen*. Utrecht, 1924[5].

Hepp, V. "De soevereiniteit Gods." in: *Tweede Internationale Congres van Gereformeerden (Calvinisten) (Second International Conference of Calvinists)*. (Reports). 's-Gravenhage, 1935.

Kolfhaus, W. *Vom christlichen Leben nach Johannes Calvin*. Neukirchen, 1949.

Kuyper, A. *Lectures on Calvinism: The Stone Lectures*. Grand Rapids, 1931.

———. *De gemeene gratie*, Vol. II. Kampen, 4th impression; year of publication not indicated.

Lecerf, A. "La souveraineté de Dieu d'apres le Calvinisme." In: *Tweede Internationale Congres van Gereformeerden (Calvinisten) (Second International Conference of Calvinists)* (Reports). 's-Gravenhage, 1935.

Wolterstorff, N. "Can a Calvinist be Progressive?" *Gereformeerd Theologisch Tijdschrift* 88 (1988): 249–58.

CHAPTER XV

The Christian Ecumenical Reception of Human Rights

Jerald D. Gort

STRUGGLE AGAINST SOCIAL DISORDER

Generally speaking, during the first sixty-odd years of its existence the modern ecumenical movement - dating from the World Missionary Conference held in Edinburgh in 1910 - did not occupy itself with human rights in the contemporary sense of the concept. As the earlier ecumenical documents amply testify, the movement did engage regularly in strong criticism of the deleterious human consequences of certain Western colonial policies and practices in Africa and Asia. There were denunciations of forced and migrant labor and immigration policies, for example, and the Secretary of the International Missionary Council (IMC), J.H. Oldham, wrote an important book entitled, *Christianity and the Race Problem*, which dealt with the question as to whether the "Church has any contributions to make to the solution of the problems involved in the contact of different races in the world" (p. vii) and which went through no fewer than eight editions between 1924 and 1926. But these problems were viewed less as human rights issues than as instances of social disorder or evil that needed to be brought to light and ameliorated, as matters of "grave menace to the peace of the world and to the cooperation and progress of its peoples" (p. vii).

In later years the IMC and particularly the Life and Work Movement and the World Council of Churches (from the very beginning of its process of formation in 1938) became deeply involved in reflection and action on a variety of issues and themes which years hence would be considered to be highly relevant to human rights, such as the threat of totalitarianism, peace among the nations, refugees, economic justice and political order in a world of human disorder, the responsible society, rapid social change, Christian responsibility in the modern world, the role of the Church in society and international relations, etc. At the 1937 Oxford Life and Work Conference the then Archbishop of York, William Temple, even anticipated a theme which would play a central role in much later ecumenical human rights discussions when he stated that the

> forces of evil against which Christians have to contend are found not only in the hearts of men as individuals, but have entered into and infected the structure of society, and there must also be combatted. (cited in Smit, 748)

Yet none of these issues, either, was at this time viewed from the special perspective of human rights and duties, though Paul Abrecht is surely right in contending that the contemporary ecumenical concern with human rights flows from the pioneering work of the Life and Work movement (cf. p. 614).

There was one human rights issue, however, that did receive steady and full attention within the ecumenical movement from the outset, namely, freedom of religion, understood as an individually distinct and separate problem area.

EMPHASIS ON RELIGIOUS LIBERTY

Initial ecumenical efforts on behalf of human rights consisted of formal and informal representations made to colonial authorities who were restricting freedom of missionary movement, particularly in Moslem areas, for purposes of preserving the social and religious status quo of the societies under their administration with a view to the protection of Western political and commercial interests. There were many instances of ecumenical missionary resistance to such policy in colonial territories.[1] And in response to anti-mission attitudes and actions on the part of civil authorities in various parts of the world the 1910 Edinburgh Conference spent a day discussing the topic *Missions and Governments* (cf. Gairdner, 154-77).

The issue of freedom of religion was explicitly raised for the first time within the ecumenical movement at the 1928 Jerusalem Meeting of the IMC. Jerusalem placed the matter of religious liberty within the framework of church-state relations: the aims of efforts in this area were understood "in terms of facilitating relationships with governments in order to enable the missionary enterprise to proceed unhindered" (*Study Paper*, 3). Calling for "a study of the relation of the principle of religious freedom to the rights of minorities under State systems of education" (*ibid.*, 20), this conference roundly repudiated "any attempt on the part of trade or of governments, openly or covertly, to use the missionary cause for ulterior purposes" (*ibid.*, 18). Jerusalem also articulated an important insight that would be echoed repeatedly in later years, for example, at the Fifth Assembly of the World Council of Churches (WCC) in Nairobi in 1975 and at the WCC Executive Committee Meeting in 1979:

> ... we would repudiate any symptoms of a religious imperialism that would desire to impose beliefs and practices on others in order to manage their souls in

[1] For an example of such reaction in colonial Northern Nigeria see Boer, 8-22.

> their supposed interests. We obey a God who respects our will and we desire to respect those of others. (*ibid.*, 18)

The Oxford Life and Work Conference in 1937 and the 1938 Tambaram Meeting of the IMC drew up comprehensive descriptive formulations of religious liberty, which are very similar to each other both as to content and to starting point. Although these statements recognize in principle "the inner urge of every world religion to reach out to those outside its community," they clearly "take their point of departure from the calling of the Christian church" (Verkuyl, 10, 11).[2] A more "universally stated" and thus "felicitous" description of the right of religious freedom is that produced in 1944 by a North American Joint Committee of missionary and church leaders (*ibid.*, 11, 12):

> Religious liberty shall be interpreted to include freedom to worship according to conscience and to bring up children in the faith of their parents, freedom for the individual to change his religion, freedom to preach, educate, publish and carry on missionary activities and freedom to organize with others and to acquire and hold property for these purposes. (*ibid.*, 12)

HEIGHTENED AND BROADENED AWARENESS

It was around this time that human rights began to emerge as a world concern. According to Weingärtner the modern concept of human rights "derives from the notion that on the grounds of the paramountcy" of certain rights of the human person "limits and duties can be placed upon authorities and the community, nationally and internationally and that these can be codified and guaranteed by law" (1991, 484). The so-called 'first generation' of human rights, consisting of individual civil and political rights (including the rights to life, liberty, citizenship and ownership, freedom of religion, assembly, association, expression, and participation in government), as well as the 'second generation' ones, consisting of economic, social and cultural rights (such as those to employment and fair working conditions, education, health care, and participation in the life of the community), had become legally established and at least formally recognized in various countries by the 1930's (cf. Zalaquett, 9). Subsequent to and as a consequence of the Second World War both of these sets of rights gained official recognition as "an international responsibility" (Weingärtner, 1991, 485).

Almost immediately after its founding in 1945 the United Nations took up the work of drafting the *Universal Declaration of Human Rights*, which was adopted on 10 December 1948. As a direct result of the war experience this Declaration posits an indissoluble link between world peace and adherence to human rights by stating in its very first sentence that:

---

[2] Translations from Dutch in this paper are mine.

> recognition of the inherent dignity and of the equal and inalienable rights of all members of the human family is the foundation of freedom, justice and peace in the world. (*Universal Declaration*)

Peace in the world, thus, does not depend solely on instruments of agreement between governments and nations: it is finally "the freedom and security of citizens of all countries that is the foundation of world peace" (Zalaquett, 9). Contrary to popular thinking, the Universal Declaration is not legally binding; it was intended to be a moral standard, a statement of human aspiration. The plan was to prepare a covenant on its basis that *would* be binding. Because agreement could not be reached on the content of such a contract, however, two separate covenants were drawn up and adopted in 1966, one for each of the two existing categories of rights: the *International Covenant on Civil and Political Rights* and the *International Covenant on Economic, Social and Cultural Rights*. These three documents together are often referred to as the International Bill of Human Rights (cf. Zalaquett, 13).

THE WORLD COUNCIL AND RELIGIOUS FREEDOM

From the very moment of its founding, the WCC had been deeply involved in the advocacy of and struggle for freedom of religion and conscience. The Commission of the Churches on International Affairs (CCIA) - which was formed in 1946 by joint decision of the IMC and the WCC (in process of formation) and in 1948 was incorporated into the WCC as that new body's department responsible for human rights - also concentrated on the right of religious freedom in the early years of its history. It was in this area that the CCIA felt "it had a special responsibility and expertise. Thus religious liberty became the point of departure for ecumenical human rights concerns" (Weingärtner, 1981, 46). In 1979 the WCC Executive Committee pointed out that careful study of WCC documents and actions in respect of this basic human right reveals that

> there has been a progressive evolution in the ecumenical understanding of religious liberty, which has been augmented and refined by the variety of concrete experiences of member churches as they live and work in vastly different environments. (*Study Paper*, 15)

The CCIA "played a significant role in the formulation of the article on 'religious liberty' in the Universal Declaration of Human Rights," (Koshy, *1038*), particularly through the direct participation of its first director, Frederick Nolde, who served from 1946 to 1948 as consultant on this matter and that of freedom of conscience to the drafters of the Declaration (cf. Weingärtner, 1991, 487). In addition, the CCIA was instrumental in effecting the establishment of the UN Commission on Human Rights (cf. Koshy, 1038) and took an active part in the composition of the two 1966 International Covenants on Human Rights (cf. Weingärtner, 1981, 44).

Nolde also led preparations for the discussion on human rights and religious liberty at the 1948 inaugural assembly of the WCC in Amsterdam. The issue of the freedom of religion was dealt with on various other occasions during the early years of WCC existence. All of the discussions and documents involved reflect certain anxieties and "bear the mark of the historical period in which they took place or were produced" (*Study Paper*, 3). The Amsterdam *Declaration on Religious Liberty* "reflects the Cold War tensions" of that time; the statement issuing from the 1949 WCC Central Committee Meeting in Chichester clearly evidences "anxieties aroused by the success of the revolution in China"; the report approved by the 1961 Third Assembly of the WCC in New Delhi, entitled *Christian Witness, Proselytism and Religious Liberty in the Setting of the WCC*, must be understood against the background of the tense issue of "Protestant-Orthodox relations, especially as regards the phenomenon of Evangelical missions in Orthodox countries"; a 1965 CCIA Executive Committee statement and the 1966 WCC Central Committee *Declaration on Religious Liberty* call attention, "in the context of the Second Vatican Council, ... to the rights of Protestant minorities in countries with Roman Catholic majorities" (*Study Paper*, 3, 4).

The *Study Paper* cited in the previous paragraph, which was prepared for the 1983 Sixth Assembly of the WCC in Vancouver, points to the utter absence of Third World influence or viewpoints in these early WCC documents on the right to freedom of religion. The only references in them to Third World regions "come in the context of concerns related to the future of Christian missions during a process of decolonization" (*ibid.*, 5). The argumentation in them proceeds on the assumption that religious liberty is "a static principle that need only be applied according to internationally recognized standards of behaviour" (*ibid.*, 6). The early documents take no account of traditional or contemporary concepts of religious freedom and the relation between religion and state or between religion and traditional social institutions in Asian and African cultural settings. Nor do they seek to discover a basis for cooperation with people of other faiths in the search for and advancement of religious freedom (*ibid.*, 5). Significant progress in ecumenical thinking regarding this right to freedom of religion would have to wait until the middle of the 1970's.

SHIFT OF EMPHASIS

In the 1960's human rights developed in a situation of great change and upheaval. During this period many events and crises took place that acted as strong catalysts of ever greater human rights awareness in the world. Increasingly, these rights were invoked in reaction to military and political developments such as the invasion of the Dominican Republic by the US in 1965 and that of Czechoslovakia by the USSR in 1968; the rise of repressive regimes in Asia, Africa and Latin America; the war in Vietnam. Colonized and oppressed peoples everywhere were clamoring for liberation. It was

> particularly the people of the 'Third World' who, through their struggle for freedom, ... impressed upon all human beings and states the urgent necessity of recognizing and realizing fundamental rights. (Moltmann, 58)

This context, these experiences, struggles and aspirations, gave rise to a *third generation* of human rights, which include the right of peoples to development and to self-determination, the right to dispose freely of their natural wealth and resources, the right to freedom from extreme want and from aggression. It was against this background and "as a result of critical reflection" as well as "the changing constituency of the World Council of Churches" that ecumenical understanding of human rights had been evolving through the years (Weingärtner, 1981, 44). But it would not be until the beginning of the 1970's that clear signs of a change of emphasis with respect to human rights, evidence of an intensification of approach began to appear within the ecumenical movement.

The year 1971 marked a turning point in WCC involvement in human rights. Although the CCIA had, of course, never been bereft of concern for human rights in the broader sense, its early efforts in this area, as shown above, took place "within the framework of the United Nations system" (Weingärtner, 1981, 44). The emphasis of the CCIA's general human rights work in the early years of its existence was especially directed toward the effort of persuading the churches and the world community to accept the norms and standards of human rights.

At its 1971 meeting in Addis Ababa the WCC Central Committee called upon the CCIA to engage in intensive "ecumenical reflection and involvement in the field of human rights," underlining "its conviction that the realization of human rights is basic to human survival itself" (Weingärtner, 1983, 13). In the document produced by this meeting, *Memorandum and Recommendation on Human Rights*, the Central Committee advocated an approach to rights more in keeping with the contemporary perception of the variety and complexity of issues involved in this field. The *Memorandum* states that "the attention of the churches will have to be centered primarily on the question of how best to implement [established] standards" of human rights (Weingärtner, 1981, 44). This represented a significant departure from the older position: the ecumenical churches were now being called to become actively involved in the effort to *realize* human rights. Weingärtner traces the immediate inspiration of this new focus to the influence of the 1968 Fourth Assembly of the WCC in Uppsala, "which expressed a strong socio-political concern" and generated "action-oriented programmes such as the Programme to Combat Racism" (*ibid.*, 44).

There continued to be a great deal of variation in the interpretation of human rights, depending on one's political, economic and geographic perspective.

Many in the Third World and Eastern Europe considered human rights to be nothing more than an instrument of North Atlantic economic policies and political goals. In July of 1971 the Executive Committee of the CCIA tried to dispel any impression that the WCC understanding of human rights "was one exclusively related to West European and North American" ideological interests (*ibid.*, 45). The Committee stated that the ecumenical perception of human rights, based on the Christian view of the "relation of God and man and the brotherhood of all men as sons of God", would of necessity have to move beyond the Western liberal preoccupation with individual civil and political rights to embrace the whole range of human rights, including broadly conceived social rights and the "collective rights of peoples to determine their own political and cultural destiny" (*ibid.*, 45).

Against the background of an enormous increase of human rights violations and abuses throughout the early 1970's the CCIA was concerned to enrich "existing narrow definitions," to put "human rights into the context of concrete historical situations" and to increase "emphasis on the essential role of member churches in the implementation of human rights in this larger perspective" (*ibid.*, 45). Despite such attempts to encourage a new enlarged common understanding of human rights and the churches' responsibility in respect of them, ecumenical consensus on this issue remained largely elusive. It was decided, therefore, to organize an international consultation on Human Rights and Christian Responsibility, with a view to working out "a commonly accepted framework for ecumenical endeavours in this field" (Weingärtner, 1983, 14). This gathering was held in St. Pölten, Austria in October 1974.

The delegates to this key consultation, who came from all parts of the world, were asked to deal in particular with the question of

> how to relate standards of human rights to the cultural, socio-economic and political settings of different parts of the world ..., emphasis being laid on finding more effective means of international cooperation for the implementation of human rights. (Weingärtner, 1981, 45)

There were two distinct positions represented at St. Pölten regarding the interpretation of the *content* of human rights and the *type of action* appropriate for Christians in the struggle for these rights. Regarding the question of content, one school of thought emphasized the inviolability of the individual person based on his or her creation in the image of God. This position defended the centrality of individual civil and political rights and argued that religious liberty takes absolute precedence on the grounds that it presupposes for its realization all other rights and freedoms belonging to this category. Economic, social and cultural *rights* do not really exist in the same sense as individual rights and should be approached by Christians from the viewpoint of service to the world. The second position stressed the relational nature of the human person, created male and female by God, who in the Christian understanding is a unity of three persons. Therefore, the individual can never take precedence over the community. According to this view human dignity is grounded in the well-being of the entire human family. Religious liberty is important, but may never be claimed as a priority by Christians so long as the community is subjected to suffering owing to the lack of collective rights. Social rights stand in a relationship of priority to individual rights since the former constitute the foundation of true personal freedom (cf. Weingärtner, 1983, 15).

With respect to the matter of appropriate type of action for human rights the first group argued the importance of denunciation and advocacy in connection with individual civil and political rights. Such rights entail a negative obligation on the part of governments and therefore are immediately demandable and can be granted by any government anywhere. Governmental infringement of individual freedoms, wherever it occurs, must be countered with formal criticism by Christians. The second position on this question was of a utilitarian nature. The only valid criterion for judging the validity of an action, it was maintained, is the possibility it offers for attaining a desirable result. Almost nothing can be achieved by the denunciation of the lack or denial of economic, social or cultural rights. It is necessary to identify the root causes of the nonimplementation of these rights - poverty, repression, exploitation, underdevelopment - and then engage in efforts to do away with these causes (cf. *ibid.*).

St. Pölten helped greatly to clarify the many complex questions and issues involved in the field of human rights. Moreover, despite the differences of interpretation represented, St. Pölten achieved considerable consensus and thus contributed very significantly to the development of ecumenical understanding of human rights and their advancement.

BREAKTHROUGH

The report of the St. Pölten consultation, *Human Rights and Christian Responsibility*, played a central role in the human rights discussions at the 1975 Fifth Assembly of the WCC in Nairobi, and its main findings were incorporated into the Assembly report, significantly under *Section V: Structures of Injustice and Struggles for Liberation* (cf. Paton, 102-07). This clearly indicates that according to Nairobi human rights cannot be properly understood solely in terms of individual rights or in isolation from the broader social, political and economic contexts in which their violations and abuse take place. Contrary to the view that human rights are primarily a humanitarian or diaconal concern, Nairobi took the position that they have a very definite political dimension, "that the struggle for human rights, even of the individual, is at root the struggle for the liberation of the entire community" (Weingärtner, 1981, 45).

Nairobi 1975 may be viewed as an important breakthrough in the ecumenical reception of human rights for two additional reasons. First, it abandoned the earlier ecumenical preoccupation with religious liberty and the idea that this freedom could be sought and implemented in isolation from other freedoms. According to J. Verkuyl the inseparable link between religious liberty and other fundamental rights had already been recognized in the general post-Second World War literature. It was understood by many that "religious liberty is nowhere in the world an isolated reality" (Verkuyl, 13):

> Religious freedom and the other freedoms die off and blossom together .... Struggle for one freedom requires struggle for the other freedoms as well, for they are interdependent. (*ibid.*, 14)

And now at Nairobi this insight respecting the indivisibility of human rights and therefore the need for an integral approach to them was explicitly recognized and endorsed by the ecumenical movement (cf. Paton, 106, par. 34). Moreover, it was clearly stated that the right to religious liberty, "though it continues to be a major concern of member churches and the WCC," may never be viewed as something

> belonging exclusively to the Church. The exercise of religious freedom has not always reflected the great diversity of convictions that exist around the world .... No religious community should plead for its own religious liberty without active respect and reverence for the faith and basic human rights of others. (Paton, 106, par. 34)

The second reason for viewing the Nairobi Assembly as an important watershed in the development of the ecumenical position on human rights is that at this gathering a consensus was reached "for the first time in ecumenical history, ... regarding the content of human rights" (Weingärtner, 1981, 46). Despite the high degree of ideological heterogeneity and geographical and cultural diversity within its membership, the WCC was able - albeit after intense debate - to reach agreement on "what constitutes, for Christian churches throughout the world, a definition" of human rights. According to Nairobi they include: the right to basic guarantees for life; the right to self-determination and cultural identity, and the rights of minorities; the right to participate in decision-making within the community; the right to dissent; the right to personal dignity; and the right to religious freedom (cf. Paton, 103-06).

There was also agreement on appropriate Christian action for human rights. Christians are said to have a special duty "to express in word and deed their solidarity with those people whose human rights and fundamental freedoms are denied" (Paton, 106, par. 37). The gospel, it is asserted, should inspire Christians to fuller participation in human rights endeavors, including the struggle against unjust social structures, which "create the conditions under which human rights are denied." It should cause them to become more and more involved in

> identifying and rectifying violations of human rights in [their] own societies, and to enter into new forms of ecumenical solidarity with Christians elsewhere who are similarly engaged. It [should lead them] into the struggle of the poor and the oppressed both within and outside the church as [the poor] seek to achieve their full human rights, and [it] frees [them] to work together with people of other faiths or ideologies who share with [them] a common concern for human dignity. (*ibid.*, 102, pars. 13, 12)

St. Pölten held that the specific role of the WCC in the area of human rights activities ought to be one of enablement rather than denunciation. The WCC could engage in the latter but only sparingly to enhance the enabling approach when necessary or useful. With respect to official WCC human rights actions the emphasis "was on sustained, long-term programmes of educational, pastoral and advocacy activities" (Weingärtner, 1983, 21). At Nairobi this became a matter of heated discussion. After the Uppsala Assembly the WCC had come under increasing fire, particularly in Western Europe and North America for what was perceived as its "selective indignation" with regard to human rights abuse and violation. Although the mandate of the Programme to Combat Racism is clearly global, most attention within its context was directed toward South Africa. Also, various Western countries were regularly subjected to sharp ecumenical criticism for certain of their policies and failings, whereas hardly anything at all was said in public about the flagrant human rights violations in Eastern Europe.

The debate intensified greatly after the signing of the Final Act of the Helsinki Conference on Security and Cooperation in Europe - held to close some of the gaps left by the absence of a concluding peace treaty at the end of World War Two - by 35 states of Western and Eastern Europe and North America on 1 August 1975, just four months prior to Nairobi. The Final Act, or Helsinki Accords, contained a so-called "third basket" of humanitarian issues. This made it now imperative, it was argued, for the WCC to take an openly critical stance against human rights failures in Eastern Europe as well, particularly those regarding church persecution and encroachments on the right to religious liberty (cf. Weingärtner, 1983, 19-21).

This dissension represented a serious threat to the achievement of agreement on human rights at Nairobi. The passing of a *Resolution on the Helsinki Agreement* no doubt helped to defuse the tension. The resolution called on the General Secretary of the WCC to consult with the member churches of the Helsinki signatory states on the matter of religious liberty. As a follow-up to this request two CCIA-organized colloquia consisting of representatives from these churches were held in Montreux, Switzerland in, respectively, 1976 and 1977. The first of these recommended the strengthening of CCIA human rights facilities and the creation of an international Human Rights Advisory Group (HRAG) within the CCIA, to help "channel and deepen the CCIA's work in human rights and provide for a network of exchange among the regions" (Weingärtner, 1981, 47).

The HRAG was set up in 1978 but, because of lack of funds, was not able to meet for the first time until the end of 1979.

The second Montreux colloquium resulted eventually in the establishment of a *Churches' Human Rights Programme for the Implementation of the Helsinki Final Act* under joint sponsorship of the Conference of European Churches, the National Council of Churches of Christ in the USA, and the Canadian Council of Churches. This programme, which received an appointed secretary in 1980 and was given a mandate until 1985, met with many objections at the very outset, notably from Third World spokespersons who took strenuous issue with the lopsided amount of energy and resources the CIA was devoting to European human rights questions with the result that the far greater problems of the Southern hemisphere were being neglected (cf. Weingärtner, 1983, 22-29).

FURTHER DEVELOPMENTS

After Nairobi 1975 there was what Theo van Boven, former Director of the UN Division of Human Rights (now the UN Center for Human Rights), called "an explosion" of human rights activities and concerns that ran in tandem with the fact that "the violation of human rights throughout the world [had] reached epidemic proportions" (Weingärtner, 1983, 7). As a result it could be said that

> ecumenical concern for human rights has derived less from intellectual elaborations at the top than from the experiences and needs of the churches and Christians engaged in often dramatic struggles for ... human dignity in their own situation. (Weingärtner, 1981, 46)

Huber and Tödt argue the same point:

> Die Menschenrechte, so fragil, antagonistisch und interpretationsbedürftig sie sind, sind in unserer Welt nicht bloss Ideale von Philosophen oder Produkte von Weltverbesserern, nicht bloss Begriffe und Schlagworte im ideologischen Kampf der Systeme. Sie sind auch und vor allem Ergebnisse von langen und schweren Verhandlungen, rechtlich gefasster Ausdruck eines mühsam errungenen Konsensus und so eben Teile des Völkerrechts. (pp. 34, 35)

And yet, it goes almost without saying that theological reflection on human rights against the background of this practical experience is indispensable. In 1981 Jose Zalaquett wrote regarding "a perceived theoretical vacuum" within the international human rights movement regarding *inter alia* "the foundation of human rights" and "the relation between different human rights" (p. 38). Within the ecumenical movement and Christian confessional world bodies this gap began to be addressed through an extensive process of joint study and reflection from the early 1970's onward.

To mention just one of the many examples that could be adduced,[3] the World Alliance of Reformed Churches (WARC) at its 1970 Uniting General Council meeting in Nairobi issued a call for a theological study of human rights. Between 1971 and 1975 a great deal of work was done in this regard, which culminated in a 1976 WARC-sponsored consultation in London. This gathering produced a report entitled, *The Theological Basis of Human Rights*, based on an impressive study paper presented there by Jürgen Moltmann. The WARC document argues for the "grounding of fundamental human rights in God's right to, i.e., his claim upon human beings" by virtue of their creation in God's image, their reconciliation through God's incarnation, and their citizenship of God's coming Kingdom. Because of this claim of God on all humans, human dignity cannot be legitimately denied or curtailed by any earthly authority, and the concern of "Christian theology is one for the humanity of persons as well as for their ongoing rights and duties" (*The Theological Basis*, 51).

The first human rights addressee of this document is the Church itself: Christian communities should be characterized by the marks of the Kingdom of God, i.e., they should strive to become an "alternative society, ... in which people can individually and collectively achieve their full human potential" (*ibid.*, 55). Freedom of religion is "paramount in the understanding of humanity as created in the image of God" and should therefore be sought for all. The statement also calls for recognition of the rights of future generations and of the natural environment. With respect to the latter it is suggested that in addition to "the existing Covenants on Human Rights of 1966 there would seem to be the need for a further Human Rights Covenant ... relating to environmental rights" (*ibid.*, 56-57). In sum, it may be said that the 1976 WARC document argues that violations and abuse of human and future-generation rights constitute violations and abuse "of that creation which has been [or will be] created in the image of God and which has been called to live in the freedom of His grace" (*ibid.*, 57) or, in the case of the natural environment, which is meant to be allowed to live and exist in the freedom of the grace of God.

The main insights and emphases of the 1975 Nairobi Assembly regarding human rights and religious freedom were repeatedly endorsed and in some cases expanded by ecumenical gatherings and agencies in later years. The 1979 WCC Executive Committee *Statement on Religious Liberty* defines this liberty - which "cannot be divorced from other aspects of human rights" (p. 23) - as

---

[3] Of the large body of ecumenical Christian literature devoted to the study of human rights, one might mention in particular the influential work of Jürgen Moltmann, e.g., in addition to the study paper referred to, *Menschenwürde, Recht und Freiheit*, Stuttgart/Berlin: Kreuz Verlag, 1979, and the fundamental study by W. Huber and H.E. Tödt (cf. bibliography), which deals not only with the theology but also the legal status and the philosophical foundation and critique of human rights; for additional information on human rights studies by world Christian communions see Weingärtner, 1983, 53-54.

> the freedom to have or to adopt a religion or belief of one's choice, and freedom, either individually or in community with others and in public or private, to manifest one's religion or belief in worship, observance, practice and teaching. Religious freedom should also include the right and duty of religious bodies to criticize the ruling powers when necessary, on the basis of their religious convictions. (*ibid.*, 24)

Registering an "alarming" increase of incidences of restriction of religious liberty during the previous two years, the *Statement* goes on to echo Nairobi's sentiments regarding appropriate action for human rights and cooperation with people of other faiths for the advancement of rights. Human rights ought to be a priority concern for all world religions and thus figure strongly in interreligious dialogue and interaction between religions, particularly in multireligious settings (cf. *ibid.*, *23*). Christians must

> be concerned about more than their own religious liberty. Our concern must extend to the defence of the human rights of all - whether they profess other religions or no religion. We have to find ways in which the common humanity of a pluralistic world can be expressed in societies which affirm the dignity and freedom of all human beings. (*ibid.*, 25, 26)

And a church which commits itself to the struggle for the realization of "all rights for all people," it is added, "has often, with surprise, rediscovered something of its essential evangelical mission" (*ibid.*, 23).

The 1980 CCIA *Study Paper on Religious Liberty*, and the 1981 Report of the CCIA *Human Rights Advisory Group* meeting in Glion, Switzerland can also be cited in this connection. Both of these documents stress the obligation to service that religious liberty entails. The Glion *Report* refers unambiguously to religious freedom as a basic human right: it may be claimed for all everywhere. It states approvingly that freedom of religion is often "taken as the yardstick by which to measure the implementation of human rights," but adds immediately that Christians should not defend this and other human rights only with an eye to freedom for their own work, "but also for the development of the whole human person and the society in which he or she lives" (*Report*, 1981, 64). In its 1980 *Study Paper* the CCIA lists ten principles or guidelines for reflection on human rights, among which is one that stresses the indissoluble link between the rights and duties of religious organizations and believers.

> Religious *rights* must be inseparably combined with religious obligations. The freedom which any church or religious community enjoys should be applied in service to the whole society. The exercise of religious liberty must be connected not only to the liturgical and mission functions of the church but also to the diaconic and prophetic functions. (*Study Paper*, 12)

These guidelines, which strongly emphasize that matters of religious liberty need to be clarified within the actual practice of local contexts, also have a clearly dialogical thrust: there is an "urgent necessity of a dialogue with people of other faiths and ideologies regarding religious liberty" (*ibid.*, 13).[4] Moreover, this document states that the concept of religious liberty implies the freedom to co-operate with people of other faiths and convictions for the advancement of justice and peace and in the struggle to relieve and redress the situation of the poor, adding significantly that "such mutual collaboration will itself increase the liberty of the partners in service" (*ibid.*). Further, the *Study Paper* posits a very important direct link between the human rights issue and theology of religion concerns. Churches may not seek only their own freedom but "should work for the rights of other religious communities" as well, on the basis of the latter's "own self-definition." Such pursuit of religious liberty for all must of necessity lead Christians to assign "a theological value to the existence of those ethnic or religious communities, rather than seeing them simply as objects of evangelization" (*ibid.*, 11).

The 1981 Glion *Report* referred to above encouraged the CCIA and WCC to continue to facilitate the process of ecumenical study on human rights, a process which should include the reflection of people directly "engaged in struggles for human rights" (p. 56) and should lay emphasis "on theological concepts and symbols which enable Christians to join in effective solidarity with people of other faiths and ideologies who share" the commitment to justice (p. 64). It also points unambiguously to the fact that the human rights situation within the churches is considerably less than ideal: even there rights "are far from universally assured" (p. 64). Reiterating a concern found in previous documents, the *Report* argues that any credible involvement in human rights by the Christian churches will have to take its departure from sincere critical examination of their own past and present life, policies and practices (cf. pp. 64, 56). Glion also made an appeal to the coming 1983 Assembly of the WCC in Vancouver to

> make a clear statement on human rights as a concern central to the churches, reaffirming the ecumenical position and giving a new mandate for the work of the WCC on human rights. (p. 56)

CONSOLIDATION

Now that numerous ecumenical instruments for participation in the human rights struggle had been put into place and it had become firmly established among

---

[4] Regarding the importance of interreligious dialogue for the interpretation of human rights see, e.g., F. Köster, 43-56.

large numbers of Christians that "concern about human rights is not ... just an option for ecclesiastical politics, but central to the wholeness of the Gospel of Jesus Christ" (Smith, 50), the CCIA became aware of the need to clarify two basic matters essential to continued effective ecumenical activity in the field of human rights. The first had to do with the identification of the main actors in the human rights struggle. Earlier gatherings had already dealt with this question but their findings were not yet accepted by all in the ecumenical family. In its report to the 1979 WCC Central Committee Meeting in Jamaica the CCIA stated emphatically that, in view of the limitations of its resources, direct responsibility for human rights would have to be assumed by the member churches of the WCC. This concept also rests

> on the realization that those who live within any given location are best qualified to interpret and analyze their own experience and are best able to prescribe strategies for the realization of human rights within their own situation. (Weingärtner, 1981, 48)

On the strength of this report Jamaica 1979 "underlined the responsibility of local ... church bodies for human rights work in their own areas (*Report*, 1982, 28), and the 1981 Glion *Report* called on the WCC to redouble its efforts to create or strengthen *national and local instruments of the churches* for human rights endeavors (cf. p. 65). By the early 1980's "all regional councils or conferences of churches" had "major human rights programmes, in most cases involving fulltime staff" (*Report*, 1982, 29). Equally important at the Jamaica meeting and in later documents, however, was the parallel emphasis on *international ecumenical solidarity*, which refers to the "responsibility of churches within the ecumenical community to support each other morally, materially and politically" (Weingärtner, 1983, 30).

The second major issue to be addressed was that of the ultimate causes of human rights abuse and infringement. Though this matter, too, had been touched upon on previous occasions, it remained a bone of no little contention among ecumenical churches. Paradoxically, human rights not only united these churches but simultaneously caused division among them. As pointed out in the foregoing, human rights efforts within the ecumenical movement and churches had often had a diaconal thrust and aim: direct relief and succor of the victims of rights violations. This approach, though in itself important and necessary, runs the risk of addressing the mere "symptoms of the ills in the world order" (Weingärtner, 1981, 50). According to the CCIA at the beginning of the 1980's, violations of human rights are not merely due to the aberrant behavior of a

> limited number of demented individuals in positions of power, but the logical consequences of social, political, economic and military systems. The link between human rights and justice (the broader biblical concept) has become more apparent. The root causes of human rights violations arise from the systems of

> injustice which have developed in the West, the East, the North, and the South .... (Weingärtner, 1983, 7)

This took up a prominent theme from the 1981 Glion *Report* which pointed out that new awareness had been gained of "the globality of human rights violations and of their causes"; more and more it had come to be recognized that "those causes are rooted in international structures" of injustice, "erected by those who wish to increase their own power and privilege," and that any attempt to approach human rights "problems in an isolated way is only to offer palliatives, not lasting relief to the victims" (p. 60).

Important sectors of the WCC constituency as well as funding agencies continued "to view human rights through the prism of individual morality," however, which left little or no room for recognition of the structural aspect of human rights infringements and therefore of the extraordinary difficulty of implementing these rights (Weingärtner, 1981, 49). The diaconal approach fails to identify and make an attempt to deal with the "intricate relationships between human rights and other key issues on the international agenda" (*ibid.*, 50), such as arms expenditures,militarism, racism, world hunger, environmental pollution, oppression of women and children, biological and genetic manipulation, repressive political and economic structures. Specific and hard questions needed to be posed in this connection. For example, what is the best way to effect a change of oppressive political systems that frustrate the realization of human rights? Is "humanitarian outside intervention" a permissible means in such situations? Or again, people in many parts of the world are being robbed of the fundamental right to life and sustenance by unjust national and international economic dependencies. What could and should be done to transform such structures?

Despite these and other remaining questions and discrepancies of interpretation, Weingärtner, writing in 1981, avers that in the previous decade the ecumenical churches had made great strides in the area of human rights.

> Compared with the situation ten years ago, church endorsement and concrete support for human rights activities has steadily increased .... The insight that concern for human rights is an integral part of the demands of the Gospel is today shared by the majority of the churches throughout the ecumenical spectrum to an extent that could not have been imagined in 1971. (p. 49)

FOCAL CONCERN

Although the CCIA continued to bear the main responsibility for human rights efforts within the WCC, it should be noted that by this time the rights issue constituted a focal aspect of the work of nearly all of the various departments of the World Council and its related organizations. Human rights had clearly become one of the major programme emphases of the entire ecumenical movement. Almost all WCC units were engaged to one degree or another in the mobilization of the resources of the churches to combat infringements and promote the implementation of human rights.[5]

General consensus regarding the modes of ecumenical action for human rights also dates from this period. These modes consist of four interdependent activities: monitoring, advocacy, the building of public awareness, and study. The primary flow of information needed for monitoring, it was determined, must come from or be channelled through the member churches of the WCC. Within this framework five regional ecumenical consultations were held between 1979 and 1981, each of which emphasized the "importance of analytical studies into the root causes of human rights" nonimplementation and argued that all "human rights problems [require] an interdisciplinary approach" (Weingärtner, 1983, 44). Ecumenical human rights advocacy, it was established, should be largely a matter of referral to local churches, various independent human rights organizations, and United Nations agencies for human rights. Awareness-building at all levels of public and church education was identified as one of the key dimensions of ecumenical human rights work, as was study, both in the form of academic research and of conciliar discussion and reflection. Areas requiring ongoing attention include such subjects as religious liberty, torture, extrajudicial execution, terrorism, racism, militarism, etc., as well as biblical-theological reflection on human rights. Some continued to insist that ecumenical human rights activity should include public denunciation of rights infringements as well.

In its report to the 1983 Vancouver Assembly of the WCC the Working Committee of the Churches' Human Rights Programme for the Implementation of the Helsinki Final Act outlined the results of a series of regional consultations it had organized in 1981 and 1982. These study encounters stressed the following concepts and priorities for churches in Europe and North America in their attempt to discover "a more profound and effective way of ... dealing with human rights within the so-called Helsinki area" and elsewhere:

> human rights are closely related with peace and détente; socio-economic justice is a prerequisite for individual and collective human rights; the churches' involvement in human rights is a sign of their obedience to God's redemptive purpose; the (industrialized) signatory states of the Helsinki Final Act bear a major responsibility for the violation of human rights in developing countries; .... (*Report*, 1983, 69)

Human rights problems needing special attention in the North Atlantic countries, this report argues, are those having to do with the position of women, the situa-

[5] For an exhaustive survey of WCC programmatic interrelationships and interdepartmental cooperation with regard to human rights see Weingärtner, 1983 (cf. bibliography), 32-36.

tion of racial minorities, work conditions and unemployment, the negative effects of the modern information revolution, and threats to religious liberty for all. Implementation of human rights in these areas is a matter of great urgency.

The 1983 Sixth Assembly of the WCC in Vancouver noted with gratification evidence of steadily increasing ecumenical dedication to the struggle for human dignity as well as the emergence of human rights cooperation "between the Christian community and people of other living faiths ... based on their common commitment to human values and social goals" (*Sixth Assembly Statement*, 27). According to Vancouver, Christians are enjoined to participate in the pursuit of human rights by the conviction that all

> human beings, regardless of race, sex or belief, have been created by God as individuals and in human community. Yet the world has been corrupted by sin, which results in the destruction of human relationships. In reconciling humankind and creation with God, Jesus Christ has also reconciled human beings with each other. Love of our neighbours is the essence of obedience to God. (*ibid.*)

In awareness of the "complexity and interrelatedness of human rights" the ecumenical churches had come to an appreciation of the "need to set individual rights and their violation in the context of society and its social structures" (*ibid.*, 28). Human rights cannot be dealt with separately but only in conjunction with other pressing issues of a national or global nature. The abrogation of human rights can and does lead to national and international disorder and instability, and conversely, political, economic and social disorder, at whatever level it occurs, leads to human rights abuse and violation. Among the many pressing problems in the field of human rights Vancouver called particular attention to the plight of indigenous people in various parts of the world and to ever more numerous occurrences of: "sophisticated forms of physical and psychological torture, ... 'disappearances' and extrajudicial executions"; curtailment of fundamental human rights on the basis of spurious appeals to national security doctrines; violation of workers' rights, especially those of migrant laborers; denial of the rights of refugees; and infringements of religious liberty (cf. *ibid.*, 28-30).

Reaffirming the common ecumenical commitment to human rights work, Vancouver appealed to the WCC and its member churches to continue their "pastoral approach" to human rights, "which combines prayer, preaching and practical efforts in action," along with the work of monitoring, advocacy, study and the raising of consciousness (*ibid.*, 30). The Assembly also reminded the churches of the need for constant self-examination: "their own structures and methods of operation" often stand in the way of the realization of the rights of "women, youth, children, and disabled persons" (*ibid.*, 28). Moreover, in the face of waxing human rights abuse throughout the world the churches "must confess in humility that they have not done enough to counter forces of evil and death, at times even being in complicity with them" (*ibid.*, 27). In the Vancouver *Statement on Peace and Justice* the ecumenical churches

> are called to confess anew their faith, and to repent for the times when Christians have remained silent in the face of injustice or threats to peace. The biblical vision of peace with justice for all, of wholeness, of unity for all God's people is not one of several options for the followers of Christ. It is an imperative in our time. (p. 132)

Since Vancouver human rights within the ecumenical movement came to be closely associated with the concerns of the Justice, Peace and Integrity of Creation process (JPIC) set into motion by that assembly and carried through the 1989 European Ecumenical Assembly held in Basel and the 1990 Seoul World Convocation on JPIC. It became commonly understood that without justice, peace and environmental well-being human rights are unattainable.

The Human Rights Advisory Group (HRAG) of the CCIA, at its 1986 meeting in Glion, reaffirmed the most important established ecumenical principles and activities in the area of human rights, calling, in addition, for the development of a "theoretical framework" to "enable churches to become more deeply committed to human rights work as part of the engagement for justice, peace and the integrity of creation" (*Priorities*, 34). Glion 1986 identified three problem areas for renewed attention: first, menaces to the survival rights of entire groups arising from the increasing use of genocide "as a systematic policy" by certain governments, military expenditures, dumping of nuclear waste, hunger and starvation, and homelessness; second, threats to religious liberty in the form of state control, cooption or rejection of religion, and interreligious animosity; and third, the undermining of the process of democratization and the pursuit of social and economic justice by militarization, the arms trade and crippling foreign debt. This gathering underlined the position

> that the violation of human rights is properly placed squarely within the *structures of injustice* and that the mission of the churches in the pursuit of human rights is therefore deeply related to the struggle against domestic and international structures of injustice. (*ibid.*, 35)

With an eye to the promotion of full religious freedom for all, particularly in multireligious settings, the HRAG recommended ecumenical cooperation to establish continuous interreligious dialogue. It called specifically for "dialogue between representatives of Islam and churches living in Islamic countries," adding that in view of the large numbers of Moslems living in Western Europe, "such dialogue should also be carried out in European countries where intolerance and racism is on the rise ..." (*ibid.*, 37).

The 1991 Seventh Assembly of the WCC in Canberra contended that Christians are called by the gospel to be active in the advancement and protection of human rights: those of women and children, those of minorities, and those of the victims of racism and economic injustice (cf. *Rapport Sectie II*, 115). Human rights at Canberra must be understood against the background and within the framework of the ecumenical JPIC process. JPIC pulls together and at the same time is an expression of the "intimate interrelatedness of ... issues that used to be dealt with by the churches and the Council as separate" matters (Keshishian, 260). Canberra reconfirmed Vancouver's designation of JPIC as a WCC-wide programme emphasis and reiterated the earlier assembly's contention that the "JPIC process is grounded on the conviction that the threats to life in the world are interlocked and thus cannot be approached singly. Justice, peace and the integrity of creation are three facets of one reality" (Van der Zee, 12).

This interconnectedness of such threats to life on earth, which of course constitute threats to human rights, makes it imperative for the ecumenical churches to "intensify and deepen concrete analysis of the root causes and institutional structures of injustice" (*Report of the Committee*, 278). Obstacles to the implementation of peace and justice on earth and therefore of individual and social human rights include "ideologies that separate subject from object, spirit from matter, and nature from culture" (*Rapport Sectie I*, 67). Another important hindrance to the realization of this aim is the division of the world into industrialized and non-industrialized nations, whereby the exertions on the part of rich countries to protect their wealth and power by all means are rewarded at the expense of the poor, and their endeavors "to increase gross *national* product" very often lead to "decrease of gross *natural* product" (*ibid.*). But the chief impediment to the effectuation of justice and thus human rights "lies in our own hearts, in our fear of change, in our tepidity, in our lack of spirituality, ... [and] trust in God" (*ibid.*). It was argued that "interracial, interregional and multicultural interaction is essential to new understanding [of] and action" for justice and human rights (*Report of the Committee*, 278).

Canberra highlighted the God-given vocation of the churches to resist all forms of injustice, whether local, regional, national or international, whether of an economic, political, cultural or social nature, whether in the area of gender, race or ecology (cf. *ibid.*, 280). It appealed to the churches to bend their efforts to the task of constructing concrete models of justice, peace and environmental integrity in their local situations, and reminded them that the concept of *justice* implies the human right to power-sharing and participation in the full life of the community and society (cf. *ibid.*, 278). In view of the severity of the present ecological crisis, one of the greatest challenges facing the ecumenical movement in the coming years will be the necessity to develop a theology of creation that will provide the churches and Christians with a new and deeper understanding of their fundamental responsibilities with respect to the natural environment (cf. *Rapport Sectie I*, 59-65, 75), which is being "misused" in an "absolutely irresponsible manner" today (Herwijnen, 56). Canberra also stressed the point that dialogue with people of other faiths and convictions "must continue to be promoted, particularly for cooperation in our common quest for justice, peace and the integrity of creation" (*Report of the Committee*, 280). Ultimately, if human dignity is to be truly honored everywhere, it will be necessary - as has been so often argued in recent years - to construct a new international order reflecting the JPIC vision.

CONTEMPORARY ECUMENICAL UNDERSTANDING OF HUMAN RIGHTS

We may now attempt a summarizing delineation of what might be termed 'the harvest' of ecumenical thought on the subject of human rights. It is of course impossible to do justice here to the entirety of the ecumenical view on this matter in all of its complex ramifications and implications. A brief recapitulation of a number of its main features and key concepts will have to suffice.

1. The *content* of human rights, while expanding steadily in ecumenical thinking since the late 1960's, has been broadened dramatically in recent times. In the view of many it now includes considerably more than the classical categories of 'first generation' individual and 'second generation' social rights. Against the background of the communication revolution of recent years, which has led to greatly increased awareness of the rapidly growing interdependence of human communities throughout the world, three additional categories of rights have begun to emerge, each of which is related to deep apprehensions about threats to peace, global injustice, and large-scale environmental destruction. They are: a 'third generation' of peoples rights to self-determination and development and to freedom from want and aggression (Weingärtner, 1991, 485); a 'fourth generation' of environmental rights; and a fifth set or category of what might well be called 'future-generation rights.' These evolving sets of rights may be understood to be derivative of "the concern of a nascent [world] community, which seeks to protect the common nest from being blown up or fouled and endeavours to use its resources for the benefit of all" (Zalaquett, 11).

These concerns are deeply shared by growing numbers of Christians and Christian churches today. Even though "the conditions of the world in which we live have become ever more turbulent" (Scott, 176), ever more complex and difficult to fathom and master, there has been an attempt within both Roman Catholic and ecumenical theology to come to grips with the biblical notion of discernment of the signs of the times.[6]

Though the notion of environmental 'rights' may continue to strike some Christians as strange, the concept is definitely biblical. In Romans 8, e.g., the Apostle Paul writes about the creation in terms eminently consentaneous to earth

---

[6] See in this connection the stimulating paper authored by the late David Bosch, 1992, listed in the bibliography.

concerns and to the idea that nature has rights. There is a distinct need, in the words of Canberra, for a "universal declaration on human obligations towards nature" (cf. *Rapport Sectie I*, 75). In addition, it is clear that "we are in a symbiotic relationship with our environment: if it suffers, we suffer, and conversely, if it prospers, we flourish" (Hulley, 133).

The fifth category of human rights referred to above is also legitimated by biblical teaching. For some time now Dutch radio has been running an environmental-awareness advertisement which concludes with the words: "After all, we only have the earth on loan from our children." And this idea rings very true from the Christian perspective. According to Christian belief this earth belongs to God, who created it, pronounced it very good, and gave it to humankind to use for its good. Today the implications of this concept are becoming better and more fully understood. There is a growing sense that each existing generation has the earth in *lend-lease* from humanity in its totality. The good earth - corrupted by personal sin and structural evil, it is true, but good nevertheless - has been transferred to us by past generations, and it is incumbent upon us to make payment for this transfer by doing our part to ensure that, when our time for using and enjoying the natural environment is over, the earth returned to humanity is at least as good as the one we received. Future generations do indeed have rights, and they have a claim upon us with respect to them.

2. The ecumenical understanding of the *relation* between human rights is that they are indivisible. This also holds for infractions of rights: problems in this field are perceived to require an interdisciplinary approach for their solution. Careful reflection shows that human rights issues constitute a web of mutually related elements. Since they are *human* rights, they cannot be said to have been truly realized if they have not been effectuated everywhere for all. Also, all rights, freedoms and duties and all categories of rights are mutually dependent and interlocked. Personal civil and political freedom mean very little if one is suffering poverty and privation or is living in a situation of inequality or economic exploitation. By the same token, social, economic and cultural rights and freedoms are hollow achievements if unaccompanied by personal freedom, rights and duties. Liberty absent justice is vain; justice absent liberty is false. True liberty and true justice presuppose one another.

Likewise, if we refuse to recognize the claims of future generations on us, *our* right to respect and honor from them will be incapable of realization, and *they* will have been robbed of the possibility of fulfilling their duty to heed the enjoinder to honor their father and mother. Or again, people could not exercise their right to know in the absence of free access to information and freedom of expression. Further, religious liberty may be viewed as a sort of linchpin or cornerstone of human rights, a yardstick by which the degree of rights implementation can be measured,[7] for without freedom of religion there is no true freedom of conscience and expression, of assembly and association. Religious liberty is essential to genuine realization of human rights. Also, since so many Christians in recent times "have suffered imprisonment, torture, disappearance and martyrdom" in consequence of their human rights involvement, the "right to be engaged in the struggle for justice and human dignity has itself become a component of religious liberty" (Weingärtner, 1991, 488). Finally, ecological rights seems to be absolutely basic, for without a sound natural environment life itself becomes impossible.

3. In the ecumenical perception the matter of the identity of the *actors* is of paramount importance for the question of determining appropriate *methodology* and *approach* in the human rights struggle. Questions of interpretation of human rights content, but in particular of strategy, type of action and prioritization in human rights implementation efforts, it is maintained, cannot be properly addressed from any one 'center' but can only be clarified in the actual practice of local settings. Human rights ought not to be perceived as an unchanging concept or principle that can simply be applied along the same lines on every occasion in all places. According to Weingärtner

> the content of human rights is open-ended, related to the forms of inequality and oppression against which individuals, groups or nations demand their rights. As new expressions of injustice arise, human rights standards must be expanded or refined. (1991, 486)

The WCC, the CCIA, and other world ecumenical bodies can, of course, and should aid local churches in their human rights endeavors. Assistance of this kind continues to be provided through the agency of the activities described above: monitoring, study, advocacy, and awareness-raising. Important examples of central ecumenical human rights support that emerged from a combination of all four of these modes of action are WCC statements such as those censuring racism (1968), torture (1977), extrajudicial execution (1982), and the death penalty (1990). Nevertheless, regional bodies and local churches bear primary responsibility for identifying rights violations in their areas and for deciding what action to take with an eye to the removal of encumbrances to the realization of rights and freedoms. Christians are strongly encouraged to seek cooperation with other religious people in pursuit of human rights interpretation and aims. Thus, according to contemporary ecumenical thinking the matter of

---

[7] For a recent defense of religious liberty as "the irreducible foundation, the *sine qua non*," in both theory and practice, "of any meaningful scheme of 'human rights'" see George Weigel, "Religious Freedom: The First Human Right," in: Richard J. Neuhaus (ed.), *The Structure of Freedom: Correlations, Causes and Cautions* (Grand Rapids: Eerdmans, 1991), pp. 34-35.

human rights must be thoroughly contextualized and enculturated. There is perhaps one single exception to this, namely, the WCC establishment of 'preferential option for the poor'[8] as strategic priority in human rights.

4. The affirmation of solidarity with the poor as priority is based on the ecumenical understanding of the *causes* of the infringement of human rights. Of course it is understood that curtailment of rights and freedoms has an immediate cause in human behavior, but it is now generally recognized within the ecumenical movement that there are also ultimate or *root* causes of rights violations, namely, unjust national and, in particular, exploitative global structures. Emphasis on such structural impediments to the realization of human rights is a very important component of present ecumenical thinking. Particularly in countries of the Third World, new formulations of human rights and duties by ecumenical churches and organizations often include explicit reference to the structural transformations deemed necessary for the effectuation of individual, social and peoples rights. As J. Van Nieuwenhove has recently demonstrated, the closing document of the Fourth General Conference of Latin American Bishops (Santo Domingo 1992) adds an important new element to discussion of structures in the context of human rights by stating emphatically that unjust political, economic and social structures not only provide opportunities for infringements of rights by individuals, institutions and governments - these structures *themselves* constitute egregious violations of human rights (cf. p. 25).

CONCLUDING REMARKS

Today the advocacy and pursuit of human rights broadly conceived are a thoroughly international concern, engaging people of many different nationalities, races and persuasions. No government, no societal institution, no business or even transnational corporation can openly ignore these rights or deny them with impunity. Human rights have become an inseparable part of "modern ethical consciousness" (Van Nieuwenhove, 15), a "household notion" throughout the world, so much so, that philosophies and religions everywhere have either "begun formulating their own concepts of rights or have stressed the connection between their respective traditions and human rights" (Zalaquett, 12). Which is all to the good since the practical violations and abuse of human rights are expanding alarmingly, not only quantitatively but also in terms of the demonic sophistication of methods used and the depth and barbarism of the outrages perpetrated. Today violation of the fundamental human rights of women and girls, namely, the literal violation of their bodies, is even being employed as a *strategic weapon of war* in what used to be Yugoslavia - strategic wholesale rape: a horror nearly beyond comprehension. And it is indeed to be feared that

---

[8] Regarding this notion see, e.g., J.D. Gort and L.D. Hulley, pp. 134-137.

advances in the area of international human rights have taken place more at the level of the *development* than of the *realization* of norms:

> Mag auch die völkerrechtliche Menschenrechtsentwicklung während der drei letzten Jahrzehnte eindrucksvoll scheinen, so muss man doch befürchten dass die Fortschritte wesentlich auf dem Gebiet der Normenentwicklung, nicht aber auf dem der Normenverwirklichung liegen. (Huber, 24)

It has in truth been aptly said "that the only universal thing about human rights, today, is their universal violation" (*The Theological Basis*, 52). At the 1983 Vancouver Assembly of the WCC, Armenian Archbishop Ajamian is reported to have "pleaded for a word of hope in the face of a thoroughly depressing human rights situation worldwide" (Gill, 138). It may be said with certitude that all instances of interreligious cooperation in the area of human rights, whether at the level of practice or dialogue and reflection, constitute especially significant signs of hope in our broken and divided world.

BIBLIOGRAPHY

Abrecht, P. "Life and Work." In: N. Lossky *et al.* (eds.). *Dictionary of the Ecumenical Movement* (hereinafter: *DEM*). Geneva/Grand Rapids: WCC/Eerdmans. Pp. 612-14.

Boer, John. *Christianity and Islam under Colonialism in Northern Nigeria*. Jos: Institute of Church and Society, 1988.

Bosch, David. "A Theology of the Signs of the Times." *Exchange: Journal of Missiological and Ecumenical Research* 21 (1992): 247-66.

Canberra 1991: De zevende assemblée. Verslagen en rapporten. 's-Hertogenbosch: Willibrordvereniging, 1991.

Gairdner, W.H.T. *Edinburgh 1910: An Account and Interpretation of the World Missionary Conference*. Edinburgh/London: Oliphant, Anderson and Ferrier, 1910.

Gill, D. (ed.). *Gathered for Life*. Official Report of the Fourth Assembly of the WCC, Vancouver, 1983. Geneva/Grand Rapids: WCC/Eerdmans, 1983.

Gort, J.D. "Gospel for the Poor?" In: *Zending op weg naar de toekomst*. Essays aangeboden aan J. Verkuyl. Kampen: Kok, 1978. Pp. 80-109.

Herwijnen, W.E.R. "Gever van leven behoud uw schepping: Ter inleiding van Sectie I." In: *Canberra 1991: De zevende assemblée*, 1991. Pp. 53-59.

Huber, W. and H.E. Tödt. *Menschenrechte: Perspektiven einer menschlichen Welt*. Stuttgart/Berlin: Kreuz Verlag, 1977.

Hulley, L.D. "Ethical Comments on JPIC." *Missionalia* 19 (1991): 131-43.

Keshishian, A. "Reflections on the Future." *The Ecumenical Review* 43 (1991): 259-261.

Köster, F. "Die Menschenrechte als gemeinsamer Auftrag." *Verbum* 28 (1987): 43-56.

Koshy, N. "Director's Introduction." In: Zalaquett, 1981. Pp. 5-6.

———. "United Nations." In: *DEM*. Pp. 1036-38.

Moltmann, J. "A Christian Declaration on Human Rights." *Reformed World* 34 (1976): 58-72.

Paton, D.M. (ed.). *Breaking Barriers*, Official Report of the Fifth Assembly of the WCC, Nairobi 1975. London/Grand Rapids: SPCK/Eerdmans, 1976.

Priorities in the Human Rights Work of the Commission of the Churches on International Affairs. Human Rights Advisory Group, Glion, Switzerland, 1986, *The Churches in International Affairs* (hereinafter *TCIA*), Reports 1987-1990. Geneva: WCC, 1990. Pp. 40-41.

Rapport Sectie I. In: *Canberra 1991: De zevende assemblée*. 1991. Pp. 59-82.

Rapport Sectie II. In: *Canberra 1991: De zevende assemblée*. 1991. Pp. 89-117.

Report of the CCIA Human Rights Advisory Group, Glion, Switzerland, 1981, Appendix II. In: Zalaquett, 1981. Pp. 52-65.

Report of the Committee on Programme Policy, Seventh Assembly of the WCC, Canberra, 1991, *The Ecumenical Review* 43 (1991): 276-81.

Report on Human Rights to the Unit Committee II, Central Committee, Geneva, 1982, *TCIA*, Reports 1979-1982. Geneva: WCC, 1983. Pp. 28-29.

Report to the Vancouver Assembly By the Churches' Human Rights Programme for the Implementation of the Helsinki Final Act, 1983, Appendix I. In: Weingärtner, 1983. Pp. 68-71.

Scott, E. *Report of the Moderator of the Central Committee*. In: Gill, 1983. Pp. 175-92.

Sixth Assembly Statement on Human Rights, Vancouver, Canada, 1983, *TCIA*, Reports 1983-1986. Geneva: WCC, 1987. Pp. 27-31.

Statement on Peace and Justice, Sixth Assembly of the WCC, Vancouver, 1983. In: Gill, 1983. Pp. 130-38.

Statement on Religious Liberty, WCC Executive Committee. Geneva, September 1979, *TCIA*, Reports 1979-1982. Geneva: WCC, 1983. Pp. 23-26.

Study Paper on Religious Liberty, Commission of the Churches on International Affairs Background Informaton (hereinafter CCIABI), 1980/4. Geneva: WCC, 1981.

Smit, D.J. "Order." In: *DEM*. Pp. 747-50.

Smith, R. "Editorial." *Reformed World* 34 (1976): 49-50.

The Theological Basis of Human Rights, Statement of the World Alliance of Reformed Churches Consultation, London, 1976, *Reformed World* 34 (1976): 50-58.

Universal Declaration of Human Rights, Final Authorized Text, UNDPI, 1950.

Van Nieuwenhove, J. *Santo Domingo: Uitsluiting of insluiting van bevrijdingstheologie?* Nijmgen: KUN, 1993.

Van der Zee, W.R. "De zevende assemblée." In: *Canberra 1991: De zevende assemblée*. 1991. Pp. 7-23.

Verkuyl, J. *Enkele aspecten van het probleem der godsdienstvrijheid in Azië*. Kampen: Kok, 1948.

Weingärtner, E. *A Decade of Human Rights in the WCC: An Evaluation*, Appendix I. In: Zalaquett, 1981. Pp. 44-51.

——. *Human Rights on the Ecumenical Agenda: A Report and Assessment*, CCIABI, 1983/3. Geneva: WCC, 1983.

——. "Human Rights." In: *DEM*. Pp. 484-488.

Zalaquett, J. *The Human Rights Issue and the Human Rights Movement*, CCIABI, 1981/3. Geneva: WCC, 1981.

CHAPTER XVI

Toward an Islamic Hermeneutics for Human Rights

Abdullahi Ahmed An-Na'im

INTRODUCTION

The central question addressed in this collection of essays is whether the various religious views of what it means to be truly human leave room for the acknowledgment of a set of *neutrally formulated* common human rights (my emphasis). It is not possible, or desirable, in my view to identify a set of neutrally formulated human rights. Any normative regime, which justifies a set of rights and provides or informs their content, must necessarily represent a commitment to a specific value system. This is particularly true, I believe, of a regime which claims to justify and formulate a set of human rights because of the organic relationship between the conception and implementation of such rights on the one hand, and the normative regime which provides or informs perceptions of human dignity, self-identity and personal experience on the other.

Nevertheless, I will argue in this paper that an 'internal' commitment to a normative regime from one point of view need not and should not be exclusive of the 'other' (however he or she is identified) with respect to a set of commonly agreed human rights. In my view, therefore, what is at issue is not the possibility of abstract or absolute neutrality from any religious, cultural or ideological regime. Rather, the question is how to reconcile commitments to diverse normative regimes with a commitment to a concept and set of universal human rights. If this is achieved, the commitment of some to one regime or another would be, in effect, immaterial from other points of view. In other words, it would be possible to achieve the benefits of neutral formulation instead of pursuing the illusion of neutrality as such.

It may be argued that seeking to exclude the requirement of neutral formulation simply begs the question of how to achieve consensus on a set of rights accruing universally to all human beings of whatever religious persuasion or lack thereof, and irrespective of gender or race (hereinafter referred to as universal human rights). From this point of view, to allow the formulation of a set of rights to be committed to a particular value system would impose that system's criteria of entitlement to rights which might *exclude* group(s) of human beings. Judging by the experience to date, the argument goes, commitment to a religious value system would almost certainly exclude those who do not adhere to that religion, or at least not accord them rights equal to those enjoyed by the adherents of the religion in question. Religious value systems also tend to deny women equality with men. This is certainly true not only of orthodox perceptions of Judaism, Christianity and Islam, it could be added, but also of other religious traditions, cultures and even ideologies. In this light, it may be concluded, the only way to achieve consensus on a set of universal human rights is through 'neutral formulation'.

As indicated earlier, however, the difficulty of achieving consensus on universal human rights is not due to commitment to a value system as such, be it religious, cultural or ideological. What is problematic is the *exclusive* nature of value systems, that is to say, their tendency to define the relationship between the 'self' and the 'other' in antagonistic or negative terms, thereby diminishing prospects for the acknowledgment of equality and non-discrimination. I would therefore argue that if and to the extent that it is possible to overcome this particular feature of the various value systems of the world today, global consensus on universal human rights would be attainable without requiring people to abandon their religious, cultural or ideological commitments in order to subscribe to this project.

In any case, it would be counter-productive to require people to choose between their religion, culture or ideology, on the one hand, and a supposedly 'neutral' universal human rights project, on the other, because most people would probably opt for the former over the latter. This choice is more likely for two reasons. First, to the vast majority of people, no human rights scheme can by itself serve as a substitute for religion, culture or ideology. Second, most people would maintain that some conception of human rights is integral to their specific religion, culture or ideology. To avoid undermining the legitimacy of a universal human rights project by placing it in direct competition with what people hold as their comprehensive fundamental value systems, I would strongly recommend a strategy of *internal transformation* of perceptions of the religion, culture or ideology in question in order to reconcile the former with the latter. Without minimizing the difficulties and risks of this approach, I maintain that such reconciliation is conceptually possible in general (cf. An-Na'im and Deng, 1990; An-Na'im, 1992) and applicable in the Islamic context (An-Na'im, 1990). In view of the greater difficulties and risks of trying to establish and implement a supposedly neutral universal human rights scheme, I would recommend attempting to achieve reconciliation at least as *one of the strategies* for legitimizing and effectuating a universal human rights project.

In this paper, I will explore the issues and prospects of such internal transformation in relation to Islam and Islamic societies in the present globalized world of diverse religious and other normative systems. To this end, I will define and outline an *Islamic hermeneutics for human rights*. However, if the proposed analysis is to be useful for a universal human rights project, it should be applicable to other religions, cultures and ideologies. I will therefore attempt to extrapolate from the Islamic case some general guidelines on the conceptual and methodological aspects of the process of internal transformation as it may apply to any religion, culture or ideology.

THE GENESIS OF EXCLUSION AND INCLUSION

As suggested earlier, the problem is the exclusive nature of religion, culture or ideology rather than these normative systems as such. But it is also clear to me that some level of exclusivity is integral to the fundamental nature and function of normative systems: the basis of the claim of each system to the commitment of its adherents and the sanction for compliance with its precepts. That is to say, people's commitment to a given normative system is usually premised on the belief that conformity with the precepts of the system in question would bring them specific moral and/or material benefits. Part of this rationale, it seems, is the belief that other normative systems will not achieve those benefits, at least not to the same degree or quality. Thus, the advantage of adhering to one system is appreciated on its own terms as well as in contrast to the disadvantage of adhering to other systems.

However, the process of achieving the perceived benefits of adherence to a normative system is normally protracted, diffused and difficult to evaluate in daily life. In the case of some religious normative systems in particular, the most significant benefits, such as becoming a moral person in this life or achieving salvation/going to heaven in the next life, cannot be verified in concrete or immediate terms. Consequently, people need to find ways of sustaining their faith in the ability of their chosen normative system to deliver promised benefits, especially during periods of mounting frustration and helplessness.

One way in which people tend to reinforce their faith in their own normative system is to exaggerate the quality or quantity of the benefits they have or will have, and the loss of those who do not adhere to the same system. In this way, many people come to have a territorial or proprietary interest in their own system and an adverse view of other systems. This self-vindicating defense mechanism often leads to a 'them' and 'us' syndrome which can easily degenerate into hostility and antagonism towards the 'them' and solidarity with the 'us' under any circumstances.

Despite the unavoidability of some level of exclusivity in all normative systems and its tendency to degenerate into hostility and antagonism towards the 'other', I would still argue that commitment to a system can be compatible with a degree of inclusion of the 'other' at another level. More specifically, I suggest that one can be fully committed to a certain religion and identify with his or her co-believers for that purpose, while also being fully committed to another normative system and identifying with co-adherents of that system for its purposes as well. In other words, people can and do have *multiple or overlapping identities* and can and do cooperate with the 'us' of each of their identities without being hostile to the 'them' of one level of identity because the latter can be part of the 'us' of another level of identity.

For example, I am a Muslim and do identify with other Muslims for the purposes of my religion. I am also a Sudanese who belongs to a certain profession and have a variety of interests and concerns which I share with other Sudanese, and with people from all parts of the world. Ultimately, and most importantly, I am a human being who is committed to protecting and promoting the values and qualities of being human. The fact that there is a variety of 'them' and 'us' at the various levels of my overlapping identities indicate to me that my relationship to the 'them' of one identity should not frustrate or diminish the prospects of relating to the same people when I need them to be part of the 'us' for me at other levels of identity.

I see the possibility and utility of overlapping identities and cooperation as integral to my faith as a Muslim, in accordance with verse 13 of chapter 49 of the Qur'an (that is, 49:13 as the Qur'an will be quoted in this paper) which may be translated as follows:

> We [God] have created you [human beings] into [different] peoples and tribes so that you may [all] get to know [understand and cooperate with] each other; the most honorable among you in the sight of God are the pious [righteous] ones.

As I understand it, this verse means that human diversity or pluralism (be it ethnic, religious or otherwise) is not only inherent in the divine scheme of things, but also deliberately designed to promote understanding and cooperation among various peoples. The last part of the verse emphasizes to me that the quality of morality and human worth is to be judged by the person's moral conduct, rather than by his or her membership in a particular ethnic, religious or other group.

However, I must admit that my choice of this particular verse of the Qur'an, and interpreting it as supporting the principle of overlapping identities and cooperation with the "non-Muslim other", are premised upon a certain orientation which may not be shared by all Muslims today. Muslims of a different orientation may choose to emphasize other, clearly exclusive, verses of the Qur'an such as 3:28, 4:139,144, 8:72-73,[1] and/or interpret the above-quoted

[1] These verses speak about 'believers' as *awliya'* (allies and supporters of) one another and 'non-believers' as *awliya'* of one another. I will address the question of criteria and rationale of reconciling apparently conflicting verses of the Qur'an below, especially in section 5 of this paper.

verse as referring to diversity and pluralism *within* the global Islamic community (*Umma*) rather than among the totality of humanity at large. A Muslim of the latter orientation may also see the last part of the verse as restricting piety/righteousness to Muslims, so that only a Muslim may qualify for honor in the sight of God in accordance with the quality of his or her personal conduct, as judged by Islamic criteria.

It should be emphasized, however, that choice and/or interpretation of verses of the Qur'an (or any other text for that matter) in relation to human experience and relationships is necessarily informed by the orientation of the person in question. Muslims, for example, have always differed, and will always differ, in their choice of verses to cite in support of their views, and also in their understanding of the verses they quote. That is one of the reasons why there are so many schools of Islamic theology and jurisprudence, with a wide variety of views within each school. This feature of Islamic discourse is often cited by Muslims with great pride as conclusive evidence of the flexibility and adaptability of Islam to the different circumstances of time and place.

By 'orientation' I mean the *conditioning of the existential or material circumstances* of the person reading (or hearing) the Qur'an or another textual source. That is to say, every person always understands the text in question, and derives its normative implications, in terms of his or her knowledge and experience of the world: perceptions of self-interests in political, economic and social contexts, realities of inter-communal and/or international relations, and so forth.

A person's orientation may also be influenced by his or her vision for change or improvement in existential or material circumstances. In other words, one need not always feel totality constrained by existing circumstances, and may wish to strive to break away from the mold of prevailing political, economic and social conditions. For such vision to have realistic prospects of fulfillment, however, it must be grounded in existing sociological, political, economic and intellectual circumstances of the society in question. This is what I will refer to in the next section as the 'historical contingency' factor in the hermeneutical process.

In my view, two conclusions can be drawn from the above analysis in relation to the thesis of this paper. First, there is no such thing as the only possible or valid understanding of the Qur'an, or conception of Islam, since each is informed by the individual and collective orientation of Muslims as they address themselves to the Qur'an with a view to deriving normative implications for human behavior. Consequently, a change in the orientation of Muslims will contribute to a transformation of their understanding of it, and hence of their conception of Islam itself.

Before considering whether modern Muslims already have, or are likely to have, an orientation which is conducive to actively supporting a project of universal human rights, I wish to clarify the concept of hermeneutical discourse in relation to Islam. This is important because the following sections of the paper deal with might be called an Islamic hermeneutics which can be harnessed, I suggest, in promoting and applying a human rights orientation among Muslims today.

HERMENEUTICS IN CONTEXT

Hermeneutics is usually defined as the art or science of interpretation, especially of Scripture, and commonly distinguished from exegesis or explanation and exposition (*Oxford Universal Dictionary*, 3rd ed., 1955). The need for interpretation as a means of understanding the purpose and normative implications of a text like the Qur'an or Bible is beyond dispute. But the precise nature and actual practice of hermeneutics, and its relationship to exegesis would, of course, vary from one religion to another, and often within the same religion over time and/or place. I would also emphasize the anthropological dimension of these processes.

For example, according to the 1992 acts of the Christian Reformed Ecumenical Council, hermeneutics is an unavoidable task of the Christian church in seeking the abiding significance of the Word of God in the constantly changing circumstances of human life and history: "Hermeneutics has to do with the interpretation of the Bible *as it applies to our own time*, taking into account the broad historical, cultural and scientific changes that have taken place, as well as the changes in basic mentality and outlook that characterize the modern world" (1992, 28-29, emphasis mine). This document maintains that it is necessary to take into account contextual and cultural factors in applying Scriptural ethical directives to concrete life situations (*ibid.*, 49-51). However, it is clear from the argument and conclusions of the document as a whole that it is cast in terms of a particular tradition within the Christianity as distinguished not only from that of the Roman Catholic church but also from earlier views within the Protestant church. The very fact that the document was issued at this point in time indicates to me that its authors felt the need to re-formulate or update the position of their own tradition on questions of hermeneutics and ethics.

It is true that each religion (and specific tradition within a religion) has its own 'framework of interpretation': a set of interpretative rules, techniques and underlying assumptions which are accepted by the adherents of the religion or tradition in question as valid or authoritative. It would therefore seem to follow that there is a 'correct' way of understanding and applying the content of the Scripture (or the Qur'an for Muslims), that is to say, a way which is consistent with the appropriate framework of interpretation (Vroom, 1993).

As can be expected, however, all participants in the hermeneutical process would claim that their understanding of the Scripture is the correct one because it is more consistent with the accepted framework of interpretation. Others may even challenge the authority of a given framework of interpretation and seek to provide an alternative. Such claims or combinations thereof underlie differences between, for example, Orthodox, Catholic and Protestant Christians, Sunni and Shi'ite Muslims, Sufi and non-Sufi Muslims, as well as among various factions within each religion.

I would therefore emphasize the need to understand the process through which the frame of interpretation is specified, verified and revised or re-formulated: how and by whom is it defined and specified? Does that process provide for reformulation or revision, according to which criteria and how can that be legitimately done? Ultimately, who is to arbitrate and mediate between competing claims about the frame of interpretation and/or its application?

In my view, the community of believers as a whole should be the 'living frame of interpretation and ultimate arbiter and mediator of interpretative rules, techniques and underlying assumptions. This seems to have been the case during the founding stages of major religions. Over time, however, a few tended to appropriate and monopolize the process of interpretation and turn it into an 'exclusive and technical science or art'. Thus, the process of religious revival and reformation is often about breaking the monopoly of the clergy or technocrats of hermeneutics and reclaiming the right of the community to be the living frame of interpretation for their own religion and its normative regime.

In the case of Islam, for example, there is no reference in the early traditions to any special requirements or qualifications for engaging in the interpretation of the Qur'an or exercising *ijtihad* (human reasoning) to derive ethical norms and legal principles. Even the founders of the major *mathahib* (schools of Islamic jurisprudence) simply stated their views for Muslims at large to accept or reject freely without claiming an exclusive right to interpretation or *ijtihad*. By the end of the third century of Islam, however, the process was rendered so technical and exclusive that the "gate of ijtihad" was said to have been closed, thereby confining subsequent generations of Muslims to the blind followers of the founding 'masters' of Islamic jurisprudence. (Hallaq, 1984). Since Ibn Taymiyya (14th century AD), various scholars have tried to break the deadlock of tradition (Kerr, 1966).

A possible reason for this failure, it might be suggested, is that the sociological, political, economic and other circumstances of the time were not ripe for a change in the orientation of Muslims which would have permitted acceptance of the proposed reforms. That is to say, the requirement of historical contingency of their hermeneutical argument was not satisfied at the time of those reform efforts. I would agree that this must have been the case since, or to the extent that, previous reform efforts were not successful as a matter of fact. But I would also emphasize that *historical contingency can only be accurately judged in retrospect*.

It is integral to any reform effort that its proponents of reform should strive to demonstrate that the circumstances of the time are ripe for change. One would also expect the opponents of reform either to dispute the validity of the proposed change as such or to claim that it is premature. Whatever one may think of the hermeneutical argument or other aspects of the case for reform, the historical contingency factor cannot be categorically judged in advance. Only time will tell whether the community in question will eventually accept or reject the proposed reform. Moreover, rejection of a hermeneutical argument for reform at any point in time should not be seen as final and conclusive, or that its historical contingency will never be satisfied in the future. Subsequent generations of 'would-be reformers' may continue to make, refine and update the argument in their own context, and may well succeed when the case for reform is made in the right or appropriate way, time and place.

AN ANTHROPOLOGICAL APPROACH TO ISLAM

The above analysis may be described as an 'anthropological approach' to the Qur'an and to Islam in general, in the sense that it is premised on an organic, dynamic relationship between the Qur'an and Islam on the one hand, and the nature of human beings (that is, their comprehension, imagination, judgment, behavior, experience, and so forth) on the other. Is such an approach valid from an Islamic religious point of view? If it is valid, what does it mean for the ways in which Muslims seek to understand Islam and try to conform to its precepts today?

An anthropological approach to the Qur'an and Islam in general is fully justified, indeed imperative, in my view, by virtue of the terms of the Qur'an itself and the experience of Muslim communities throughout their history. According to Muslim belief, the text of the Qur'an contains the final and conclusive message of God to the whole of humanity. This is explicitly stated in verses 107:21, 1:25; and is also clear from the many verses (such as 168:2, 138:3, 31:7 and 13:49, quoted above) in which the Qur'anic form of address is "Oh, humankind" or "Oh, Children of Adam".

The Qur'anic form of address is also directed mostly to the individual person, or to community in some cases, without the intermediacy of clergy or officials of the state. In so doing, the Qur'an constantly emphasizes that people should reflect and consider what is being said, should think about this or that, and so forth, as in verses 219:2, 266:2, 191:3, 3:1-4:13, 44:16, 24:10 and 8:30. In fact, verses 2:12 and 3:43 declare human reflection and understanding to be the whole purpose of revealing the Qur'an.

Two further points can be added in support of the validity of an anthropological approach to the Qur'an and Islam in general. First, human agency is simply unavoidable in understanding the Qur'an and traditions of the Prophet, and in deriving ethical norms and legal principles from those sources to regulate individual behavior and social relations. Ali bin Abi Talib, one of the leading earliest Muslims and the Fourth Khalifa, is reported to have said "The Qur'an does not speak, it is people who speak on its behalf." Second, and as noted earlier, the actual rich and complex diversity of Islamic theology and jurisprudence clearly demonstrate the dynamic relationship between the scriptural sources of Islam, on the one hand, and the comprehension, imagination, and experience of Muslim peoples, on the other.

Thus, there is nothing new about an *Islamic* anthropological approach to the Qur'an and Islam in general. What is at issue, in my view, is what this approach means for the ways in which Muslims seek to understand Islam and try to conform to its precepts today. Given the fact that the specific historical context has always affected the perceptions and practice of Islamic principles by Muslims of the past, how does the modern context affect the perceptions and practice of present-day Muslims? More importantly for the purposes of this paper, what is the *orientation* through which Muslims should understand the Qur'an in the modern context?

It is obvious that the orientation of modern Muslims should be different from that of earlier generations because of the radical transformation of the existential and material circumstances of their life today in contrast to those of the past. For better or for worse, Muslims now live in a globalized world of political, economic and security inter-dependence, and mutual social/cultural influence. Their conception of Islam, and efforts to live by its precepts, must be conditioned by modern perceptions of individual and collective self-interests in the context of this radically transformed world. Whatever vision Muslims may have for change or improvement in the present realities of the world today must also be grounded in the circumstances and conditions of this world. That is, their perceptions of the range of options available to them must take into account the facts of interdependence and mutual influence.

A central issue that modern Muslims have been struggling with over the last two centuries is how to adapt their orientation and transform their conception of Islam in an *authentic and legitimate* manner. Whether in terms of issues of modernity, democracy, human rights, economic development or some other concern, the central issue has often been the need for legitimizing and rationalizing desired normative or material objectives in terms of the traditions of Islamic societies. It is obvious that there is more to these traditions than the Islamic dimension, but to the extent that Islam is integral to the circumstances of these societies, there seems to be a spectrum of opinion on issues of political, economic and social change.

At one end of the spectrum, there is what might be called the traditionalist or 'fundamentalist' approach, which insists on strict conformity to Shari'a as an essential prerequisite for accepting the proposed change. At the other end, there are those who wish to avoid the question of conformity to Shari'a altogether, usually out of a conviction that reconciliation between their objectives and the relevant principles of Shari'a is not possible. For example, some advocates of universal human rights in Islamic societies prefer to base their position on the present international standards of human rights, irrespective of the conformity of those standards with principles of Shari'a. Between these two poles of the spectrum, there is a variety of positions which seek to reconcile universal human rights with Shari'a, or with Islam in general, in one way or another.

While I agree with those who see Islamic authenticity and legitimacy as imperative for wide and effective acceptance and implementation of universal human rights, I believe that their reconciliation with Shari'a is neither possible nor required. Reconciliation is not possible because Shari'a is premised on a fundamental distinction between the rights of Muslims and non-Muslims, and those of Muslim men and women, which totally repudiates the principle of equality and non-discrimination upon which universal human rights are fundamentally premised. That is to say, it is simply impossible for Shari'a to acknowledge any set of rights to which all human beings are entitled by virtue of their humanity, without distinction on grounds of religion or gender. Since what is required is Islamic authenticity and legitimacy, rather than conformity with Shari'a as such, I believe that this requirement can be satisfied without necessarily reconciling universal human rights with Shari'a. In other words, I argue that it is possible to achieve Islamic authenticity and legitimacy for a set of human rights by distinguishing between Islam and Shari'a.

THE DIVINITY OF ISLAM AND TEMPORALITY OF SHARI'A

In my view, as a human understanding of Islam and hence necessarily limited by circumstances of time and place, Shari'a should not be identified with the totality of the religion itself. As explained earlier, any reader of the scriptural sources of Islam would always understand those texts and their normative implications in terms of his or her knowledge and experience of the world. Since that knowledge and experience, and indeed the world itself, tend to change over time, Islam should not be bound by any particular understanding of its scriptural sources. I believe that this view is not only consistent with the Muslim belief in the divinity of the Qur'an and finality of its message, but is in fact essential for maintaining the practical relevance of that divinity and finality to the lives of Muslims through the ages.

One often hears in Islamic discourse the proposition that "Islam is suitable (valid) for all times and places". For this maxim to be true, however, there must be flexibility and change in the understanding and implementation of Islam over time and place. More specifically, and given the radical transformation of Islamic societies and the whole world around them, it is simply impossible for the same principles of Shari'a formulated by Muslim jurists more than thirteen centuries ago to remain the only valid and applicable law of Islam. It would therefore follow that Shari'a principles must be reformed and reformulated before they can be applied today, whether in themselves or as criteria for accepting and implementing a normative system of universal human rights.

This obviously valid proposition is usually stated in modern Islamic discourse as a critique of what is known as *fiqh* (the juridical and theological opinion of early Muslim jurists) rather than of Shari'a itself. Moreover, advocates of reform would also call for a modern exercise in *ijtihad* in order to change those aspects of *fiqh* which they find objectionable or problematic today. Such calls for *ijtihad*, however, are rarely followed by actual application and concrete derivation of specific new principles of Shari'a. Space does not permit much elaboration, but I wish to state briefly two objections to this sort of reasoning from the point of view of the advocacy of universal human rights in modern Islamic societies.

First, since universal human rights are untenable in view of some clear and categorical verses of the Qur'an itself, such as verse 4:34 of the Qur'an, often cited as the basis of the inequality of women to men, the problem is one of Shari'a and not merely *fiqh*. Second, since the traditional principle of *ijtihad* is confined to matters on which there is no clear and categorical text of the Qur'an, it cannot challenge a principle of inequality based on such a text. In other words, there is a need to reform the principle of *ijtihad* itself before it can be used to resolve incompatibility of Shari'a and universal human rights where conflict between the two is due to a clear and categorical text of the Qur'an rather than *fiqh* as the opinion of early jurists.

I believe that *ijtihad* should be applied even to matters governed by clear and categorical texts of the Qur'an, as suggested by the late Sudanese Muslim reformer, *Ustadh* Mahmoud Mohamed Taha. According to Taha's methodology of reform, the Qur'an itself should be seen as containing two messages, one intended for immediate application within the historical context of the seventh century and after, and another message for subsequent implementation as and when the circumstances of time and place permit (Taha, 1987). An historical approach to the Qur'an in general can be supported by some of the rulings of Umar ibn al-Khatab, the second Khalifa, who decided that clear and categorical verses of the Qur'an should not apply when the objectives intended to be achieved by the revelation are no longer valid (An-Na'im, 1990, 28). Taha has developed that approach into a comprehensive methodology of Islamic reform which would enable modern Muslim jurists to select and interpret verses of the Qur'an in order to develop a modern version of Shari'a (An-Na'im, 1990).

Taha's methodology may appear to be too radical to many Muslims today, but I am not aware of any alternative which will adequately resolve the crisis in modern Islamic reform, especially in relation to universal human rights. Those who wish to achieve Islamic authenticity and legitimacy for universal human rights must overcome theological objections, and political and sociological resistance, to an adequate reform methodology, be it that of Taha or any other viable alternative. My own preference to date is the methodology proposed by Taha and explained in the sources cited earlier. I remain open, however, to accepting any alternative methodology which will achieve what I believe to be the necessary degree of Islamic reform.

This is as far as theory is concerned. In the next section, I will offer some reflections on aspects of the political and sociological resistance to approaches which seek to develop and present an Islamic rationale for universal human rights in modern Islamic societies. In my experience, much of so-called theological or hermeneutical objections to reform methodologies such as that of Taha are in fact a product of political and sociological factors. Whatever may be their nature or motivation, I believe that all obstacles to genuine commitment to universal human rights must be identified and overcome by the proponents of universality, each working within his or her own context as well as in collaboration with others.

PROSPECTS OF UNIVERSALITY IN GLOBAL CONTEXT

Resistance to an Islamic rationale for universal human rights in Islamic societies today may be traced to several sources, some pertaining to regional and international considerations while others relate to local dynamics of power relations. It is also important to note that this resistance is mostly reactive to perceived threats or other concerns, whether internal or external to the region. It is not possible, of course, to discuss all aspects of this phenomenon, but it may be useful to highlight the following aspects with a view to suggesting ways of overcoming resistance to universality of human rights.

First, there is the problem of perceiving universal human rights as yet another element of a 'Western' conspiracy to undermine the integrity and independence of Islamic societies. The best defence these societies have against this neocolonial attack, the argument goes, is a strong and uncompromising assertion of a distinctive Islamic identity and culture. Thus, while all Muslim advocates of universal human rights are seen as agents of foreign domination and Western cultural imperialism, those who seek to base their advocacy on an Islamic rationale are even more 'dangerous' because they undermine the distinctive Islamic identity and culture as vital defence.

Related to this factor are popular perceptions of the double-standard of Western governments, media and public at large regarding Muslim concerns, especially in relation to Palestine and, more recently, former Yugoslavia, in contrast to devastating and decisive action against Iraq. These perceptions enhance the view that the West is not interested in universal human rights except where they serve its geo-political and economic interests.

There is also the perception that the existing international human rights standards, and mechanisms for their implementation, in fact reflect a Western bias in favor of individual civil and political rights, over against economic and social rights and collective human rights. Besides reinforcing apprehensions of cultural imperialism, this bias is also used to argue that the values and priorities of Islamic societies are not served by the existing international standards.

At the local or internal level, there is resistance from those who feel that their vested interests are threatened by universal human rights. These include ruling classes and groups, men and Muslim majorities at large who would normally tend to resist any threat to their privileged position. The usual argument used by these groups is that human rights are alien to the culture and traditions of Islamic societies. Thus, the perceived threat is even more serious when it claims an Islamic rationale, thereby seeking to undermine the rationale of the defence itself.

Strategies for overcoming these and other causes of resistance must be founded on a realistic understanding of the internal logic and perceived basis of opposition to universal human rights. For example, the facts and aftermath of Western colonialism and present domination and exploitation must be admitted and confronted, the facts of internal power relations and perceptions of vested interest must be understood and redressed, and so forth.

The key to any effort in this regard, however, is the credibility of advocates of universal human rights in the eyes of their own local constituencies. These advocates must be able to draw on the symbols of their own culture and history, speak the 'language' of their own peoples, know and respect their concerns and priorities. In so doing, advocates of universal human rights should appreciate and utilize the 'ambivalence and contestably' of their cultures, seek out and explore new options and rationales for advancing the cultural legitimacy of universal human rights. All of this will have to be through what might be called an internal Islamic discourse. Outsiders can assist such an internal discourse by supporting the right of all Muslims insiders to engage in it, as well as by holding their own (Christian, Hindu, Buddhist or other internal religious) discourses to resolve the conflicts and tensions between their respective religions and universal human rights. Universality of human rights can also be enhanced through a cross-cultural dialogue to promote an over-lapping consensus on global moral foundations of these rights (An-Na'im and Deng, 1990; An-Na'im, 1992).

All the major religions of the world agree that there is an organic and dynamic relationship between ends and means, so that legitimate objectives can only be realized through appropriate methods and processes. I would therefore conclude that, in the final analysis, the acknowledgment and implementation of universal human rights should be seen as a co-operative process as well as an a common objective - a global joint venture and not an attempt to universalize a particular cultural or religious model.

BIBLIOGRAPHY

An-Na'im, A.A. *Toward an Islamic Reformation: Civil Liberties, Human Rights and International Law*. Syracuse: Syracuse University Press, 1990.

——. (ed.). *Human Rights in Cross-Cultural Perspectives*. Philadelphia: University of Pennsylvania Press, 1992.

——— and F.M. Deng. (eds.). *Human Rights in Africa: Cross-Cultural Perspectives*. Washington: The Brookings Institution, 1990.

Hallaq, Wael B. "Was the Gate of Ijtihad Closed?" *International Journal of Middle East Studies* 16 (1984): 3-41.

Kerr, Malcolm H. *Islamic Reform: The Political and Legal Theories of Muhammad Abduh and Rashid Rida*. Berkeley and Los Angeles: University of California Press, 1966.

Reformed Ecumenical Council. *Acts of the Reformed Eumenical Council: Athens 1992*. Grand Rapids: The Reformed Ecumenical Council.

Taha, M.M. *The Second Message of Islam*. Syracuse: Syracuse University Press, 1987.

Vroom, H.M. "Scripture Read and Interpreted: The Development of the Doctrine of Scripture and Hermeneutics in Gereformeerde Theology in the Netherlands." *Calvin Theological Journal* 28 (1993): 352-71.

CHAPTER XVII

'Ali Shari'ati and Human Rights

Anton Wessels

> The *shahid* (martyr) is the heart of history. The heart gives blood and life to the otherwise dead blood-vessels of the body. Like the heart, a *shahid* sends his own blood into the half-dead body of the dying society, whose children have lost faith in themselves, which is slowly approaching death, which has accepted submission, which has forgotten its responsibility, which is alienated from humanity, and in which there is no life, movement, and creativity. The greatest miracle of *shahadat* is giving to a generation a renewed faith in itself. A *shahid* is ever-present and ever-lasting.
>
> (From "After Shahadat," 'Ali Shari'ati)

INTRODUCTION

The discussion on 'Islam and Human Rights' often focusses on the issue of whether Moslems should formulate their own Islamic declaration of human rights (cf. Mayer, 1991). One can refer, for instance, to the 1981 Islamic declaration issued in Paris (*Islamochristiana*), or to the more recent conference in Cairo - "The Cairo Declaration on Human Rights in Islam" (5 August 1990) - which called for special Islamic emphases in pronouncements on human rights (Dwyer, 1991).

In this paper, I shall deal with the significance of the contribution made by 'Ali Shari'ati - sometimes hailed as the precursor of the Iranian revolution, or even "the chief ideologue of the Iranian islamic revolution" (Algar, 7,8) - to reflection on 'Human Rights and Islam'. His own rights were often violated and he is thought to have been a victim of the Savak, the Shah's secret service, when he died in a hospital in London on 19 June 1977 of heart failure, according to the official report. He was arrested for the first time in 1957 because he participated in the activities of the National Front led by Muhammad Mosaddeq (d. 1967) (Akhavi, 125). Upon returning to Iran in 1964 after a stay in France, he was arrested at the border because of his membership in the Liberation Movement (*Nihzat-Azadi*), a religious nationalist group founded by Mehdi Bazargan (who would later be prime minister for a brief period under Ayatollah Khomeini). He was arrested after the Husayni-ye Irshad, the institute where he taught and delivered most of his lectures to large crowds ('Ali Shari'ati, 1980, 8, n. 2; cf. 1986, 103-60), was closed in 1973, and he spent eighteen months in prison without being properly tried. His body was buried in Damascus. The well-known Lebanese Shi'ite leader, Imam Musa Sadr, who himself 'disappeared' in August 1978 in Libya under mysterious circumstances, officiated at 'Ali Shari'ati's funeral.

My aim here is to show how an important and influential thinker like 'Ali Shari'ati expressed himself with respect to human rights in the context of his interpretation of the meaning of Islam in modern society. We will first give a brief account of his life, but the focus of the paper will be an examination of his work, *The Pilgrimage* (*Al-Hajj*), in which he relates his own experiences and comments on and analyzes the different stages of the *Hajj*, "this social and mystical act" ('Ali Shari'ati, 1982, 119).

BIOGRAPHY

'Ali Shari'ati was born in 1933 in Mazinan, a suburb of Meshed in eastern Iran, into a family of religious scholars. His grandfather was a well-known *'alim*, and his father Muhammad Taqi Shari'ati was a religious teacher in Meshed and is still highly respected.

'Ali Shari'ati received his initial education in Iran. He attended a Teacher's Training College in Meshed and after graduation studied part-time at the faculty of literature at Meshed. Being a teacher brought him into contact with the poorer strata of the society in the city. He taught in a centre that had been founded by his father: The Institute for the Spread of Islamic Truth. In 1959 he received a scholarship for doctoral studies in Islam and sociology in Paris. He studied with well-known French scholars Jacques Berque - although Berque did not notice him at the time (cf. 'Ali Shari'ati, 1982, 11) - and Louis Massignon. In Paris, where he remained until 1964, he obtained a doctoral degree in medieval Iranian philology under professor G. Lazard - not in sociology as is often thought (Akhavi, 126). While in Paris he became acquainted with the Algerian resistance leaders and wrote articles for an Algerian nationalist newspaper (*ibid.*, 126). He read Franz Fanon's *Les Damnées de la terre*, an analysis of the psychological damage and cultural alienation that resulted from colonialism. He knew Fanon personally and translated his book into Persian ('Ali Shari'ati1986, 19). Among the Western thinkers who influenced him were Jean Paul Sartre and Albert Camus. After his return to Iran in 1964 - and his imprisonment - he taught on a temporary basis at different schools and institutions, such as the department of sociology at Meshed University where he attracted many students. He later had to move to Teheran where he taught at the Institute for Religious Learning, the *Husayniya-yi Irshad* (founded by Bazargan and Sayyid Husayn Nasr). His taped lectures were very popular even among young literate men in the villages (Mottahedeh, 353).

He is well known in Iran where he is currently 'claimed' by the present-day revolutionary leadership, although he died in 1977 well before the revolution (1979). His interpretation of Islam is of a much more 'progressive' nature than that of Khomeini. 'Ali Shari'ati is called the spiritual father of the *Mujahiddin al-Khalq*, 'the Fighters of the People', an urban guerrilla movement that has been active since the sixties and more openly in the seventies. It is not certain that he had any connection with this movement, even though it appeals to his authority. Several of the extensive number of lectures he gave have been published and translated into numerous European as well as other languages, such as Bahasa Indonesian (cf. 'Ali Shari'ati, 1982, 11-20; Kielstra, 1992 70-71).

THE PILGRIMAGE OF HUMANKIND

In his book on the *Hajj* 'Ali Shari'ati explains his views concerning the significance of pilgrimage (p. xi). This work was not intended to be a practical guide for pilgrims but rather to deal with the *hajj*'s significance for the everyday life of Moslems in society, in which every day is seen as the day of sacrifice, every month as Dhu-Hijjah (the twelfth month of the year and the month of the yearly pilgrimage) and every land as Mina (where the concluding rites of the pilgrimage take place). The whole of life should be like the *Hajj* (p. 146). Ali Shari'ati reflects on how the pilgrimage can be put into everyday practice. He states how, "with the passage of time and the influence of various forces of the social system which disregard human rights and duties," the human character has changed. Humankind, which is supposed to be God's trustee on earth, has became alienated (p.3).[1]

The human family has been dramatically divided right from the very beginning, as exemplified by the two sons of Adam: Cain and Abel. God was the sole owner of creation and all people were considered equal. People adhered to the morals of Abel and lived like him. But Cain later became a farmer and claimed the land as his own, thereby restricting its use. Adam was succeeded by Cain, a son not worthy of his father; he was a non-believer, a greedy usurper and murderer. Abel, the poor shepherd, was killed by his wealthy landlord brother Cain, whose descendants brought division into Adam's family, and the unity of humankind was broken. It became divided into races, nations, classes, subclasses, groups, and families (pp. 8, 9). Throughout history, the children of Cain have been the rulers of humankind.

---

[1] Cf. Sura 2:30 (28): "And when thy Lord said unto the angels: Lo! I am about to place a viceroy in the earth (*khalifa fi ard*), they said: Wilt Thou place therein one who will do harm therein and will shed blood, while we hymn Thy praise and sanctify Thee? He said: Surely I know which ye know not."

The murderer Cain, who rules the children of Abel, has three faces: Pharaoh, Croesus and Balaam (pp. 124, 125).[2] In modern society Cain, the ruler, has hidden his face behind politics, economics and religion and has created the three major powers, oppression, wealth, and hypocrisy, which have given birth to despotism, exploitation and brainwashing techniques. These three powers can be described as follows: Pharaoh is the symbol of oppression, Croesus (Korah/Qarun)[3] is the symbol of capital/capitalism, and Balaam is the symbol of hypocrisy. *Polytheista* summons people to worship them instead of the Almighty God.

The three oppressors are the three faces of Cain, the landowner, who killed his brother Abel, a shepherd, and became the guardian of Abel's orphaned children. The poor and oppressed on this earth are the orphans of history; the children of the martyred Abel are the true believers in God. It is remarkable, according to 'Ali Shari'ati, that all the Abrahamic prophets who proclaimed monotheism and justice were shepherds - the true heirs of Abel during the first common era. The last of these messengers, the illiterate prophet Mohammed, was also a shepherd (p. 127). Cain divided humankind into two races and society into two classes, made history bi-polar and converted the existing unity into duality. Cain further changed unity into trinity: he is the symbol of the one ruling class that has three faces (p. 129).

During the pilgrimage, however, the pilgrim is called to model his action on that of Abraham, "the man of faith and the founder of true unity" (p. 35): "Lo! Abraham was a nation obedient to God, by nature upright, and he was not of the idolaters" (Sura 16:120 (121)). The pilgrims are invited to do away with the three idols as Abraham did: "O follower of Ibrahim and soldier of Tawhid, destroy the three idols!" (p. 101).

'Ali Shari'ati points out that the Qur'an begins with an invocation of the name of God and ends with an invocation of the name of the people (1979, 117; Cragg, 82). He emphasizes and provides a special interpretation of the last chapter of the Qur'an, Sura *al-nas* ("Humankind"), which reads:

> In the name of God, the Merciful, the Compassionate.
> Say: I seek refuge in the Lord of mankind (*al-nas*),
> The King of mankind (*al-nas*),
> The God of mankind (*al-nas*),
> From the evil of the sneaking whisperer,

---

[2] The Qur'an does not mention Balaam by name, although it does possibly allude to him in 7:175 (174), 176 (175). The latter phrases are used by mystics such as al-Muhasibi to turn Balaam into the prototype of the spiritual man led astray by lust and pride. Cf. "Bal'am," in: *Encyclopedia of Islam*.

[3] All three, Pharaoh, Haman and Korah (or Qarun), said that Moses was a "lying sorcerer". Cf. Sura 40:24 (25); 43:49 (48); 28:76-82 and Numbers 16:1-35 (in the Bible).

> Who whispereth in the hearts of mankind (*al-nas*),
> of the jinn and of mankind.[4]

'Ali Shari'ati (1982, 19) translates *al-nas* (repeated several times) as "the masses" and calls God "the God of the masses" and further identifies the oppressors who rebel against God and disrespect human rights with the trinity of oppressors.[5]

'Ali Shari'ati sees monotheism (*tawhid*) and polytheism (*shirk*) as two philosophical theories that are at the heart of human socio-economic struggles of all ages. Polytheism is the dominating faith of history, the opium of the people (*Hajj*, 124). But the worst tragedy to befall humankind is that polytheism often conceals itself behind the face of monotheism: *Iblis* (the devil) disguises himself as a holy man; *tawhid* is in the service of *shirk* (*ibid.*, 132-33).

He explains how neocapitalistic and neocolonial intellectuals and sociologists today know how to manipulate science in order to achieve their ends and to promote ignorance in the name of civilization, how to corrupt the nation's culture, faith, will, consciousness and leave the hearts of people empty (*ibid.*, 140).

> Today's conscious humanitarian workers care for human beings and humanitarian rights! They are the ones who realize what the effects of colonization mean, the stealing the natural resources of poor nations of the third world, and when cruel agents are appointed to run these countries disregarding humanitarian rights. All these are true tragedies caused by outsiders. The really fearful tragedy is what is happening in the hearts of people. (*ibid.*, 140-41)

The most dreadful tragedy threatening the world population is the "alienation of mankind" - humankind becoming inhuman. The whisperer does not only damage the body, but the spirit as well. This is what frightens the conscious and responsible intellectual in the present, the intellectual who understands the severity of "alienation":

> He has seen 'humanity' sacrificed wherever 'humanitarian rights' are disrespected. He is then one who knows the evildoers and makers of idols who can't always be seen. Sometimes they are hidden or they may be a mysterious

---

[4] This sura is quoted together with the earlier one when 'Ali Shariati reflects on *al-mu'awwidatani*, the two chapters against evil. One could compare this with the Moslem habit of quoting Sura 16:8 (100): "And when thou recitest the Qur'an, seek refuge in God from Satan the outcast."

[5] Strictly speaking, one can argue that the Qur'an is not attacking the Christian doctrine of the Trinity but rather tritheism - the belief in three gods (God, Jesus and Mary, cf. Sura 5:116) - which the Christian church also condemned. Cf. Rudolph, 86 f.

> power. They don't have to use the yoke of slavery; they can whisper in one's heart. Covertly and quietly, they may enter the mind, disturb it, change one's personality and replace it with another! This is alienation! Yes, the danger lies in ambush, worse than ever, not hidden in the rocks or mountains, but deep in one's heart or conscience. It is not an ambush on one's life or money, but on one's faith, humanity, knowledge, love, victory, struggle, the inheritance of one's history, one's possibilities of becoming like Ibrahim, and one's approach to Almighty God. (*ibid.*, 141)

The three eternal false Gods are more oppressive than ever. Today's Pharaoh is not a person but a system; Croesus is not one but a class; Balaam no longer speaks of faith but of science, ideology and art (*ibid.*, 142-43). Surprisingly, the Qur'an speaks in the second to last chapter, according to 'Ali Shari'ati, of three evils that are unique in that they share one characteristic:

> In the name of God the Merciful, the Compassionate
> Say: I seek refuge in the Lord of Daybreak
> From the evil that which He created;
> From the evil of the darkness when it is intense,
> And from the evil of malignant witchcraft,
> And from the evil of the envier when he envieth.
> Sura al-Falaq (The Daybreak). (cf. *Hajj*, 143)

'Ali Shari'ati mentions the evils of oppression, brainwashing, deception, murder and plunder. These evils deny people human rights and freedom, enslave them and keep them poor and ignorant. Humans will survive the heavy pressures of these tragedies somehow, but it is a greater tragedy at present when these anti-human superpowers try to paralyse human values by emptying the hearts of the people for their own exploitation. History has taught these powers that if they want to conquer economically and politically, they have to destroy those values cherished by people and then change their human nature. In other words, people must become alienated (*ibid.*, 143).

The "whisper" is a deadly poison injected into the human body by this three-headed snake. The *Khannas* (the sly whisperer) represents the three idols and his mischief is much more tragic. The last chapters of the book of revelation teach that he is more dangerous than the three idols. A heavenly consciousness will cut the dark curtain of night at dawn to fight the three powers that enslave humankind (*ibid.*, 143).

To oppose the satanic power of the *Khannas*, one must seek refuge in unity (*tawhid*). To eradicate the structure of polytheism (*shirk*) in human consciousness and in society, people must recognize that the three powers of ownership, sovereignty, and divinity exist in Almighty God alone. This will result in the establishment of an Abel-like society, i.e., a society based on the equality and oneness of humankind. An "exemplary community", of the type prophesied by

Abraham, has to be built, and Mohammed, the last prophet, gave Moslems this responsibility. Because Moslems understand the tragedy, 'Ali Shari'ati argues, it is their responsibility to resolve it. Because they are the heirs to the tradition of Abraham, they must teach his message to an intellectual generation that is struggling for social justice (*ibid.*, 144).

'Ali Shari'ati writes further: "You are like Abraham who in the history of mankind was a great fighter against idolatry. He came out of the house of Azar - in the Qur'an the name for Abraham's father, 6:74 -, the idol-maker of his tribe. He broke the idols; he broke Nimrod" (*ibid.*, 149).[6] Again, "Abraham's life was filled with struggle when he reached this point - breaking the idols, fighting with Nimrod, braving his fire, struggling with Iblis, sacrificing his son Ishmael,[7] migration, homelessness, loneliness, torture, passage from the stage of prophecy to the stage of leadership (*Imamat*), going from individuality to collectivity and from the house of Azar to being the builder of the house of unity (Ka'ba)" [cf. Sura 2:125 (119), 127 (121)] (*ibid.*, 150). He was the founder of unity in this world and had the responsibility of leading his people:

> You, the builder of Ka'ba, the architect of the house of freedom, the founder of unity, the enemy of idolatry, the tribal leader, the fighter against oppression, ignorance and disbelief - now you, pilgrim, are building a house, not for yourself, not even a shelter for your son, not a house for the people. It is a shelter for those homeless people who are wounded, tortured or victims of oppression and have no place to go. Nimrod is following them everywhere. (*ibid.*, 151)

'Ali Shari'ati continues,

> Now that you are standing in Abraham's position and are going to play his role, live like him; be the architect of the Ka'ba of your faith, rescue your people from the lagoon of their life. Re-breathe life into their bodies that are numb and dead from the suffering of oppression and the darkness of ignorance. Encourage them to stand on their feet and give them direction. Call upon them to come to *hajj*, to *tawaf* (circumambulation). After entering *tawaf*, denying selfishness and purifying yourself to adopt the characteristics of Ibrahim, you have promised God to follow his path. God is your witness. (*ibid.*, 151)

---

[6] Cf. Sura 2:258 (260). According to the commentary of Jalalayn, Nimrod, mentioned in Gen. 10:8-9, is the one with whom Ibrahim disputes. The reference is taken from Jabr and Jansen, 33.

[7] The Qur'an is not quite clear as to which of the two sons, Isaac or Ishmael, Abraham was prepared to sacrifice (Cf. Sura 37:102-107). Usual Moslem opinion favours the latter. Cf. Paret, 417.

EVALUATION

'Ali Shari'ati is not a systematic thinker who has produced a finished work, and those writings that do exist have not yet been fully edited. Although his contribution to Islamic thought and human rights remains as fragmented as his life, it is extensive and important enough to draw certain conclusions.

His primary audience, of course, are his fellow Moslems, but that does not mean that others are denied access to Islamic insights for modern society. Although he knew and was influenced by Fanon, he did not agree with Fanon's antireligious sensitivities. In his opinion Fanon's experience, which was related to Europe, could not be extended to the Islamic world ('Ali Shari'ati, 1986, 19). He was neither a sociologist nor a social scientist but a socially-committed Moslem. According to him an Islamic revolution was impossible without a revolution of Islam itself ('Ali Shari'ati, 1982, 16).

'Ali Shari'ati could be called a kind of Moslem 'Liberation theologian' (cf. 'Ali Shari'ati, 28, n. 15) or a 'Moslem for Socialism', although he was clearly opposed to Marxist ideology (cf. 'Ali Shari'ati, 1981a, 26). He replaced Marxian determinism with the Shi'ite millenarian restoration of the universe: the conflict will end, according to him, only with an "inevitable revolution" that will restore "the system of Abel" in the world. This will be a unitarian as opposed to a polytheistic system; a religion of consciousness, movement and revolution, as opposed to one of deceit, stupefaction and justification of the status quo; it will be a system of human justice and unity as opposed to that of class and racial discrimination (Enayat, 158). 'Ali Shari'ati was a Moslem thinker who, from an Islamic Third World perspective, defended the rights of those in his part of the world who had become alienated as a result of the internal and external oppression to which they had been subjected. He called for "an Islam of the aware", by whom he meant those "who registered injustice and alienation, who have shed the blinkers of idle piety or scholastic complacence, and were alive to the crisis of contemporary man, chronically misread and exploited by the West" (Cragg, 80).

In order to understand and evaluate 'Ali Shari'ati's position *vis á vis* 'Islam and human rights' it is necessary to understand how he relates belief in the unity of God (*tawhid*) with the unity of humankind over against polytheism and the role the Prophet Mohammed played in it. 'Ali Shari'ati speaks of Mohammed's ministry as prophet in the following way:

> The mission and characteristics of the Prophet are clearly set forth in the Qur'an, and they consist of conveying a message [cf. Sura 16:35 (37)]. He is responsible for conveying a message; he is a warner and a bearer of glad tidings. And when the Prophet is disturbed by the fact that people do not respond and he cannot guide them as he would wish, God repeatedly explains to him that his mission consists only of conveying the message, of inspiring fear in men, of giving them glad tidings, of showing the path; he is not in any way

> responsible for their decline or their advancement, for it is the people themselves who are responsible [cf. Sura 3:20 (18)]. In the Qur'an the Prophet is not recognized as the active cause of fundamental change and development in human history. He is depicted rather as the bearer of a message whose duty it is to show men the school and the path of truth. His mission is then completed, and men are free to choose the truth or to reject it, either to be guided or to be misguided. ('Ali Shari'ati, 1981, 48)

This vision reminds one in part of that of the Egyptian religious scholar (*'alim*) 'Ali 'Abd al-Raziq and his book, *Islam wa usul al-hukm* ("Islam and the Foundations of Government") and of the more recent Sudanese Mahmoud Taha and his, *The Second Message of Islam* (cf. Renaud).

With reference to Maxime Rodinson, who called Mohammed the armed Prophet, 'Ali Shari'ati acknowledges that this was indeed the case. He was not a prophet who only announced the revelation and then retired into silenc. He was also concerned about the implementation of the revelation and was prepared to suffer and fight for it and to face opposition because of it (cf. 1981c): "He leaves Mecca to reply to the question, 'What is to be done?'" (Abedi and Legenhausen, 180). Mohammed embodied both prophethood and imamate: "His invitation was addressed to the people and was concerned both with this world and with the hereafter. 'Better life' means both God and bread, both worship and justice." (*ibid.*, 202)

'Ali Shari'ati emphasizes that the prophet Mohammed, like the other Abrahamic prophets, "arose from the mass of people. This means that the prophets were only human beings, not angels or supernatural beings with fantastic powers. They were appointed from among the ordinary mass of people rather than from a special noble, and selective class of society" (*ibid.*, 155). That which can be said about the prophet Mohammed also holds true for his companions. They were all men of the sword, concerned with improving their society, men of justice (*ibid.*, 81). There will be no prophet after Mohammed, but the person who is aware is the prophet's heir ('Ali Shari'ati, 1982, 28, cf. 19).

The great concern of the prophet's ministry was the unity of God. The first half of the Moslem confession of faith is that "there is no God but God", which is directed against idolatry. The greatest sin is *shirk*. 'Ali Shari'ati spoke of the unity of God with all creation, although he did not understand this in a pantheistic or mystical way. His objection to mysticism was that it had too often become an excuse for immobility and oppression (1982, 16). He was not thinking here of *fana'*, the absorption or annihilation of the person in the One God, but he was critical of the quietist attitude which was popular among his fellow shi'ite countrymen, as if they only had to be "caretakers of graveyards ... beggars at the door of the innocence of martyrs" (1980c, 87, cf. 22, 33). He quotes Imam 'Ali who said: "Be the enemy of the oppressor and the friend of the oppressed" (1982, 53).

For 'Ali Shari'ati *tawhid* was not an abstract theological question disconnected from the concrete reality of humanity and society. *Tawhid* cannot be a bare assertion: "It has to be an enterprise. It is not a concept of number but an issue of sovereignty. It is an active subduing of 'whatever powers, systems and relations' deny or defy it" (Cragg, 88). The biblical teaching of Jeremiah that to know God is to do justice (Jer. 22:15, 16) is also taught by the Qur'an and Islam. Islam has a clear concern for a just society. *Salat* (ritual prayer) and *zakat* (the giving of alms) are often mentioned in the Qur'an in one and the same breath:[8] the spiritual and social obligations are intricately connected.

> The Prophet of Islam came to confirm the universal doctrine of *tawhid* and to bring that unity into human history, to all races, nations, groups, families and social classes, and to eliminate the discord brought by polytheistic religions. (*ibid.*, 157)

Islamic theology is described as *'ilm al-tawhid*, the science of the unity of God. The Mu'tazilites, members of one of the most important theological schools, were called the *ahl al-'adl wa-tawhid*, the 'people of the justice and unity of God'. What is fascinating is that 'Ali Shari'ati connects this belief in the unity of God, so crucial for the Qur'an and for Islam as such, with the unity of humankind:

> *Tawhid* may be said to descend from the heavens to the earth and ... enters the affairs of society. It poses the various questions involved in social relationships, class relations, the orientation of individuals, the social structure, the family, politics, culture, economy, ownership, social ethics and the rest. (1980c, 32)

And,

> Monotheism is the torch of this hope and the signal of the prophecy which was carried on the shoulders of the shepherd throughout history. They transferred this flag from hand to hand and from generation to generation. It went from Abel to Abraham, from Abraham to Muhammad, from Muhammad to Hussayn and from him to everywhere and everyday until the very last day, the day of judgment! (*ibid.*, 133)

'Ali Shari'ati is thus in line with those modernists who "turn the meaning of *tawhid* from a mere theological formula into a comprehensive system of faith and political action" (Enayat, 9).

---

[8] Sura 13:22; 22:35 (36); 14:31 (36); 35:29 (26); 2:3 (2); 8:3; 42:38 (36).

It is thus quite interesting how he elaborates on the idea of *shirk*, the opposite of *tawhid*. According to 'Ali Shari'ati the children of Cain have directed human destiny throughout history. This pole operates in the three areas of economics, politics, and religion, which 'Ali Shari'ati associates here and elsewhere with three Qur'anic and Biblical figures: Pharaoh (power), Croesus [Korah/Qarun] (riches), and Balaam (the clergy who monopolize religion) (1981a, 19). The three classes of this order, the powerful, the rich, and the clergy, will continue to rule history (*ibid.*, 20). He then speaks of what he calls "social polytheism" (*ibid.*, 21) and sees this polytheistic worldview transformed into 'Trinity' not only in India, Greece, Rome or Persia, but also in Judaism, Christianity and Islam (*ibid.*, 21): "The three idols are involved in alienating and brain-washing mankind with the help of their experts and advanced technology" (*ibid.*, 138). The unity of God is irreconcilable with the class division between rich and poor. A true 'Ali'te, shi'ite society stands opposed to Safawid society (represented, in 'Ali Shari'ati's opinion, by the Shah and his Pahlevian dynasty). The Abel-like society is one in which the Cains (in their three representations) no longer rule. 'Ali Shari'ati translates the *tawhid* into its social implications for society.

He defended himself against the criticism that he had spoken of the 'God of the oppressed' through his suggestion that the aristocracy and rulers have a different God by referring to the last chapter of the Qur'an where God is called, "Lord, King and God of the masses" (1986, 26, 27, n. 1). 'Ali Shari'ati refers to the *nass*, the people or masses, with the anti-*nass* as its opposing pole. In his opinion, the Qur'an always addresses *al-nas*, the people: "The Prophet is sent to *al-nas*; he addresses himself to *al-nas*, it is *al-nas* who are accountable for their deeds; ... in short, the whole responsibility for society and history is borne by *al-nas*." 'Ali Shari'ati sees Islam as "the first school of social thought that recognizes the masses as the basis, the fundamental and conscious factor in determining history and society" (1979, 49).

In his view, religions, including Islam, can play an ambivalent role. He refers to Imam 'Ali who "for many years struggles and strives against polytheism within his ranks, a polytheism which has cloaked itself in the dress of *tawhid*. He has to grapple with the *kafir* who has assumed the mantle of Islam and who positioned the Qur'an on the point of a lance" (Abedi and Legenhausen, 161). Religion (in its ambivalent role) destroys and revitalizes, puts to sleep and awakens, enslaves and emancipates, teaches docility and revolt. In short, the history of humankind is the history of the struggle of 'religion against religion' and not of religion against atheism. The history of Islam itself is the story of these contradictory roles of religion among various social classes. It is the history of the war of Islam against Islam and even the war of the Qur'an against the Qur'an (1986, 48). After having quoted Sura 21:105 ("... My righteous slaves will inherit the earth") and Sura 28:5 ("And We desired to show favour unto those who were oppressed in the earth, and to make them examples and to make them the inheritors"), 'Ali Shari'ati says that these words constitute

> the pledge of the future leadership of human society. The class of people who were always and everywhere deprived of their human rights will inherit the palaces of power, the treasures of wealth and the fortunes of education! What a similarity between the words 'the oppressed people of the world' and 'the wretched of the earth', which is the title of a book by Franz Fanon. (*ibid.*, 77-78)

The world view of *shirk* forms its basis in society "with its discrimination among classes and races." *Tawhid* negates all forms of *shirk*: it bestows on human beings independence and dignity (1979, 85-87). The struggle between Abel and Cain, or between *tawhid* and *shirk*, is one "between justice and human unity on the one hand, and social and racial discrimination on the other" (1979, 108-09). In other words, according to 'Ali Shari'ati, Islam's purpose is thus to be understood in terms of 'atonement', provided one takes the concept in its original sense of at-*one*-ment.

'Ali Shari'ati speaks of God as addressing 'humankind' (*al-nas*) and not just Moslems. This should not be read or understood to mean that 'Ali Shari'ati wants all people to become Moslems in the sense of establishing 'an Islamic state' in one way or another. He defends rather an 'Abel-like society' which he does not present as a specific 'Islamic' society or an Islamic *umma* in the narrow or exclusivistic sense of the word. His use of Qur'anic and Islamic images like Abel, Cain, the *hajj* (pilgrimage) is recognizable to those familiar with biblical imagery and can therefore be more universally understood and interpreted. His view contains a criticism of religion that includes or even is primarily directed against the Islamic religious establishment. Exploitation and alienation can be brought about not only by economic and political means but by religious ones as well. The 'evil whisperer' can conceal itself in the garb of truth, which is one of its most terrible methods. Therefore 'Ali Shari'ati was opposed not only to the political establishment during the time of the Shah but to the religious establishment as well.

One does not need to be a 'fundamentalist' to claim that "a universal concept of human rights must come from the philosophical vision of all peoples" (Dwyer, 43). As far as an understanding of 'human rights' from an Islamic perspective is concerned, 'Ali Shari'ati's insights are an indispensable and valuable contribution for a real ecumenical understanding of human rights in the world.

BIBLIOGRAPHY

Abedi, Mehdi and Gary Legenhausen, (eds.). *Jihad and Shahadat: Struggle and Martyrdom in Islam. Essays and Addresses by Ayatullah Mahmud Taleqani, Ayatullah Murtada Mutahhari. Dr. 'Ali Shari'ati*. Houston, 1986.

Akhavi, S. "Shariati's Social Thought." In: Nikki R. Keddie, (ed.). *Religion and Politics in Iran; Shi'ism from Quietism to Revolution*. New Haven/London, 1983.

'Ali 'Abd al-Raziq. *Islam wa usul al-hukm*. Cairo, 1925.

'Ali Shari'ati. *On the Sociology of Islam: Lectures by 'Ali Shari'ati*. Tr. H. Algar. Berkeley, 1979.

——. *Exploition und Raffinierung der kulturellen Quellen*. Bonn, 1980.

——. *Marxism and Other Western Fallacies: An Islamic Critique*. Tr. R. Campbell. Berkeley, 1980.

——. *On the Sociology of Islam*. Berkeley, 1980.

——. *Zivilisation und Modernismus: Botschaft der islamischen Republik Iran*. Bonn, 1980.

——. *Man and Islam*. Tr. Fatollah Marjani. Houston, 1981.

——. *Die vier Gefängnisse des Menschen*. Bonn, 1981

——. *Zur westlichen Demokratie*. Bonn, 1981.

——. *Histoire et destinée*. Tr. F. Hamed and N. Yavari-d'Hellencourt. Paris, 1982.

——. *What is to be Done: The Enlightened Thinkers and an Islamic Renaissance*. Houston, 1986.

——. *Hajj*. Tr. Ali A. Behzadnia and Majla Denny. No place or date of publication indicated.

Algar, H. In: Ali Shari'ati. *Marxism and Other Western Fallacies: An Islamic Critique*. Tr. R. Campbell. Berkeley, 1980.

Cragg, Kenneth. *The Pen and the Faith: Eight Modern Muslim Writers and the Qur'an*. London, 1985.

Dwyer, K. *Arab Voices: The Human Rights Debate in the Middle East*. London/New York, 1991.

Enayat, H. *Modern Islamic Political Thought*. Austin, 1982.

Fanon, Franz. *The Wretched of the Earth*. New York, 1963.

Jabr, Asad and J.J.G. Jansen. *De Koran*. In de vertaling van J.H. Kramers. Amsterdam, 1992.

Keddi, N.R. *Roots of Revolution: An Interpretative History of Modern Iran*. New Haven, 1980.

——. *Religion and Politics in Iran; Shi'ism from Quietism to Revolution*. New Haven, 1983.

Kielstra, N. "Voorloper van de Iraanse revolutie." In: R. Peters and R. Meijer (eds.). *Moslimse intellectuelen over de Islam*. Muiderberg, 1992.

Mayer, Ann E. *Islam and Human Rights: Tradition and Politics*. London, 1991.

Mottahedeh, R. *The Mantle of the Prophet: Religions and Politics in Iran*. London, 1985.

Paret, R. *Der Koran: Kommentar und Konkordanz*. Stuttgart/Berlin/Cologne/Mainz, 1971.

Renaud, E. "Mahmud Taha and the Second Mission of Islam." In: *Encounter* (Documents for Muslim-Christian Understanding (May 1986)). Nr. 125.

Rudolph, W. *Die Abhängigkeit des Qorans von Judentum und Christentum*. Stuttgart, 1922.

Taha, M. *The Second Message of Islam*. Tr. A.A. An-Na'im. New York, 1987.

Part 4

Concluding Observations
Strategies for the Future

CHAPTER XVIII

Religions and Rights: Local Values and Universal Declarations

John Clayton

The discourse of 'rights' is peculiarly modern and uniquely Western in origin. Talk of human rights can be linked historically to the decline of the feudal order, the emergence of national states and market economies, and to the invention of *the autonomous individual* in European imagination at the origins of modernity. It would not have occurred to ancient Greek philosophers to speak of 'human rights', even though the texts that record their musings exhibit a profound concern about right conduct in respect to other persons. Formative or classical Hindu, Buddhist, Jewish, Christian and Islamic sources refer more typically to *duties* than to *rights*. Just such traditional duties are still liable sometimes to be cited to justify blatant violations of what in the Universal Declaration of Human Rights are heralded as inalienable. Traditional *religious anthropologies*, therefore, would seem to be infertile ground in which to try to cultivate an ethos of *human rights*.

On the one hand, the very fact that contributors to a volume on human rights and religious traditions can look for *and find* positive 'human rights' embedded in the traditional moral discourses of diverse religions rooted deep in the pre-modern past, itself demonstrates that the reception of religious traditions in the present has not been left untouched by the spirit of modernity. On the other hand, the fact that contributors have taken the opportunity to insist that the traditions under scrutiny offer resources to correct some of the perceived deficiencies of modern 'rights' discourse in the public domain demonstrates that the process of re-interpretation is not mere acquiescence in the spirit of the times. The act of drawing on the resources of the past in order to come to terms with the issues of the present is the means whereby the spirit of every time creates itself afresh.

Suspicion of the moral discourse of modernity, with its pretensions to 'neutrality' and 'universality', does not in itself betray a reactionary counter-modernism, as champions of what is now commonly called the 'Modern' or the 'Enlightenment project' may openly fear; nor does suspicion about the discourse of 'human rights' automatically excuse governments from acting responsibly under the instruments of international law, as the complacent or the unscrupulous may secretly hope.

Such persons can certainly take no comfort from this volume. For its contributors want to make more effective the practical implementation of the legal instruments of human rights. However much they may differ on strategy, their aim remains to push beyond modernity and its discontents in order to achieve an enhanced vision of common life on a shared planet. In pursuing that goal, most contributors discover elements in the religions surveyed that would contribute to the enrichment of life in a global context, even while allowing that no one religion has all the answers or lives up to its own professed ideals.

To judge from the vast volume of literature on human rights to have appeared in recent years, the subject has never been more topical. Nor does one have to reflect long on the current geo-political context to see why this might be the case. Yet in the thousands of publications to have appeared within the past two or three years, few are devoted to considering the positive rôle religions might play in defining and implementing human rights. The assumption seems widespread that religious convictions are more often a factor in the infringement than a force in the implementation of human rights. It is easy enough, to be sure, to think of instances when religious authority has been invoked in order to legitimate the violation of human rights. And it is likewise easy to think of further instances when religious rivalries may have exacerbated conflicts that have other, more specifically economic or social origins, even if one cannot always be certain just how to order cause and effect in all such situations.

Even so, most contributors to this volume maintain the view that the religious traditions examined not only have an interest in the quality of human life on this earth, but also have resources to enhance life beyond the minimalist expectations of some advocates of human rights. As more than one contributor has remarked, in comparison to the image of the good life projected in the authoritative texts of many religious traditions, the narrowly secular discourse of rights looks decidedly thin.

Why have those richer resources not been taken more seriously by advocates of human rights? One main reason why the positive rôle religions can play in defining and enforcing human rights has tended to be ignored in international discussions on human rights must surely be sought in the popular presumption that the discourse of rights is *universal* in scope and ideologically neutral in respect to underlying principles. The moral discourses of religious traditions are perceived in contrast as parochial or *local* in scope and as being grounded in context-specific commitments. They may carry conviction at some time and in some place, but not at all times or in all places.

This commonsensical view is not without justification. For *human* rights - entitlements all persons are supposed to possess simply in virtue of being persons - would seem by definition to be rights whose authority cannot be contingent upon limiting circumstances, historical or cultural. Human rights are presumed to trump any place-specific privileges to which persons may be entitled because of their position in some society or some sub-group within a society.

But the diverse moral discourses of religious groups more typically spell out duties which are specific to the members of their own communities and which could not even in principle be reasonably extended as requirements for persons beyond their perimeters. And legitimation of group-specific duties derives ultimately from some authority that is accepted as authority only by that group. Such moral discourses express group-specific norms and not 'universal maxims', whether in a Kantian or some other sense.

Any talk of 'human rights' and 'religious anthropologies' must, therefore, deal with the dilemma of universal and local in at least these two interrelated aspects: how group-specific duties relate to human rights and how human rights are legitimated. The question in respect to legitimation is whether human rights claims must always be grounded only in reasons that can be reasons for everyone, or if in some circumstances they might also be grounded in reasons that are recognised as such only by participants in some localised community of interest. This dilemma faces anyone engaged in discussion about human rights, but it is made more acute by the extravagant claims religious groups often make for their moral discourse and its unique grounds. And on this issue, contributors to the present volume do not speak with a common voice.

What sorts of strategy might be adopted to deal with the tension between the universal pretensions of human rights and the local limits of group-defined duties? Variations on at least five distinct but occasionally overlapping strategies have found advocates amongst those writing in this volume.

1. First, some hold that the concept of 'human rights' is a kind of shared universal, arrived at by different cultural routes but expressing nonetheless a kind of *consensus gentium*. For people who hold this view, the main contribution of religious anthropologies to human rights has typically less to do with setting standards than with providing motives for adopting and implementing independently established standards. This might take the form of proposing a reading of traditional texts to show that they somehow anticipate the concept of human rights, or that they are at least compatible with what is now understood by that concept. One could search the base-texts of some religious tradition, for instance, selecting those passages that seem to commend behaviour or attitudes similar to those engendered by the modern discourse of human rights. When dissonance is registered, harmony is re-established if possible through a reinterpretation of the traditional text. But in cases of irreconcilable conflict between the *local* moral practices of some religion and the *universal* norms of human rights, 'local' custom is transposed to suit 'universal' tastes.

2. Whereas advocates of the first strategy allow 'universal' reasons to trump 'local' ones, those of the second reverse the direction, insisting that local reasons be given priority over the general. Both the concept and the practice of

human rights are measured by criteria that have been established by some authoritative religious standard. What are allowed as rights and what count as their grounds are derived from resources uniquely available to some religious tradition, not from some 'universal' or 'independent' concept of rights.

This kind of strategy leads necessarily to considerable variety in practice. One community might want to ground human rights in the sovereignty of God, whereas another might do so in the sacredness of life. Both of them might with equal vigour oppose the anthropocentrism of the ancient dictum (attributed to Protagoras) that "man is the measure of all things". But the one would do so in the name of a *theo*-centrism, and the other in the name of a kind of *zoe*-centrism. Such differences, however, inform not just the *foundations* of rights, but their *edifice* as well. Two such communities might still be able to co-operate on many human rights issues, but their co-operation would remain limited and strategic and would have no basis in an agreement about the nature or the grounds of such rights.

3. Advocates of the third strategy promise to point a way between the first two by insisting that the *underlying principles* of human rights are universal, whilst allowing that the discourses of rights vary according to local preference. In line with the first strategy, religions are viewed as providing motives to implement the relevant international legal instruments. In line with the second strategy, however, there is recognition that particular rights might be given different priorities according to the demands of local circumstance. The main difficulty facing this strategy arises whenever an attempt is made to explicate the common principles that are supposed to underlie the variety of moral discourses that function in different religious and cultural contexts. It then becomes evident that different sorts of constructions are supported by different kinds of foundations.

4. Whereas the third strategy assumed common underlying principles for diversely formed human rights, the fourth allows differently laid foundations to support a limited set of *core rights* that transcend their local provenance and achieve universal consensus. These core rights, however few in number, are treated as 'non-negotiable'. The problem confronting this fourth option, however, is similar to that which faced the third. When people attempt to agree a list of core rights, it becomes all too clear that consensus is less universal than one might imagine. The problem is unintentionally illustrated in this volume by one contributor's having named the prohibition against killing one's mother as an example of a universal moral value, only to be contradicted by a second who, in illustrating a point of his own, had occasion to remind us of the duty felt in some societies to ease the way of one's elderly parents into the next world when they are no longer capable of looking after themselves in this one.

Different foundations of human rights support different kinds of value structures. Even a right - such as the right to life - that may be reasonably expected to appear on virtually everyone's list of 'core rights' will not be understood by everyone to have precisely the same entailments. There is no consensus about when 'the right to life' actually begins (at conception or at birth or at some moment in between?), nor about its proper bearers (individuals only or also groups?), nor about the circumstances, if any, in which it may be justifiably infringed (combatants in battle?) or lawfully forfeited (capital punishment?) or even perhaps voluntarily relinquished (euthanasia?). And a Buddhist or a Hindu would want to insist that the right to life extends beyond the limits of the species-specific discourse of narrow *human* rights.

5. This type of problem has led other contributors to draw back slightly and to maintain only that there is *some degree of overlap*, falling short of consensus, about what count as core rights. But such rights might be said to overlap in either of two ways. On the one hand, there is the tighter sort of overlap required by those who insist that there must be some point, however fine, at which agreement is present in order for a right to be counted as a core right. On the other hand, there is a looser kind of overlap sufficient for those who, possibly in a more Wittgensteinian mood, are content to find a relatively coherent pattern of the kinds of rights that appear on different lists of core rights, even if no one right appears on every list. This latter sense of overlapping softens the claim that particular rights are universal and creates room for manoeuvre in approaching the dilemma of universal rights and local values.

That dilemma, in the form stated above, presumed that secular rights discourse is in some strong sense *universal* and *neutral*, but the competing moral discourses of determinate religions are *local* and *partisan*, being confined to the communities of interest that embrace them. Yet the secular discourse of 'rights' (especially that of human rights) is itself a construction of a specific historical and cultural circumstance. And the idea of 'rights' encoded in such discourse is also tied to the place in which it is formed or gains endorsement. 'Human rights' are historical constructions, not natural kinds.

For instance, John Locke, a major contributor to the modern formation of rights discourse, could by subverting the idea of rights defend in his *Second Treatise of Government* the institution of slavery, according to which persons "are by right of nature subjected to the absolute dominion and arbitrary power of their master" (VII, § 85). A later upholder of the Lockean tradition of human rights may have been more ambivalent in his attitude toward the institution of slavery, but Jefferson cannot have had foremost in mind his own slaves when he extolled in one of the most eloquent documents of his age the 'unalienable' rights of *life, liberty and the pursuit of happiness*.

Surely none could claim that Locke's or Jefferson's understanding of rights was 'universal', whether in the sense of being an equal entitlement to everyone or in the sense of gaining general endorsement by everyone. Nor could one reasonably think that its underpinning was ideologically neutral. Human slavery may not yet be entirely eradicated, but it no longer has morally earnest defenders. What has changed since John Locke's or Thomas Jefferson's time to make slavery indefensible, however, is not just that a further item or two has been added to the short-list of so-called 'core rights'. What has occurred, more crucially, is a transformation of what is meant by a 'right' and what it is to be a 'rights-bearer'.

Every understanding of 'rights' is bound to a time and place. This holds for our own notion of human rights as much as it does for that of Locke or Jefferson. Over time, the concept of rights may develop or be stretched or altered to fit some new circumstance or it may be finally abandoned as outmoded. But it does not stay fixed in stone. The discourse of human rights is itself *temporal* and not 'eternal', *local* and not 'universal'. And this applies to the *Universal Declaration of Human Rights*, no less than it does to the American *Declaration of Independence* or the French *Déclaration des droits de l'homme et du citoyen*, whose datedness is perhaps more readily evident.

The 1948 Universal Declaration was a *historic* document. It is rightly regarded as a key moment in shaping the post-war world. In the meantime, however, it has become also a *historical* document. It can now be seen to mirror the concerns of that time and to embody its asymmetry of political power. The understanding of what count as 'human rights' it presumes has now been altered, stretched, and developed by ensuing *Conventions, Charters, Declarations* and *Protocols*. The discourse of rights has continued by this means to create itself afresh. And rival conceptions of human rights compete for wider endorsement within an increasingly global *culture of rights*.

This feature of the modern discourse of rights brings it nearer to the competing moral discourses of the determinate religious communities which, according to the Enlightenment self-image, the tradition-neutral language of rights was itself supposed to supersede. The dilemma of universal and local seems, therefore, to end in a proliferation of localised norms, vying with one another in the world's market place.

Any challenge to the universality of human rights norms raises the spectre of relativism. During the recent World Conference on Human Rights held in Vienna, the U.S. Secretary of State warned against allowing cultural relativism to become the last refuge of repression. But some delegates listening to Warren Christopher on that occasion may have harboured their own worry that such insistence on universality could easily become the last refuge of imperialism. Many thoughtful people from mainly Asia and Africa, including some who attended the workshop in Amsterdam, find cause to complain that the West in general or the United States in particular uses its preferred priorities in 'human rights' as a means of imposing its own political ideology and economic policy on the rest of the world. It would be misguided to hear their complaint as no more than a defence, opportunistic or otherwise, of some variety of 'relativism'.

In any case, resorting to relativism is ultimately self-defeating. It fails to provide adequate reasons for adopting some position and it fails to provide a convincing account of how claims (epistemic or moral) can be contested across cultural boundaries. But the case against relativism, and the course of the debate about rationality generally, is too familiar to require being rehearsed again here. That debate, moreover, has grown stale in virtue of having been conducted too much at the level of high theory, rather than at the level of the practical operations of reason in different contexts. The tension in human rights discussions between universal declarations and local values, by contrast, exhibits practical reason at work where it really counts.

More significant than the perceived threat of 'relativism' in matters moral is the simple fact that the discourse of rights has become in modern times, and pre-eminently since World War Two, the recognised global currency in which to negotiate our different views about what weight attaches to competing entitlements due to persons. In this fact is to be found the key to undo the deadlock between local and universal in regard to religious traditions and human rights.

This is not to say that there is a consensus about the rights we have or the values which underpin them. The discourse of rights has nonetheless established itself as the language in which competing values are publicly justified and, in the face of opposition, publicly contested. Protagonists on both sides of the abortion debate, for example, will each claim to be champions of 'human rights' and will define their position in terms of competing rights, typically summed up as 'the right to life' and 'women's rights'. Their dispute in effect has to do with *which* kind of right has the greater claim to priority in such circumstances.

'Human rights' has been able to become a universal discourse in large measure because of its elasticity. The concept of rights has been expanded and stretched to encompass aspects of human life that were once beyond its limits. In addition to an individual's civil and political rights that constitute its traditional core, the concept of 'human rights' has been extended to cover not only economic, social, cultural and other group rights, but also environmental rights and the rights of 'future generations'.

For philosophers, this makes up an untidy series of disparate goods. For jurists, the list presents difficulties of a different kind, since such diverse rights cannot all be honoured in like measure at any one time. Above all, it poses for everyone a problem of priorities. The 1981 "African Charter", for instance, places the collective rights of peoples alongside the personal rights of individuals without indicating how the two kinds of rights relate to one another or how their competing entitlements are to be reconciled when they come into conflict. Which human rights, and under which circumstances, are to be allowed to trump other human rights?

In response to that question, it is not helpful to insist, as Western public officials are sometimes inclined to do, that the priorities fit for one's own local constituency have inherent universal validity. No one would deny that the most appalling violations of human rights regularly occur in every part of the world - violations that are beyond all reasonable defence, no matter which set of norms and priorities are adopted in respect to human rights. But there are also genuine disputes among peoples about the proper order of priorities among human rights in differing circumstances. During the 'Cold War', it was sometimes observed (a little simplistically, but not without justification) that in the West or the 'First World', civil and political rights were given highest priority; in the then East or 'Second World', economic and social-welfare rights were ranked first; and in the South or 'Third World', group rights or development rights tended to take precedence over individual rights or social rights. Our world no longer looks just like that, but the point remains that differing local circumstances can influence the hierarchy of human rights.

For this reason, it is more helpful to treat such disputes over priorities as differences *within the discourse of rights*, than to regard them as conflicts between those who are committed to human rights and those who are not. It is more helpful not least because the language of rights itself provides a public medium within which disparate communities of interest, religious and secular alike, can test the soundness of the other's position and have their own position contested in return. For instance, if one wished to argue for the priority of personal rights over, say, development rights, then one approach might be to try to show that the curtailment of individuals' civil and political rights impedes economic development and that the developing countries that have the best record in protecting civil rights show also the highest rates of economic development, and so forth. Or if one wished to argue for the priority of group rights over individual rights, then one strategy would be to try to show that in, say, pluralistic societies the protection of the rights of minority groups is the best way to protect individuals' rights against majoritarian tyranny.

Such moves cannot be said to occur in some neutral space or to be based on value-free reasoning. For there is no place which is not some place in particular and there are no reasons that are not reasons for someone. Nor can they be expected to lead to global consensus on prioritization in the hierarchy of rights. But they remain strategies that can be pursued within the medium of the universal discourse of rights. And the price of participating in this medium is *not* agreement to set aside all attachments and commitments in order to achieve universality and neutrality. The price of participating in this medium is no more than the willingness to be a reasonable partisan.

Testing and being contested - by this means the discourse of rights creates itself afresh and the hierarchy of rights is subjected to public scrutiny. By this means basic human rights are more likely to be implemented than if one insists on some prior consensus about core rights and the hierarchy of specific rights.

CHAPTER XIX

Human Rights and Religious Anthropologies

Workshop Statement
Free University of Amsterdam

We, a group of jurists, social scientists, theologians, philosophers and students of the phenomenology and history of religions, coming from Asia, Africa and the North Atlantic, have reflected intensively on the matter of the relation between human rights and religion, particularly from the point of view of Christianity, Islam and Buddhism. We have come to the following common understanding.

Human rights constitute the basic wherewithal for human beings, individually and collectively, to protect their well-being, i.e., their spiritual, mental and physical integrity. Most states subscribe to human rights but fail to act accordingly.

Modern Western culture evinces strong individualistic tendencies, which leads to the neglect and alienation of many people and groups in Western societies. The affluent and permissive society exploits peoples in other parts of the world and neglects its responsibilities with respect to the world's poor, whose economic, social and cultural rights are daily violated. The environmental problems caused by industrial irresponsibility and mindless consumerism are of a very grave nature. All of this calls the individualistic, secular, and liberal ethics of Western culture into serious question. Elsewhere, for example in Asia and Africa, some governments, in order to escape their responsibilities, claim that human rights are a merely Western invention and that the attempt to globalize them represents a form of neo-colonialism.

The chief problem today does not consist of the lack of human rights values and norms but rather of the need to implement existing human rights standards within the process of present global development with its diverse cultural dimensions. Human rights implementation requires not only the existence of certain socio-political institutions and legal instruments but also the active acceptance of the concept of human rights by people of various cultural traditions. The cultural implementation of the human rights idea is one of the most pressing problems confronting the contemporary world. That being the case, support of human rights by the several religious traditions of the world is of the utmost importance. And this clearly implies that Western culture must be prepared to accept other, supplementary interpretations of human rights and human rights issues.

Many central cultural concepts and practices, such as those of caste, group dharma, subjugation of women, religious liberty, primacy of religious communities, etc., are closely bound up with the interpretation of holy scriptures and with concepts of what it means to be truly human. That is why it would be utterly futile to attempt human rights implementation in various cultures without taking religious attitudes and beliefs into account.

Religious traditions are not static entities; they develop in interaction with the rest of culture and other traditions with which they come into contact. Religions have a capacity for change which should not be underestimated: it is distinctly possible for a religious tradition which was previously not particularly supportive of human rights to become a strong advocate of this cause and to contribute to the further development of the moral foundations of human rights. Though acutely aware of the serious problems that certain religious concepts and practices present in terms of human rights, we would nevertheless argue that religious traditions are capable of advocating and supporting human rights as a matter of principle. In pursuit of this goal, adherents of the religions should engage in internal discourse with an eye to the reinterpretation of elements in their traditions which form encumbrances to the positive reception and implementation of human rights.

Religious traditions are ambiguous. The practice of religious communities is certainly not always consistent with their professed adherence to lofty ideals. And when such communities fail to live up to their own standards, they must be subjected to criticism. But they should also be encouraged to provide support for human rights in every corner of the globe. The worldwide reality of religious inspiration underlying the search for a genuinely human way of life forms a powerful potential source of support for all of those whose freedoms have been denied and whose rights have been forgotten. In consequence of its narrow view of human rights as consisting mainly of individual civil and political rights and its failure to take religion into account in the struggle for human rights, Western secular culture may well stand in the way of the acceptance of these rights in other cultures.

In light of the foregoing we urge students of various academic disciplines to engage in study of the beliefs and convictions, the anthropologies and ethics of the world's religions, and we strongly encourage the administrative boards and other authorities of universities and institutions of higher education to stimulate and support such interdisciplinary research.

We urge governments, international governmental organizations and international and national non-governmental organizations to stimulate public discussion of the ethics of the various religious traditions of the world and to acknowledge their dependence on world-and-life views for the establishment and sustentation of truly human and humane societies.

We urge religious communities to engage in reflection on the concept of human rights and the possibilities open to them for participation in the advancement of the cause of these rights. We urge them to engage in public debate and inter-religious dialogue regarding their conception of what constitutes true humanity and a genuinely human way of life. Such public and interreligious discourse is the most promising means for achieving sustained, long-term support for human rights, for it can very definitely lead to religious reinterpretations consentaneous to the notion and implementation of human rights; to the discovery and acknowledgment of areas of conceptual and experiential overlap among religious faiths and faith articulations; to common recognition of the value of human life and the need to preserve nature from the consequences of human greed.

APPENDIX I

An Illustrative Checklist of Indicators of Political Freedom[1]

PERSONAL SECURITY

- *Arbitrary arrest and detention* — Are there arrests without a warrant or probable cause; detentions without a prompt hearing before a court or other independent body; unreasonably long detentions before trial or conviction; arrests and detentions of people for their political beliefs? Is anyone detained incommunado?
- *Torture or cruel treatment or punishment* — Are there acts of torture (mental or physical)? Is there cruel, unusual or degrading treatment or punishment? Are there inhuman prison conditions? Does police brutality exist?
- *Arbitrary killing* — Are there any executions without due process of law by the police, the security forces or state officials? Are there any killings by non-governmental forces with government acquiescence or compliance? Are there killings, either of civilians or of captured or wounded combatants, in violations of the laws of war?
- *Disappearances* — Are persons abducted and held in unacknowledged detention by order of, or with the complicity of State or opposition forces, without their family or friends having any knowledge of where they are and how they are faring? Do family members have effective judicial or administrative mechanisms for determining the whereabouts and status of abducted persons?

RULE OF LAW

- Fair and public hearings — Are there fair and public hearings in the determination of criminal charges? Is every person charged with an offence tried without undue delay, and with adequate time and facilities for the preparation of his or her defence?
- *Competent, independent and impartial tribunal* — Is the judiciary free of outside pressure or influence? Is there corruption in the judiciary? Is the procedure

[1] Supplied by P.J.I.M. de Waart; source: *Human Development Report 1992*, 31.

for selecting judges an open one in which opinions outside the executive can be heard? Do judges have security of tenure?

• *Legal counsel* — Does everyone have the right to capable and independent defence counsel in the determination of any criminal charge against him or her? Does everyone have the right to have legal assistance assigned to him or her in any case where the interests of justice so require, and without payment by the defendant if he or she lacks the necessary means? Do they have the right to consult with counsel immediately on arrest, before interrogation begins?

• *Review of conviction* — Does everyone convicted of a crime have the right to have his or her conviction and sentence reviewed by an independent judicial tribunal?

• *Failure to prosecute* — Do state prosecutors also prosecute government officials, or members of pro-government forces, who violate the rights and freedoms of other persons?

FREEDOM OF EXPRESSION

• *Restriction in law and practice* — Is freedom of expression a constitutionally or legally protected right? Are there legal restrictions on freedom of opinion and expression other that what is necessary to protect the rights of others? Are journalists or others who have infringed such laws prosecuted? Are the punishments prescribed severe in proportion to the offence?

• *Media censorship* — Is there direct censorship of any of the media? Is there indirect censorship by such means as withdrawal of government advertisement revenue, licensing laws, or restrictions on the supply of materials? Are there threats to, or harassment of, publishers, editors or writers? Is there destruction of media outlets by State or non-State forces? Has the government shut down any newspapers on the grounds of their legitimately expressed views?

• *Media ownership* — Are the media (particularly TV and radio) wholly or partly owned by the government? If so, do the media tend to reflect or favour government policy? Is independent ownership of the media permitted?

• *Freedom of speech* — Is there any censorship of mail, phone-tapping or government surveillance? Are there any restrictions on freedom of speech? Are there government controls on book publishing or the arts, other than to safeguard public morality or in the legitimate interests of national security or public order?

POLITICAL PARTICIPATION

• *Political participation* — Is there freedom of association and assembly? Are multiple parties allowed in law and in practice? Is there violence against, or harassment of, political opponents?

- *Free and fair elections* — Is there a universal adult franchise? Are there procedural irregularities by government, such as the exclusion or intimidation of voters, the rigging of votes, or violence against candidates or opponents of government? Do the voting procedures permit political parties and independent observers to monitor balloting and vote counting?
- *Continuity of the democratic system* — Are free elections a recent introduction or a long-standing tradition? What are the prospects for the continuation of a democratic society? Do elections occur at reasonably regular intervals?
- *Community and local decision-making* — Are political decision-making powers decentralized? How much public participation is allowed in local bodies and at the community level?

EQUALITY OF OPPORTUNITY

- *Legal guarantees* — Are there constitutional or statutory guarantees of equality, regardless of gender, race, colour, descent, tribe, religion or national or ethnic origin?
- *Violence against or harassment of particular groups* — Does the State always prosecute those responsible for violence or harassment (State or non-State) against particular groups?
- *Political participation* — Are any groups excluded or hindered from participation in voting or government? Does the State support or condone this, or does it make serious efforts to combat it?
- *Economic participation* — Are there inequalities in pay and employment as a result of discrimination? Are there discriminatory restrictions on economic participation? Does the State support or condone discrimination, or does it make serious efforts to ensure equal treatment?

APPENDIX II

Draft Illustrative Checklist of Social Freedom[1]

PARTICIPATION

- *Democratic transformation* — Are there any obstacles to a democratic transformation of existing political, economic and social policies and structures which are conducive to the full and effective participation of all persons, groups and peoples in decision-making processes on social order and on a fair distribution of economic and political power among all sectors of national society?
- *Effectiveness* — Is effective participation ensured of all the elements of society in the preparation and execution of national plans and programmes of economic and social development?
- *Increasing popular participation* — Are there measures for an increasing rate of popular participation in the economic, social, cultural and political life through national governmental bodies, non-governmental organizations, co-operatives, rural associations, workers' and employers' organizations and women's and youth organizations, by such methods as national and regional plans for social and economic progress and community development?
- *Social information and mobilization* — Is public opinion mobilized by the dissemination of social information to make people aware of changing circumstances in society as a whole, and to educate the consumer?
- *Social and institutional reforms* — Are there legislative, administrative and other measures to ensure the promotion of democratically based social and institutional reforms and motivation for change basic to the elimination of all forms of discrimination and exploitation and conducive to high rates of economic and social progress, to include land, trade, services and technology, in which ownership and use of all national resources will be made to serve best the objectives of social justice and economic development?
- *Vulnerable sectors* — Are there special measures to ensure full participation of particularly vulnerable sectors of society, such as children, rural people, and

---

[1] Supplied by P.J.I.M. de Waart. The indicators for measuring social freedom were derived from the international human rights instruments published in *Human Rights: A Compilation of International Instruments*, UN doc. ST/HR/1/Rev.3, June 1988. Indicators that were selected are those which are not more difficult to apply than the ones in the UNDP checklist of political freedom.

the extremely poor, as well as those which have traditionally experienced exclusion or discrimination, such as women, minorities, and indigenous peoples?

EMPLOYMENT

• *Right to work* — Are legislative, administrative and political measures taken to achieve the full realization of the right to work including technical and vocational guidance and training programmes, policies and techniques?

• *Employment policy* — Is there an active government policy to promote full, productive and freely chosen employment without discrimination of any kind as to race, colour, sex, religion, political or other opinion, national or social origin, property, birth or status? Is such policy formulated in close and effective consultation with representatives of employers and workers? Is the employment policy based on reliable analytical studies of the present and future size and distribution of the labour force, employment, underemployment and unemployment? Does the employment policy maintain a proper balance between rural and urban development?

• *Trade unions* — Do all workers have the freedom of association, including the right to bargain collectively and to strike? Do trade unions enjoy full democratic freedoms? Are trade unions subjected to limitations other than those prescribed by law and which are necessary in a democratic society in the interests of national security or public order or for the protection of the rights and freedoms of others?

• *Forced labour* — Is there absolutely no question of forced or compulsory labour as a means of political coercion or education or as a punishment for holding or expressing political views, as a means of labour discipline or of racial, social, national or religious discrimination, as a method of mobilizing and using labour for purposes of economic development or as a punishment for having participated in strikes?

• *Child labour* — Is there a national policy in place to ensure the effective abolition of child labour and to raise progressively the minimum age for admission to employment to a level consistent with the full physical and mental development of young persons, i.e. a minimum age not less than 15 years?

• *Disabled persons* — Are appropriate measures instituted for the rehabilitation of mentally or physically disabled persons in respect to education, vocational and social guidance, training and selective placement?

DISTRIBUTION OF WEALTH

• *Poverty* — Are legislative, policy, administrative and other measures taken to eliminate poverty and to assure a steady improvement in levels of living and of a just and equitable distribution of income?
• *National income* — Is equitable (re)distribution of national income achieved by such means as, *inter alia*, the fiscal system and government spending?
• *Adequate standard of living* — Are appropriate steps taken to ensure the right of everyone to an adequate standard of living for himself and his family, including adequate food, clothing and housing and to the continuous improvement of living conditions?
• *Favourable conditions of work* — Is remuneration ensured which provides all workers, as a minimum, with fair wages and equal remuneration of equal work without distinction of any kind, in particular women being guaranteed conditions of work not inferior to those enjoyed by men, with equal pay for equal work? Are rest, leisure and reasonable limitation of working hours ensured as well as periodic holidays, with pay, and remuneration for public holidays?
• *Social security* — Are comprehensive social security and insurance systems as well as social welfare services provided for all persons who, because of involuntary unemployment, illness, disability or old age, are temporarily or permanently unable to earn their living?
• *Working mothers* — Are measures provided to safeguard the income of working mothers during pregnancy and the infancy of their children such as maternity, paternity or parental leave and allowances without loss of employment or wages?

HEALTH CARE

• *Standards* — Are legislative, policy, administrative and other measures taken to eliminate hunger and malnutrition and to guarantee the right to proper nutrition? Are there means to achieve the highest standards of health and the provision of health protection for the entire population, if possible free of charge?
• *Free health services* — Are free health services as well as adequate preventive and curative facilities and welfare medical services accessible to all?
• *Occupational safety and health* — Is there a coherent government policy on occupational safety, occupational health and the working environment? Is such policy formulated, implemented and periodically reviewed in consultation with the most representative organizations of employers and workers? Are occupational health services provided by laws, regulations of collective agreement or otherwise agreed upon by the employers and workers concerned?
• *Specific risks* — Are measures taken to protect workers and the population as a whole against specific risks caused by toxic substances and agents, machinery, air pollution, noise and vibration? Are measures taken to protect workers against

risks in given branches of activity such as building industry, commerce and offices, and dock work?

FOOD

• *Production* — Are legislative, policy, administrative and other measures taken to improve methods of production, conservation and distribution of food by making full use of technological and scientific knowledge, by disseminating knowledge of the principles of nutrition and by developing or reforming agrarian systems in such a way as to achieve the most efficient development and utilization of natural resources?
• *Distribution* — Do legislative, policy, administrative and other measures take into account the problems of both food-importing and food-exporting countries, to ensure an equitable distribution of world food supplies in relation to need?

EDUCATION

• *Illiteracy* — Are legislative, policy, administrative and other measures taken to eradicate illiteracy?
• *Levels of education* — Is primary education compulsory and free to all? Is secondary education in its different forms, including technical and vocational secondary education, made generally available and accessible to all by every appropriate means, and in particular by the progressive introduction of free education? Is higher education made equally accessible to all, on the basis of capacity, by every appropriate means, and in particular by the progressive introduction of free education?
• *Employment needs* — Do policies and programmes of vocational guidance and vocational training take due account of employment needs, opportunities and problems, both regional and national? Do they also take due account of the stage and level of economic, social and cultural development; and the mutual relationships between human resources development and other economic, social and cultural objectives?
• *Liberty of parents* — Do parents and, when applicable, legal guardians, have the liberty to choose for their children schools other than those established by the public authorities, which conform to such minimum standards as may be laid down or approved by the state and to ensure the religious and moral education of their children in conformity with their own convictions?
• *Information media* — Are national information media developed, expanded and rationally and fully used towards continuing education of the whole population and towards encouraging its participation in social development activities?
• *Brain drain* — Are national and international policies and measures formulated to avoid "brain drain" and to obviate its adverse effects?

• *Human rights* — Does education strengthen the respect for human rights and fundamental freedoms? Does education enable all persons to participate effectively in a free society, promote understanding, tolerance and friendship among all nations and all racial, ethnic or religious groups, and further the activities of the United Nations for the maintenance of peace?

CULTURE AND SCIENCE

• *Universal access* — Are legislative, policy, administrative and other measures taken to assure the right to universal access to culture? Are there obstacles to everyone's participation in cultural life?
• *Scientific progress* — Are steps taken that everyone can enjoy the benefits of scientific progress and development? Are there measures for the conservation, development and diffusion of science and culture? Can everyone benefit from the protection of moral and material interests resulting from any scientific, literary or artistic production of which he or she is the author?

TECHNOLOGY

• *Public interest* — Are appropriate measures taken to ensure that the results of scientific and technological developments are used in the interests of strengthening international peace and security, freedom and independence and for the purpose of the economic and social development of peoples and the realization of human rights and freedoms? Do such steps prevent the use of scientific and technological developments to limit or interfere with the enjoyment of human rights and fundamental freedoms of the individual? Are steps taken to extend the benefits of science and technology to all strata of the population and to protect them, both socially and materially, from possible harmful effects of the misuse of scientific and technological developments, including their misuse to infringe upon the rights of the individual or of the group, particularly with regard to respect for privacy and the protection of the human personality and its physical and intellectual integrity?
• *Preventing abuses* — Are steps taken to prevent abuses which might result from the exercise of exclusive rights conferred by patents, for example, failure to work or insufficient operation? Are there legislative, policy, administrative and other measures to prevent restrictive business practices in transfer of technology, for instance, requiring the acquiring party to refrain from challenging the validity of the patent; imposing acceptance of additional technology, future inventions and improvements, goods and services not wanted by the acquiring party; restrictions on research, use of personnel, adaptations, publicity or export?
• *Patent regime* — Are measures taken to prevent the patent regime from negatively affecting the welfare of people(s) by involving immense costs through, *in-*

ter alia, subverting and distorting scientific endeavour, slowing down diffusion and retarding global technological progress?

SUSTAINABLE DEVELOPMENT

- *Intergenerational equity* — Are legislative, policy, administrative and other measures taken in respect of rights and obligations for the use and conservation of natural resources and environmental protection? Do these measures secure that the state exercises its permanent sovereignty over natural resources in the interest of the peoples belonging to its territory and without causing substantial injury to the economy of other states or damage to the environment of other states or of areas beyond the limits of national jurisdiction?
- *Natural resources* — Are there measures to maintain biological diversity of the ecosystems and ecological processes essential for the functioning of the biosphere?
- *Social costs* — Are steps taken to mitigate social costs of adjustment and privatization and to meet the minimal essential needs of people for employment, food, energy, shelter, water supply, sanitation and health care?
- *Self-determination* — Does the government comply with the right to self-determination of peoples within its territory in such a way that it represents the whole population? Is the right to self-determination of peoples within a state respected by the government in such a way that each people may choose its road to development without injuring the same right of the other people(s)? Are measures taken for the peaceful settlement of a conflict between the right to self-determination and the prohibition of secession?

APPENDIX III

Motion for a Resolution of the European Parliament[1]

A.
The committee on Youth, Culture, Education, Information and Sport hereby submits to the European Parliament the following motion for a resolution together with explanatory statement:

MOTION FOR A RESOLUTION
on the activity of certain religious movements within the European Community

The European Parliament,
- accepting the principle laid down in Article 9 of the European Convention for the Protection of Human Rights and Fundamental Freedoms,
- having regard to the Treaty of Rome and in particular Article 220 thereof,
- having regard to International Youth Year 1985,
- having regard to the motions for resolutions on:
    - distress caused by Sun Myung Moon's Unification Church (Doc.1-2/82),
    - the activities of the Sun Myung Moon's Unification Church (Doc.1-109/82),
-having regard to the report of the Committee on Youth, Culture, education, Information and Sport and the opinion of the Legal Affairs Committee,

A. having regard to the concern felt by individuals and families in the Community at the activities of certain organizations described as 'new religious movements' insofar as their practices infringe human and civil rights and are detrimental to the position in society of those affected;

B. stressing that full freedom of religion and opinion is a principle in the Member States and that the Community Institutions therefore have no right to judge the value of either religious beliefs in general or individual religious practices;

---

[1] Supplied by Reender Kranenborg.

C. convinced that in this instance, the validity of religious beliefs is not in question, but rather the lawfulness of the practices used to recruit new members and the treatment they receive;

D. whereas the problems arising from the emergence of certain 'new religious movements' have attained world-wide dimensions, occurring in all Member States, although to different degrees, and having already prompted investigations, government action and court judgments in various Member States;

E. whereas the abandonment of their previous way of life by the members of these movements raises social issues and issues connected with Labour Law, adversely affecting not only the individuals involved, but also the community and the social system;

1. Considers it necessary for the Councils of Ministers responsible, that is to say the Ministers of the Interior and Ministers of Justice meeting in European Political Cooperation, and the Council of Ministers for Social Affairs, to hold an exchange of information as soon as possible on the problems arising from the activity of certain new religious movements with particular reference to the following areas:
   (a) procedure applied in conferring charity status and tax exemption on such movements;
   (b) compliance with the laws of the individual Member States, for example Labour Law and social security legislation;
   (c) consequences for society of failure to comply with these Laws;
   (d) attempts to find missing persons and the possibilities of cooperation with third countries for this purpose;
   (e) ways in which the rights of members to personal freedom are infringed;
   (f) creation of centres to assist those leaving these organizations by providing legal aid and assistance to reintegrate into society and find employment;
   (g) existence of legal loopholes owing tot the differences in legislation in the individual countries which enable proscribed activities to be pursued from one country in another;

2. Considers it necessary to apply the following criteria in assessing these 'new religious movements':
   (a) persons under the age of majority should not be induced on becoming a member of a movement to make a solemn long-term commitment that will determine the course of their lives;
   (b) there should be an adequate period of reflection on the financial or personal commitment involved;

(c) after joining an organization contacts must be allowed with family and friends;

(d) members who have already commenced a course of education must not be prevented from completing it;

(e) the following rights of the individual must be respected:
- the right to leave a movement unhindered;
- the right to contact family and friends in person or by letter and telephone;
- the right to seek independent advice, legal or otherwise;
- the right to seek medical attention at any time;

(f) no one may be incited to break any law, particularly with regard to fund-raising, for example by begging or prostitution;

(g) movements may not extract permanent commitments from potential recruits, for example students or tourists, who are visitors to a country in which they are not resident;

(h) during recruitment, the name and principles of the movement should always be made immediately clear;

(i) such movements must inform the competent authorities on request of the address or whereabouts of individual members;

(j) new religious movements must ensure that individuals dependent on them and working on their behalf receive the social security benefits provided in the Member States in which they live or work;

(k) if a member travels abroad in pursuit of the interests of a movement, it must accept responsibility for bringing the individual home, especially in the event of illness;

(l) telephone calls and letters from members' families must be immediately passed on to them;

(m) where recruits have children, movements must do their utmost to further their education and health, and avoid any circumstances in which the children's well-being might be at risk.

3. Calls on the Commission:
- to submit a compilation of data, if necessary using a data bank, on the international ramifications of new religious movements, including those using cover names and front organizations, and on their activities in the Member States specifically indicating the measures taken by government bodies, especially by the police and the courts, in response to infringements of the law by these movements, as well as the findings of government commissions of investigation into certain new religious movements;
- to submit proposals to the Councils of Ministers responsible with a view to securing the effective protection of Community citizens;

4. Invites the Councils of Ministers responsible to discuss, on the basis of the Commission's data and proposals for action, the problems arising from the activities of the said movements, thereby enabling the Member States to cooperate with each other, if possible on the basis of Article 220 of the Treaty of Rome, in protecting the rights of their citizens;

5. Considers, moreover, a common approach within the context of the Council of Europe to be desirable and calls, therefore, on the governments of the Member States to press for appropriate agreements to be drawn up by the Council of Europe which will guarantee the individual effective protection from the machinations of these movements and their physical and moral coercion;

6. Instructs its President to forward this resolution to the Commission and Council of the European Communities, to the Governments and national parliaments of the Member States, and to the Council of Europe.

APPENDIX IV

Recommendation of the Council of Europe[1]

Recommendation 1178 (1992) on sects and new religious movements

1. The Assembly is concerned at certain problems connected with the activities of sects and new religious movements.

2. It has been alerted by various associations and families who consider that they have been harmed by the activities of sects.

3. It has taken account of the invitation, given to the Council of Europe by the European Parliament in the Cottrell report, to consider this problem.

4. It has asked all the member states to indicate what practices they follow and what the legal problems are.

5. It considers that the freedom of conscience and religion guaranteed by Article 9 of the European Convention on Human Rights makes major legislation on sects undesirable, since such legislation might well interfere with this fundamental right and harm traditional religions.

6. It considers, however, that educational as well as legislative and other measures should be taken in response to the problems raised by some of the activities of sects or new religious movements.

7. To this end the Assembly recommends that the Committee of Ministers call on the member states of the Council of Europe to adopt the following measures:

   I. The basic educational curriculum should include objective factual information concerning established religions and their major variants, concerning the principles of comparative religion and concerning ethics and personal and social rights;

[1] Supplied by Reender Kranenborg.

II. Supplementary information of a similar nature, and in particular on the nature and activities of sects and new religious movements, should also be widely circulated to the general public. Independent bodies should be set up to collect and circulate this information;

III. Consideration should be given to introducing legislation, if it does not already exist, which grants corporate status to all sects and new religious movements which have been registered, together with all offshoots of the mother sect;

IV. To protect minors and prevent abductions and transfers abroad, member states which have not yet done so should ratify the European Convention on Recognition and Enforcement of Decisions concerning Custody of Children and on Restoration of Custody of Children (1980), and to adopt legislation making it possible to implement it;

V. Existing legislation concerning the protection of children should be more rigorously applied. Additionally, those belonging to a sect must be informed that they have the right to leave;

VI. Persons working for sects should be registered with social welfare bodies and guaranteed social welfare coverage, and such social welfare provision should also be available to those deciding to leave the sects.

Index of Authors and Names

Contributors

MASAO ABE, Buddhist Philosophy, Department of Philosophy, Purdue Univer sity, USA.

ABDULLAHI AHMED AN-NA'IM, Human Rights Watch: Africa, Washington, DC, USA.

ARNULF CAMPS, OFM, Third World Theology, Faculty of Theology, University of Nijmegen, The Netherlands.

JOHN CLAYTON, Philosophy of Religion, Department of Religious Studies, University of Lancaster, United Kingdom.

BAS DE GAAY FORTMAN, Political Economy, Institute of Social Studies, The Hague, The Netherlands.

PADMASIRI DE SILVA, Buddhist Philosophy, Information and Resource Center, Singapore.

P.J.I.M. DE WAART, International Law, Faculty of Law, Free University of Amsterdam, The Netherlands.

ANDRÉ F. DROOGERS, Cultural Anthropology, Faculty of Social-Cultural Studies, Free University of Amsterdam, The Netherlands.

REIN FERNHOUT, Comparative Religion, Faculty of Theology, Free University of Amsterdam, The Netherlands.

JERALD D. GORT, Missiology, Faculty of Theology, Free University of Amsterdam, The Netherlands.

JACQUES H. KAMSTRA, Comparative Religion and the History and Phenomenology of Non-Christian Religions, Faculty of Theology, University of Amsterdam, The Netherlands.

REENDER KRANENBORG, New Religious Movements, Faculty of Theology, Free University of Amsterdam, The Netherlands.

JOHANNES S. REINDERS, Ethics, Faculty of Theology, Free University of Amsterdam, The Netherlands.

VICTOR A. VAN BIJLERT, Indology, Department of Religious Studies, State University of Leiden, The Netherlands.

CORSTIAAN J.G. VAN DER BURG, Indology, Faculty of Theology, Free University of Amsterdam, The Netherlands.

AAD VAN EGMOND, Systematic Theology, Faculty of Theology, Free University of Amsterdam, The Netherlands.

HENDRIK M. VROOM, Philosophy of Religion, Faculty of Theology, Free University of Amsterdam, The Netherlands.

ANTON WESSELS, Comparative Religion and Missiology, Faculty of Theology, Free University of Amsterdam, The Netherlands.